MODERN GERMANY

Society, economy and politics in the twentieth century

Modern Germany

Society, economy and politics in the twentieth century

Second edition

V. R. BERGHAHN

Professor of History, University of Warwick

CAMBRIDGE
UNIVERSITY PRESS

Published by the Press Syndicate of the University of Cambridge
The Pitt Building, Trumpington Street, Cambridge CB2 1RP
40 West 20th Street, New York, NY 10011-4211, USA
10 Stamford Road, Oakleigh, Melbourne 3166, Australia

First published 1982
Second edition 1987
Reprinted 1988 (twice), 1989, 1990, 1991, 1993, 1994, 1995

Printed in the United States of America

Library of Congress Cataloging-in-Publication Data is available

British Library Cataloging in Publication applied for.

ISBN 0-521-34505-7 hardback
ISBN 0-521-34748-3 paperback

Contents

Contents

Maps

Preface

The first edition of this volume contained rather a brief preface in which, in the limited space that was then available to me, I tried to bring out some of the salient features of my attempt to make sense of the confused and confusing history of modern Germany and to delineate how this study differed from other, older textbooks of this kind. This second edition provides me with an opportunity not only of expanding and updating Chapter 6, the Statistical Tables and the Select Bibliography, but also of elaborating on the perspectives I am trying to offer.

As I argued in the first edition, all textbooks tend to have a framework and to operate with broader underlying hypotheses. Their main themes reflect, in different ways, the authors' overall views of recent German history. Seen in this light, it seems fair to say that the books listed in my bibliography were written essentially in a 'failure-of-liberalism' mould. This was clearly also the perspective of Gordon Craig's *Germany*, which, conceived twenty years earlier, was finally published in 1978 and which, significantly, took the year 1866 as its starting point, later ending with the following 'message':

> Adolf Hitler was nothing if not thorough. He destroyed the basis of the traditional resistance to modernity and liberalism just as completely as he had destroyed the structure of the *Rechtsstaat* and democracy. Because his work of demolition was so complete, he left the German people nothing that could be repaired or built upon. They had to begin all over again, a hard task perhaps, but a challenging one, in the facing of which they were not entirely bereft of guidance. For Hitler had not only restored to them the options that they had had a century earlier but had also bequeathed to them the memory of horror to help them with their choice.

Methodologically Craig and the other authors before him were indebted to political history, blended with a strong dose of intellectual history which had emerged as a genre in its own right in the United States during the 1950s. It was not that these books ignored social and economic developments, but the balance was clearly in favour of politics, diplomacy and high culture. At least it does not seem accidental that Craig, for example, started off with the following paragraph:

Is it a mistake to begin with Bismarck? So much is written these days, and so insistently, about the primary importance of economic and social forces in history that one runs the risk of being considered old-fashioned if one gives too much prominence to personality. Yet it is certainly unnecessary to apologize for introducing Bismarck's name at the outset. If he had never risen to the top in Prussian politics, the unification of Germany would probably have taken place anyway, but surely not at the same time or in quite the same way as it did. Whatever may be said about the movement of economic forces, there is no burking the fact that the decision concerning the form unification would take was made, not in the area of economic and commercial policy, but on the battlefield of Königsgrätz on 3 July 1866.

It is for two reasons that I would like to draw the reader's attention to these aspects of textbook-writing. To begin with, it would appear to be important to make the question of overt or covert assumptions the subject of classroom discussion, so that nobody is under the misapprehension that textbooks are straightforward summaries of objective knowledge. They are products of the general state of research reached by a particular time and of broader perceptions of Germany and its history prevalent in the Anglo-Saxon world. They can do no more than synthesise available knowledge and are more likely to reflect the wider scholarly *Zeitgeist* about the country in question than overturn the existing consensus. I would certainly ask readers to bear this in mind when they use this particular textbook.

However, I am not proposing to analyse how Germany, by failing to adopt liberalism and parliamentary democracy in the 1860s, ended up on the path of authoritarianism and, finally, of brutal dictatorship. Instead this volume approaches Germany from the angle of an industrialising and industrial society. Problems of socioeconomic change lie at the heart of my analysis, even if a good deal of space is, and indeed must be, devoted to dealing with the repercussions of rapid industrialisation at the level of domestic and external politics. In this sense, a textbook-writer is under an obligation to be comprehensive and cannot leave out questions of centralised power and influence, however fascinating 'grass-roots' history may be. The level of politics would seem to be all the more important because it provides a yardstick by which we may be able to measure the tensions and conflicts stemming from socioeconomic change. This yardstick is the intensity of violence manifested in German society at various times. As we shall see, the propensity to resort to high levels of violence, mostly directed towards the 'internal enemy', but twice in this century also towards external ones, was very considerable at least up to 1945. This is also why this book refuses to make a strict analytical distinction between domestic policy and foreign policy, between civil war and foreign war. Both are manifestations of a deeper internal crisis and hence offer a gauge with which to examine German history both before and after the Second World War.

This approach implies that Germany is seen here as a society in which socioeconomic and political power was unevenly distributed. However, I have shied away from operating with a dichotomous model of stratification which draws a dividing-line between those who own the means of production and those who do not. A one-sentence definition of the divisions and structured inequalities in German society is therefore not given here. Rather it is hoped that there will emerge from the first twenty pages or so what I would consider the peculiarities of that society. At this point only one crucial aspect shall be highlighted in anticipation of that later analysis which is also a recurrent theme in subsequent chapters: industrial Germany, though no doubt a class society, did not have a ruling class. Deep as the gulf between various classes was, at least in the first half of this century, there was also a lack of cohesion at the top of the socioeconomic and political pyramid. Time and again, as will be seen, the groups which possessed greater power and influence than the strata lower down the social scale found themselves disunited over how to deploy their superiority and over whether to deploy it towards a reformist adaptation to a changing societal environment or towards a stopping of the historical clock. In other words, if industrialisation led to the relentless growth of a large industrial working class and if this growth, in turn, was bound to have a destabilising effect on the existing social and political system, the question was as to whether a consensus could be forged among the power elites over how to deal with these developments 'from below'. Were the new social groups which had the vote and now demanded greater and genuine participation in the decision-making processes at all levels to be integrated by a policy of concessions? Or were they to be ghettoised, politically emasculated and violently repressed?

This book is ultimately about the solutions found to these problems. It is therefore about winners and losers not only in the conflict between larger social collectives but also in the struggles between the reformists and the counter-revolutionaries at the top. We shall see that the balance, though precarious at various points, tended to tilt in favour of the latter camp in the first half of the twentieth century, with the reversal of the tide finally occurring in the second half. To trace this highly dramatic process which deeply affected the course of modern German history and, through two world wars, also the history of Europe and the rest of the world, was one of the considerations behind taking the chronology of this account beyond 1945. Apart from a conceptual, there was also a pragmatic reason: I thought the time had come to cover the past four decades and not just the Hohenzollern monarchy, the Weimar Republic and the Third Reich. This is also why I was only too glad to respond to the suggestion of the publishers to expand Chapter 6; for, having badly overshot the original word-limit for the first edition, there was no room left in 1980–1 for writing more than a brief survey of the 1960s and

1970s, self-consciously entitled 'Aspects of Contemporary Life in Two Germanies'.

The last chapter, I hope, is now more substantial, although technical constraints prevented me from changing and improving Chapters 1–5, except for a number of corrections of factual errors. This still leaves some glaring gaps. Some of these I would like to stand by, and not merely because I wanted to keep this book within manageable proportions. Thus I mentioned in my first edition that I had taken a number of deliberate short-cuts in my analysis of the Nazi dictatorship. A few reviewers picked this up and then charged me – I think, quite unfairly – with not having said enough about the Holocaust. The short-cut I actually took and had in mind was to say nothing about *culture* in the Third Reich. This was not because there is insufficient material on this topic, but rather because I wanted to emphasise the barbaric character of the Hitler regime. On the other hand, there are omissions which I now regret more than ever before, the most important being a more balanced treatment of women in German society. To some extent my present regrets are the result of a wider changing consciousness concerning the importance of this field. But looking back, I also remember wishing ten years ago that more research had been available. Clearly, future textbook-writers must, and will, take more seriously the task of integrating gender history into general German history, and there may even be some recasting of current modes of analysing the development of modern Germany. They will be assisted in this by a wealth of empirical material which has become available in recent years or is now in the pipeline. They may even be helped by the publication of a synthesis, produced by a courageous soul, which pulls the available detailed research together. Maybe Ute Frevert's excellent *Frauen-Geschichte* (Frankfurt 1986) will soon be available in English.

Meanwhile the basic framework of this textbook remains unchanged. My book is an attempt to pursue the themes of social and political conflict and modes of conflict-resolution against the background of rapid industrialisation, and I remain painfully aware of the gaps in my analysis. Naturally, these inadequacies are my responsibility and not that of a number of friends and colleagues who helped me in my efforts to write a fresh account of modern German history. In particular I would like to thank Marion Berghahn, Ian Farr, Mary Fulbrook, Robin Lenman, Tim Mason, Willie Paterson, Hartmut Pogge, Jill Stephenson, Barbara Weinberger, Bernd Weisbrod and Jay Winter.

University of Warwick   V. R. BERGHAHN

Abbreviations

ADGB	*Allgemeiner Deutscher Gewerkschaftsbund*
AEG	*Allgemeine Electrizitäts-Gesellschaft*
AGVK	*Arbeitsgemeinschaft Vaterländischer Kampfverbände*
ATB	*Arbeiter-Turn- und Sport-Bund*
BdA	*Bundesvereinigung deutscher Arbeitgeberverbände*
BDF	*Bund Deutscher Frauenvereine*
BdI	*Bund der Industriellen*
BDI	*Bundesverband der Deutschen Industrie*
BDM	*Bund Deutscher Mädel*
BHE	*Bund der Heimatvertriebenen und Entrechteten*
BKV	*Betriebskollektivverträge*
BP	*Bayern-Partei*
BVP	*Bayerische Volkspartei*
CDU	*Christlich-Demokratische Union*
CSU	*Christlich-Soziale Union*
DAF	*Deutsche Arbeitsfront*
DDP	*Deutsche Demokratische Partei*
DFU	*Deutsche Friedens-Union*
DGB	*Deutscher Gewerkschaftsbund*
DKP	*Deutsch-Konservative Partei*
DKP	*Deutsche Kommunistische Partei*
DNVP	*Deutsch-Nationale Volkspartei*
DP	*Deutsche Partei*
DP	Displaced Person
DRP	*Deutsche Reichspartei*
DVFP	*Deutsch-Völkische Freiheitspartei*
DVP	*Deutsche Volkspartei*
DWK	*Deutsche Wirtschafts-Kommission*
ECSC	European Coal and Steel Community
EDC	European Defence Community
EEC	European Economic Community

Abbreviations

ERP	European Recovery Programme
FDGB	*Freier Deutscher Gewerkschaftsbund*
FDJ	*Freie Deutsche Jugend*
FDP	*Freie Demokratische Partei*
FVP	*Fortschrittliche Volkspartei*
GARIOA	Government Appropriations for Relief in Occupied Areas
GDP	Gross Domestic Product
GDR	German Democratic Republic
GHH	*Gutehoffnungshütte*
GNP	Gross National Product
HO	*Handelsorganisation*
KdF	*Kraft durch Freude*
KPD	*Kommunistische Partei Deutschlands*
KRA	*Kriegsrohstoff-Abteilung*
LAG	*Lastenausgleichsgesetz*
LDPD	*Liberal-Demokratische Partei Deutschlands*
MTS	Machine Tractor Station
NATO	North Atlantic Treaty Organisation
NLP	*Nationalliberale Partei*
NPD	*Nationaldemokratische Partei Deutschlands*
NSDAP	*Nationalsozialistische Deutsche Arbeiterpartei*
NSV	*Nationalsozialistische Volkswohlfahrt*
NVA	*Nationale Volksarmee*
RDI	*Reichsverband der Deutschen Industrie*
RP	*Reichspartei*
RSHA	*Reichssicherheitshauptamt*
SA	*Sturmabteilung*
SAP	*Sozialistische Arbeiterpartei*
SDS	*Sozialistischer Deutscher Studentenbund*
SED	*Sozialistische Einheitspartei*
SHAEF	Supreme Headquarters Allied Expeditionary Forces
SPD	*Sozialdemokratische Partei Deutschlands*
SRP	*Sozialistische Reichspartei*
SS	*Schutzstaffel*
USPD	*Unabhängige Sozialdemokratische Partei Deutschlands*
VVVB	*Vereinigte Vaterländische Verbände Bayerns*
WAV	*Wirtschaftliche Aufbau-Vereinigung*
WP	*Wirtschaftspartei*
ZAG	*Zentralarbeitsgemeinschaft*

Glossary

(This glossary is designed to help students with some of the German, French or other unfamiliar terms in the text and is based on a list compiled by Professor L. E. Hoffman (Virginia State University). I would like to thank her for suggesting this aid and for making her list available for inclusion in this edition.)

passim	*bürgerlich(e)* (adj.): bourgeois; of or pertaining to the middle classes
p. 7	*nouveaux riches* (n., pl.): people newly rich
p. 8	*Mittelstand* (n., s.): the middle classes
	Old: the professions and merchants, artisans
	New: industrial entrepreneurs, technical experts
p. 11	*Summus Episcopus* (n., s.): supreme bishop, or the head of a religious denomination
	Kulturkampf (n., s.): 'culture struggle'; Bismarck's persecution of the Catholic Church in Germany, 1872–8
p. 14	*Volksschulen* (n., pl.): elementary or primary schools
	Mittelschule (n., s.): intermediate school, either academic or technical
	höhere Schule (n., s.): secondary school, either academic (*Gymnasium*) or technical
	Abitur (n., s.): examination taken on leaving secondary school and, by extension, the certificate earned by passing it, a necessary qualification to enter university studies
p. 24	East Elbia: the territory east of the Elbe River that constituted the traditional heart of Prussia and the domain of the *Junker* aristocracy
p. 29	*Weltpolitik* (n., s.): global politics; the policy aimed at establishing Germany as a major world power
p. 49	*va-banque* policies: to break the bank, go broke; to spend without thought of tomorrow
p. 60	*sauve qui peut*: everyone for himself; a disorderly retreat
p. 64	ideal-typical: in the sociology of Max Weber (German, 1864–1920), an 'ideal type' is a theoretical model which displays all of the most characteristic qualities of a particular kind of thing or person
p. 68	*Zentralarbeitsgemeinschaft* (ZAG): Central Labour Association
p. 71	*Gesindeordnungen* (n., pl.): Labourers' ordinances, traditional laws which regulated the rights and terms of employment of domestic servants and farm-hands, usually to the advantage of employers
p. 72	rentier (n., s.): a person who receives a fixed, unearned income, such as rents from land or dividends from stock

Glossary

p. 80   *Bürgerbräukeller* (n., s.): beer-hall found in many German towns; specifically, the one in Munich where Hitler and Ludendorff launched their right-wing revolt of 1923, which is therefore known as the Beer Hall Putsch

p. 82   *Stammtisch* (n., s.): table reserved for regular customers, common in neighbourhood beer-halls or cafes; by extension, the people (generally men) who sit there

p. 84   *neue Sachlichkeit*: the 'New Objectivity', an art style of the 1920s which stressed representational realism in reaction to abstract art

p. 86   *Arbeiter-Turn- und-Sport-Bund* (ATB): Workers' Gymnastics and Sports Association

           Volksbühne: the people's theatre, or popular theatre movement

           l'art pour l'art: art for art's sake, for no practical or educational purpose

p. 88   *Bund der Industriellen* (BdI): the Manufacturers' League

p. 90   *völkisch(e)* (adj.): pertaining to racial nationalism. The *Volk*, in German right-wing politics, were the tribal group, the ethnically 'pure' Germans

p. 91   *Vernunftrepublikaner* (n., s. & pl.): 'rational republicans', people who supported the Weimar government for practical reasons rather than out of true belief in democracy

p. 103   *Reichsverband der Deutschen Industrie* (RDI): National Association of German Industry

           Herr-im-Hause: the master of the house; can refer both to the father of a family, or to the owner of a business; in either case, implies paternalistic control

p. 105   *Allgemeiner Deutscher Gewerkschaftsbund* (ADGB): the German League of Trade Unions

p. 106   *Hirsch-Dunckerschen Gewerkschaften*: The Hirsch-Duncker trade unions, founded in the late nineteenth century and always small, were politically liberal (as distinct from the more conservative Christian unions and the more left-wing Socialist ones) and pursued gradual improvement of working conditions through negotiation with employers, not strikes or revolution.

p. 107   *Ruhreisenstreit*: the 1928 conflict in the iron and metal-working industry of the Ruhr area

p. 109   *Gutsherren* (n., pl.): the lords of the manor, the *Junker* landowners who had extensive powers over their tenants

           Osthilfe (n., s.): 'help to the East'; programme of subsidies to the large landowners East of the Elbe, demanded by the Nationalists

p. 110   *Mein Kampf*: 'My Struggle', Hitler's autobiography and declaration of principles, written in prison in 1924

p. 111   *Reichslandbund*: German Agricultural Association

p. 116   redundancy: in British usage, to be out of work because one's labour is no longer required; laid off

p. 117   attentist: attitude of watchful waiting for some significant event (from French 'attente', waiting)

p. 119   *Stahlhelm*: 'Steel Helmet', a paramilitary organisation founded in late 1918, mainly of nationalistic veterans; the largest such group in Germany during the 1920s. It opposed the Versailles settlement, favouring an authoritarian regime to replace the Weimar Republic. Officially independent of political parties, but increasingly allied with the Nationalists.

p. 122   *Reichsbanner*: the paramilitary organisation of the parties of the Weimar coalition, primarily the Socialists; very large but never as ruthless as the extremists, and never trusted by army leaders

p. 124   front bench: the main leaders; from the British parliamentary system, where the government ministers sit on the front bench in the House of Commons

p. 130   *Kampffront Schwarz-Weiß-Rot*: political coalition of the conservative parties in the 1933 elections, named for the colours of the monarchist flag (black, white, and red)

p. 134   *Jungvolk*: Nazi organisation for young boys
            Jungmädelbund: Nazi organisation for young girls
            Bund Deutscher Mädel: league of German Girls; Nazi organisation for teenagers

p. 135   *Hochburgen* (n., pl.): chief cities

p. 141   ersatz (adj.): imitation, synthetic

p. 147   *Rüstungsbetriebe* (n., pl.): armaments factories

p. 149   *Volksgenossen* (n., pl.): folk or racial comrades; Nazi term for fellow Germans

p. 151   *Weltmachtflotte*: world class navy

p. 153   *Grossraumwirtschaft*: closed economy based on domination of the entire continent of Europe

p. 161   *telos*: aim; ultimate purpose or goal (Greek)

p. 162   OKW: *Oberkommando der Wehrmacht*, or high command of the armed forces; replaced both the civilian war ministry and the general staff after 1938, bringing the armed forces under Hitler's personal command. General Keitel was subservient to Hitler.
            Reichssicherheitshauptamt (RSHA): central state security office of the SS, created 1939, headed by Reinhard Heydrich (to his death, 1942), became the central agency of the SS state, with power over both criminal and political offenders

p. 163   *franc tireurs*: snipers

p. 164   *Denkschrift*: memorandum or written opinion
            Untermensch (plural *Untermenschen*): subhuman; a term Nazis applied to members of 'inferior' races, especially the Slavs

p. 166   helots: slaves (from classical Greek)

p. 169   Reichsbahn: German railway agency

p. 170   *Ausrottungspolitik*: policy of extermination (of Jews)

p. 171   *Gerichtsverfassungsgesetz*: law governing the judicial branch of government, judges and courts

p. 172   *Volksschädling* Decree: law of November 1938 branding Jews as 'parasites on the *volk*' and thus excluding them from most economic activities and imposing a huge collective fine

p. 173   *SD-Inland-Nachrichtendienst*: SS domestic intelligence service, interested in the situation within Germany

           Berichte zur innenpolitischen Lage: 'Reports on the Internal Political Situation'

           Sportpalast: sports palace or coliseum (in Berlin)

p. 175   *Machtergreifung*: Nazi seizure of power, 30 January 1933

p. 186   *Land* (plural *Länder*): state(s) within the Federal Republic, West Germany

p. 188   *Volksstaat*: republic, representative democracy

p. 199   *Sozialstaat*: social welfare state

p. 201   *Schützen-, Kegel-* and other associations: rifle clubs, bowling clubs, etc.

p. 202   *Wohlstand für alle*: prosperity for everyone

           131er-Gesetz: Article 131 of the Basic Law of the Federal Republic

           déclassé: having come down in the world, lost social status

p. 204   *Marktwirtschaft*: market economy, competitive capitalism

           Kartellgestz: legislation outlawing cartels

           Rhein-Ruhr-Klub: club of manufacturing and business leaders from the western industrial districts

p. 205   *Deutscher Gewerkschaftsbund* (DGB): (West) German Trade Union Association; federation similar to the AFL-CIO

p. 206   *Mitbestimmung*: worker participation in company management

           Bundesvereinigung deutscher Arbeitgeberverbände (BdA): Federation of German Employers' Associations

p. 209   *Bundeswehr*: West German armed forces, created as part of NATO

p. 210   *Dienststelle Blank*: Department Blank

p. 216   démarche: announcement of a change in policy

p. 217   *troika*: trio, in Russian; originally a sled pulled by three horses, now refers to a ruling group of three

p. 233   *Erziehungsgesellschaft*: society oriented around education

           Hochschulen (pl.): colleges, universities

p. 237   *Kleinbürgertum* (collective noun): lower middle classes

p. 243   *Vermögensbildung*: plan for wealth formation in the hands of the mass of the population

           Konzertierte Aktion: forum for collective economic policy planning involving the Economics Ministry, industrial associations and unions

p. 248   *Sozialistischer Deutscher Studentenbund* (SDS): German Socialist

	Student Association, left-wing organisation especially active in the 1960s
p. 249	*Mitteleuropa*: Middle or Central Europe; a term often used by German expansionists to refer to their aim of German domination of the entire area
	Grundvertrag: basic treaty between East and West Germany ratified in 1973
p. 253	*Ihr da oben – wir da unten*: 'You up there – we down here'
p. 254	*Aufbruchstimmung*: optimistic mood to make a fresh start
p. 256	*'Realos'*: 'Green' realists
	'Fundamentalos': 'Green' fundamentalists
p. 261	*Illustrierten* (pl.): glossy weekly in the style of *Life*, but more sensationalist
p. 264	*Trümmerfrauen* (pl.): literally 'rubble women', who lived in, and cleared up, postwar cities
p. 267	*Radikalenerlass*: decree against radicals in the Civil Service

1 Wilhelmine Germany, 1900–1914

Rapid industrialisation and its impact on society

The development of modern Germany is best understood against the background of the Industrial Revolution which affected Central Europe with full force in the final decades of the nineteenth century. Britain had experienced the blessings and traumas of industrialisation earlier and more slowly, but nowhere else in Europe did the transition from an economy based on agriculture to one dominated by industry occur with the same rapidity as in Germany. Inevitably, the Industrial Revolution also had a profound effect on social structures, on the life-styles and political behaviour of people as well as on their perceptions of the world around them. These, too, changed more rapidly in Germany than in other European countries. Seen from the perspective of the late twentieth century, the links between economic, social and political transformation may seem obvious enough. While it is not easy fully to appreciate the highly dynamic situation which had developed in Germany by the turn of the century, it is nonetheless fundamental to an understanding of the subsequent course of the country's history, and this is why these changes require brief discussion here.

Although the economic, social and political factors which generated these energies must be perceived as being in constant interaction with one another, it is convenient to start with the purely economic aspects of German industrialisation. A first, very general impression of dramatic economic transformation may be obtained from a glance at the output of coal between 1880 and 1913 which rose more than fourfold and has to be set against the British figures for the same period (Table 9). Even more staggering is the figure for steel production which by the year 1913 had far outpaced Britain, the first industrial nation, and had grown more than tenfold since 1880 (Table 9). The production indices of key industries confirm this picture and expand it to the extent that the growth figures include not merely the industries of the First Industrial Revolution (coal, iron), but also of the Second Industrial Revolution in which the chemical and electrical engineering industries came to play an ever more

1

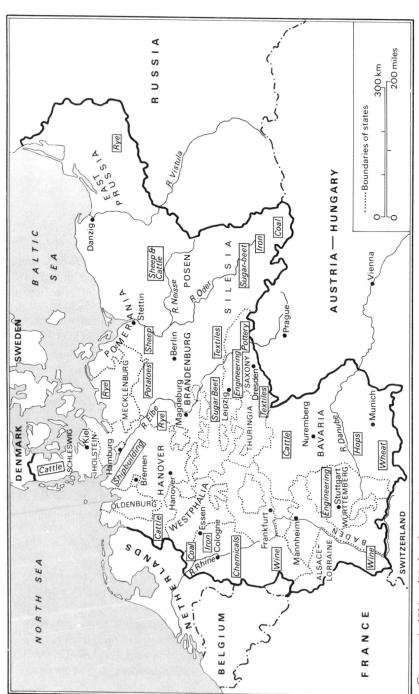

1. Germany in 1914: political and economic.

important role (Table 8). In the case of Germany, these two 'revolutions' occurred in such quick succession that they virtually merged into one. Scientists and entrepreneurs were certainly quick to recognise the potential of the new industries in which Germany began to lead the world before 1914.

Taken together, the various tables in the Appendix give a rough impression of the highly dynamic industrial economy that had emerged in the heart of Europe around the turn of the century. Many parts of the country were bustling with economic activity. Especially in the valleys of the Ruhr and lower Rhine rivers, in Saxony, Silesia, Berlin, along the Neckar river in the south-west and in the Saarland, more and more as well as increasingly larger factories kept on producing, and not merely for the domestic market. By 1913 Imperial Germany was one of the major trading and exporting nations of the world whose volume of exports and imports had grown fourfold between 1880 and 1913 (Table 10). It would be wrong to assume that economic growth was uninterrupted and that agriculture, in the long run the main victim of industrialisation, was the only sector to experience difficulties. In fact, there were a few years when the growth rate was as high as 7 or 8 per cent, but it fell to zero or below in the late 1870s, 1891, and 1901. Nevertheless, the overall trend was in a positive direction. The shift towards an industrial economy was irreversible. The machine age was there to stay.

However, industry needed people to operate the machines. As in Britain earlier in the nineteenth century, the great industrial centres of Germany became magnets for millions of men and women who moved there to toil in the factories and workshops. Hand-in-hand with a vast expansion of industrial production and technology the country experienced a demographic revolution. There are two aspects to this. First, Germany's population grew by leaps and bounds from 41 million in 1871 to 49.7 million in 1891 and 65.3 million by 1911 (Table 1). Some three million of these, it is true, joined the stream of European emigrants to North America and other parts of the world between 1871 and 1911, but the figure declined markedly in the decade after the turn of the century. Within a generation, more than 20 million additional people inhabited the country, of whom more than 12 million were looking for employment in the economy.

A growing number of these were born in the cities where the rates of increase were frequently significantly higher than those in the countryside. They were the first group to seek jobs in the factories. Secondly, and no less importantly, Germany, like Britain before her, witnessed great population movements from the rural areas to the towns and cities (Table 2). The extent of the movement was so great that in 1907 only just over half of the then 60.4 million Germans still lived at their birth-place. Two-thirds of the 29 million migrants, it is true, had resettled in the vicinity of their childhood residence. Nevertheless, some 8.9 million people had moved to other parts of the country, with the largest number streaming from the eastern provinces into the Ruhr and Berlin regions. The census of 1907 counted 512,700 people of eastern German origin in Rhineland-Westphalia and 1,116,900 in the Berlin area. A mere three years later these figures had grown by a further 300,000 and 750,000 respectively. The population of some cities, like Düsseldorf, Duisburg, Essen, Frankfurt, Kiel and Leipzig increased by between 300 and 500 per cent (Table 3). Through births and migration, the population of Saxony rose from 2.5 million in 1871 to 4.8 million in 1900. The population of the Rhineland also doubled in the same period, whereas that of agricultural East Prussia typically showed but a small overall growth of just over 200,000.

Another way of looking at the enormous levels of geographical mobility and the great trek into the urban centres is in occupational terms, by taking the percentages of those employed in agriculture on the one hand and those in industry on the other (Table 15). In 1871, 49 per cent of the population worked in agriculture. By 1907, this figure had declined to 35.2 per cent. In the same period the proportion of those employed in industry rose from 31 to 40 per cent. The remaining quarter worked in the service sector. An enquiry into the causes of this demographic shift reveals that people moved into the urban centres in the hope of participating, however marginally, in the wealth generated by industrial and commercial activity. Agriculture was incapable of matching the greater productivity and prosperity of industrial enterprise. Wages and work conditions outside agriculture, however low they may have been by present-day standards, were considerably better than in the country-side, apart from other attractions which will be described in a moment.

It is important to bear the relativity of these town-and-country comparisons in mind. The actual number of people employed in agriculture continued to rise up to 1913 (Table 16). There was still money to be made in agriculture (Tables 6 and 19), but it was less than in industry and commerce. Above all, what was required was a willingness and ability to adapt to the changing patterns of the market and to modernise production methods. Many farmers found this most difficult to do, though for different reasons. In the west and south of Germany the pattern of land tenure was predominantly that of small-holders producing a large variety of crops. Dairy farming and meat production were also concentrated here. This peasant economy in which 3.5 out of 5.5 million owned less than 5 acres had not been particularly viable for some time. Its survival into the late nineteenth century and in particular after the Great Depression of the 1870s and 1880s was in large part due to the fact that it could rely, at modest levels of profitability, on the labour force of the entire family, including those children who, as so-called *Nahwanderer*, continued to live at home while commuting to work in local industry. Thus the agricultural structure remained generally intact without being able genuinely to increase its productivity.

4

The surplus population which this kind of small-scale agriculture could not maintain flooded into the urban centres in search of a livelihood. In the eastern provinces, the structure of ownership was rather different by comparison with the west and south-west. Some 20 per cent of the units were very large and many of them were managed by the *Junker*, the traditional ruling elite of Prussia. Since the mid-nineteenth century their ranks had been infiltrated by bourgeois elements who, during the boom period of large-scale farming in the 1850s and 1860s, saw grain-growing as a profitable investment. In other words, it would be wrong to see East Elbian agriculture as being completely untouched by the developing market economy and modern production methods. On the other hand, Prussian agriculture never embraced capitalism with unbridled enthusiasm, and older traditions of economic conduct lingered on. These conditions made the *Junker* vulnerable to the vagaries of the market which they supplied with a single crop: grain. Trouble started in the 1870s when, with the development of the American Midwest and of the Ukraine for cereal crops, the world market was hit by what can only be described as a crisis of overproduction. This crisis, which came on top of the structural problems of agriculture as a result of industrialisation, began seriously to threaten the economic position of the estate owners.

The decline of the *Junker's* own economic fortunes inevitably also adversely affected the livelihood of those men, women and children who had worked and had been forced to work for them: tied peasants, agricultural labourers and migrant workers from the Polish parts of Russia. A number of the peasants had succeeded in freeing themselves from their service obligations to the local landlord and had set themselves up as independent small-holders, eking out a meagre existence. The others, with their already low wages being held down by the erosion of their employers' and masters' income, simply packed their few belongings and absconded to the great industrial centres of Berlin, Saxony and the Ruhr, if they did not emigrate overseas. Thus, while industry succeeded in achieving growth, albeit an uneven one, the rot had set in for German agriculture, with far-reaching non-economic repercussions.

Up to now, the focus of our analysis has been exclusively on the major economic aspects of industrialisation and demographic change. We must now consider the sociological and social implications of Germany's rapid transition from an agricultural to an industrial economy. It is clear from what has been said so far that this transition resulted in a society in which millions of lower-class people were on the move. Most of them sought economic advancement as a means of achieving upward social mobility, and industry appeared to be offering this opportunity more easily than agriculture with its more inflexible stratification. Especially in rural Prussia, many of the patriarchal structures of the pre-industrial period had survived, supported by legal rights which put the landlord in a very powerful position. On the great estates, people simply stayed in 'their place', even if there was a growing number of younger men and women in particular who refused to 'know their place'. They moved away, and their response shows that the expectation of economic advancement cannot be separated from their desire to escape from the rigidly stratified society of the eastern provinces. Although most migrants entered industry as unskilled or semi-skilled labourers, for the ambitious among them it was easier to enhance the status of some of their children, if not their own.

There were, as we shall see in a moment, definite limits to an upward mobility. Imperial Germany was, and remained to the end, a society which might be crudely divided into a traditional upper class, an increasingly differentiated middle class and an agricultural and industrial working class. Few succeeded in surmounting these major barriers although it was possible to move up (and down) within the confines of one of these strata. In particular the expanding industrial economy with its increasingly complex organisation and pressures for rationalised production in larger units using the latest technologies provided room for upward movement of the skilled and the specialist. In the industries of the Second Industrial Revolution the systematic use of the applied sciences created the need for new skills and hence new opportunities. Commerce, banking and insurance also expanded rapidly (Table 16).

It would therefore be quite wrong to portray Wilhelmine society as stagnant and petrified. There was rapid change and great diversity which does not make it easy to generalise about the state of that society. What complicated the situation even further were regional variations, resulting from the federal structure of the country, the persistence of pockets of traditionalism and denominational divisions, mainly between Protestants and Catholics. Thus, at one end of the spectrum people continued to live very much in the same conditions and with the same perceptions of the world as their parents and grandparents. Provinces like Pomerania or parts of Bavaria remained extremely rural and isolated. Villagers rarely looked beyond the parish pump. The local priest or the landlord were the dominant figures, socially, economically and politically. The age of deference was far from over, occasional rebellions at the ballot-box or riots by village youths (*Haberfeldtreiben*) notwithstanding. Traditional life-styles, old hierarchies and patronage networks also survived into the twentieth century in many provincial towns. On the other hand, we have seen that even the more remote areas experienced change, if only in the sense that large numbers of people were opting out of this small universe and moving to the urban centres. Life in the cities, on the other hand, proceeded at a very much faster and unsteady pace. Because of the demographic upheavals, they found themselves constantly in a state of economic uncertainty and social commotion. To be sure, class lines were clearly discernible in the cities as well, and some were more equal than others.

For the shrewd and dynamic merchant or entrepreneur there was a great deal of money to be made. Despite repeated fluctuations, there was a general upward trend in income from investments. In the commercial centres like Frankfurt, Hamburg or Cologne, wealth had been accumulated over a longer period and was, perhaps, also less conspicuous. But new wealth was being generated very fast in places like Berlin, the capital of the German Empire and a major industrial and commercial centre. It was also acquired in the Rhineland in heavy industry, in Saxony and Silesia, or in Mannheim and Stuttgart with their growing engineering industries. Munich and Leipzig are other examples of cities which saw a good deal of affluence. In 1896, the Prussian Inland Revenue counted 9,265 taxpayers with an income of 30,500–100,000 marks and 1,699 with an income of over 100,000 marks per annum. By 1912 these figures had risen to 20,999 and 4,456, an increase of 126 per cent and 162 per cent respectively. And the *nouveaux riches* of the Industrial Revolution enjoyed showing off this wealth. In the late 1870s, the Krupps built their famous Villa Hügel like an English stately home on the southern fringes of Essen, overlooking the Ruhr valley and surrounded by quasi-royal splendour. Gerson Bleichröder, Bismarck's banker, was also doing quite well, as Benjamin Disraeli, not exactly a visitor from an underdeveloped country, had occasion to witness:

The banqueting hall, very vast and very lofty, and indeed the whole mansion, is built of every species of rare marble, and where it is not marble it is gold. There was a gallery for the musicians who played Wagner, and Wagner only, which I was very glad of, as I have rarely had an opportunity of hearing that master. After dinner, we were promenaded through the splendid saloons – and picture galleries, and a ballroom fit for a fairy-tale, and sitting alone on a sofa was a very mean-looking little woman, covered with pearls and diamonds, who was Madame Bleichröder and whom he had married very early in life when he was penniless. She was unlike her husband, and by no means equal to her wondrous fortune.

Indeed Bleichröder's was a very different story from that of the Prussian *Junker* who saw their economic position disintegrate while trying to maintain the life-style to which they were accustomed. As one of them, Elard von Oldenburg-Januschau exclaimed in 1904: 'Being poor is no misfortune, but lapsing into poverty is one!' Meanwhile, in 1895, Udo Count Stolberg-Wernigerode, scion of an old Prussian landowning family, was forced to sell his town-house in Berlin because he was unable to afford the rates. This social humiliation provides a telling contrast with Bleichröder's affluence and illustrates what the Industrial Revolution was doing to the agrarian upper class on the one hand and the well-to-do bourgeoisie on the other.

Lower down the social scale there were the white-collar workers in private industry and commerce and at different levels of the Civil Service. The promotion prospects and opportunities for status advancement of the former

7

increased greatly in those expanding industries which relied on technical–scientific and managerial skills and qualifications. The so-called New *Mittel-stand* emerged, taking pride in its expertise and developing its own social aspirations.

Yet it was not all optimism and prosperity in the non-agricultural sector of the German economy. In particular the artisans and members of the so-called Old *Mittelstand* found it difficult to keep up with the dynamics of a modern capitalist–industrial system, except for those who established themselves as specialist suppliers to industry. Many families of the well-to-do Wilhelmine bourgeoisie had once themselves started their businesses in a small workshop, but they had succeeded in expanding their activities. Mergers and takeovers increased. By the late nineteenth century there was a strong trend towards larger units and factories, aided partly by the German system of banking and external industrial finance, but also by the rise of the joint stock company (Table 17). The less successful and enterprising among the self-employed who continued to operate from a damp backroom soon found themselves squeezed between the wage demands of their two or three employees and the competition by the larger manufacturers and traders who had more capital to play with and were less vulnerable to temporary recessions.

Initially, the expansion of the market had also afforded many of the smaller businesses improved opportunities. But the concentration of economic power soon affected not merely the manufacturing side, but also retailing. In the small towns away from the industrial centres, artisans and traders lost much of their former business because of the above-mentioned population movement. However, decline also came because they were less adaptable to a changing market situation. We shall have to analyse in a moment how these various *Mittelstand* groups, the prospering as well as the hard-pressed ones, reacted to their socioeconomic predicament. Yet this reaction cannot be understood without a prior look at the position of the industrial working class.

The working class had not only experienced a rapid growth in numbers (Tables 14 and 16), but also a precarious improvement in their living standards. Contrary to the gloomy predictions of many social revolutionaries in the nineteenth century, wages had experienced a long-term rise (Table 23). The index of annual real incomes for employees in industry and commerce which was at 100 points in 1895 had moved up to 114 by 1905 and to 125 by 1913. However, the material benefits of industrial growth were very unevenly distributed. According to Prussian income statistics, the number of taxpayers who earned between 900 marks and 3,000 marks per annum rose by 167 per cent between 1896 and 1912, from 2.5 million to 6.8 million. On the other hand, there were still some 8.2 million employees with annual earnings under 900 marks, only 5 per cent less than in 1896. In all, more than half of the 15.7 million taxpayers in Prussia, the largest State of the Reich, were in the lowest income category. Fluctuations of the economy tended to affect many workers very immediately, and it appears that living conditions experienced a deterioration shortly before the First World War. This implies that working-class families, most of whom fell into this low-income category, still found it extremely difficult to make ends meet, and relative improvements were often achieved only because several family members went out to work. Furthermore, the poverty trap into which these families were liable to fall in case of illness or redundancy was still wide open (Table 18). These were still the days when the State provided no more than the most rudimentary social security 'net'. Some 30 per cent of all family households in this prosperous Second Empire lived in destitution and abject misery. Yet even those whose income was sufficient and who kept it above the rate of inflation did not enjoy a particularly comfortable life. Over half of the weekly wage packet was spent on food, with bread being the main item in the diet. What more than anything else made their daily existence so arduous were not only the ten to twelve working hours (Table 31), often in very unhealthy conditions, for six days of the week, but also their housing conditions.

After their long workday, industrial workers needed their leisure time primarily for sheer physical regeneration. But the accommodation they returned to in the evenings, often after a long walk from their workplace, was rarely conducive to this need. The urban explosion had, not surprisingly, led to a desperate housing shortage. The building industry could not keep up with the influx of people and market demand dictated the price. Since the overwhelming majority of people (in 1895 = 93.35% in Berlin) did not own their accommodation, most families had to put aside as much as one quarter of their income for rent. Most of them had to be satisfied with one-room or two-room flats. Later, three-room units became more common, but as late as 1905, 12.1 per cent of the families took in overnight lodgers (*Schlafgänger*) to help pay the rent, and in some cities the figure was even higher. Heating facilities tended to be restricted to one room although winters could be bitterly cold and the problem of overcrowding became even worse during these months when outdoor life was impossible. Rent increases and other economic pressures forced families to move frequently.

It is worthwhile pausing for a moment to try to visualise the effects of these conditions on marital relations, the education of children and health, but also on group consciousness. Maybe these housing conditions still compared favourably with those of the rural labourers and maids who lived in tiny cubby-holes above the stables. But even where differences between town and country were more marginal, the fact remains that migrants came to the industrial centres in search of a better life and, once they had found their feet in Berlin, Leipzig, Essen or Stuttgart, they were hoping for their life chances to improve. It was here that the most serious social problem began.

Wilhelmine Germany, 1900–1914

Stratification and social mobility

Sooner or later the workers and their families discovered that opportunities of economic betterment and upward mobility were strictly limited, and limited by sociocultural as well as political barriers. It is more difficult to be precise about the former than about the latter, largely because the mechanisms of social and cultural stratification in Wilhelmine Germany were fairly subtle. Furthermore, they were not merely rooted in tangible differentiations of wealth, income and power which have been mentioned above, but also in *perceptions* of class and status of one group by another. This is an area of social history which historians of Germany have only just begun to explore. Nevertheless, there is little doubt that there existed marked differences in the way in which people organised their life outside their workplace. Here traditions, customs and social consciousness weighed heavily. From childhood on, people had been social-ised into a milieu in thousands of small ways and these experiences had an important influence on their perceptions of the world around them. Depend-ing upon their position within the social structure, men, women and children would eat, speak and dress in a certain way. They had their own peculiar habits of furnishing their rooms and of spending their leisure time. Cultural and social differences of this kind provided as much a frame of reference by which people 'recognised' others inside or outside their own group as did their job and income.

Although it is not unproblematical for the historian to draw upon the visual arts and literature as primary sources, the paintings of Heinrich Zille or, in a different way, of Käthe Kollwitz and the writings of Carl Zuckmayer or the Mann brothers do provide useful, if stylised, insights into the cultural environment of divergent social groups. However, there were two currents which tended to cut across the stratification of Wilhelmine society in terms of a specific class culture. These cross-currents complicated the overall picture because they did not act to reinforce existing divisions along class and intra-class status lines, and they were: regionalism and denomination.

The importance of regionalism and local consciousness cannot be empha-sised too strongly, the more so as it was institutionally supported by the federal structure of the Constitution of 1871. The German Empire was composed of twenty-two principalities and three Hanseatic cities. At the one end of the scale were States like Schaumburg-Lippe with 39,000 inhabitants living in a territory of 340 sq. kilometres, and tiny entities like Reuß ä.L. or Schwarzburg-Sondershausen; at the other end was the Kingdom of Prussia which in 1890 had 30 million citizens and occupied 349,000 sq. kilometres, 64 per cent of the total Reich territory. Within Prussia resided Pomeranians, Hanoverians, Hessians and Westphalians. Some of these people lived in very remote areas, just as it must be remembered that, rapid industrialisation and demographic change notwithstanding, some 40 per cent of the population spent their days in closely knit communities of under 2,000 people as late as 1910 (Table 2). The effect of all this was that most Germans saw themselves and others not exclusively as peasants, textile workers, shopkeepers, white-collar office workers or aristocrats, but as *Bavarian* peasants, *Württembergian* shopkeepers, *Hanoverian* office workers or *Silesian* aristocrats. Regionalism, in other words, created a strong sense of separateness *vis-à-vis* other parts of Germany, perpetuated by linguistic variations and the observance of regional custom, tradition and folklore. Local uniformity of a particular accent has occasionally been taken as proof that regionalism was a stronger bond than class. Wilhelmine Germany was deemed to be less class-ridden than Edwardian England where the accent immediately betrayed a person's social background. It may be that a Bavarian felt particularly Bavarian in Berlin or Cologne; but this did not mean that he or she had lost the capacity or propensity to place other Bavarians within the Empire's overall social structure. He might be pleased to meet a fellow-businessman from Munich in Prussia. Yet he was as unlikely to befriend a Bavarian factory worker outside Bavaria as he was to have social intercourse with him back home.

Religious belief was the second factor which cut across class and status barriers, albeit less and less so. The percentage of formal affiliation to one or other of the denominations was high. In 1910, some 40 million out of 64.5 million Germans were members of the Protestant churches; 23.8 million belonged to the Catholic Church, and there were some 615,000 Jews (Table 5). Although the spiritual hold of the churches over their flocks was diminishing under the impact of urbanisation and industrialisation, the local religious community continued to act as a focus which was able to exert a pressure on people's behaviour, especially in small towns and villages which lacked the greater anonymity of cities. Here the churches were openly opposed to the changes resulting from the transition to an industrial society. Catholic priests took their cue from the conservative policies enunciated by the Vatican. In Prussia the Evangelical Church had long enjoyed the status of a state institution, with the monarch acting as *Summus Episcopus*. This gave church leaders an important voice in education and other public matters, and the existing major division into Protestants and Catholics gave denomination a tangible weight in politics and popular consciousness. As in the case of regionalism, religion could thus act as a powerful cross-current which interfered with socioeconomic hierarchies.

This influence is particularly striking in the case of the Catholics where the *Zentrum* emerged as the party-political arm of German Catholicism. The Centre Party, internally strengthened by the confessional struggle (*Kulturkampf*) against National Liberal Protestantism and Reich Chancellor Otto von Bismarck in the 1870s and nursing its long memories of that struggle, attracted the votes of industrial workers as well as the middle and upper classes simply because they were Catholic. However, as subsequent references to the Centre will show, after the turn of the century, denominational cohesion became increasingly eroded by a more intense class consciousness among industrial workers. In short, what, by 1914, determined social and political behaviour and interaction much more than religious upbringing or regionalism were the perceptions of 'them' and 'us' in terms of class and status. One indication of this trend as far as industrial workers are concerned is the degree of unionisation. Catholic trade unions had come into existence in the 1890s side by side with socialist-orientated unions and anti-Marxist liberal workers' associations, known as *Hirsch-Dunckerschen Gewerkschaften* (Table 46). However, after 1910 they were unable to sustain their growth of members in the same way as the Free Unions. Catholic workers increasingly accepted Social Democrat interpretations of social structure and Wilhelmine politics as more plausible.

With regionalism and religion as integrating factors declining and working-class criticism of social and economic conditions rising, nationalism and imperialism came to be employed as devices to paper over the fissures of class and status. Yet instead of acting as a unifying force, nationalistic propaganda and the appeal to strengthen Germany's defences did much to simplify into a bipolarity the rather more complex picture of social and ideological division. However much people might disagree on other political issues, where the question of upholding German interests in a world of hostile foreign powers was concerned the pressure to conform was tremendous. Lukewarm support for the country's foreign and armaments policy would put a person outside this consensus into the camp of the 'unpatriotic fellows' on the Left.

We shall have to come back to the evolution of this polarity in our discussion of Wilhelmine politics. The point to bear in mind here is that pre-1914 Germany was a clearly stratified society in which upward mobility beyond the class boundary was difficult. With the process of rapid industrialisation and urbanisation creating so much disruption at the grass-roots of society, the upper strata reacted all the more strongly against what they perceived as dangerous 'levelling' tendencies. The reaction was to maintain social barriers and to deny social recognition to those who had succeeded in acquiring the material prerequisites of entry into the higher class. Thus a Berlin businessman who had amassed enough wealth to buy himself an estate north-east of the capital would more often than not fail to gain social recognition by the local Prussian nobility and squirearchy. Similar would be the fate of a successful family butcher who sought access to the exclusive circles of Bremen's patrician families. As Hartmut Kaelble put it in his survey of social mobility in twentieth-century Germany: 'It is clear that, even in the long run, Germany did not become a new land of unbounded opportunities: the large majority of working-class sons did not leave their class; the majority of the lower middle class continued to come from lower-middle-class origins.'

The position was not much better higher up on the social ladder. In 1903, 30 per cent of the candidates for the Prussian Higher Civil Service had fathers who were themselves in this category. Another 15 per cent had fathers in the officer corps; 22 per cent were the sons of estate owners, and 16 per cent offspring of the business elite. Only 4 per cent of the fathers were middle-ranking civil servants and there were no lower-middle-class or working-class candidates. As various studies on the social composition of the Prussian officer corps, once the preserve of the nobility, have shown, officers of middle-class background succeeded in making substantial inroads here. By 1913, they accounted for no less than 70 per cent of the total officer corps. However, these percentages again tell us little about the problems which these men encountered in respect of promotion and social intercourse with fellow-officers of noble background. Often they found themselves shunted off to command posts in remote areas; or they discovered that they could gain advancement only in the low-prestige artillery and the engineering corps. In 1900, 60 per cent of all colonels and 70 per cent of all General Staff officers were noblemen. As late as 1913, four out of five posts in the cavalry were occupied by the nobility, as against 40 per cent in the artillery. The institution of marriage consent tended to put a stop to rapid upward mobility in the female line.

Similar practices existed, albeit less formalised, among the business elite, the medical and legal professions and virtually all the way down the middle-class scale. In short, demographic change and economic upward mobility were not accompanied by a perceptible flattening of the class and status pyramid. It is not possible to describe the mechanisms by which the advancement of 'undesirable elements' could be impeded. Occasionally, it is true, they were also applied to people of the 'wrong' regional or denominational background. It could be a disadvantage to be born in Saxony or to be a professing Catholic living in Prussia. To be of Jewish ancestry tended to be an even worse handicap. However, more often social recognition was difficult to obtain because a person's family was considered too humble by his superiors. Additional obstacles existed in the public services. By the turn of the century, the Civil Service was experiencing a further narrowing of its recruitment base after stern political criteria had begun to dominate selection and promotion. People who were suspected of not being staunchly monarchist and conservative were not admitted, and all too often a lower-class background was sufficient to nourish such suspicions.

The role of the educational system is of obvious significance to social mobility. Germany was one of the first countries to develop a system of compulsory education from the ages of six to fourteen. This system was no doubt effective in transmitting basic reading and writing skills, despite class sizes of around 60 pupils (Table 37). Illiteracy rates were, so far as is known, lower than in Britain and France, although the state of official statistics and regional variations makes it difficult to provide absolutely reliable figures. *Volksschulen* were moreover important for inculcating the mass of the population with the dominant values of the Wilhelmine age. However, beyond the elementary level, barriers were in operation and it required more than an above-average intelligence to overcome them. Money was indispensable. In 1872 Prussia introduced the *Mittelschule*, but parents had to pay a fee. The same applied to the highly selective *höhere Schule*. In the years before 1914 it cost at least 130 marks a year to go to high school, and the long years up to the *Abitur* (A-level certificate) in one of the three types of *höhere Schulen* were trying for parents and pupils. Pedagogical principles were authoritarian and the drop-out rate was high. What made the attainment of the *Abitur* so arduous for children of lower-class background was that, apart from the financial burdens it imposed upon the pupil's family, it required a domestic environment which was supportive of academic study. In this system, it was no less difficult for a girl of any social background to get a higher education than it was for the 'bright lad' from a lower-class family. Consequently, the number of high school students rose after the turn of the century to only slightly above half a per cent of the population.

The *Abitur* certificate gave automatic access to university – again for those whose families could afford it. Academic demands were high, and studies could take four or even six years, often lengthened by the concept of academic freedom and moves between different universities. Still, at the end of the educational ladder beckoned the prospect of a career in the professions, the higher echelons of industry or the civil service. In the decade after 1901, the total number of students increased by 20,000 to some 70,000, of whom about three or four per cent were women (Table 38). If being a *Primaner* (sixth-former) or a university student carried with it improved social status, it is not surprising that those involved in the educational system on the teaching side fought hard to preserve its high degree of selectivity, which provided them with better pay and enhanced prestige. Meanwhile, primary school teachers, on salaries half as large as those of their colleagues in the high school sector, tried in vain to obtain a more flexible training system and career structure with promotion prospects to a higher level. Similarly the gate to a university post remained closely guarded.

The preceding discussion of social mobility and educational opportunities in Germany was intended to explain rather than condemn or praise the principles of stratification by which Wilhelmine society operated. Of course, there was nothing extraordinary about these principles, as other European countries applied similar filters which retarded social mobility in an age of rapid economic and demographic change. Nevertheless, these details enable us to

14

appreciate more clearly the psychological repercussions which this system of structured inequalities had on the individuals and groups living in this kind of society. On the one hand, there are not many groups in history which have abandoned privilege and power without fairly pugnacious resistance. On the other, it is understandable that those who came up against the strong ceilings of stratification would harbour resentments and struggle to demolish them. The discovery that there were other people whose privileged position was also threatened or, conversely, whose advancement was similarly blocked, created feelings of solidarity which worked to reinforce the sociocultural group identities based on language, life-style, employment and tradition.

This was particularly true of a group which had most to gain from a dissolution of existing hierarchies and which, because of its aspirations and its potential numerical strength, was regarded by the groups above it as the most dangerous threat to the status quo: the German industrial working class. Its sense of 'them' and 'us' had become heightened not merely by the experience of economic discrimination and cultural separateness, but also because of its deliberate 'ghettoisation' by the middle and upper classes. The notion of 'ghetto' points to differences and conflicts beyond the bounds of material differentiation and social stratification. Nowhere did these conflicts manifest themselves more tangibly than in the legal and political sphere.

Seen from the perspective of the upper classes, more direct means were available to 'keep people in their place' than the mechanisms of social and economic discrimination described so far. The power of the 'State' could be deployed. There were the police, the judiciary and the Army, and Bismarck had used them to implement and maintain the anti-socialist laws against the German working-class movement between 1878 and 1890. During this period the repressive arm of the State had been purposefully mobilised to contain the threat of 'revolution'. Indeed, the Chancellor knew how to draw upon the fears this threat engendered. It was perceived to be real and serious enough by the rest of society. However, we are here primarily concerned with the impact of twelve long years of proscription and class hostility, not merely upon the organised part of the working class (which was obviously most directly affected by it), but also upon those workers who did not or dared not commit themselves to the Social Democratic Party (SPD). As to the middle and upper classes, the agitation prior to the ratification of the anti-socialist laws of 1878 did much to sharpen the belief in the 'red menace'. In subsequent years the parliamentary debates relating to the renewal of the laws, as well as anti-socialist propaganda, served to perpetuate prevailing fears. As one scholar put it: 'Excited minds in the upper echelons of the bureaucracy envisaged socialist level-crossing keepers and pointsmen interfering with the movement of troop trains.' The lapse of the anti-socialist laws in 1890 and the reappearance of the working-class movement in the streets and

15

factories further intensified deeply ingrained suspicions of both the Social Democrats and of the unorganised 'masses'.

For a loyal member of the SPD, on the other hand, the 1880s were very hard times indeed. W. L. Guttsman has described the system of repression in the following words:

Generally police surveillance and prosecution operated fairly strictly, especially in Prussia. The police regularly invoked the provision of the 'minor siege' to harass those suspected of pro-socialist sentiments and activities. Even innocent-seeming glee clubs, gymnastics associations and general cultural and vocational societies were subject to constant harassment and prohibition.... Legal prosecutions took place under the slightest pretext, often on a charge of lese-majesty or incitement to public disorder. It has been estimated that during the years of the repressive legislation, 900 persons were expelled from their homes and place of work and that 1500 men were sentenced to varying terms of imprisonment, totalling 1000 years.

The persecution of alleged 'socialist agitators' invariably brought physical and emotional suffering to their families, who often had to rely on relatives or neighbours for support. Experience of the anti-socialist laws was therefore not merely confined to professing Social Democrats and their relatives. News of some police action against someone from their midst was bound to create worry and uncertainty, on the one hand, and spontaneous offers of help, on the other, as working-class communities tended to be geographically self-contained and closely knit. Above all, proscription increased the feeling of ostracism and 'societal loneliness' which, together with the experience of conflict at the workplace, fostered group consciousness. After 1890, when opinions could be expressed more freely again, this increased solidarity found its political expression in a growing identification with the SPD and the trade unions (Table 46). In the 1898 elections to the German Parliament (Reichstag) the Social Democrats gained 2.1 million votes and 56 seats; fourteen years later 4.25 million men gave them their support at the polls. The SPD had become the largest party in the Reichstag, with 110 deputies (Tables 40 and 41). Trade union membership likewise rose from 278,000 in 1891 to 2,549,000 in 1913.

The unions were confronted by powerful employers' organisations, most of which were totally opposed to the organising efforts of the workforce and refused to grant unions any official status. Although collective bargaining practices started in some smaller branches of industry, most owners and managers tried to run their factories in a firmly autocratic fashion. They were quick to impose a lock-out in response to strikes or to call the police to move strike-breakers through the picket-lines (Table 44). Social Democrat 'agitators' were unceremoniously sacked and blacklisted. Industrial relations were particularly poor in some of the heavy industries. Employers' attempts to curb trade union influence were supported at the national level by an effective interest-group representation which had emerged since the late 1870s. These organisations saw to it that the views of industry were taken into account when it came to questions of economic and social policy, and on most issues they tended to take a hard line, particularly where labour problems were involved. Not surprisingly, these realities did much to foster a desire on the part of the workers to join a union, even if it could not do much to protect them. As social tensions increased towards 1914 and employers became tougher, the working-class movement gained more recruits.

It would hence be misleading to explain the growth of the working-class movement simply in terms of the demographic explosion. The point is that more and more people of working-class origin came to regard the SPD and its various associations as the only legitimate political representation of their interests. Moreover, and no less importantly, Social Democracy offered them something like a spiritual home. Although its essentially Marxist ideology was purveyed in a large variety of interpretations, it succeeded in offering an explanation of the present socioeconomic predicament of the German workers and raised their hopes for a better future. It appears that, on the basis of their own experiences, they found the orthodox views of the class character of Wilhelmine society, as expounded in the Erfurt Programme of 1891, most plausible. In particular they subscribed to the basically dichotomous view of existing society espoused in the first part of that Programme. They may have felt more ambivalent about the call for a political struggle against exploitation, and indeed the Party ultimately dodged the question of whether the much-vaunted new society which was to emerge from this struggle would be born in a revolutionary upheaval or would result from gradual change and reform.

The second part of the Erfurt Programme contained many demands which could be achieved through gradualism, a strategy which the majority of the members and SPD voters clearly preferred to radical revolution. One of these demands was a reduction of work-hours which may appear to be very modest and reasonable today. But it is worth putting these aspirations into a contemporary context and to remember E. Halévy's dictum that 'when I was fifteen, the demand for the eight-hour day seemed one of the most striking utopias of revolutionary socialism'. This was certainly the view of many trade unionists who regarded improvement by small steps in the field of wages and conditions of employment as the real task. Using strikes as a political weapon to bring the economy to a halt and to undermine and ultimately destroy the existing order, as advocated by Rosa Luxemburg and a few others on the Left of the SPD, was rejected as dangerous and self-defeating, however much the unions may have agreed in principle with the notion that the German workers lived in a rigidly stratified, exploitative and repressive class society.

Nothing did more to strengthen the position of the reformists than the impression of a slow improvement in living conditions and the SPD's

17

successes at the polls. Did electoral trends not confirm that it was merely a matter of time before the Social Democrats would also have the majority of seats in the Reichstag, notwithstanding the various handicaps which the peculiarities of the voting system imposed? But this question also touches upon the central issue of the Wilhelmine constitutional system, namely whether this achievement would have brought the reformists in the working-class movement any nearer to their political objective of gaining a decisive say in the decision-making processes of the Wilhelmine Empire as a prerequisite of their objective to initiate further social and economic change. Had Germany possessed a fully fledged parliamentary system, similar to the British one at this time, prospects of achieving this objective might be considered bright. The majority party in Parliament would have formed a government and would have been in a position to introduce bills on a whole range of economic and social matters to create a more egalitarian and democratic society.

The Prusso-German political system and its political culture

However, the German political system was not to be compared with the British one. The Reichstag was not the hub of power and the executive was not responsible to it. Although the Bismarckian Constitution of 1871 was a highly complex structure, it is clear that its centre of political gravity lay outside the parliamentary sphere. Thus the right to conduct the country's foreign policy and to decide upon the deployment of the armed forces in war and peacetime was in the hands of the German Emperor (Kaiser) and the ministerial officials appointed by him. The Kaiser also had the power to nominate and dismiss the Reich Chancellor and the heads of other Reich offices. While the Crown was hence involved in major areas of executive decision-making, Wilhelm II was also king of Prussia and in this capacity was able to select the members of the Ministry of State and the Civil Service. As head of the Prussian government he was also involved in the legislative process in Prussia. All bills had to be approved by three constitutional organs, the king, the upper chamber (*Herrenhaus*) and the lower chamber (*Landtag*), with the right to initiate legislation resting with the monarch.

It is true that bills, in passing through the legislative process, were liable to be amended by the deputies in the two assemblies. However, it was not too difficult to engineer a consensus between all three organs and hence to secure the passage of a particular bill. The upper chamber was dominated by the nobility and conservative representatives loyal to the Crown. The deputies of the lower chamber were elected by means of a complex three-class voting system based on income, with the wealthier groups producing two-thirds of the representatives and the mass of the male population the remaining third. This system saw to it that representation in the lower chamber would likewise be dominated by the conservative forces of Prussia, who were unlikely to oppose the equally conservative legislative initiatives of the monarchical Prussian government. Nor would they object if the king decided to preserve the status quo by legislative inaction, an equally important political device.

Similar legislative and electoral arrangements existed in the other States. Restrictive suffrage systems limited the ability of the mass of the population to participate through their elected representatives in the decision-making processes both of large States like the kingdoms of Bavaria or Saxony or of dwarf principalities like Schaumburg-Lippe. The Hanseatic cities of Hamburg, Bremen and Lübeck were dominated politically by a patriciate engaged in trade and commerce which – not unlike the landed nobility of Prussia – did its best to cement the oligarchical structures of their city governments. This was not always easy in some of the States where, against the main trend led by Prussia, forms of parliamentary government began to develop towards 1914, thus further complicating the picture. On the other hand, there were the city-fathers of Hamburg who, worried about the growth of the SPD vote after the lapse of the anti-socialist laws, went so far as to curtail local suffrage rights and to bring them more into line with the Prussian class franchise. Whereas the majority of the voters were thus constantly made aware of their reduced political status and the hierarchical nature of Wilhelmine federal politics, representation in the Reich was by universal manhood suffrage.

Introduced by a Prussian conservative, Otto von Bismarck, this was indeed a surprising, if not revolutionary feature of the Reich Constitution. Bismarck, to be sure, had his own 'Bonapartist' reasons for opening the flood-gates of mass politics. That he wanted to rely on the conservatism of the rural population and did not foresee the rise of a dissatisfied industrial working class who could now express their demands for political change at the polls, earned Bismarck frequent criticism from his successors, who found it increasingly difficult to stem the leftward drift of Reich politics (Tables 40 and 41). It was only consistent with the rising fear of Social Democracy that conservative politicians time and again demanded the abolition of universal suffrage. No doubt this cry would have been even louder had the Reich electoral system not prevented the full translation of votes into parliamentary seats. For example, governmental inaction ensured that no changes were made in constituency boundaries after 1871. Given the huge shifts of populations that took place prior to 1914, the effect of this was that in some depopulated constituencies a few thousand voters elected their deputy. In the densely populated city of Bochum, on the other hand, the number was over 40,000. Thus, 'at the turn of the century, Germany's largest electoral district, Berlin VI, which voted overwhelmingly for the Social Democrats, contained nearly as many electors as the fifteen smallest constituencies' (W. L. Guttsman). In short, a vote in the rural areas, often dominated by the conservatives, could be worth several times as much as one cast in the industrial Ruhr district.

The principle of universal suffrage was further undermined by a split-ballot system which permitted the weaker parties to pool their resources in the second ballot once the strongest party had been identified in the first round. Above all, it was the patriarchal conditions in many rural constituencies that tended to work against the idea of the franchise. In particular in Prussia, where many landowners had retained judicial and other rights over their workforce and the local population, it remained the practice to troop the labour force to the polling station, issue them with a ballot paper for the Conservative Party and tell them what to do with it. Of course, such practices were fraught with dangers in that they could also be applied by the Social Democrats in constituencies in which they held a strong position, and doubtless some arm-twisting of voters did take place there too. It is interesting that when conservative politicians, fearful of SPD successes, suggested in 1913 that Reich Chancellor Theobald von Bethmann Hollweg abolish the secret ballot, the latter rejected the idea by pointing to the double-edged nature of such 'reforms'.

None of these handicaps prevented the SPD from becoming the largest party in the Reichstag in 1912. As this had been anticipated for some time, it was a relief for the conservative forces in German society to know that the constitutional powers of the Reichstag were strictly limited and not comparable with those of the House of Commons across the Channel. The nomination and dismissal of the Reich government was independent of those who commanded the parliamentary majority. As far as legislation was concerned the deputies had to wait for a lead from the executive, and even then a bill would not reach them before it had been approved by the *Bundesrat* (Federal Council). This constitutional body was an even more exclusive circle than the Prussian Upper House. It was composed of the delegates of the twenty-two Federal Princes and three Hanseatic cities. And even here some princes, all of whom had their own governments and bureaucracies within their territories, were more equal than others. Bismarck had specifically secured a sufficiently large number of block votes for Prussia, by far the largest Federal State, for it never to be outvoted by the other States in matters of constitutional reform. According to Article 78, legislation to change the Constitution was defeated if 14 block votes opposed the proposed revision. Prussia had 17 such block votes. We shall have to remember this clause when we examine the question of whether the Prusso-German political system might have evolved into a parliamentary monarchy.

Once a bill emerged from the *Bundesrat* – where it had usually been subjected to months of bargaining and redrafting – it was sent to the Reichstag. In passing through the various readings and committee stages, it would be further modified, sometimes so much so that the Reich government objected and fresh negotiations became necessary. Ultimately all bills that became law therefore represented a compromise between the Reich Chancellor, the Federal Council and a majority of the Reichstag parties. If compromise proved impossible, the bill might be withdrawn altogether or the Kaiser might invoke Article 24 of the Constitution (dissolution of the Reichstag) in the hope that fresh elections would lead to gains by parties which were prepared to co-operate with the government. However, it was always possible that the vote would go in the opposite direction and that the government would find itself confronted with an even more hostile Parliament. If so, and if a further round of elections offered no prospect of easing the situation, Wilhelm II and his advisers would rapidly be forced down the same road of constitutional conflict with the representative assembly which his grandfather had taken in 1861/2. At the end of this road the Crown had the choice between giving way (in which case the Reichstag would have won a major shift in the balance of power opening the way to a Western-style parliamentarism)˙ or putting up a fight (i.e. calling out the Army, closing down the representative assembly, abolishing the Constitution and establishing autocratic rule). The third solution was applied by Bismarck in Prussia in the 1860s when he carried on without the support of the Diet and, after winning the war against Austria in 1866, decided to hold elections. These elections, held on the day after the Battle of Königsgrätz, resulted in a massive swing towards the conservative parties. These were prepared to conclude a compromise with the Crown. The famous Indemnity Bill, by which the Diet retroactively approved the Prussian budget and 'forgave' Bismarck for his ruthlessly anti-parliamentary domestic policy of the previous four years, was passed on 3 September 1866.

The peculiarities of the highly complex Prusso-German political system have been outlined here in some detail because they are crucial for an understanding of the development of Wilhelmine Germany in the decades before 1914 and during the First World War. The point is that most modern governments are reluctant to rely exclusively on physical force to maintain stability and order. In the twentieth century even autocratic regimes try to legitimate their policies by gaining the support of the majority of their subjects. A more than temporary erosion of popular support consequently tends to weaken the system's long-term viability, to undermine the authority of the leadership and to sharpen internal conflict. It is at this level that the most fruitful comparisons may be made between Wilhelmine Germany and Western Europe during the pre-1914 period. If we had undertaken here an analysis of stratification, mobility and structures of inequality in France or Britain of the kind provided above for the Reich, the overall conclusion would not have been markedly different: all European societies at this time displayed quite rigid social and economic divisions which economic and technological change had done much to exacerbate. The gap between the rich and the poor was wide everywhere. Industrialisation and urbanisation had put the traditional social fabric under strain; it had led to the emergence of sizeable groups which were dissatisfied with existing conditions and advanced programmes for a better future.

It would be difficult to decide with any degree of accuracy whether social conflict was markedly more acute in France, Britain or Germany. Possibly the situation was more tense in German society because of the greater speed of socioeconomic change. But although listing the number of strikes and lock-outs or analysing contemporary intellectual currents may provide pointers, it is in the political arena that these tensions can be most directly observed and that divergent constitutional arrangements in different European countries began to count. The fact that France and Britain had developed parliamentary systems in which the representative assembly, rather than a monarch, was the power centre profoundly influenced the political behaviour both of those in power and of those aspiring to gain it in the next election. It pushed the major political forces in the direction of compromise and moderation. The fact that the Reichstag was not the power centre in Wilhelmine Germany and that the Prusso-German political system remained, up to the end of the First World War, a quasi-autocracy with little taste for compromise furthered polarisation. More and more people ultimately began to search for solutions *outside* the existing constitutional structure (Table 41).

The notion that the citadels of executive and legislative power in Berlin could be conquered by patient exploitation of the universal suffrage – that dysfunctional element in the Bismarckian Constitution – may have seemed very persuasive to many reformists in the SPD and the left liberal splinter parties. Yet it ignored the fact that a peaceful shift in the balance of power between Crown and Parliament would have had to be enshrined in legislation amending the Constitution's key clauses. Given the tenacious and increasing opposition of the Federal Princes and the conservative groups supporting them, it is difficult to see how the development of a British-style parliamentarism might have come about in Wilhelmine Germany without a political revolution. As the experience during the First World War was to demonstrate, when pressures for constitutional change were greater than they had ever been in peacetime, the shift in the balance of power came about only when collapse was imminent. At this moment, the Kaiser and his advisers staged a political revolution 'from above'. They found it convenient to put the burden of military defeat upon the shoulders of the country's elected representatives. Taking account of this experience, it is hardly plausible that the monarchy would have made concessions when there was no imminent threat of a revolution 'from below'. Even if the Reich Chancellor might have been prepared to make a move, there were still the Federal States and, above all, Prussia to contend with.

There would hence appear to be truth in Wilhelm Liebknecht's dictum of 1871, which defined the Prusso-German political system as 'a princely insurance company against democracy', and one efficiently administered by a conservative bureaucracy. Forty years later, the position had altered to the extent that the bulk of the middle classes, motivated by their fear of rising Social Democracy, had been induced to take a stake in the preservation of the monarchy. By 1913 Wilhelmine politics had become polarised into those forces which hoped to turn the Reichstag into the power centre and those who fought hard either to preserve the existing monarchical order or, if necessary, even to cause it to evolve in a more dictatorial direction. There was no question for the latter of giving the 'masses' a genuine participatory role in the decision-making processes of the Reich. Analysing the Wilhelmine working-class movement, some historians have pointed to its moderation and lack of revolutionary fervour, and indeed there can be little doubt that those who wished to turn everything upside-down remained in a small minority.

However, this is not how the Social Democrats appeared to their contemporaries who identified with the political parties of the Right and the middle. To them the SPD was a thoroughly pernicious force for whose destruction all resources were to be mobilised. With the benefit of hindsight, it is clear that these fears were hopelessly exaggerated. Nevertheless, misperceptions of reality were a powerful political force. If our previous analysis is correct, it was the issue of parliamentarism on which the political positions adopted by divergent political parties became irreconcilable. Given the structural anti-parliamentarism of the 1871 Constitution, reform was not a matter of tinkering, but required a qualitative leap. And rather than open up this latter possibility and thereby create a new basis which took account of political changes since 1871, those who were in the position to initiate reforms preferred to sit tight while turning Social Democracy into a bogey which allegedly threatened the foundations of the whole society. Thank God, there were the Army, the police and the bureaucracy.

To be sure, not all opponents of the working-class movement saw physical repression as the only solution. Considerable differences of opinion arose over tactical questions. Remedies stretched from a policy of 'killing by kindness' to wholesale arrest of SPD leaders and ruthless proscription. While the basic anti-socialist consensus among the upper and middle classes acted as a powerful bond between them, it would nonetheless be misleading to say that tactical disagreement over treatment of the SPD was the only point of friction among the parties of the Right and the middle. In fact, the party system reflected divergent economic and political interests within Wilhelmine society. Traditional patterns of regional, denominational and social fragmentation, as well as the electoral system, had prevented the emergence of two or three omnibus parties similar to the British or American models. Rather there existed at the turn of the century a welter of parties, each of which had become, for all practical purposes, the parliamentary front organisation of particularist group interests. Broadly speaking, all parties appealed to specific classes and status groups, with only the Catholic Centre Party cutting across the socioeconomic divides.

Thus the *Deutsch-Konservative Partei* (DKP) was strong in the Prussian countryside and was rightly regarded as the organ of the large-scale farming community, especially of East Elbia. Staunchly agrarian in outlook, it claimed to uphold the traditions and ethos of the Old Prussia against the alleged evils of industrialisation and urbanisation. In foreign policy matters it favoured a continental orientation, relying on the Army as a power-political instrument. At heart it was opposed to colonialism and the Kaiser's *Weltpolitik* (world policy) with its emphasis on naval building. The Free Conservatives, who competed in national elections under the name of *Reichspartei* (RP), tended to attract support from rather a small stratum of people who, though frequently of agrarian background, did not feel so uneasy about industrialisation. In fact some of them had even become engaged in industrial enterprise. The RP also drew support from some conservative representatives of heavy industry for whom the National Liberal Party (NLP) was, for a variety of reasons, unacceptable. Although it retained a foothold in rural constituencies, the NLP was the party of the industrial and commercial bourgeoisie. It was hetero-geneous in its views on major problems of domestic policy, but throughout the Wilhelmine period united in its support for imperialist expansion overseas and an armaments policy which would give Germany's considerable international aspirations military clout. On the left-centre of the political spectrum, there existed in 1900 a number of smaller parties which merged in 1910 to form the Progressive People's Party (FVP). Its main support came from reformist intellectuals and academics and from left-liberal sections of the Hanseatic and south-west German bourgeoisie. The Progressives advocated an opening-up of the political system. They wanted a reconciliation of the working-class with the Prusso-German State at home, combined with a popularly based foreign policy to secure Germany's position as a manufactur-ing and exporting nation.

The Centre Party was the only political movement which, if one ignores the small parties of the national minorities (Poles, Danes, Alsatians), cannot easily be fitted into this picture. Its support, as we have seen, was based not so much on socioeconomic interest as on denominational ties, strengthened during the 1870s by Bismarck's *Kulturkampf* against the Catholic Church. Thus it would attract support from industrial workers in the Ruhr, Bavarian peasants, Cologne businessmen and Silesian landowners, provided they were Catholic.

The minority position of Catholicism in a predominantly Protestant Reich largely explains the relative stability of the Centre Party which held around 100 seats in the two decades before 1910. It was only towards the 1912 elections that Catholic workers increasingly began to ignore the denominational appeal and turned towards the SPD in the conviction that their interests were better represented by a movement whose propaganda emphasised the class divisions of the Wilhelmine Empire. In 1898 the Centre Party won over some 80 per cent of all Catholic Reichstag voters; in 1912 the figure had declined to 55 per cent; its claim to be a 'people's party above the classes' had fallen prey to growing class tensions. Although the leadership tried to stem the defection of voters by adopting a more critical stance *vis-à-vis* the inflexible brand of Prussian conservatism and by propagating the social doctrine of the papal encyclical *Rerum novarum* (1891), the drift of Catholic workers towards the Social Democrats was a telling confirmation of the growing deadlock in German domestic politics.

However, by 1912 the Social Democrats were also making inroads among rural labourers as well as among some sections of the white-collar New *Mittelstand*. The latter, employed in the dynamic industries of the Second Industrial Revolution, found the Kaiser's dependence on the agrarians and the general immobilism increasingly objectionable. In this way voters became consolidated in large blocks divided by deep socioeconomic and ideological cleavages. The divisions did not stop there. More and more political mobilisation also occurred outside the party organisations in the narrow sense. The Social Democrats were the first to destroy the concept of a party as a loosely organised association of notables in a particular community and became what Sigmund Neumann called an 'integration party'. He added: 'It has been said, jokingly, that it accompanies the member from the cradle to the grave, from the proletarian infant welfare organisation to the free-thinking cremation association.'

Indeed, by the turn of the century there was barely a field of economic, cultural or political activity for which the Social Democrats did not provide an organisational forum. They became active in the areas of sports and leisure; they made major efforts to encourage cultural activity through choral societies and people's theatres (*Volksbühnen*); they also established a large network of extramural education providing evening classes in a large variety of arts and science subjects; they also opened lending libraries. And the response was remarkable. Around 1910 various socialist sports organisations had a membership of some 300,000. Another 192,000 were members of the *Deutscher Arbeitersängerbund* in 1912. Some 48,000 subscribed to the *Neue Freie Volksbühne* at Berlin. A total of 559,199 people attended some 848 theatre performances in 1911/12. During the same year, more than 100,000 went to concerts, recitations and song evenings. Having been rejected by the rest of society and above all by

25

its political, military and economic elites to a point where there was virtually no social contact between Social Democrats and people of other ideological persuasions, the working-class movement established its own ghetto culture. This self-contained world, it is true, did not amount to an autonomous counter-culture. All too often the values, tastes, customs and traditions of the dominant cultural groups percolated through into the educational and leisure activities of working-class organisations. Nor was it highly politicised. Marxist classics were borrowed less frequently from libraries than folk literature, travel descriptions or pulp novels portraying some bourgeois idyll.

It may even be that, in a paradoxical way, the interdependence between the working class and the rest of Wilhelmine society extended further. Guenther Roth has argued that this ghetto culture was 'negatively integrated' into the dominant system because, by its very existence, it provided a framework and vehicle 'for the controlled expression and dissipation of conflict and thus contributed, for decades of peacetime, to the stability of the Empire'. But even if it is correct that Social Democracy furthered political moderation and discipline and that this prevented the working class from displaying greater militancy, it did not mean that its perceptions of and feelings about the hostile world in which it lived had been blurred. After all, workers experienced this world day in and day out at their place of work and in politics. They also read about it in the Social Democratic press, which took considerable care to expose the inequalities and biases of the Prusso-German monarchy. By 1913, the ninety or so SPD newspapers had some 1.5 million subscribers. The various cultural and theoretical journals of the party sold a further 900,000 copies. Some books and pamphlets achieved a very high circulation or were frequently taken out of the lending libraries. The popularity of writers like Émile Zola would seem to indicate that his social criticism struck a responsive chord among his German working-class readers.

In short, it is the emotional significance of these organisational efforts and cultural activities outside the narrow party-political sphere which is of the greatest interest here: they emphasised the notion of an enforced separateness which increasing numbers of industrial workers sensed to be the key to their existential predicament in Wilhelmine society. For in each field of SPD activity there existed corresponding associations and publications which wooed the members of other social groups. Implicitly, if not overtly, they appealed to the anti-socialist views of these groups. Thus, by the end of the Bismarckian era there was hardly a sphere of human cultural activity which had not produced its own class-based organisations. The roots of the middle-class sports and athletics movement went back to the beginning of the nineteenth century. Bowling and clay-pigeon shooting associations (*Kegel-und Schützenvereine*) likewise enjoyed continued popularity, and in many small towns and villages it was a must for the local burgher to belong to one or more of them. In the educational sphere, some high school associations (*Gymnasialvereine*) and student fraternities (*Korporationen*) had a long history, but the movement mushroomed in the Wilhelmine period. Other clubs tried to spread the German language and culture outside the Reich.

Taken as a whole, this large variety of organisations might be seen as an encouraging sign. It testifies to the fact that the Industrial Revolution did not merely unleash economic energies, but also unlocked a great store of intellectual and cultural creativity in German society. Indeed it would be quite wrong to view the monarchy as a sullen police state which allowed no freedom of expression. Central Europe was not a part of Tsarist Russia. Germany was illiberal enough to generate social and cultural criticism and dissent, but at the same time sufficiently liberal not to stamp it out immediately and permanently. It was an atmosphere which may have been particularly conducive to formulating unorthodox ideas and organising like-minded people. At any rate, in the twilight zone of police repression and toleration there emerged a truly flourishing cultural life. Writers and visual artists engaged in hectic experimentation, sometimes saying and doing outrageous things. Major ideas about society and scientific discoveries were developed inside and outside the universities. People got together to pursue, in odd collections of clubs, the most way-out nonconformist objectives. Youth was no barrier to joining in collective experiments, and by 1914 thousands of youngsters were members of the Youth Movement in its various forms, romantically searching for new symbols and alternative ways of living together. The Wilhelmine period was not an intellectually boring time.

Nor did women abstain from the great organising endeavour. Feminism emerged and reformist demands were promoted through a number of organisations, some more radical than others. August Bebel's *Die Frau und der Sozialismus* (1883) was republished in 1910 and sold 135,000 copies. By 1914, 175,000 women had joined the SPD. Indeed, it was not just the vote and equal access to higher education which women had yet to achieve. However, the whole question of the position of women in an industrial society also provides a good illustration of the tensions and controversies which lay behind each of the demands for cultural and political change. These tensions surfaced in the wrangles between the divergent feminist organisations themselves and, even more violently, between them and their male opponents. The new *Vereinsgesetz* (association law) of 1908 allowed women to join political organisations and to attend political meetings. Yet the effect of this law was to promote a sharp division between a radical women's movement on the Left and the bulk of women of middle-class background who became affiliated to the *Bund Deutscher Frauenvereine* (BDF). Nothing is more indicative of the political orientation of the BDF than the fact that among the associations absorbed by it was the *Deutscher Frauenbund* which had once been founded as the women's section of the League Against Social Democracy. For every argument advocating a change of the status quo between the sexes, there existed a counter-argument which defended the existing arrangement, and where such fundamental issues were concerned, no 'scientific' certainty was hare-brained enough not to find a proponent. Thus in 1900 the Leipzig neurologist, Dr Paul Möbius, published his tract on *The Physiological Feeble-Mindedness of the Woman* which postulated a correlation between the size of the female skull and her alleged low intelligence. It is not surprising that those who aimed to preserve the patriarchal structures which existed in Wilhelmine family life, politics and economics welcomed such findings and the conservative conclusions drawn from them.

Given these wider implications, it would also be naive to view the large number of associations of whatever persuasion as unpolitical, just because their activities took place in the cultural and pre-political arena. In different ways, clubs, fraternities, clay-pigeon shooting organisations, Youth Movement (*Wandervögel*) were agents of socialisation into a particular milieu and the world-view related to it. Thus they contributed – at times subtly, occasionally through crude indoctrination – to shaping a member's ideas about Germany's past, present and future. And they acted as barometers of the level of social and ideological conflict. In this connection another set of organisations must be mentioned which also mobilised people with considerable success: the patriotic leagues. They purported to stand above the political parties; but in reality they were highly political and their impact on domestic as well as foreign politics during the decade before the First World War was profound. The *nationale Verbände* (national associations) reflected well the growing crisis of Wilhelmine policy both at home and abroad. Among the most influential in stimulating nationalistic feelings were the Pan-German League and the Navy League. The *Wehrverein* (Defence League) rose to prominence after 1912. Their leaders may not have known much about the country's precise military–strategic needs, but they built up powerful propaganda machines agitating for huge armaments budgets and a more assertive foreign policy; they may have found it difficult to agree on the best remedies for the country's perceived domestic ills, but they all believed that Social Democracy had to be fought vigorously. Accordingly, known or suspected Social Democrats were refused membership, and similar restrictions were also applied in other clubs. Such polarising practices, which did much to force the working class to retreat further into its ghetto, were accompanied by press campaigns to contain the threat from the Left and to prevent the rise of 'democracy', if necessary by repression and by a restructuring of the political system in an authoritarian direction. The duties of the patriot in the face of the 'unpatriotic fellows' on the Left were thus clearly defined.

Weltpolitik *and the spectre of encirclement*

In trying to explain the foreign policy of the Second Empire, generations of historians have tended to subscribe to the pronouncements of Bismarck and his successors, who regarded Germany's diplomacy as being primarily determined by her exposed geographical position and the pressures exerted on her frontiers by other powers. The primacy of foreign policy, the Bismarckian 'nightmares of hostile coalitions', were assumed to explain not only the supposedly defensive character of German foreign policy between 1871 and 1914, but also to account for the country's heavy emphasis on military preparedness. The monarchy's social and political organisation had to be tailored to the international power constellation. One of the first historians to challenge this orthodoxy was Eckart Kehr who, after analysing the background to the Reich government's decision to embark upon *Weltpolitik* and naval construction in the late 1890s, concluded that the peculiar shape of Wilhelmine foreign policy can only be understood in terms of the 'primacy of domestic politics'. He argued that the turn of German diplomacy against both Britain and Russia and the subsequent confrontation with the Triple Entente was rooted in socioeconomic conflicts between three major forces (agrarians, commercial and industrial bourgeoisie and the industrial working class) whose respective material positions during the period of rapid industrialisation have been examined above.

This triangular conflict which marked the early reign of Wilhelm II ended, according to Kehr, in a somewhat uneasy and far from stable compromise between the agrarians and the commercial and industrial middle classes. The agrarians lent their support to the Navy Laws of 1898 and 1900, which had been promoted by industry as a military back-up to its conquest of overseas markets; in return, the industrial and commercial bourgeoisie gave its backing to the agrarians' demand for higher protective tariffs against foreign competition. Above all, both forces combined in their fight against the organised working class. This peculiar alignment of social groups and their party-political front organisations, Kehr continued, had far-reaching diplomatic implications. Since the naval build-up had a poorly concealed anti-British orientation, it was bound to provoke a power-political response from across the Channel. Agricultural protectionism, on the other hand, was partly aimed against Russian producers and thus pushed the Tsarist Empire into an antagonistic posture.

Kehr's interpretation of the roots of Wilhelmine *Weltpolitik* was rejected by most of his colleagues when it was published in 1930. Fifty years later and with the controversy on the nature of Wilhelmine imperialism which the Hamburg historian Fritz Fischer unleashed in the 1960s behind us, his position has won wider acceptance. At the same time the 'primacy' debate has yielded a broad consensus on a related issue raised by Kehr's work, that is, that the foreign policy of Wilhelmine Germany was at no time a monolithic entity, but an outgrowth of compromises between divergent social forces which succeeded in forming a majority block and thus in defeating the foreign policy alternatives advanced by other groups. The interdependence of foreign and domestic policy, as postulated by Kehr, also implies that the foreign policy precepts of class organisations harmonise with the overall world-view and programmatic objectives of those organisations. As far as the Prussian agrarians were concerned, this connection was neatly put by Otto von Völderndorff, a friend of Reich Chancellor Chlodwig zu Hohenlohe:

We must keep away [he wrote] from international rivalries; we must confine ourselves to securing our country against the two neighbours [France and Russia]. Greatest parsimony (except for the Army) and a rebuilding of the Reich upon the only reliable estate, the rural population. Our industry is not worth much anyway. It is in the hands of the Jews; its products are . . . 'cheap and bad'; it is a seedbed of Socialism. . . . Moreover, we are coming too late; all valuable overseas possessions are in the hands of others who hold on to them. We are also not wealthy enough to carry on the great power policies we have embarked upon in 1870.

The air of resignation that it might be too late to turn the tide was not shared by other conservatives who advocated a more combative approach towards their opponents at home and abroad. Nor were they convinced that growth in agriculture was the answer to Germany's problems. Indeed, they saw the economic advantages of industrialisation, but were not prepared to accept its social and political consequences. In particular, they remained irreconcilably hostile towards the growing working-class movement and the need to accommodate its demands. Hence there emerged side by side with the Old Right more radical groups and organisations to whom the use of force against Social Democracy at home (the 'internal enemy') was merely the reverse side of their equally strong proclivity to pursue an aggressive foreign policy against the country's 'external enemies'. It is not easy to be precise about the social composition of the New Right. But it appears that the bulk was made up of the Protestant middle and lower middle classes. Sympathisers with its aims could be found among academics, farmers and the representatives of heavy industry.

On the other hand, there always remained a sizeable group of people who rejected the apostles of violence and promoted a strategy of social appeasement of the working class. Whereas the advocates of violence saw autocracy as the prerequisite of a successful foreign policy, the moderates believed that only a reconciliation of the mass of the working class with a reformed monarchy would provide the popular underpinning of *Weltpolitik*. Yet throughout the pre-1914 period this remained a minority view, and what weakened it was the common conviction among all middle-class groups, whether Catholic or Protestant, that the dynamic of the industrialisation process pushed Germany beyond the European continent towards overseas markets. They also shared a Social Darwinist notion of international politics which made it seem logical that the Reich needed a fleet to protect its interests and to gain further colonies. Consequently their attempts to pursue a less offensive diplomacy *vis-à-vis* Britain and Russia at the turn of the century or a decade later were time and again overruled by the Anglophobes and Russophobes. And defeat was also the fate of the foreign policy recipes of the SPD. Its mainstream inter-nationalism and rejection of the Kaiser's *Weltpolitik* as well as of agricultural protection corresponded with its domestic programme of political reform and public investments in welfare schemes rather than armaments, on the one hand, and its resistance to the 'penny on the loaf' to the detriment of wage-earners and for the benefit of agriculture, on the other. It has been argued that the external pressures of the international situation around the turn of the century represented a crucial determinant of *Weltpolitik*. The question is whether these were really so strong and loomed so large in people's minds. After all, *Weltpolitik* was inaugurated at a time when Germany's international situation was more propitious than it had been for some time. Hence, there existed no compelling foreign policy reasons why the Kaiser and his advisers should, at this particular moment, have started a massive naval building programme that was bound to antagonise Britain, followed in 1902 by agricultural protection which offended the Russians.

All this leads to one central analytical point: if one wants to understand Germany's peculiar diplomatic strategy, it is imperative to look at her internal condition, for there was a link between how divergent social groups envisaged the Reich's development within the international system and how they wished to see society and politics ordered at home. Later, towards 1914, when domestic and diplomatic crises began to chase one another, it became virtually impossible to disentangle the constant interaction of foreign and domestic affairs. It was different, however, at the turn of the century when the Kaiser's *Weltpolitik* was inaugurated. At that time the most powerful impulse behind Wilhelmine diplomacy and the build-up of armaments came from those political forces which, against considerable opposition, aimed to bring about a fundamental change of the international status quo in order to preserve the socioeconomic status quo at home.

We have seen that this was a period of particularly rapid industrialisation, accompanied by a population explosion and demographic upheaval. Looking behind the splendid façade of the Hohenzollern monarchy, we have also discovered a society full of tension and potentially centrifugal conflicts. On the one hand, there were those social groups, and above all the industrial working class, which aspired to change the existing distribution of economic wealth

31

and political power. On the other, there were those forces which resisted any such reform. This dichotomy, which threw up the whole question of the long-term viability of the Prusso-German political system, found its most distinct expression in the political arena and in the relationship between the executive and the Reichstag. Even if the Reich government had wanted to adopt a different strategy, the power position of the conservative elites time and again forced it to pursue conservative policies in the face of an increasingly reformist Parliament. To get its legislation, and in particular the budget, passed, the Chancellor required conservative majorities. Yet faced with a welter of middle-class and agrarian parties, almost all of which, their common anti-socialism notwithstanding, saw themselves as representatives of specific interests, the government could never rely on a stable majority as in the two-party British system. The political problems resulting from this parliamentary situation were quite formidable. It was difficult enough to generate a consensus over proposed legislation among the princes in the *Bundesrat*; welding together conservative parliamentary majorities was even more arduous and became well-nigh impossible in 1913–14.

The fact that the Reich government was nominated by the Kaiser merely exacerbated the problem: since the parties were not responsible for forming the government, they could afford to push sectional interests in an 'irresponsible' fashion, knowing that the Reich Chancellor had to concede their counter-demands in order to get his bill passed. They felt little incentive to hold back for fear of jeopardising legislation. In particular, the Conservatives were prone to exploit these constitutional peculiarities of the Prusso-German political system with more than the usual dose of partisan ruthlessness. They knew that no minister of His Majesty could contemplate creating a centre-left majority for the passage of legislation. The right-wing parties *had* to be included in any scheme, even though their electoral base was shrinking. In view of these constraints, it became increasingly difficult to cobble a majority vote together.

For it was a matter of simple arithmetic (Table 41): as long as the SPD had no more than some 35 seats in the Reichstag, as against the 93 seats of the two Conservative parties after the 1890 elections, different anti-socialist combinations were conceivable. By the turn of the century the balance of parliamentary forces was such that nothing could be done without the support of the Centre Party, which knew how to exploit its key position. The outcome of the 1907 elections enabled Chancellor Bülow to form an uneasy alliance between the Conservatives and the Liberal parties, excluding the Catholics. After 1912, none of these shifting coalitions were viable, because the strength of the SPD's 110 seats required a rallying of virtually all the remaining major parties. Yet while these parties were all agreed with the Kaiser that co-operation with the Social Democrats was unthinkable, they found it impossible to develop common ground with the Reich government over vital legislation. In short, the legislative process was in considerable disarray, while reactionary Conservatives had the ear of the monarch. The way forward seemed blocked.

Bearing in mind these complications, which were a reflection of growing political crisis and the leadership's inability to respond flexibly to changing political conditions, we can now return to the interconnection between Wilhelmine domestic politics and foreign policy. European statesmen and politicians had long discovered the unifying effect of grandiose and audacious diplomatic moves which relied on the integrating effect of nationalism. The proliferation of a 'yellow press' and the refinement of propaganda techniques towards the end of the nineteenth century had made it even more tempting to try to rally people and parties of different persuasions behind causes which were proclaimed to be in the common national interest. Campaigns to strengthen defences against some outside enemy had likewise frequently been launched before and had successfully unified political forces that were otherwise divided by disagreements over domestic policy. In the parliamentary systems of Western Europe such policies had become well-worn ploys to win elections. Although the relationship between the monarchical government and the party system was different in Germany, the effect of nationalist propaganda was the same. Accordingly, Bismarck as well as his successors tried to play this card more than once in the hope of creating viable centre-right coalitions and of weakening the Left.

What made the use of foreign and military policy as an integrating device all the more tempting in the case of Germany was that the parties of the Right and the middle always enthusiastically supported patriotic ventures or improved defences. It was the instrumentalisation of nationalism and armaments policy which, backed by agitational pressure groups and newspaper propaganda, enabled the Reich government to find parliamentary majorities for its major pieces of legislation at the turn of the century. Yet the long-term effects of these laws were disastrous; Wilhelmine *Weltpolitik* and naval building caused Britain to re-evaluate her international position and to revamp her system of alliance commitments. Russia had been allied to France, Germany's arch-foe, since the early 1890s. In 1904, the Entente Cordiale established the link between Britain and France. Three years later, the triangular relationship to contain the restive and bustling nation in the centre of Europe was sealed by the Anglo-Russian agreement of August 1907.

In the eyes of the Kaiser and his advisers, this completed the 'encirclement' of the Reich which left them with the ramshackle multi-national empire of Austria-Hungary as their only firm alliance partner. However, before the encirclement' theory is accepted, it is worth remembering that the creation of the Triple Entente was a response to the anti-British orientation of *Weltpolitik* some seven years earlier. But the Kaiser's foreign policy had been designed not merely to secure a key position for Germany within the international system of the twentieth century, but also to unite divergent political forces against the SPD and to stabilise the position of the monarchy at home. The viability of the Prusso-German political system had always been threatened at parliamentary level by the difficulty of finding acceptable majorities for the passage of legislation. Yet behind this problem there loomed the conflicts and tensions between divergent social groups in a dynamic industrial society. Faced with these conflicts, it was beyond the imagination of the Kaiser and most of his advisers that they might be solved by means other than repression of the working-class movement and reliance on the unifying force of nationalism and agitation for stepped-up armaments. They succeeded to the extent that not only the nationalist associations, but also the agrarians, various *Mittelstand* organisations and heavy industry, all of which were becoming increasingly obsessed with the threat of 'revolution', were likewise committed to fighting the Left. Even if it was not always easy to unite divergent interests, anti-socialism, anti-parliamentarism and nationalism did prove a potent ideological cement in a period of growing instability.

In the long run whipping up middle-class resentments and fears was not a wise way of dealing with the industrial workers. It merely alienated the latter further. Worse, it contributed to mobilising, on the Right, more radical nationalist and anti-socialist forces, which it became impossible to control. With the diplomatic situation deteriorating at an alarming pace from 1905 onwards, pressures mounted from the nationalist associations to step up the provision of armaments, thus unleashing a very costly arms race with escalating demands for relentless military preparations.

Soon yet another factor began to affect the Wilhelmine practice of instrumentalising foreign and military policy for the purposes of strengthening the country's defensive position and of generating support for the increasingly unpopular monarchy: taxation. Like other people, the Germans did not like paying taxes. Fiscal policy, particularly the way tax burdens were distributed, became a more explosive issue than ever before when the Kaiser's *Weltpolitik* and naval building programme turned out to be prohibitively expensive. Additional money had to be found and the battle over how it was to be raised became increasingly fierce. The tax debate in Wilhelmine Germany is therefore an excellent ground on which to test the monarchy's capacity to overcome social and political divisions and to generate a majority consensus of opinion. To anticipate the outcome: taxation and the way the whole issue was handled politically did much further to polarise Wilhelmine society and to accelerate the disillusionment of many voters with the existing monarchical order.

In 1906, the government had introduced a first major reform bill of Reich finances in an attempt to create additional revenue (80–90% of which was spent on defence) (Table 34). The bill was largely a flop, partly because the

34

parliamentary parties chopped and changed it extensively, partly because the expensive Navy Law of 1908 quickly undermined its revenue calculations. In the summer of 1908 Chancellor Bülow started again and this time he was looking not merely for increased indirect taxes, the traditional means of raising money, but also for direct taxation to be levied by the central government. His reasons for this radical departure were both fiscal and political. Indirect taxes were being raised on basic items of consumption such as bread, beer or tobacco which took up the largest proportion of the weekly budget of the lower classes. Any tax increases to pay for additional armaments were therefore bound to hit the 'masses' more severely than a tax on wealth and property of which they had very little or none. The issue of indirect taxes had provided the SPD with plenty of political ammunition before and had been a major plank in its agitation against the 1902 protective tariffs on grain and other agricultural produce.

Worried about the divisiveness of these problems, Bülow believed that it was time for the better-off to be seen to be making a tangible financial contribution to defence. Hitherto the pattern had been for the parties of the Right and the middle to vote for costly diplomatic and military ventures and to accuse the opposing Social Democrats of lack of patriotism. Yet when it came to distributing the financial burdens of *Weltpolitik* they would vote higher indirect taxes which were more painful to the 'masses' than to themselves. Bülow wanted to effect a moderate change in this practice by proposing that one-fifth of the required 500 million marks be raised by means of a death duty. His plan foundered on the rocks laid by the Conservatives who opposed a direct levy on inherited wealth. In collaboration with the Centre Party they drew up and passed a modified finance bill which reverted to the old policy of indirect taxation. It is not difficult to imagine how much bitterness this move generated, although it was only in the 1912 elections that the voter was able to give effective expression to his disillusionment. As we have seen, the SPD became the largest party in the Reichstag while the Conservatives were heavily defeated.

There was also fierce opposition from the Conservatives when Bethmann Hollweg, Bülow's successor, proposed a direct tax as a one-off contribution to the costs of the 1913 Army Bill. However, the political situation had changed drastically in the meantime and there was no hope for the Right to have its way as in 1909. The Conservatives were no longer strong enough to block the ratification of the 1913 Finance Bill with its wealth tax component. It would be wrong to assume that they accepted this defeat gracefully. Their propaganda campaign against the bill was frantic. Ernst von Heydebrand und der Lasa, the leader of the DKP and 'uncrowned king of Prussia', accused the Reich government of having engineered the introduction of a Reich property tax. This, he argued, had undermined the position of the Federal States 'in favour of the democratic convention rule of the Reichstag'. It seems significant that he should make these allusions to the French Revolution. To many people on the Right the outcome of the 1913 tax battle had indeed raised very fundamental questions concerning the future of German society. It fits into this picture of growing instability that one retired general and leader of the Pan-German League sent a memorandum to the Crown Prince (who in turn forwarded it to the Kaiser) in which he proposed a violent solution to the growing domestic deadlock. Bethmann Hollweg, asked by Wilhelm II for his views, was appalled by what he thought could only mean civil war. Germany's external enemies, he added, would use the turmoil inside the Reich as the golden opportunity to wage war on her.

By 1913 the question of civil war and foreign war had indeed become the two sides of the same coin in the minds of the Kaiser and his advisers, and it is virtually impossible to decide which issue obsessed them more. They felt encircled not merely by the Triple Entente, but also by the forces of change. Germany's internal and external enemies, they believed, wanted to destroy them and the monarchical order. Some Conservatives proposed to retreat to the Prussian bastion which seemed more secure because of its three-class voting system, patriarchal conditions in the countryside and its Conservative bureaucracy. Thus on top of all the other conflicts which shook the country in the last years before the war, the split widened between the Reich and its largest Federal State. While the news was bad on the domestic front, it was arguably even worse on the international one. The diplomatic isolation of Germany which had started in 1904 had worsened and while Bethmann Hollweg was making efforts to ease some of the pressure, the generals could only think of further armaments expenditure as a remedy. The 1913 Army Bill, which had now unleashed yet another major domestic conflict over the distribution of tax burdens, had in part been a response to growing tensions in the Balkans and the weakening of the position of the Dual Alliance in that part of the world. In view of these developments, it seemed even more urgent to Helmuth von Moltke, the Chief of the General Staff, to fill the gaps which the 1912 Army Bill had left.

Yet, rearm as strenuously as they might, the German military were unable to check the deterioration of the Reich's international predicament by trying to shift the military balance in their favour. The Triple Entente quickly responded in kind. Faced with French and Russian army bills that more than matched the German effort, Moltke and his entourage were overcome by deepening gloom. In a few years time, by 1915 or 1916, he believed, Germany would have lost whatever military edge she had over the Triple Entente. It is in this atmosphere of pessimism that Wilhelmine foreign policy became inexorably militarised. Worries about the future military balance and the fear that the country's opponents might try to turn their military superiority into power-political and economic advantages that would throttle German power produced a mentality disposed towards waging a preventive war.

The assassinations of Archduke Ferdinand and his wife at Sarajevo on 28 June 1914 appeared to present the German generals with the opportunity of cutting the Gordian knot of 'encirclement' before it was too late. Bethmann Hollweg, on the other hand, more wary of the great risks involved, favoured a localisation of the July Crisis to a confrontation between Austria-Hungary and Serbia from which the Great Powers could be kept away. When it became clear from the middle of July that this limited strategy would fail, the generals took over and escalated the crisis into a world war. The Fischer Controversy of the 1960s has at least yielded this much and the historian does not any longer have to undertake a round-trip through the capitals of Europe to locate those primarily responsible. They were sitting in Berlin.

The German diplomatic and military documents contain many telling phrases to show how deeply worried the leadership had become about the country's international and strategic position. Clearly, the Kaiser's colonial and naval dreams of the turn of the century had evaporated long before 1914. Nor had nationalist agitation and the mobilisation of defensive instincts among the population been able to reverse this. The government's increasing reliance on propaganda and chauvinistic associations points back to German domestic politics where the prestige and position of the Hohenzollern monarchy was likewise disintegrating at great speed. The political conflicts which arose over the question of Reich finance were but one powerful reflection of rising tensions at home. The friend–foe dichotomy with which the Kaiser and his advisers interpreted the international world around them and which generated a strangely neurotic fortress mentality had its mirror image in the way in which they viewed the monarchy's internal predicament. With their popular base dwindling, they saw themselves beleaguered by hostile social and political forces which were believed to be bent on revolutionising the Prusso-German political system and all it stood for.

By 1914 it was deemed to be too risky to try to defeat these dangerous forces in a civil war, a great reckoning. However, the Army was deemed to be just about capable of winning a foreign war. No doubt a victory over the Triple Entente would have stabilised Germany's international position. But it would also have checked and perhaps even reversed the advance of those social groups which had been excised from the national consensus by a two-nations strategy that had likewise failed by 1914. This is why the calamitous course of Wilhelmine foreign policy cannot be understood without reference to the dynamic developments inside this rapidly industrialising society and its pent-up conflicts.

2 War and civil war, 1914–1923

The political and military situation at the beginning of the war

The declaration of war on France and Russia in August 1914 was greeted with immense enthusiasm throughout Germany. Thousands of men spontaneously flocked to the nearest assembly points to board the trains to the front. They were seen off by their wives and girl-friends – some of them apprehensive, no doubt, but also carried away by the wave of patriotic fervour. Meanwhile the parties in the Reichstag voted almost unanimously for the hastily introduced war credits in an atmosphere of elation. Most Social Democrats, hitherto the alleged 'enemies of the State', supported the government's request for funds; and many soldiers who were going off to the trenches belonged to the class which fellow-Germans thought to lack patriotism. No one was more surprised by the attitude of the SPD leadership and its supporters than the military. For many years they had prepared the Army not merely for a foreign conflagration, but also for civil war. The officer corps represented the most hardline conservatism among the Wilhelmine elites, viewing itself as the main pillar of the monarchical system in a sea of revolutionary ferment and as the last bastion of the existing order, should the Left ever dare to challenge it directly.

It was this mentality which had produced on various occasions suggestions of preventive action against the working-class movement as long as the risks were still supposed to be calculable. In fact many officers probably never lost their conviction that the day of reckoning was bound to come sooner or later. Trained to see the world in neat military categories, they tended to perceive domestic politics in a black–white polarity: whoever was not a totally loyal monarchist must be a subversive revolutionary. The notion of gradual change and reformism was alien to most of them. The belief that the SPD posed a fundamental threat to the status quo even influenced their assessment of what should be the appropriate numerical strength of the Army. Thus, during the fifteen years following the 1893 Army Bill, many top generals and military advisers of the Kaiser were not unhappy that the Navy received a disproportionately large share of the defence budget. Up to 1910/11 there was no insistent pressure for major increases in the size of the land forces, not so much because the generals felt particularly secure on the European continent, but because they feared that further numerical expansion would undermine the reliability of this pillar of the monarchy as an instrument of civil war. Between 1894 and 1910 the percentage of the population serving in the Army declined from 1.13 to 0.96 per cent.

This concern was to some extent born from a fear that the enlargement of the officer corps would result in an even larger intake of aspirants from a middle-class background who would erode the social and ideological homogeneity of the corps. These suspicions, which were also reflected in the promotion policies of the Military Cabinet, are interesting not only because they were largely unjustified, but also because they echo the problems of stratification and mobility of Wilhelmine society discussed in chapter 1. Probably more justified was the other assumption that a numerical expansion of the Army would lead to an increase of working-class recruits who might refuse to arrest striking fellow-workers or fire on insurgents and demonstrators. It was for this reason that the commanding generals tried to keep their working-class intake small and decided carefully to screen their recruits to spot Social Democrat 'agitators' among them. It also explains why the rank-and-file frequently had their lockers checked and were ordered to keep away from pubs that were assumed to have a working-class clientele. Furthermore, it was always possible to subject recalcitrant youths to special drilling exercises and other more subtle means of army discipline. Conversely, if one looks at the SPD's campaign against Prussian militarism and the literature on the maltreatment of recruits (*Rekrutenschinderei*), it is clear that the officer corps' distaste for the Left was heartily reciprocated. Nor did the role of the Army in breaking up demonstrations and strikes in the last years before 1914 do anything to ease tensions. After the notorious Zabern Affair* of 1913, even many people of middle-class background began to harbour feelings of bitterness against the reactionary and arrogant demeanour of the military. In this wider sense, 'Zabern' was not a minor incident but a national scandal demonstrating the erosion of support for the Prusso-German monarchy and the polarisation of political opinion.

Indeed Alsace-Lorraine was not the only region where civil–military relations had been deteriorating, and although the contingents of Bavaria and Württemberg were not under the Kaiser's command in peacetime, all local

---

* In the autumn of 1913, army officers stationed in the small town of Zabern (Saverne) in Alsace-Lorraine took the law into their own hands on the flimsy pretext that order could no longer be secured by the civilian authorities. Proclaiming a state of siege, they arrested and maltreated people and generally overreacted in the face of local hostility which they had themselves provoked. The incidents became a major scandal when the Kaiser sided with the military and condoned the illegalities committed by them.

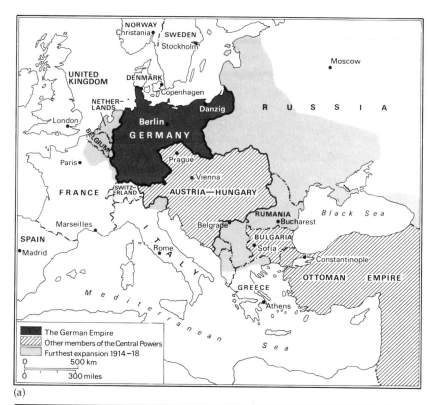

(a)

(b)

2. Maximum extent of the German State in (a) 1914–18 and (b) 1937–45.

commanders kept their instructions for dealing with civil disorders in good order. It is against the background of these deeply ingrained hostilities between the military elite and the Left that the domestic events following the delivery of the Austro-Hungarian ultimatum to Serbia on 23 July 1914 must be seen. When this document was published, there were spontaneous demonstrations in Berlin and various other cities aimed at warning Vienna against pursuing an adventurous policy. The Social Democrat press similarly took a pacifist line. These popular moods were bound to alarm the generals at a time when they began to scrutinise their mobilisation charts. However, the solution which they proposed to the problem of domestic criticism on the Left was symptomatic of their unbending conservatism: now the wholesale arrest of the SPD leadership and a clamp-down on the Social Democrat press was being mooted in army circles. The leaderless masses were then to be drafted into the Army where they would be under the strict discipline of the military penal code. Bethmann Hollweg, hearing about these plans, was appalled. Less than a year previously he had warned the Kaiser against getting involved in a civil war and a foreign war at the same time. Without delay his State Secretary for the Interior, Clemens von Delbrück, was sent to the War Ministry and at the end of July 1914 succeeded in persuading the military leadership to drop their plans as long as the Chancellor was involved in negotiations with the SPD. The aim was to gain the support of its leadership by pointing to the dangerous international predicament of the Reich, especially in the face of the Russian threat.

The Reich Chancellor's strategy worked well. Having been told that Germany might have to wage a *defensive* war in response to Russian aggression, the SPD executive promised their support. It was thus the somewhat selective information which Bethmann Hollweg fed to the SPD which stopped the earlier press criticism and secured a consensus on the basis of which all Germans were able to rally to the defence of the Fatherland. It was also helpful that Russia was identified as the main aggressor since hatred of the repressive Tsarist regime had been traditionally strong in the German working-class movement. Finally, many party leaders who had come to see Social Democracy as a reformist movement and were yearning to leave the social and political ghetto, saw the July Crisis as an opportunity of winning acceptance by the rest of society. For all their reservations about the Prusso-German monarchy and the inequities of the existing social order, the nationalism of the pre-1914 era had not left them untouched. There was a strong patriotic streak in them, reinforced by a pride in Germany's cultural and economic achievements and in their own organisational success. The Reich government succeeded in tapping this pride in the hour of extreme external crisis. It was a shrewd move on the part of the civilian leadership which, unlike the generals, was more acutely aware of the changed nature of modern war.

41

There were no arrests and no bans on Social Democrat newspapers. There were, as the Kaiser put it in his speech on 4 August 1914, no more political divisions, 'only Germans'. It was a sentiment which was repeated many times from the pulpit, in the classrooms and by men of influence and prestige in the press and the market-place.

However, this spirit of civilian co-operation did not mean that the military would henceforth leave domestic politics to the politicians. On the contrary, on the day when martial law was proclaimed, the commanding general in each of the military districts took over large areas of civilian authority. The legal basis of their activities was the Prussian Siege Law of 1851, a relic of an earlier age which, significantly enough, had never been modernised by Reich legislation after 1871. Thus, in the moment of emergency, the Old Prussian military state began to rear its head again behind the civilian constitutional façade of the Hohenzollern monarchy, just as foreign war and civil war had always been closely connected in military thinking. In August 1914 the commanding generals became responsible by law not merely for providing the back-up services for the front-line armies, including the requisitioning of war-essential goods and the drafting of fresh recruits and reservists; they were also empowered to secure law and order in their district, supervise censorship, observe opponents of the regime and prop up popular morale. The local civilian administration became subordinate to the commanding generals. Only at the highest political level in Berlin existed a dualism between the military and the civilians which the Kaiser as supreme commander and head of state was supposed to bridge. Yet, as we shall see, the civilians always found it difficult to assert themselves against the military, the more so the longer the war lasted.

For the moment, however, there were no major divisions over policy. The enthusiasm for a defensive war against Germany's longstanding enemies France and Russia sustained the *Burgfrieden*, the domestic peace which had been concluded in August 1914. Most Germans were confident that the war would be over by Christmas. The ordinary soldier trusted the military leadership in the conviction that a foolproof plan for swift victory had been worked out. Few people in the know appear to have been concerned that this plan, based on the ideas of Alfred von Schlieffen, violated Belgian and Luxemburgian neutrality. Nor did they all realise that by 1914 the German offensive was eight army corps short of the minimum deemed necessary for success on the western front. Nevertheless, the German campaign went fairly well at first. The French, supported by the British Expeditionary Force, were on the retreat until they launched a counter-offensive which initiated the famous Battle of the Marne. The French attack might well have come to grief, had not the Germans – believing that they had dangerously over-extended their own lines – in a sudden panic at Headquarters ordered a general retreat to take up new positions along the river Aisne.

There has been much speculation as to what might have happened if the Battle of the Marne had ended in a German victory. But in view of the deadlock that developed it seems more pertinent to ask why Moltke and his advisers abandoned the battle. In this respect it must be remembered that the German generals had taken a tremendous gamble when they pressed the politicians to escalate the diplomatic crisis of July 1914 to a world war. It was only in their more optimistic moments that they themselves thought Moltke's adaptation of the Schlieffen Plan might work. Yet having betted everything on the proposed great breakthrough in the west which was to throw the enemy into total confusion and provide Germany with the opportunity of annihilating France, the German planners in turn developed an obsession about the French pulling off a similar feat further south in Alsace. Indeed it was not difficult to imagine what would happen if France achieved further south what the Germans were hoping to do in northern France. To cover himself against this eventuality, Moltke had left a strong force in the south-west of the Reich which was sorely missed on the Marne at the beginning of September. Instead, and in yet another departure from the Schlieffen Plan, he ordered it to move towards Nancy.

It was a further sign of German overall inferiority that the revised Schlieffen Plan was also based on the assumption that it would take weeks for the Russian war machine to mobilise and that, having defeated France in the west, the bulk of the Army could be transported to the east in time to confront and destroy the Tsarist forces. However, the Russians opened their offensive more quickly than anticipated; by the end of August the Germans found themselves involved in major battles in the east, forcing Moltke to dispatch two further army corps from the western front. Although this force helped Paul von Hindenburg, the eastern commander, to push the Russians out of East Prussia, the net result of what had all too soon become a war on two fronts was to destroy what little initial optimism the German General Staff may have felt.

The retreat from the Marne led to a stabilisation of the western front along the hastily dug and subsequently greatly improved network of trenches in northern France. Meanwhile Hindenburg was unable to exploit his eastern victories during the autumn and winter of 1914/15, so that Russia was not knocked out of the war either. Although the battle-lines continued to be flexible in the east, by the end of 1914 the war of attrition had begun which was to last for the next four years with social, economic and political consequences which will be discussed in a moment. It was not that everybody was taken totally unawares. A few people had occasionally written about war between industrialised nations before 1914; yet their warnings remained largely unheeded. Certainly there was hardly anyone who was either intellectually or emotionally prepared for what happened between 1915 and 1918. It was a war which depended upon technologies whose destructive potential was only gradually appreciated; a war which relied on the mobilisation of all the human and material resources of the participant countries. As, given the degree of industrialisation of Europe, these resources were considerable, the end of that war was more likely to come from gradual physical and mental exhaustion and desperation on the part of one side or the other than from some splendid victory on a single battlefield. The alternative was to conclude a peace on the basis of a compromise which the Kaiser and most of his advisers refused to contemplate.

The strains of total war

Unable to accept either a compromise settlement or a war of attrition, the German generals (like their Allied counterparts) committed themselves to a strategy which, they hoped, would shift the struggle back to the type of warfare which they had learned to wage in their staff exercises. It was a strategy which was as unimaginative as it was costly and fruitless: the year 1915 saw the first attempts to break the stalemate in the west by sending thousands and tens of thousands of soldiers across no man's land into the barbed wire 'and machine-gun fire defending the enemy trenches. These attacks were preceded by an artillery bombardment which was supposed to put the front line of the enemy out of action. The result of all these offensives was not the hoped-for, decisive breakthrough, but a lunar landscape dotted with the bodies of men who, if they had not been killed instantly, were left to die a slow and agonising death. Meanwhile the defenders, though they usually managed to ward off the attack, also suffered terrible casualties.

It is not possible to describe here in detail the horrors of warfare in the age of the machine-gun, poison gas and artillery saturation bombardment. Its experience by millions of Germans of the generation of 1914 was so profound, however, that its impact can hardly be exaggerated. Among the 9.8 million people who lost their lives in the course of the First World War, Germany counted some 2.4 million casualties. An estimated 300,000 civilians also died, many of them of disease or malnutrition. There were hence few families which did not mourn the death of the father and husband or a son and brother, of an uncle or cousin. Furthermore, tens of thousands had been severely mutilated, many of them so badly that they spent the rest of their lives on crutches and in wheelchairs, afflicted by frequent illness or phantom pains. The advances of medicine had saved them from death. But now they barely survived on a meagre pension and often found their life expectancy cruelly curtailed. Those for whom the psychic strains of trench warfare had been too much and who had simply cracked up were no luckier. During the war thousands had wandered off, aimlessly, to the rear in a state of shell-shock and were apprehended and court-martialled for desertion. If they did not face the firing-squads or were sent to a mental asylum, they would return to civilian society with deeply disturbed personalities.

Even those who came out of the war without visible damage to mind or body were in one way or another traumatised. The experience of war contributed to turning many of them either into advocates of left-wing radicalism to fight for abolishing war altogether and building a classless co-operative society or into followers of right-wing ideologies which reinterpreted the experience of the trenches as something heroic and sublime, a model for the future organisation of society on militaristic lines. It is not too difficult to imagine why the screams of the wounded and dying or the inevitable 'Why-not-me?' question which the survivors asked themselves triggered the search for some higher sense and purpose behind the ordeal of total war. Historians of the war experience have rightly pointed to the creation of elaborate myths and symbols invented by the participants on both sides to explain the inexplicable. There is much that is plausible in the interpretations of the 'cult of the dead' and the 'appropriation of Nature' (G. L. Mosse). But it may be necessary to differentiate some of these findings by class and social background. If the results of British social history of the First World War provide any parallels or guide, it is possible that German soldiers of working-class background, though better able to cope with the day-to-day hardships, privations and the frequent boredom of military service, had their views of prewar Wilhelmine society broadly confirmed when they became subjected to the hierarchical structures of the Prusso-German Army. On the one hand their reactions to the bloodshed were probably similar to those of a man of middle-class background next to them, perhaps merely more fatalistic. There can also be no doubt that there developed in the thick of the fighting a strong sense of solidarity which momentarily levelled all status differences.

On the other hand, there were also long spells of inaction when soldiers simply sat in the trenches. Life became routinised; there was time to ruminate upon the war and deeply ingrained social habits reasserted themselves. Soon rumours were rife about the high life in the officers' messes and often they were justified. 'Them-and-us' attitudes of the prewar days perpetuated themselves. Just as the home front was a 'class society' (J. Kocka), soldiers were conscious of hierarchies at the front, and more so once the *Burgfrieden* began to falter. Many young officers, it is true, shared the mud-splattered and blood-stained conditions with their men and spearheaded the shocktroops out of the trenches across the barbed wire towards the enemy. But the higher ranks rarely saw the discomforts of trenches. In these circumstances, it did not take trained 'agitators' to whip up feelings against the venison-eating and champagne-drinking at the top and to generate a sense that, when this war was over, fundamental changes to society would have to be made. Such convictions among the bulk of the front soldiers were reinforced by the notion that the once much-maligned and ostracised 'unpatriotic' workers now bore the brunt of the fighting. This realisation only served to strengthen their determination not to accept, for example, the inequalities of restricted suffrage systems after their return from the front. Nor would they be prepared to condone the continuation of the old practices of industrial relations under which most employers had refused to recognise the existence of trade unions and collective bargaining rights.

From what little we know of attitudes to the war and wartime politics, it would seem safest to assume that ordinary soldiers tended to react to their experience in more simple, pragmatic terms and not by resorting to metaphysical debate. It would certainly be rash to believe that the literature on the war, the poems, novels and diaries published afterwards by middle-class intellectuals, reflected the feelings of the soldiers of working-class background. However, this is necessarily an educated guess derived from research on other participant countries. More is known in this respect about the impact of the war at sea upon the different ranks in the Imperial Navy. It has already been mentioned that its internal atmosphere and hierarchies were not dissimilar to those of the Army. Not even the growing importance of engineering skills to deal with the complex technologies of Dreadnoughts brought about an opening-up of the career structure. Thus, the Navy went to war with little change to its established traditions of conduct, and dissatisfaction and frustration soon reached boiling point. During meal times, when the ratings were served turnips and an indigestible soup called *Drahtverhau* (barbed wire), they could see the better provisions being sent along to the wardroom. Idleness and boredom which the naval strategy of keeping the fleet in port imposed left plenty of time for discussion and contemplation, ultimately leading to an erosion of discipline.

The inactivity of the Kaiser's Navy was a telling proof of the failure of Tirpitz's earlier policy. The arms race against Britain had been lost well before 1914 and, apart from a few half-hearted sorties, the High Seas Fleet remained at anchor in Kiel and Wilhelmshaven for fear of defeat by the Royal Navy. The Kaiser's grand strategy of the turn of the century was now replaced by submarine warfare, at first selective and later unlimited. The effects were barely less disastrous than those of *Weltpolitik*. No other German policy in the First World War did more to bring the Americans into the war, yet failed to force Britain to her knees. With the war at sea lost before it had even begun and the Army unable to achieve a decisive breakthrough on the western front, Germany's future came to depend on her ability to sustain a war of attrition on land. Industrial production, in other words, became a crucial factor, even though the generals had not really included it in their original preparations. However, there were a number of industrialists who, by virtue of their direct familiarity with a complex industrial economy, had a better appreciation of this factor. So it did not take them long to voice their worries about the inadequate organisation for a total war effort.

It was on the initiative of civilians (among whom Walther Rathenau, the chairman of the AEG electrical engineering concern, was the most vocal and prominent) that the War Raw Materials Department (KRA) was established in the middle of August 1914. Operating under the auspices of the Prussian War Office, the KRA quickly expanded into a large bureaucracy which, by 1918, supervised some two dozen war raw materials companies. These private companies were responsible for the acquisition, stock control and distribution of specific vital raw materials to the industries where they were most needed for the war effort. As the war unfolded and failed to go well for Germany, armaments production was inevitably given higher and higher priority, culminating in August 1916 in the adoption of the Hindenburg Programme. Supported mainly by heavy industry, the Programme laid down greatly increased production targets and initiated the further militarisation of the German economy. The concomitant tendency of the military to intervene in the economy through the allocation of raw materials and price regulation quickly generated resentment among the employers. It was not so much that they saw the mechanisms of a capitalist market economy being destroyed. As far as the regulation of prices and production was concerned, many branches of industry had already evolved an elaborate system of restrictive practices. Cartels and syndicates had become an important instrument of reducing competition and maintaining high prices to the disadvantage of the consumer. However, what did encounter opposition was the attempt by the generals to intervene in those and other areas of industrial self-administration, and in particular to curb war profiteering. At the same time, the concern of the government and the military for the efficient running of industry opened up new possibilities for influencing politics. The Hindenburg Programme with its emphasis on maximum output had greatly increased the weight of heavy industry in the governmental decision-making machinery at the expense of other branches. And while essential industries were doing well out of the war after an initial shock in the autumn of 1914, the damage done to the economy as a whole was enormous.

The dynamic growth of German industry before the First World War had been largely dependent on the country's involvement in the world market. In August 1914 the banking system was badly disrupted; export-orientated industries and commercial houses not only lost their overseas assets, but were also cut off from their markets by the Allied blockade. Although there were several loopholes in the net cast around the Central Powers, especially those provided by Dutch and Scandinavian neutrality, and although Germany was no more than a partially beleaguered fortress, the war and the fixing of production priorities by the Reich government proved catastrophic to those who had depended on the world market and had been involved in the production of consumer goods. In a more general way, the production of guns and ammunition inevitably eroded national wealth. Slowly but surely the country slithered into austerity and ultimately economic collapse.

Another consequence of the pressures of total war was that the inflationary spiral began to accelerate. Between 1913 and 1918 inflation rocketed sky-high despite increasingly tough controls on rents, prices and wages. The retail price index more than doubled in the same period. However, it was not merely heavy industry charging high prices to a government desperately dependent on arms production and the mass of ordinary citizens chasing increasingly scarce goods for civilian consumption which boosted inflation. The value of the mark was also rapidly eroded by the government's fiscal policies. The whole gigantic war effort, after all, had to be financed. One way of obtaining additional revenue which in theory was open to the Kaiser and his advisers would have been to increase direct taxation. The adoption of such a policy, apart from hitting the rich more than the poor, would have had the added advantage of siphoning off purchasing power to reduce inflation.

Yet, as we have seen, the imposition of a direct Reich tax had been a thorny issue before 1914, and resistance to introducing it after 1914 continued to be strong. Faced with this opposition, the Reich government pushed up indirect taxes to unprecedented levels to finance ordinary recurrent expenditure (Table 34), with the military budget being accounted for separately and financed by means of the more expensive and dangerous device of war loans. This reliance on bonds was more expensive because, unlike taxes, they were tied to a promise to repay the loan plus interest after a certain time-span; they were more dangerous than taxes because it was clear that they could be honoured only in the event of victory. After victory, the defeated Allies could have been made to pay for the Reich debts incurred by the war effort. It was only logical, therefore, that the government prepared the imposition of swingeing reparations – a technique which must be borne in mind when the problem of Allied reparations demands against Germany and of Nazi fiscal policies in the 1930s and 1940s is considered.

The immediate effect of the issuing of war bonds was a positive one, however. Many a patriotic citizen carried his gold marks to the bank in 1915 and 1916. He was given a certificate which, by 1918, had already lost much of its nominal value because of wartime inflation. Accordingly enthusiasm for signing war bonds proved volatile, and undersubscription rose from -2.1 million in 1916 to -39 million in 1918. When the war was lost and it was impossible to impose harsh reparations on the Allies, the government that succeeded the bankrupt Hohenzollern regime and was left to clear up the economic mess left by the Kaiser's fiscal policy had no choice but to renege on the promise to the holders of war bonds. By the time postwar inflation had been brought under control and the currency had been stabilised, the wartime certificates were worth no more than a fraction of their original value in gold.

Although there were other factors which contributed to the hyperinflation of 1923 and which will be analysed below, the roots of what amounted to an expropriation of savings must be traced back to the war and the methods which the Reich government adopted to finance it. It is tempting to call these *va-banque* policies reckless. However, it was not the first or the only time that the short-term interests of powerful social groups which feared the erosion of their economic position through direct taxes overruled more far-sighted policy options. Holding on to their savings and spending them on the black market was, of course, the way in which the middle classes were able to equalise the fall in their real income. The experience of these social groups was by no means uniform. Self-employed artisans who succeeded in becoming suppliers to larger firms essential to the war effort modestly participated in the profits to be made from producing for the Army. Although it is difficult to provide precise figures, it seems that most of the larger firms, joint stock companies as well as family enterprises, were able to keep ahead of inflation. On the other hand, there were many small producers who were forced into liquidation or, after 1916, had their workshops closed by the government. Retailers were also badly affected, especially when rationing and price controls were introduced and they had to compete against black marketeers. White-collar employees saw their living standards decline too. At the very beginning of the war there was the shock of unemployment owing to a marked slump in output. Later on, once this initial recession had been overcome, they never recovered their 1913 level of real income. Civil servants, while protected against redundancy, also saw their income eroded, especially in the higher echelons (Table 24).

Finally, the mass of the wage-earning population felt the effect of the war's drain on national wealth no less directly (Table 24). Most workers and their families experienced a cut in their living standards, with the exception of a few categories of labourers who worked in essential industries. They found their bargaining power considerably strengthened, as both government and employers had a vital interest in keeping armaments production uninterrupted by strikes or frequent movements of labour to other firms which offered higher wages. This powerful leverage made it easier for some workers and their trade union representatives to avoid a drastic fall in their real wages. It also gave them a degree of recognition as organised groups which would have been quite unthinkable before 1914. Tacitly, though not yet formally, trade unions gained recognition from government and employers. However, it was given grudgingly and the employers always resented the newly won strength of industrial workers. In view of this, the Patriotic Auxiliary Service Law, introduced in December 1916, was not merely a response on the part of the Reich government and the military aimed at mobilising Germany's labour reserves for the total war effort, but also an attempt on the part of industry to regulate the labour market and to exert pressure on wage levels.

The Law introduced a labour service for all men between the ages of 17 and 60. It also restricted the mobility of labour, even though workers retained the right to move to a better-paid job. Industry's insatiable appetite for workers to cope with increasing arms production coupled with the growing difficulty to obtain draft exemptions for able-bodied and skilled men also led to an attempt to fill the manpower gap by means of foreign labour, imported mainly from Poland and Belgium. The recruitment drives in those countries, which soon degenerated into deportations, took thousands of poorly paid and ill-housed slave workers into the Reich until the programme was abandoned in February 1917. The labour force was finally supplemented by a growing number of women who flocked into the factories. Some of their wage levels kept up with inflation and hence work in armaments factories proved attractive. Yet as they were not covered by the Patriotic Auxiliary Service Law, the appearance of women in industry was really an indication of the pressure on lower-class families trying to make ends meet at a time of rising inflation and austerity.

Life was particularly difficult for the urban 'masses' as food became scarcer and increasingly expensive. Rationing, first introduced for flour and bread in February 1915 and successively extended to other items, brought some relief. However, until 1916 the agricultural producers successfully opposed any more determined state intervention into the food market and when the War Nutrition Office was finally set up to simplify and regulate the supply system, its measures proved inadequate. Farm produce and meat failed to reach the regulated market and reappeared on the black market instead. To make an already bad situation worse, overall food production declined further after poor harvests in 1916 and 1917. Thus grain production, already well below its prewar levels, slumped from 21.8 million tons to 14.9 million tons in those two years. During the unusually hard winter of 1916/17, the home front and especially the urban population experienced a catastrophic nutritional crisis, accompanied by a lack of heating materials. The poor, the weak and the elderly were very badly hit, whereas the better-off who had savings were able to obtain supplies on the black market at exorbitant prices. Infant mortality rose dramatically, and according to some estimates more than 700,000 people died of starvation or hypothermia.

Firm government action might have done something to alleviate the suffering in the cities. But even if the political leadership and the military had been prepared to act, there were formidable vested interests to be overcome. Although politics did come to play an important role in increasing social tensions in wartime Germany, one does not have to stray from the economic sphere to comprehend the sources of the explosive situation that was developing from 1915. The gap between rich and poor, which had been large enough before 1914, appeared to be widening. Conflicts also arose between the urban population and the farmers over the food question, with the latter being accused of unscrupulously exploiting the desperation in the cities. Food riots, demonstrations and strikes occurred, and the *Burgfrieden* of 1914 did not withstand the strains of the unfolding economic crisis for very long. The emergency of total war failed to create genuine inter-class solidarity, but furthered group egotism. While people were starving to death in their thousands, others wined and dined on newly acquired riches; while many male workers in armament factories had to work 60 hours a week and many women worked up to 57 hours a week under most difficult conditions and with the concomitant disruption to their family lives, Berlin's amusement establishments, as one report by the local military command noted, were over-crowded with ladies wearing eye-catching make-up and dresses; while hundreds of thousands held the front line in muddy trenches, the Crown Prince, who was one of their commanders, celebrated the completion of his stately home, the *Cäcilienhof*, on the outskirts of Potsdam.

Reaction, reform and revolutionary ferment

Of course there were also people among the country's elites who were appalled by the plight of the mass of the population, on the one hand, and on the other the haughty talk in the officers' messes and elsewhere about the need to keep the lower orders in their place. To these critics it was self-evident that this crisis, when the survival of the nation was at stake, was a time for vigorous intervention against war profiteering and for an equalisation of economic burdens; it was a time for reducing class barriers rather than raising them. Above all, it was a time for tangible concessions and political reform. However, the point which has been made before and will have to be made again and again in subsequent chapters also applies to the history of German society in the First World War: the reformists remained in a minority, whereas those whose influence and power would have made a crucial difference continued to use their positions to block all policies of reason and change. They knew only how to wield the stick and did not hold out even a carrot.

As the diaries of Kurt Riezler, the Reich Chancellor's private secretary, show, nowhere was a die-hard conservatism more apparent than at Imperial Headquarters and at the High Command, increasingly the political power-house of Germany. Under the Constitution, the Kaiser was the supreme warlord and head of both the military and the political decision-making apparatus. Yet, not only was he full of conservative prejudice and out of touch with the mood of the country, but his self-confidence and determination to assert himself against the hardliners around him had been badly shaken long before 1914. Here was a man, potentially very powerful, who had always wanted to see himself as a well-beloved People's Kaiser; yet even in the supreme crisis of the First World War he remained no more than a figurehead of an authoritarian government, distant from and barely concerned about the suffering of the so-called masses. Nor did he act as a bridge and mediator between the Reich government and the military, whose powers had been vastly expanded under the State of Siege Law. With the mobilisation of the economy for total war and the regimentation of politics in full swing by 1915, Bethmann Hollweg and the civilian ministers began to lose ground against the generals. The erosion of their influence was completed when Hindenburg and Ludendorff took charge of the High Command in August 1916 and, for all practical purposes, became the 'silent dictators' of Germany. It was a symptomatic difference between wartime Britain and France, where the charismatic leaders were *civilians* who could base themselves on a broad national consensus, and the Second Reich, where *military* men rose to occupy comparable positions and with their popularity increasingly confined to no more than a dwindling section of the population.

From the beginning of the war, the political leadership of the country was confronted with two basic problems: how to achieve a decisive victory at the front, and how to stop the erosion of popular support for the monarchy. The military dilemma resulting from the failure of the offensive in the west has already been mentioned. As for the second problem, the proclamation of war aims in preference to the granting of economic and political concessions increasingly came to be seen as a panacea. While the link which the historian Fritz Fischer established between the country's prewar territorial ambitions and Bethmann Hollweg's Memorandum of September 1914 may continue to arouse controversy, there can be little doubt about the important domestic function of the war aims issue during the war. This function was indicated very perspicaciously by Alfred Hugenberg, a director of Krupp and leading right-wing politician, at a meeting of the sub-committee of the War Boar (*Kriegsausschuss*) of German Industry in November 1914. Looking at the problem from an employers' point of view, he explained:

The consequences of the war will in themselves be unfavourable for the employers and industry in many ways. There can be no doubt that the capacity and willingness of the workers returning from the front to produce will suffer considerably when they are subordinated to factory discipline. One will probably have to count on a very increased sense of power on the part of the workers and the labour unions which will also find expression in increased demands on employers and for legislation. We would therefore be well advised, in order to avoid internal difficulties, to distract the attention of the people and to give fantasies concerning the extension of German territory room to play.

However, it was not merely the industrial relations sphere which would come under this kind of pressure. It was to be expected that those who had given their utmost to the defence of the Fatherland would return home to demand major political, legal and educational reforms and push for more than cosmetic changes to the existing power structure. Hugenberg's idea of setting people's eyes upon plans to acquire a great empire was therefore seen to be an attractive device to be employed not merely by industrialists, but also by political and military leaders who were most worried about the democratising effects of the war. The unifying and distracting force of imperialism was definitely considerable and had been exploited before. But never in the past had it succeeded in generating a broad popular consensus comparable to the *Burgfrieden*. Nor was it intended to achieve this. In fact, it merely helped to clarify a misunderstanding on which the domestic peace of 1914 had been based; for its unifying force had rested on diametrically opposed inter-pretations of the *Burgfrieden* by divergent political forces. To the Social Democrats it implied an undertaking on the part of the other classes to reform the worst aspects of the Wilhelmine system in return for working-class support against the Allies. For most Conservatives and National Liberals the truce of 1914 was tantamount to a promise by the working-class movement to step into line and not to touch the existing distribution of power at home. The proclamation of war aims did not lend itself to such misunderstandings. It meant a denial of reform and an exhortation to concentrate all energies on the achievement of a military victory. War aims were hence openly divisive and destructive of the *Burgfrieden*.

No one was more acutely aware of this than Bethmann Hollweg. He believed the promotion of polarisation to be a disastrous policy and was therefore loath to start a debate on Germany's war aims for fear of unveiling the ambiguity of the truce of 1914 and of dividing the nation into those who advocated a 'victorious peace' (*Siegfrieden*) with annexations and those who supported the notion of a compromise peace on the basis of the territorial *status quo ante*. However, once adverse military, economic and political developments began to undermine the domestic peace of 1914, the question quickly became one of the balance between the forces of victory and of peace. Hugenberg and others who shared his pessimistic views may initially have hoped that the lure of 'fantasies concerning the extension of German territory' would prove so potent as to attract the great majority of the population. This turned out to be an illusion, but did not stop the annexationists from pursuing their demand for a public discussion of the issue.

Their persistence, which ultimately defeated Bethmann Hollweg and the temporisers, was partly motivated by a belief that Germany needed an expanded base, but partly also by the way in which a split of the population which they promoted would occur sociologically. If war aims were to distract people from the question of internal reform, then their promotion could also be used as a weapon against those Germans who refused to be distracted and who, by fighting for a peace without annexations, were also struggling against the hardline domestic conservatism of the annexationists. There hence exists a dialectical relationship between attitudes towards the war aims issue and internal reform, with the division, sociologically speaking, being a fairly familiar one: on the one hand, there were growing numbers of workers calling for an immediate peace and change at home. They were reinforced by sections of the white-collar employees, some of whose organisations took an anti-annexationist line and were prepared to collaborate with the Left. At the other end of the spectrum rallied large sections of the middle and upper classes to campaign for a *Siegfrieden*. They did so not merely because they had visions of empire or because victory was the only way of getting their war bonds reimbursed, but also because they opposed reform of the existing domestic order.

Of course, this polarity did not develop overnight. What began as a carefully controlled debate in 1915 turned into a more determined organised propaganda effort in 1916 and finally into hectic agitation, progressively mobilising the political forces ranged behind the annexationist and anti-annexationist positions. Time and again Bethmann Hollweg and other moderates manoeuvred to avoid further polarisation. Much of his diplomacy may be seen in this context. Through various channels he explored possibilities of a negotiated peace with the Allies. For even if these explorations were unsuccessful, not least because of the annexationist clamour at home, they served to reassure the anti-annexationists that the Reich government kept on trying. At the same time he moved to appease the annexationists when he publicly proclaimed that the incorporation of Belgium into the German sphere was not negotiable. It was indeed a precarious balancing act in which to engage. The Chancellor also attempted to relieve mounting internal conflict by holding out the prospect of political reform, to be implemented not immediately, but after the war. In March 1917 a parliamentary committee was set up to examine the question of constitutional change, 'especially with regard to the structure of the representative body of the nation and its relationship with the government'. Finally, on 7 April 1917 he succeeded in persuading the Kaiser to proclaim that the Prussian three-class voting system would be reformed after victory. Yet, in view of the continuing economic crisis and of government action in other spheres of politics, such promises were too non-committal to reverse the division of German society into two hostile camps. By the summer of 1917, Bethmann Hollweg found himself beleaguered on both sides and faced with irreconcilable demands which were being advanced more and more impatiently.

The Peace Resolution which the parties of the Left and centre-Left tabled in July 1917 and the subsequent founding by the Right of the Fatherland Party, encouraged by Hindenburg and Ludendorff and financed by Army and industry, are a good illustration of the dynamic interaction of opposing political forces. On the one hand, the Reichstag was called upon to resolve that Germany was prepared to enter into peace negotiations without forced annexations, a resolution which was supported by the same forces that also promoted a parliamentarisation of the Prusso-German monarchy. The Fatherland Party, on the other hand, was established as a movement outside the existing party system to counter the idea of a compromise peace and, significantly enough, of political reform at home. It also advocated the ruthless repression of the critics of the High Command's policies, by now the decisive factor in the decision-making machinery. By 1918, the Fatherland Party had increased its membership to 1.2 million, providing the generals with a popular backing for their two-pronged attack against the threatening disintegration of the monarchy: annexations abroad and dictatorship at home.

In forcing Lenin's revolutionary government to sign a punitive peace treaty at Brest-Litovsk, the High Command, assisted by a civilian government which was a mere puppet of the military, implemented the eastern half of the annexationist programme by occupying vast areas of Russia. There were, it is true, also economic considerations behind the incorporation of these territories. There were also some people who, as a long-term strategy, preferred indirect domination by Germany to the method of military occupation adopted by the Ludendorffians. However, seen in relation to German domestic policy, the formal colonialism in the east neatly complemented the policies of tough regimentation and increasing repression at home.

By 1917, the extensive powers of the military under the State of Siege Law had been fully mobilised to facilitate centralised policy-making and to stamp out any signs of dissent from the High Command's line. Bethmann Hollweg's earlier attempt to steer a middle course was abandoned completely. He was replaced in July 1917 by Georg Michaelis, a colourless civil servant and a pawn in the hands of the supporters of Ludendorff's ideas. The military showed little understanding of the causes of popular dissatisfaction and unrest which found expression in a growing number of strikes, demonstrations and insistent press criticism (Table 44). The first massive walk-outs had occurred in April 1917, when no less than 200,000 workers struck in Berlin alone. Since then, with deprivation and disillusionment growing, civil unrest in some part of the country had become an almost daily event. One reflection of this growing radicalisation of the 'masses' was that the Social Democrats found it impossible to contain the organised working class within their own ranks. In April 1917, a group of left-wingers led by Hugo Haase, hitherto joint chairman of the SPD together with Friedrich Ebert, finally left the fold to form the Independent Social Democratic Party (USPD). Even further to the left a small band of militant democratic socialists around Rosa Luxemburg and Karl Liebknecht constituted themselves into the Spartacus League.

However perceptive many of the left-wing criticisms of the existing regime may appear in retrospect, the High Command was not prepared to listen. Nor were they bothered about the effect of their policies of regimentation and escalation. To the generals, and their civilian supporters inside and outside the Fatherland Party, the agitation for peace and domestic reform was the work of dangerous revolutionaries who were to be apprehended and locked up. They engaged in a vigorous campaign of counter-propaganda. Rallies were organised, millions of leaflets distributed. A programme of Patriotic Instruction was introduced in the Army. There was a major ideological war to be fought and soon the search for scapegoats who were allegedly responsible for the weakening of Germany's position was in full swing. Jews became an even more easily identifiable group than Social Democrats, and just as the anti-Semites before 1914 had blamed them for Germany's difficult predicament, the traditional scapegoat mechanism worked even more effectively in wartime. There was a marked increase in anti-Semitism, with the Jews being accused of draft-dodging, war profiteering and generally undermining the strength of the country. The tracts which espoused these ideas and became increasingly pervaded by conspiratorial theories of history make depressing reading. But what is even more depressing is that so many people on the Right were ready to believe them.

The same applies to the propaganda on other subjects: the hallucinations about empire, the megalomaniac proposals for territorial expansion, the ruthless anti-Slav racism and open advocacy of dictatorship, the demands for relentless anti-socialist repression. Many of the authors were educated people, even academics, whom one might have expected to be too intelligent to purvey such views. But fears and passions blinded them and blocked a rational assessment of causes and effects. More alarming was that their arguments were not merely picked up by other people of right-wing disposition whom the course of events since 1914 had left in bewilderment, but also taken seriously in the corridors of power and tentatively converted into practical policies. What ultimately inspired them all – propagandists of a *Siegfrieden*, their followers and those who tried to realise their ideas – was the growing anxiety, so well expressed by Hugenberg in November 1914, that the way in which prewar society had been ordered would disappear; that socioeconomic advantage and political privilege would be swept away by the expectations of the soldiers returning from the front and the deprived sections of the population at home.

Yet by the spring of 1918 it had also become clear that no amount of agitation and intimidation could stop the erosion of loyalty to the monarchy. Many tired and desperate people merely vented their grievances in private or more openly in bread queues or in their local. Others tried to co-ordinate and organise their protest. In January 1918, widespread strikes involving more than a million workers, had flared up in Berlin and other major cities. The authorities quelled them remorselessly. Ebert, the leader of the SPD, who had attempted to contain the movement by putting himself at its head, was tried and sentenced for treason. It was an almost classic constellation, with the SPD executive – basically conservative and worried about radicalisation at the grass-roots and the schism of the working-class movement – hoping to channel popular protest and to keep it from exploding into an uncontrollable revolution. It was faced by a military and civilian establishment, including a monarchist judiciary, which had no sensitivity for the predicament of the 'masses' and merely saw the world in terms of friends or foes. Ebert, of course, was seen as a subversive revolutionary and enemy of the State. The seriousness of these demonstrations nonetheless raised the question of how long law and order could be upheld. By the spring of 1918 it was clear that only a military victory against the Allies could save the existing political system from collapse. After the conclusion of the Treaty of Brest-Litovsk the moment seemed propitious to attempt a decisive breakthrough in the west. Although some 1.5 million soldiers remained tied up in the east to police the occupied territories, the bulk of the eastern army was free to be transported to northern France. The High Command began to prepare for the final great offensive. The onslaught on the French and British armies, reinforced by then by some 300,000 Americans, started on 21 March 1918. The Germans made some territorial gains, but the attack soon ground to a halt. By July, the Allies had regrouped to launch their counter-offensive, in the course of which the Germans were thrown back to their pre-March positions. Spurred by their initial successes, the Allied armies continued a slow advance towards the Reich border with the Germans retreating before them. By the beginning of September it dawned on Ludendorff that the war might be lost.

The Revolutions of 1918/19

Faced with this possibility, there now began a great debate among the decision-makers at Headquarters over the best political strategy to be pursued. Gradually a faction led by the State Secretary in the German Foreign Ministry, Admiral Paul von Hintze, gained the upper hand. They argued pessimistically that the war was definitely lost and that it was time to initiate a 'revolution from above' before the monarchy was swept away by a 'revolution from below'. If an armistice were to be signed as soon as possible, there was, in Hintze's view, only one way in which the domestic crisis following the announcement of such negotiations could be contained: by involving a broadly based government representing also the parties of the centre and the Left. At a crucial meeting on 29 September, Ludendorff, who in previous weeks had been wavering between military optimism and political panic, agreed to Hintze's proposals and Hindenburg fell into line. The Kaiser subsequently also concurred and the Reich Chancellor, who had, typically, not been involved in these discussions, resigned to make room for a man who enjoyed the confidence of the political parties. The man chosen was Prince Max of Baden, whose moderate views were well known.

His appointment brought a change to the entire constitutional structure which can only be called momentous. We have repeatedly referred to the problem of parliamentarisation in the pre-1914 period and seen that the Kaiser and the political forces supporting him had fought tooth and nail against a shift in the balance of power away from the Crown towards the Reichstag. Among the royal prerogatives which had been defended with great tenacity was the power to nominate and dismiss ministers without consulting Parliament. Since 1916, it is true, the Reichstag had expanded its control functions and begun to play a greater role in the governmental process. Thus, a fifteen-man parliamentary committee had been constituted in connection with the Auxiliary Service Law to help monitor its implementation. A few months later, in March 1917, Reichstag participation had been secured for the constitutional discussions. By the summer of that year, co-operation between SPD, Left-Liberals and Centre Party, which together commanded a majority of seats, had stabilised sufficiently to enable the passage of the Peace Resolution (see above, p. 54) and, in November 1917, to force the resignation of Reich Chancellor Michaelis. But the majority parties continued to be too disunited and weak to impose a successor of their choice. Nor did the man who became Chancellor because he suited the High Command do much to adhere to the programme which had been formulated after consultation with the Reichstag. Both in power-political and in constitutional terms the balance continued to be tilted in favour of the Crown and the generals who had come to stand in for the politically impotent Kaiser. Given the state of mind of the military, it is likely that, had Germany won the war, they would have used their then greatly strengthened prestige and power to block domestic reform, not to mention the treatment they would have meted out to the country's neighbours.

However, in October 1918, when defeat was certain, the situation was radically different. The Kaiser consented to what amounted to the conversion of the Prusso-German political system into a constitutional monarchy similar to the British one. After years of military-dominated government, it was now for the civilian politicians, elected on the basis of a universal suffrage, to sign the armistice and hence shoulder the burden of defeat. Even in the hour of bankruptcy, the generals showed a remarkable ability to uphold the self-interest of the Prussian military state. As Ludendorff put it at the meeting of 29 September, as many people as possible were to be held responsible for the humiliation of defeat – with the exception of those who had been instrumental first in unleashing the war and then in conducting it uncompromisingly.

The leaders of the majority parties accepted Ludendorff's offer although they realised its dangers for their own future. They did so from both a sense of responsibility and of the opportunity, belatedly presented to them, of assuming control of the executive. They also agreed because they hoped that Allied peace terms might be more lenient if the representatives of the old order had been removed. Finally they were worried about the possibility of a 'revolution from below'. Their concern was not merely with the people who had already become totally alienated from the monarchy, but also those who had continued to believe in the official victory propaganda and the optimistic reports from the front. The sudden announcement that the country had to sue for peace was likely to destroy what little faith in the leadership was left in them. Their dejected reaction was bound to have a destabilising impact on the existing order which only parliamentarisation might be able to arrest. Even many moderate Social Democrats, Ebert among them, basically did not wish to see more radical constitutional reforms than those introduced in October 1918. While the civilians grasped the nettle in the hope of saving what was left from the wreckage for the sake of a better future, Ludendorff was looking for scapegoats on whom the regime's abysmal failure might be blamed. Addressing the section chiefs of the High Command on 1 October 1918, he put forward the case for the inclusion of left-wing representatives in the executive as follows:

I have asked His Majesty to bring those people into the government who are largely responsible for things having turned out as they have. We shall, therefore, see these gentlemen enter the ministries, and they must now make the peace which has to be made. They must now eat the soup which they have served us!

It was the theme which Ludendorff, who ought to have known better than this, later reiterated on many occasions and with tremendous effect when he became one of the champions of the Legend of the Stab in the Back. Other officers' opinions were summed up by the Bavarian military attaché who reported to Munich that 'on the domestic political situation one often hears the opinion expressed that it is a good thing that the left-wing parties will have to incur the odium for peace. The storm of indignation of the people will fall on them.' Then he also alluded to the rationale behind the move: 'One hopes that then one can get back into the saddle and continue to govern according to the old recipe.'

It is not inconceivable that such calculations might have worked and that the shift in the political balance of power would have been more marginal than it turned out to be. Up to November, nothing had happened to plough up the existing structures of socioeconomic domination. All the 'masses' had gained was access to political decision-making through the traditional parliamentary parties. Furthermore the Prussian three-class voting system had been eliminated. Ministers had been made responsible to the Reichstag. The Crown's prerogatives over the Army and Navy were practically abolished. These constitutional reforms, spirited through the *Bundesrat* by Prince Max of Baden, gave the majority parties a chance to legislate social and economic reforms. If this was what they wanted, it was bound to be a long-drawn-out process in the course of which plenty of opportunities would arise for the old opponents of the Reichstag majority to obstruct change. With parliamentary government installed, it is conceivable that a much more far-reaching 'revolution from below' might have been staved off if there had been a greater unity of purpose among the conservative elites. However, upon realising the certainty of defeat, many of them abandoned themselves to the fatalism which also paralysed the erstwhile middle-class supporters of a *Siegfrieden*. Others took a *sauve qui peut* attitude and retreated. Only the naval officer corps refused to lapse into passivity. Instead they embarked upon a course of action which not only undermined the long-term chances of success of the 'revolution from above', but also virtually unleashed the 'revolution from below'. What moved them was not so much the survival of the Hohenzollern monarchy and its main pillar, the Army, but their own future.

It has already been mentioned that morale in the Imperial Navy was very low, both because of the rigid hierarchies and the tensions they engendered and because the battle-fleet had made no tangible contribution to the war effort. Submarine warfare had been relatively more successful although it failed to knock Britain out of the war. Instead, unlimited submarine warfare had brought the United States with its superior economic resources into the war, further diminishing Germany's chances of victory. Given that so much importance had always been attached to the battle-fleet and so much prestige had been invested in it, the admirals had been worried for some time about the long-term consequences of the fleet's inaction. Vice-Admiral Franz von Hipper had warned against these dangers in May 1916 just before the Battle of Jutland, the only major engagement against the Royal Navy. He added that 'for this reason alone I wish that we may soon be able to do battle'.

It is against the background of such considerations that the Admiralty, in October 1918, began to plan a final sortie to meet the British in the North Sea. Reinhard Scheer, the Chief of the Admiralty, argued in a secret memorandum that the 'honour and existence of the Navy' demanded a sortie of the fleet at this late stage. He admitted that 'the course of events cannot thereby be significantly altered'; in fact the admirals even realised that their policy would directly undermine the efforts of the civilian government to sign an early armistice. However, the naval leaders had come to the conclusion that they did not 'need an armistice'. To them it was more important to try and lay the foundation of a future Navy. Without informing the Reich government, they gave orders for the High Seas Fleet to seek a do-or-die battle against the Royal Navy. Although orders to this effect were merely given verbally, ships' crews in Kiel and Wilhelmshaven quickly suspected what was in store for them. They were in no mood to join in a suicide mission. Ratings failed to return from shore leave or refused to move the ships moored at Wilhelmshaven.

Hipper, whom this rebellion caught quite unprepared, finally decided that there was no hope of getting the fleet to sail. Instead he dispersed the ships, sending the Third Squadron to Kiel where the sailors immediately went ashore to organise demonstrations and to demand action against those responsible for ordering the mission. Soon political demands were added. The protest movement now spread like wild-fire from north Germany to every larger town and city in the Reich. The 'revolution from below' had got underway. Meanwhile the admirals demonstrated a capacity to identify scapegoats which matched that of Ludendorff. Grand Admiral Prince Heinrich, the Kaiser's brother, having fled from Kiel on a lorry flying a red flag, blamed British money which was supposed to have instigated the sailors' revolt. Three days earlier, Admiral Adolf von Trotha had told Scheer that, in his view, the 'Bolshevik movement' was behind the events. But the realities of the situation were different and there was little Bolshevism in the country. Although there was a potential for radicalisation, the tens of thousands of people who could be seen milling in the streets of Germany's urban centres were looking to the Social Democrats and the USPD for leadership. They wanted the conclusion of an early peace and the initiation of domestic reforms. Yet, after years of material deprivation and the pent-up bitterness against the old regime, the emotionally charged and volatile situation was deteriorating rapidly. For the next week or so, those civilian and military leaders who had not yet withdrawn from the scene and hoped to channel the revolutionary movement repeatedly found themselves to be acting too late.

Thus, on 6 November, a crucial meeting had been called between a delegation from the Imperial Headquarters led by General Wilhelm Groener, and Social Democrat and trade union leaders, the only politicians who still appeared to be having some influence with the 'masses'. The conference was held against the backdrop of a telephone call from Gustav Noske, who had been dispatched to try to bring the continued demonstrations in Kiel under control. Noske reported that the situation there was 'almost hopeless. General chaos is imminent and power is slipping more and more into the hands of the revolutionary sailors.' With Kiel in this state, Ebert as the spokesman of the civilian delegation thought it sufficient for the Kaiser to 'declare his abdication, if possible today or at the latest tomorrow and make one of his sons . . . Regent'. In other words, he still hoped to preserve the monarchy and the October Settlement. But Groener refused 'to undertake any steps with regard to the abdication of the Kaiser or even to present this demand' to the monarch.

While this debate was still going on, another SPD leader, Philipp Scheidemann, burst into the room with the words: 'The question of abdication has been overtaken by events. The Revolution is on the march. . . . Gentlemen, it is no use having discussions now; action is required. We do not know whether we'll be sitting on these chairs tomorrow.' Ebert refused to be moved and declared 'that nothing had been decided yet'. He added that, although he was a confirmed Republican, 'the question: monarchy or republic would only be of theoretical importance'. In practice he would be satisfied with a parliamentary monarchy and would therefore 'urgently advise General Groener to seize this last opportunity for the salvaging of the monarchy and to see that one of the Imperial princes would be entrusted with the regency without delay'. Groener replied firmly that this was impossible.

Yet what was unacceptable to Groener on 6 November, did occur three days later when the Kaiser was virtually thrust into his exile in Holland by his generals. By then it was no longer a question of nominating a regent. The Hohenzollern monarchy itself and the unity of the Reich were at stake. In Bavaria, Kurt Eisner proclaimed a Socialist Republic after seizing power in Munich on 7 November. Two days later, Max of Baden announced his own resignation in Berlin together with the abdication of the Kaiser *before* the generals at Imperial Headquarters had persuaded Wilhelm II to bow out. Shortly afterwards, Scheidemann appeared on the balcony of the Reichstag building to proclaim a republic to an impatient crowd. The Prusso-German monarchy, even in its parliamentarised form of October 1918, had failed to withstand the onslaught of the 'revolution from below'. What had been unthinkable only a few days earlier had now become reality.

Max of Baden's resignation on 9 November had been followed by an odd ceremony in the Chancellor's palace in the presence of Ebert, the SPD leader: the Prince handed over business to the Social Democrat who had been called to see him. It was an act of great political significance in that it provided the semblance of continuity which enabled the civilian and military bureaucracies of the Reich to serve under a new 'legitimate' government headed by Ebert. On closer inspection, however, Prince Max's move was constitutionally irrelevant because he had no powers to legitimate Ebert in this way. The monarchy as a political system had definitely collapsed when he and the Kaiser resigned. A republic had been proclaimed. What then was the basis of legitimacy of the political leaders who emerged from the confusion of 9/10 November? What gave them the authority to try to govern a country in turmoil? Since it has sometimes been denied that Germany experienced a revolution in 1918, the answer to these questions helps to clarify this issue.

In effect, what might be called the 'Ebert government' did not emerge from the encounter in the Reich Chancellor's palace, but from a hastily concluded agreement between the leaders of the SPD and the Independent Social Democrats who had split off from the Social Democrats in April 1917. This left-wing coalition received its confirmation in office on the following day.

10 November, by the assembled Workers' and Soldiers' Councils of Berlin, claiming to represent the Council movement which had sprung up throughout the country. These Councils had had no place in the previous political system. They had been formed spontaneously in the early days of November, although their origins went back to the activities of the Revolutionary Shop Stewards, a group of militant trade unionists who had organised the first massive strikes of the summer of 1916. By the spring of 1917, so-called Workers' Councils had begun to function in various cities side by side with strike committees. The Revolutionary Shop Stewards were also instrumental in unleashing the strikes of January 1918. It was the pattern established by the organisers of these strikes in Berlin which served as a blueprint for the formation of the Councils ten months later. Wherever rallies had been held in squares and factories, committees had been elected on an *ad hoc* basis to articulate and organise the demands of the demonstrating 'masses'. There can be no doubt that the Councils were genuine organs of the Revolution and by seeking and obtaining approval by the Berlin Councils of the SPD–USPD coalition agreement of 9 November, the 'Ebert Cabinet' (or Council of People's Deputies, as they called themselves) derived its authority to act both from the two main working-class movements and from spontaneously organised institutions of the 'revolution from below'.

In view of their central importance to an understanding of the events of 1918/19, the Councils have attracted considerable interest. For a long time, it was taken for granted that they were very radical organs of the Revolution led by people who were aiming to exploit the chaos of November 1918 to repeat in Germany what Lenin had achieved by means of the Soviets in Russia in 1917. The Soldiers' and Workers' Councils were seen as front organisations of German Bolshevism. More recent closer investigations of the phenomenon at regional and local level revealed several surprises, however. To begin with, although there were some radicals among the Council delegates, they were mostly in the minority. Thus, on 10 November, it was the soldiers' delegates, together with moderate workers, who blocked plans for the formation of a Socialist government without SPD participation and approved the composition of the Council of People's Deputies led by Ebert and Haase. In most other parts of the country, the balance of power was even more firmly weighted against radicals. Accordingly, the objectives of the overwhelming majority of the Councils were also moderate, comprising no more than the traditional catalogue of demands of mainstream Social Democracy. Nor did they view themselves as an autonomous power factor, as in Russia, where the Soviets had set themselves up in competition with the Provisional Government of Prince Lvov. Rather they were almost desperately eager to leave the initiation and execution of policies to the People's Deputies and to provide the 'Cabinet' with a mass-democratic backing to push through reforms.

However, Ebert and his colleagues in the SPD executive did not regard themselves as spearheads of a Council democracy. They wanted political and economic gains for the German working class, but aimed to achieve them within the framework of a parliamentary-representative system. The introduction of parliamentarism in Germany and the formation of a government led by the largest party required, if nothing else, a *political* revolution, at least as long as the Kaiser and his advisers flatly rejected evolutionary constitutional change. But this revolution had meanwhile taken place and with the changes of October 1918 and the proclamation of the Republic a representative framework had been created. In Ebert's view it was now for a National Assembly, elected by all Germans once order had returned and demobilisation had been effected, to frame the details of a new constitution and to provide a forum from which a parliamentary government would emerge. It was therefore not merely the Russian precedent which caused Ebert and his colleagues to misperceive the different character of the German Council movement and to engineer its early destruction.

Although this factor is important for understanding their profound suspicions of the movement, they also considered that there were certain irreconcilable differences of principle between parliamentarism as well as the type of representation system which had grown up in the SPD and the trade unions, on the one hand, and the Council model, on the other. And in a sense they were right: there were differences between parliamentary democracy and Council democracy which could not easily be reconciled.

Councils were based on the idea of constant democratic involvement and permanent answerability of delegates to their constituency. They favoured an imperative mandate and rejected the concept of liberal representative democracy by which a deputy, once elected, was subject only to his conscience and the party whip when it came to voting on legislation. To this extent the Council idea was directed against parties and, by the same token, against party bureaucracies and appointed officials. The same applied to trade unions with their hierarchies of permanent functionaries. In short, the ideal-typical political and economic organisation of society behind the Council model was rather different from parliamentarism. Whereas these differences were blurred at the beginning of the Revolution, they began to take more concrete shape in the following weeks.

One reason for the initial confusion was that many Councils, composed of heterogeneous forces as they were, themselves advocated elections to a National Assembly. Only a small minority of people on the extreme Left promoted the idea of a Council system as an alternative to a parliamentary republic. There were some, like Eisner in Bavaria, who hoped to combine the two models. But in the circumstances this was barely realistic as a polarisation of the revolutionary forces set in. Even the moderates expected the People's

Deputies to tackle immediate reforms and in particular a democratisation of the economy as well as of the civilian and military bureaucratic machinery. They believed that in this respect the Councils continued to have an important role to play. They insisted that their demands be taken seriously, which Ebert and some of his Social Democrat associates were less and less prepared to do. Suspicious of the Council movement as a whole and alarmed by the pronouncements of the more militant spokesmen within it, the SPD leaders pressed for early elections to a National Assembly prior to the initiation of major reforms. The result of this interaction of divergent aims and policies was the disintegration of the Council movement, which split into those who supported Ebert's parliamentary strategy and those more radical elements who aimed to turn it into an autonomous instrument for a fundamental reorganisation of German society. The split was reflected on the government side in the departure of the USPD leadership from the 'Cabinet'.

In the escalating crisis which had developed between the Social Democrats and the Councils it is virtually impossible to separate cause from effect. By December the two sides were heading in quite different directions. With the Ebert government unwilling to rely on the Councils, the activists who wished to retain the initial momentum of the November days gained the upper hand in certain key areas of the country. The moderates among the Council supporters left, thereby accelerating the process of radicalisation. The situation was now rapidly deteriorating and moved towards a confrontation between the 'Ebert Cabinet' and the radical revolutionaries. A new and violent phase in the history of the German Revolution began. The question was: who was Ebert to rely on, if his authority were physically challenged by the extreme Left?

It is at this point that the role of the Army after the abdication of the Kaiser must be considered. Unlike many conservative politicians and the Federal Princes who simply retreated from the scene, Hindenburg and Groener, Ludendorff's successor, did not take the easy way out. They were concerned to organise the orderly return of hundreds of thousands of soldiers after the signing of the armistice. But they were also determined to prevent the home front from slipping into revolutionary chaos. The best way of achieving this objective seemed to be to support the Social Democrat leaders who, together with the Independent Socialists, were the only people in Germany whom the crowds in the streets were still willing to follow. On 9 November Groener therefore telephoned Ebert from Headquarters at Spa and offered him the support of the Army, if help was needed in maintaining law and order. Ebert accepted. The famous Ebert–Groener Pact was complemented by another accord, the Stinnes–Legien Agreement, struck between the employers and the trade unions on 15 November. In it, the industrialists recognised the unions as the official representation of labour and as bargaining partners. Restrictions upon the right of association were declared inadmissable. The employers promised to refrain from supporting company unions and to re-employ returning soldiers in their former jobs. The accord also stipulated that all firms with fifty or more workers should have an elected committee to represent the labour force and to oversee, together with the management, the implementation of collective agreements. The latter were to contain provisions for arbitration boards on which employers and employees would be equally represented. Finally the two sides of industry agreed to introduce the eight-hour working day. In return for these concessions, the trade unions gave an undertaking not to touch the existing property structure. The government was also able to count on the co-operation of the civil servants, most of whom stayed in office.

With these heterogeneous, but influential allies behind him, Ebert was in a better position to deal with the radicalised Left. Financed by industry and constituted by Army officers, volunteer units, the Free Corps, were set up to quell left-wing challenges to government authority. The first clash of arms came early in January 1919 when the militant Spartacus League, embittered and frustrated by the course of the Revolution since November, staged a revolt. They did not have a chance against the Free Corps. The Workers' and Soldiers' Councils were the next in the firing line. The first four months of 1919 saw a number of attempts by militant workers and left-wing intellectuals to establish some form of Council system in various parts of the country. However, they did not succeed in resisting the advance of the Free Corps units which soon appeared on the scene.

While the Free Corps were engaged in brutal mopping-up operations against the extreme Left, the preparations for the National Assembly were being completed. The result of the elections of 19 January 1919 are shown in the following table.

The National Assembly elections of 19 January 1919

	USPD	SPD	DDP	Centre	DVP	DNVP	Splinter groups
No. of votes (000s)	2,317	11,509	5,642	5,980	1,346	3,121	484
% of vote	7.6	37.9	18.6	19.7	4.4	10.3	1.3
Seats	22	163	75	91	19	44	7

These figures demonstrate an overwhelming support for a Republican parliamentary system. The three 'Weimar' parties, the SPD, the Centre Party and the German Democratic Party (DDP) gained 76.2 per cent of the votes and 329 out of 421 seats in the new National Assembly. The Constitution which was drawn up and subsequently ratified neatly reflected the changes that had taken place since the autumn. Although the powers of the Reichstag were counterbalanced by those of a popularly elected Reich President, the government was now directly responsible to the national Parliament.

We shall have to come back to the structure of the Weimar Constitution in the next chapter. Only the final section is of immediate interest here in that it contained a list of articles which indicated a shift in the balance of political forces. Whereas most of the clauses were concerned with the guarantee of basic political and religious liberties, others established social and economic rights which reflected the strength of the Social Democrats and trade unions in the constitutional compromise. What the moderates in the German working-class movement had been fighting for, since the Erfurt Programme of 1891, had now become enshrined in the document which set the political framework for the new German Republic. The question was whether these rights would remain on paper or, through legislative action, could be given real force. The outcome of this question depended to a considerable extent on the mandate of the electorate, now that a parliamentary-representative regime had been created. It also depended on the attitudes of the elites.

Economic dislocation and counter-revolution, 1919–1923

If the broad reformist consensus of the November days had persisted, the SPD and the trade unions would have had some reason for optimism. However, the civil war of the subsequent months had done much to polarise opinion. Above all, it had given the conservative forces time to recover from the shock of 9 November. The radicalisation of the Left had already driven the Ebert government into the arms of the former representatives of the monarchy. For the moment, the generals, industrialists and bureaucrats were happy to help Ebert to destroy the extreme Left. Yet their success was not only encouraging to them, but also to the politicians on the Right and the middle who, in the elections of 1919, were once more given an opportunity to appeal to their former voters. To many of them, the Social Democrats were just as dangerous as the Spartacists and the sooner a complete roll-back could be effected the better.

Given the great potential of the counter-revolution, as yet barely tapped, much depended on economic developments. It is not difficult to see that the lost war had saddled the Republic with almost insuperable problems. There was first of all the harsh Peace Treaty which the Allies handed down at Versailles. Under its terms, Germany lost 13 per cent of her territory, comprising 10 per cent of her population. Her colonies became mandates under the League of Nations. Nine-tenths of her merchant fleet was taken away. The armed forces were to be reduced to 100,000 men. The country's prewar export markets had largely disappeared. In 1919 industrial production reached an all-time low (Table 7). Meanwhile millions of demobilised soldiers reappeared on the labour market. Under the Stinnes–Legien Agreement their jobs were to be kept open. But there were also many young people who had been born during the prewar baby boom. Still, unemployment remained relatively low (Table 18), although the demographic shift from the countryside to the cities had continued (Tables 2 and 16). Furthermore the war had accelerated the trend towards larger firms and the decline of the self-employed (Tables 17 and 15). By 1925, 56.3 per cent of the national income was earned in salaries and wages, as against 45.3 per cent in 1913.

The advance of industry with its greater productivity, however, also raised fresh possibilities of economic growth. An attempt could be made to reopen former export markets to German goods and to unfreeze assets abroad. The home market was likewise starved of goods after five years of total war and austerity. Yet these opportunities could only be exploited if industrial peace could be maintained and a relapse into the class-war positions of the Wilhelmine period could be avoided. It was clear that the might of the trade unions had increased and that the repressive arm of the State was less easily available to employers than it had been before the war. In these changed circumstances it was in the interests of industry to continue to enhance the co-operation between the two sides of industry which had been established at the end of the war and formalised in the *Zentralarbeitsgemeinschaft* (ZAG) on 6 November 1918. After protracted, but ultimately successful negotiations, the Works' Council Bill was ratified on 4 February 1920. It provided for the election of employees' representatives in firms with more than 20 employees. These representatives had to be consulted about working conditions, proposed redundancies and welfare questions. The expansion of the system of wage agreements also increased the protection of the workforce. Between 1920 and 1924 the number of employees included in collective agreements increased from about 6 million to 13 million. In an effort to establish collective bargaining as a universal principle in industry and to reduce the use of strikes and lock-outs as a weapon in industrial disputes, a system of arbitration was introduced. The position of the industrial workforce was also improved by the creation of a network of social security and unemployment benefits. In short, the war and the Revolution had resulted in some tangible improvements to the legal and economic position of the working class by comparison with its erstwhile pariah status.

Yet these gains were never secure, not even during the early period of relative strength of organised labour. This was partly due to the postwar economic crisis and the subsequent hyperinflation. However, one must not underestimate the determination of many employers in major branches of industry to launch offensives against the gains of the working-class movement and to resort to the powerful weapon of lock-outs to change the postwar industrial balance in their favour. The abolition of the eight-hour workday in 1923, one of the major and long-fought-for gains of 1918, and the collapse of the ZAG in 1924 provide strong pointers that old hostilities continued to be very deep. Although the methods of the industrial roll-back were different from the ones that were simultaneously deployed in the political sphere by the anti-Republican Right, the employers' moves must be seen within the broader context of the counter-revolution of the early 1920s.

There is also the important area of wages and living standards. Viewed over a period of several years, G. Bry is probably correct in concluding that real wages were 'substantially below' the pre-1914 figure. But, perhaps surprisingly, the situation does not appear to have been too bad in 1920/1, although there were considerable variations between different branches of industry (Table 24). Thus some recent calculations would suggest that hourly paid workers in the Frankfurt area succeeded in keeping ahead of the cost-of-living index, if only just, during the 20 months after July 1920. Many skilled men in Hamburg also did fairly well. However, from March 1922 the economic situation became so volatile that real wages fell well below prewar levels. By the summer of 1923 the position on the wage front had become so chaotic that all figures ceased to be meaningful indicators of anything more than the suffering which hyperinflation during that year inflicted upon the 'masses'. This is also confirmed by the fact that civilian health reached an all-time low, with cases of tuberculosis and rickets rising rapidly. Nevertheless, it appears that there was no catastrophic decline in real wages up to 1922. The early postwar period was a phase of relative boom in German industry and the unions were prepared to use their newly found strength, while employers were anxious to avoid constant conflict over wages (Tables 7, 8, 18 and 44).

It also helped the wage-earning population that some basic foodstuffs continued to be rationed and that the rigid wartime rent controls were maintained. Nor, for the same reason, were there any sharp increases in heating and electricity prices. As the average working-class family spent a considerable proportion of its income on these items, continued regimentation and a more or less successful use of the collective bargaining right shielded workers and their families from the worst. It also worked to their advantage that the government's economic policy was expansionist. As long as the rumblings of a social revolution could still be heard, it was probably rightly felt that the country could not bear a further austerity programme with high unemployment after five years of wartime hardship. The social costs and dangers would have been too high. Hence the Reich government went for growth and industrial production in response to democratic pressures and assisted industry to reconquer export markets lost during the war. It is a reflection of the changed balance of power that this policy could assert itself, although it suffered from a serious drawback: it fuelled inflation and complicated the already strained relations with the Western Allies concerning the reparations problem.

We have seen earlier that the way in which the Hohenzollern monarchy had financed the war had not only led to inflationary pressures before 1918 which price, wage and rent controls had barely been able to stem, but had also mortgaged the future owing to its reliance on war bonds. If victory failed to come and reparations which the Kaiser had been planning to impose upon the defeated nations were not available, Germany's finances were bound to be in an unholy mess. One way of honouring the wartime debts of the previous regime, and also of finding the money for reparations now being demanded by the victorious Western Allies, would have been to raise taxation. Yet the sums required were so large that, apart from depressing the economy and increasing unemployment, the new taxation levels would have been socially unacceptable. Inflating the mark therefore had the dual advantage of enabling the government to overcome the postwar demobilisation crisis and to rid itself of its debts *vis-à-vis* both the holders of war bonds and the Allies.

The disadvantage was that it was bound to infuriate the latter, who began to suspect that the Germans were deliberately wrecking their currency to avoid reparations payments. And as far as the holders of war bonds and people with savings were concerned, inflation would ruin their wealth. Worse, many of them were likely to come from those middle-class groups whose earnings from other sources had been more seriously eroded by war and postwar crises than those of the working class. Thus the salaries of higher civil servants in big cities had been reduced to 46.8 per cent of their 1914 value in real terms by 1918 and to 35.6 per cent by 1922 (Table 24). The respective figures for the Lower Civil Service, who had actually had some of their earnings restored in 1919 and were only some 10 per cent worse off than in 1914, were 69.6 per cent (1918) and 72.9 per cent (1922) (Table 24). The decline in middle-class living standards is reflected in consumption habits where, on the few statistics available, there appears to have been a marked drift away from meat, butter and fruit towards rye bread and potatoes. The professionals and self-employed did not fare any better. On top of having to rebuild their business connections which had often been shattered by the war, they were haunted by the threat of bankruptcy.

Another group which was badly hit were professional soldiers or those who had been hoping to make service in the armed forces their postwar career. The military clauses of the Versailles Treaty stipulated a reduction of the officer corps to 4,000 and hence drastically curtailed the career expectations of many younger men who had been rapidly promoted during the war. Some of them joined the Free Corps in the hope of being taken over into the regular forces. A year later they faced dismissal when, from the summer of 1919 onwards, the Allies began to press the Reich government to implement the military clauses of the Peace Treaty and to disband the volunteers' units. Thus thousands who had learned nothing besides the military profession were forced into early retirement and neither their promotion to the next higher rank nor the corresponding increase in their pension would mollify them.

Agriculture, which had temporarily benefited from the wartime food crisis and the black market economy, emerged from the war with its prewar structural problems unresolved, if not worsened (Tables 6 and 19). It took until the late 1920s for production to recover its 1912 level and then only because of a disproportionate growth in the production of potatoes and beetroot. In 1921 grain production was still 8.1 million tons or some 30 per cent below the 1912 figure. Meat and milk production also rose but slowly. Farmers and in particular the larger landowners found their economic viability weakened by the refusal of the early Weimar governments to continue the Wilhelmine practice of special subsidies and other *Liebesgaben* ('gifts of love'). Worse, they had their profits further eroded by increases in labour costs resulting from the abolition of all *Gesindeordnungen* which, dating back to the nineteenth century, barred land-labourers from going on strike and from joining a union. These discriminations were now lifted and replaced by a code, introduced on 24 January 1919, which gave land-labourers the same legal rights as those enjoyed by industrial workers. The year 1919 also saw the ratification of a bill which obliged the States to establish agricultural settlement associations which were endowed with the priority right of purchase of farms beyond a specified size. Although there was no land reform and expropriation in 1918/19 (which some left-wingers demanded) – a fact that tells us much about the limited nature of the German Revolution – the measures that were taken by the People's Deputies and later by the early Weimar governments did not endear the farming community to the Republic. In fact it was the landowners in particular who, still ensconced in their former estates, but with their local and national power position greatly weakened, were soon to be found in the vanguard of the counter-revolution. The scapegoats had been quickly identified by them, and the DNVP became the main agrarian instrument to fight them inside and outside the Reichstag.

Although figures are difficult to come by, mention must finally be made in this survey of economic conditions in the early postwar period of the plight of war widows and their children. As we have seen, some 2.4 million soldiers had been killed on the German side and although not all of them had families of their own, it is clear that hundreds of thousands of children grew up without a father and with their mothers drawing no more than a meagre pension. To this number must be added the crippled soldiers and their families. The sight of men on crutches with war decorations sitting as beggars or newspaper sellers on street corners was not an uncommon one.

There was only one sizeable group which actually emerged from the postwar

71

crisis with its economic position strengthened: entrepreneurs with productive assets and factories. It is not difficult to see that there existed a considerable need for industry to invest and modernise after the wartime years of round-the-clock production for the armed forces. But although there was some reinvestment of profits, most of the capital was found in the money markets. It was advantageous to take up loans with which machinery could be modernised, but whose value diminished with inflation. By the time credits had to be repaid they were worth only a fraction of their original value. In the long term, the modernisation boom led to overcapacities which created problems after 1923. For the moment, however, manufacturing industry and its owners were among the few who held and possibly even increased their share of the national income. They gained not so much at the expense of the mass of the wage- and salary-earning population, but of the rentiers and people with liquid assets. It was among these latter groups that the inflation ravaged really disastrously. In so far as their money had been invested in war bonds, the worthlessness of the certificates had virtually been decided by the outcome of the war. Yet not all savings had been converted into bonds and it was these that were now wiped out by postwar hyperinflation. In 1914, one dollar could be bought at 4.20 marks. By July 1919, the exchange rate was 14 marks to the dollar. Some 18 months later the ratio was 64.90:1, deteriorating quickly to 191.80:1 in January 1922, to 17,972.00:1 in January 1923 and to 4,420,000,000,000:1 in November of that year.

We have spent some time charting postwar economic developments in Germany and their effects on the material life of various social groups. We have done so not merely because it seemed intrinsically interesting to look at how people fared between 1919 and 1923, but also to provide the background to an understanding of the psychological reactions to these crucial developments; for it should be clear by now that in 1918 the traditional social order whose fissures have been described above was thrown into great confusion. Downward social mobility had increased. Thus many businessmen who had enjoyed a gratifyingly high status in their local community were forced into bankruptcy and had to join the army of dependent employees, if not the dole queues. Landlords, whose income was squeezed by continued rent controls on housing, inevitably felt bitter. So did rentiers who had lost their savings or civil servants and teachers who had their salaries cut by ministerial fiat. Officers, who had been regarded as the first estate in the country, found themselves dismissed, humiliated and socially degraded. Other middle-class groups reacted to the impact of the war in a similar way, the more so since it appeared to them that the 'proletariat' had succeeded in narrowing the gap which had been so carefully maintained during the Wilhelmine period, both by means of income differentials and by the maintenance of political, legal and educational obstacles against the assertion of the 'masses'. Some of these obstacles were now disappearing or might soon be removed by legislation, should the balance of seats in the Reichstag shift towards the Left.

For the historian, analysing the early postwar years with the benefit of hindsight, it may be possible to provide explanations for the changes in German society which are perfectly plausible today. Yet this does not mean that they were acceptable to those who experienced this period of upheaval. Indeed, it was much easier to search for scapegoats than to try and comprehend the complex processes which lay behind the decline of specific social groups. And just as the former leaders of the monarchy, Ludendorff most prominently among them, had already displayed a highly developed capacity to blame others for defeat and misery, the middle classes soon joined the campaigns, conducted in private at the local beer hall and in public in the press and election propaganda, against those who were patently least responsible for the crisis. The war, it was argued, had not been started by the Germans, but by the Allies; the war had been lost, not because the Army had been militarily defeated; on the contrary, it was alleged to have been unvanquished on the battlefields. Nor had the country been defeated and driven into the revolutionary upheaval because of the leadership's reckless and inflexible policies; instead the collapse of the home front had allegedly been caused by a minority of left-wing revolutionaries and Jews who, financed by the Allies, were supposed to have undermined popular morale. Worse, in November 1918 this minority was said to have seized power by toppling the monarchy and establishing a republic. It had also signed the 'nefarious' Treaty of Versailles in which Germany was held responsible for unleashing the war and was forced to pay exorbitant indemnities. It was with the help of such arguments that the causes of the postwar crisis became psychologically manageable. Had it not been brought on by the corrupt and incompetent 'November criminals' and the reparations payments to the Allies? Inflation was seen as a vicious device of the 'revolutionaries' for expropriating the middle classes and for preparing the country for a socialist dictatorship. All in all, these arguments amounted to a fundamental rejection of the Weimar Republic, and more generally of everything that had happened in the fields of foreign and domestic policy as well as the economy since the collapse of the Hohenzollern monarchy.

Some of these anti-Republicans, it is true, even thought they had identified specific groups of fellow-Germans. Those who had been anti-Semites before were inclined to view the events of 1918/19 as part of a vast international 'Jewish conspiracy'. Others regarded the Social Democrats as the basic evil. The fact that a whole range of anti-Republican arguments of this kind were repeated so often and propagated in the right-wing press and by many 'respectable' people, many of them academics, professionals and churchmen, merely lent them greater weight. With the destruction of the Council movement accomplished and a parliamentary system established, two parties in particular were free to capitalise on these emotions among the bewildered middle and upper classes and to reinforce their prejudices by casting them into persuasive campaign slogans: the German Nationalist People's Party (DNVP) and the German People's Party (DVP). Both rejected the Republic and demanded a restitution of the monarchy; their foreign policy programmes were rabidly revisionist, advocating non-fulfilment of the Versailles Treaty and an overthrow of the Peace Settlement at the earliest opportunity.

It cannot be emphasised too strongly that this was not a 'loyal opposition', that is, one which was prepared to operate within the existing constitutional framework and to abide by its rules. What the so-called 'National Opposition' aimed at was the substitution of the Republican system by a monarchical and an autocratic one. In the field of foreign policy, they wanted to replace the Versailles order by a German power bloc. Differences of opinion arose merely over the tactical question of whether change was to be effected by violent overthrow or by conquest of parliamentary majorities which would permit basic constitutional reform by legislation. A similar split occurred with reference to the best revisionist diplomacy to be adopted. Up to 1923, these two factions continued to compete against each other, after which date the putschist option receded into the background together with the idea of an early revanchist war. However, these divergencies do not change the crucial point that there existed a sizeable number of people on the Right of the political spectrum who did not consider a parliamentary Republic to be the appropriate political system for Germany or 'fulfilment' of Versailles the correct diplomacy. Their number was swelled by men and women from a very different social and ideological background on the extreme Left, whose proposals for the political and economic organisation of the country could also not be accommodated within the Weimar structure. In other words, there was also a 'disloyal opposition' on the Left which agitated against the Republic and its leaders not because they had allegedly toppled the monarchy and stabbed the Army in the back, as the Right asserted, but because they had not been radical enough and had 'betrayed' the Revolution.

However, this type of anti-Republican agitation was never as successful as that of the Right. How strong a chord the emotional scapegoat propaganda of DNVP and DVP struck among sizeable sections of the middle-class population may be gauged from the results of the 1920 elections. In them, the three Weimar parties (SPD, Centre and DDP) lost heavily, retaining only 43.6 per cent of the vote and 206 out of 459 seats in the Reichstag (Table 42). The DNVP, DVP and the new Bavarian People's Party (BVP) clocked up 33.3 per cent of the vote and 157 seats. The extreme Left obtained 20 per cent and 87 seats. Weimar, as has often been observed, had become a 'republic without Republicans', i.e. a political system with which a majority of the population did not wholeheartedly identify.

This shift in the balance of political forces is even more astonishing if one remembers that it occurred only a year after the elections to the National Assembly and three months after the Kapp Putsch of March 1920, the first major right-wing attempt to overthrow the constitutional order by force. In the narrow sense, this putsch was a revolt by Free Corps units stationed near Berlin and led by General Walther von Lüttwitz and naval Captain Hermann Ehrhardt to forestall their dissolution. But, backed by their military power, their aims quickly expanded and they proceeded to install a government headed by a former Prussian civil servant and founder member of the wartime Fatherland Party, Wolfgang Kapp. The Republican Cabinet and President Ebert as commander-in-chief of the armed forces asked General Hans von Seeckt, the top Reichswehr officer, to stop the rebellion. But they were told that 'Reichswehr does not fire upon Reichswehr'. This refusal of the Army to support the elected and legitimate government of Germany forced the ministers to flee to Weimar and then on to Stuttgart. It looked as though the Weimar order had come to the end of the road only a year after its creation. What saved it was a general strike proclaimed by the working-class movement. This strike proved so effective that it quickly paralysed the Kapp regime. Unable to establish its authority and to administer the country, Kapp and Lüttwitz threw in the sponge within four days. Yet peace did not return immediately. For several weeks civil war raged in various parts of the country, especially in the Ruhr area where the extreme Left had mobilised an army of 50,000 volunteers. Having been challenged by the anti-Republican Right, the government now faced a challenge from the extreme Left.

It is a measure of the radicalisation of sections of the working class and the persistence of its disappointment with the outcome of the Revolution that a force of this size was thrown into the battle against the Reichswehr, forcing it to retreat temporarily from the Ruhr area. Seen in conjunction with the performance of the USPD and the newly founded Communist Party (KPD) in the June 1920 elections, the civil war in the Ruhr was no doubt a major event; and so was the defeat of the insurgents by the Reichswehr which had been so reluctant to intervene against the putschists on the Right. Once reinforcements and volunteers' units had been brought in, the uprisings were suppressed with a ruthlessness that had also characterised the civil war between the extreme Left and the Free Corps in the previous year. When law and order had been restored, the remaining volunteers' units found that the Republican government had lost all taste for maintaining them any longer. The victims of this purge, which was also extended to the Reichswehr itself, were too weak to resist their dismissal. But they were able to flout the order that they hand in all their weapons. The authorities could also do little to prevent Free Corps fighters from reconstituting themselves in private clubs. Attempts by the police to contain the illegal paramilitarism which soon flourished, especially in the eastern provinces, met with great hostility not only by activists, but also by sympathisers who provided shelter and financial aid. Whoever 'betrayed' arms caches to the authorities was liable to be murdered by private liquidation (*Feme*) squads. Republican politicians likewise became victims of assassinations which demonstrated that the secret societies on the Right interpreted 'treason' very broadly to include such well-known politicians as Matthias Erzberger who had been among the signatories of the 1918 Armistice and Walther Rathenau, who, as Foreign Minister, advocated fulfilment of the Versailles Treaty.

Possibly even more alarming was that these continued manifestations of civil war and a poisoned political life enjoyed the tacit support of many 'respectable' people. As has been mentioned above, they too felt no love for the Republic. The judiciary presents a particularly glaring example. Kapp, though he died while awaiting his trial, would not have had to fear a heavy sentence. Lüttwitz suffered no worse than being sent into retirement on a general's pension. Ehrhardt was allowed to escape to Austria. The trial against Adolf Hitler and Ludendorff following their abortive putsch of November 1923 was marked by a similar leniency towards right-wing plotters: Ludendorff was acquitted altogether; Hitler was sentenced to five years, but released after less than 12 months. Leaders of left-wing risings against the Republic were not treated so leniently. Eugen Leviné and some of his associates who established a short-lived Soviet Republic in Munich in April 1919 were either executed or given long prison sentences. Max Hölz, who staged a Communist coup in the Mansfeld region in the spring of 1921, was imprisoned for life. That judges were motivated by political considerations is revealed most clearly in the statistics of sentences passed against activists of the Right or Left. Up to 1921, 13 murder cases involving left-wingers were brought to court which imposed eight death sentences and a total of 176 years' imprisonment; by contrast some 314 murders committed by right-wingers led to one life sentence and a total of 31 years' imprisonment. Also in later years, a political murder perpetrated by a Communist earned either a high prison sentence or the death penalty; right-wing *Feme* murderers, on the other hand, tended to be let off very lightly.

Overt or covert sympathies with putschism varied from region to region. In Prussia, the SPD-led government had succeeded in instilling the police and Civil Service with a measure of loyalty. It was a different matter in Bavaria where traditional separatism, memories of Eisner's Socialist Republic and even more of Leviné's Soviet Republic and, thirdly, a deep resentment against all that the Berlin 'November Republic' was assumed to stand for, merged to produce a strong current of radical right-wing politics. With the majority of the Bavarian population living either in the countryside or in small towns far from

Germany's industrial centres, they had quickly come to accept the propaganda that was being spread by the DNVP and BVP about the treachery and corruption in the capital. Proudly they saw themselves as a bastion against the pernicious influences of Republicanism and Social Democracy further north. Radical anti-Republicans who had the Prussian police following too closely on their heels found a haven in and around Munich. They were welcomed by a welter of paramilitary organisations which enjoyed the official support of the Bavarian government. The German south became the operating ground of reactionaries with either black–white–red or white–blue (Bavarian) propensities, restless tramps of the counter-revolution, former Free Corps mercenaries, Kappists and airy-fairy 'national revolutionaries'.

By 1922, three major factions had emerged among the paramilitary associations there. In November 1922, the high-school teacher Hermann Bauer created the *Vereinigte Vaterländische Verbände Bayerns* (VVVB) which had strongly federalist and monarchist leanings and favoured Gustav von Kahr. Bauer's organisation was rather lax and did not attract the genuine activists who either joined the *Sturmabteilungen* (SA) of Captain Ernst Röhm or similar radical groups, all of which combined in January 1923 in a cartel under the name of *Arbeitsgemeinschaft Vaterländische Kampfverbände* (AGVK). The AGVK had taken courage from the events in Italy in 1922 and were dreaming of a march on Berlin. Finally, there was a third force in northern Bavaria which was earmarked for 'border protection' against the 'red' north.

Yet the developments in Bavaria were not the only events to worry the Reich government. A crisis had been brewing for some time over reparations, fixed by the Reparations Commission at 132 milliard gold marks in April 1921. A week later, a schedule of payments was drawn up which laid down the detailed terms of German liabilities. The first cash payment of one milliard gold marks was made in full in the summer of that year. However, subsequent instalments were much reduced and in the following year the London Schedule was thrown into total confusion. The Reich government claimed that the sums were more than the country could afford. The Allies, on the other hand, experiencing the often intolerably obstinate demeanour of German negotiators and pointing to the Republic's expansionist financial and economic policies, increasingly came to suspect that the Germans deliberately ruined their currency in order to obtain a more favourable reparations settlement. The accuracy of this claim has been the subject of much historical debate which cannot be recounted here. What is undisputed is that Germany was defaulting on her cash payments and, as the Reparations Commission concluded in December 1922, was also failing to make agreed deliveries in kind. Disagreement now arose among the Allies over what should be done about this, with the French pressing for a drastic show of strength. In January 1923 France, supported by Belgian soldiers, occupied the Ruhr area in response to which the

Berlin government proclaimed a policy of passive resistance. The economic heart of Germany virtually came to a standstill. The resistance was a tremendous drain on the country's financial resources, further fuelling inflation. It was clear that sooner rather than later this policy would have to be called off. Hyperinflation was ruining the middle classes at a frightening pace and hunger drove the industrial population out on to the streets. Confidence in the Republic was at its lowest ebb. It seemed that the Reich was about to fall apart and fresh Communist uprisings loomed on the horizon.

Thus what the Bavarian government had set up along its northern border was officially designed to stop civil war from spreading south. However, the growing private army inside its own territory was not without serious danger either. In September 1923, one of the paramilitary leaders suggested that 'it cannot go on like this. The cities are like overheated boilers, we must now march with our rifles and our machine-guns and our few guns. And if we are not given the horses we require, we shall pull [the guns] through Thuringia ourselves.' Made nervous by such statements, the Bavarian government proclaimed a state of emergency and nominated Kahr as *Generalstaatskommissar*. Three days later, Kahr had Captain Ehrhardt of Kapp Putsch fame brought from exile at Salzburg in a Bavarian Reichswehr car and put him in charge of the northern border police at Coburg.

There is little doubt that Kahr, too, had begun to think of the possibility of a march on Berlin which hypnotised most anti-Republicans at this time. Various rifts between the AGVK and Ehrhardt's troops notwithstanding, by the autumn of 1923 the attack upon the capital had become the objective of all right-wing forces in Bavaria. While the preparations for it were in full swing, Kahr and his supporters were on the look-out for allies in the north. Obviously, in order to assure the success of a coup the mistakes of the Kapp Putsch would have to be avoided. In particular, no move was possible without the explicit support of the Reichswehr which, since 1920, had been transformed into a powerful instrument under the command of Seeckt. Like many other officers, he had never accepted the Versailles Settlement as final. He also subscribed to the right-wing views of the causes of the 1918 Revolution and remained a monarchist at heart who hoped for the eventual return of the Hohenzollerns. In short, he was a revisionist both in matters of domestic and foreign policy, although he was shrewd enough to realise that the country was too weak to challenge the Versailles Peace head on.

What could be done, however, was to try and lay the foundations of a military instrument that might be used to unhinge the Versailles system at a later date. The manpower problem of the Army which had resulted from the enforced reduction of its size to 100,000 men was to be overcome by training illegal contingents of volunteers drawn from the private armies of the post-Kapp era. This Black Reichswehr was organised by local commanders, especially in the eastern provinces. Under the Treaty of Versailles, the Reichswehr was also forbidden to develop tanks, planes and other modern weapons. Seeckt had found a means of circumventing these stipulations by establishing links with the Red Army. The Russians proved to be useful partners in these secret attempts to fill the technological gap that threatened to open up between the Reichswehr and the Western Allies. They provided the Germans with research and development facilities as well as training grounds on Soviet territory in return for access to German military expertise.

Seeckt finally tried hard to imbue the Army with an ethos of service – not to the German Republic, but to an abstract notion of the German State. The advantages of this ideology were that it permitted the officer corps to distance themselves from the existing constitutional order. They were assumed to be working for a national interest which transcended the Republic. Given the ambiguous stance of the Reichswehr and its claims to a leading political role, it is not surprising that men like the former Pan-German leader Heinrich Class should approach Seeckt about the possibility of a dictatorial solution when the economic and political crisis reached its peak in the autumn of 1923. By this time, inflation was completely out of control. The Reich government had lost its support among the majority parties. The time seemed ripe for a move to scrap the Constitution and to establish an autocratic directorium on the ruins of the Republic. Various names were tossed about as members of the proposed putschist government, among them Friedrich Minoux, a former director of the Stinnes concern. However, it appears that not only heavy industry, which had never wholeheartedly supported the ZAG experiment, but also Seeckt were prepared to cut ties with the Republic.

The rumours of feverish plotting in Munich and Berlin were deeply disturbing for the SPD-led provincial governments in central Germany. They became convinced that a fascist dictatorship was imminent. On 10 October two Communist ministers entered the Cabinet of Erich Zeigner in Saxony. Thuringia followed suit and this promptly provoked discussions of an impending left-wing coup. Zeigner moreover decided to publish details of Germany's secret rearmament measures, which proved deeply embarrassing to the Reichswehr. At this point the Reich government, trying to regain control of the situation, resolved to postpone dealing with the Bavarian problem. As so often in later years, the 'red peril' was considered more dangerous than right-wing plotting. Reichswehr contingents were ordered to march against Saxony and Thuringia. The Zeigner government was removed on 29 October; the Thurigian left-wingers survived until 2 November.

The removal of the 'red belt' between Berlin and Bavaria advanced but also confused the putschist cause. There was no discord over whether a move to overthrow the Republic should be undertaken. The crucial factor was whether the Bavarians or the anti-Republicans in the north should act first. Kahr procrastinated, waiting for a signal from the north; the northerners pressed the Bavarians to move, hoping that this would sway Seeckt. However, Seeckt was perturbed by the radicalism of the Bavarian movement, and a number of events in the south had caused him to make his own independent preparations. On 4 November, he invited Otto Wiedfeldt, the German ambassador in Washington, to join a directorium under him. Simultaneously he outlined his own plans in a long letter to Kahr in which he warned against precipitate action. In particular he wished to avoid further violence and full-scale civil war.

While these multilateral negotiations were still going on, the most radical elements around the SA, which had been excluded from the talks because they were deemed to lack respectability, resorted to a desperate action which ultimately wrecked the various directorium plans. Impatient with Kahr and his conservative allies, they decided to precipitate the march on Berlin by forcing the *Generalstaatskommissar* to proclaim the beginning of the 'national revolution'. The latter agreed in the course of a bizarre encounter in a smoke-filled backroom of the Munich *Bürgerbräukeller* when pushed by two of the leaders of the radicals: Hitler and Ludendorff. When the news of the events in Munich reached him a few hours later, President Ebert summoned Seeckt to his office and put him on the spot. Endowing the Reichswehr chief with full emergency powers to resolve the crisis, he asked him to choose between putschism and the defence of the Republic. Instead of arresting the President, Seeckt decided to use the Reichswehr to save the existing constitutional system.

However dramatic and fascinating the developments of early November 1923 may have been, the main point to be made here is that the Weimar order came very close to destruction. It was threatened by the extreme Left, but this danger remained relatively small when compared with the strength of anti-Republican feeling on the Right and with the physical power and financial and political influence it could bring to bear. It was in this period that it became clear how little the position and influence of the traditional elites had been touched by the Revolution of 1918 outside the parliamentary sphere. A representative system and a liberal constitution had emerged from the upheavals of 1918/19. But the structures of socioeconomic power had been only marginally affected. The shifts in the balance which had occurred were not protected against a roll-back. The state bureaucracy and the legal, military and educational institutions had seen little change, with the possible exception of some areas of government in Prussia which was to remain a bastion of the Republic until July 1932 and attempted a number of bold reforms, especially of the school system (Table 37). Nor did it augur well for the future that the parliamentary system had found so little acceptance among the people of education and influence in industry, agriculture and the professions. On the other hand, it is true that the Weimar order had survived in the face of problems which would have stretched other political systems to their limits. In this sense, the outcome of the crisis of 1923 was heartening to the supporters of the Republic. Its radical critics had failed, at least for the time being. The period of open civil war and putschism came to an end. An era of relative stability and optimism began which lasted until the onset of the World Depression in 1929/30.

3 The Weimar Republic between stabilisation and collapse, 1924–1933

Intellectual and cultural activity

The picture which has been painted so far of German history in the early twentieth century is one of a society racked by social tensions and violent political conflicts. It was a development which cannot be separated from the experience of rapid economic change since the late nineteenth century, followed by total war, defeat and civil war. What exacerbated these tensions and the violence which accompanied them was the inflexible conservatism of the country's agrarian, industrial and educated elites. Time and time again they thwarted even moderate reformist change and frustrated the aspirations of a growing number of working-class Germans. It was a conservatism which stemmed not merely from a perceived threat to established social, political and economic positions from below, but a more general obsession with an alleged undermining of accepted values and social morality resulting from the advent of 'mass society'. Invariably, the cities were identified as the main source of moral corruption and decay, not only because they were seen as seedbeds of socialism and 'low culture', but also because they had become, already before 1914, centres of alternative life-styles, artistic experimentation and radical debate among coffee-house intellectuals.

It is not easy to describe how hostile and philistine were the reactions of the upper classes, and also of many petty bourgeois *Stammtisch* politicians in the provinces to these tendencies. Literary movements or *avantgarde* artistic activity provoked almost universal indignation. Long before 1914 Reich Chancellor Hohenlohe gave telling expression to this in his diary after viewing Gerhart Hauptmann's *Hannele's Himmelfahrt*. 'A monstrous wretched piece of work,' he noted, 'social-democratic realistic, at the same time full of sickly, sentimental mysticism, nerve-racking, in general abominable. Afterwards we went to Borchard's to get ourselves back into a human frame of mind with champagne and caviar.' Wilhelm II likewise had little patience with modern art and tried to sack the director of the National Gallery because he disapproved of the latter's acquisitions policy. This remained the dominant attitude towards artists and intellectuals. On the other hand, the Prussian police was not as efficient in containing artistic activity as it was in its surveillance of Social Democrats. The Bavarians were even more lax. There was hence a good deal of artistic freedom in Germany and the authorities were never consistent in their cultural policies. It was in this peculiar atmosphere of semi-autocracy that cultural activity thrived, turning Berlin and Munich into major meeting places of the *avantgarde*.

Peter Gay has reminded us that in terms of cultural production 'the Republic created little; it liberated what was already there'. Although this may be too extreme a statement, it is true that the 1920s saw an unprecedented flourishing of artistic activity. Aided by the adoption of a liberal official policy, even towards the most provocative experiments, these years came to be known as the 'golden years' of Weimar culture. Berlin was one of the world's most important cultural cities. It is not possible here to offer a comprehensive survey of this rich intellectual life. Much of it was moved by purely aesthetic concerns and it is always risky to try to establish a link between artistic creation and society. Expressionism in particular, however momentous its influence in different art forms may have been, was probably too heterogeneous and directionless a movement to permit relating it to the societal conditions in which it grew up. On the other hand, much of the writing, visual art and musical output clearly reflected aspects of the human predicament in the twentieth century. The recurrent themes of alienation, sickness, dissonance and chaos did represent a form of social criticism. Dadaism perhaps went furthest in trying to unmask the absurdities in the life of modern man. 'Weimar Culture' therefore raises the question of whether its richness and its frantic creativity were more than a reflection of the Republic's liberal policies towards the arts; of whether it was conceivable outside the context of a society torn by many contradictions and affected by many intellectual currents. After total war and violent revolutionary upheaval, to quote Helmut Kuhn, 'nothing and no-one was in its place any more; everything had become possible'. Conversely, it might be asked how far the often vitriolic criticism by Weimar intellectuals, by members of the *avantgarde* establishment, mirrored the basic instability of Germany in the 1920s. Ideas never exist in a vacuum. These at least would seem to be the most interesting broader questions raised by 'Weimar Culture' which should be borne in mind when we come to consider social, economic and political developments later in this chapter.

Of course, it was not too difficult to ridicule and criticise. Yet the satirising of modern life and even less the denial of art did not provide a plausible alternative to prevailing conditions. Nor did the portrayal of the machine age in Fritz Lang's famous films do more than inspire fear and horror of the future. The architecture of the Bauhaus, by contrast, tended to take a more constructive view of the potentialities of industrialism and urban dwelling. Its use of new materials for building and furniture reflected a conscious step in this direction, while making at the same time an effort to reknit the earlier links between art and handicraft. No doubt it was, as James Joll put it, a 'confused, confusing and contradictory' period: 'On the one hand, [Germany] was a society in which the *neue Sachlichkeit* – a rational aesthetic which preached a new simplicity and respect for the materials in art and design – led to the foundation of the international style in contemporary architecture while in other intellectual disciplines ... new and rewarding methods and theories were being developed.' Yet, on the other hand, 'it was a milieu in which every kind of irrational and exotic belief, from harmless cults of astrology or medicine or health foods to darkest and most sinister racial theories, could find a ready audience'. Literature was one of the fields in which the transition from a vague societal criticism and ruminations upon the future shape of the industrial age to a preoccupation with contemporary social and political problems became clearly discernible. This was particularly true of some writers who had been politicised by the experience of industrialised war in northern France. Their way of trying to cope with the memories of horror was to relive it on paper or on the stage. Their realism was in effect a mode of pacifism. 'No more war' was the message of Erich Maria Remarque's *All Quiet on the Western Front*.

Yet not all Germans who read the novel or saw the film reacted in a pacifist mould. They had formed a different view of the lessons of the First World War which came to be represented in the highly successful writings of Ernst Jünger. He derived from the experience of the trenches the vision, not of a peaceful world, but of a martial and militarised society. Other writers experienced their political awakening in the face of mass misery and revolutionary upheaval on the home front. There were first of all those who took the developments of the second decade of the twentieth century as further evidence of the decay of the bourgeois world. Deeply suspicious of the 'masses', they viewed this alleged decline with fatalistic pessimism and tacit fear. It would, they believed, all end in chaos, in the collapse of individuality and established hierarchies. Others attempted to visualise, through their writings, the emergence of a society which reconciled and integrated the 'masses' within the concept of a 'German socialism'. In terms of quantity of output and influence upon the dominant political culture of Weimar Germany, the creativity which was ultimately inspired by a fear of the modern industrial age was clearly more important. It may not always be easy to press all of these artists and intellectuals into a traditional right–left pattern. Yet in their majority they must be placed in the camp of those who wanted to reverse the historical trends of the past two hundred years, even if they revelled in the contradictions of the Conservative Revolution. What united them was their elitism and rejection of liberalism and Marxism, of rationalism and 'materialism'. They were the counter-revolutionaries of this period and hence different from yet another group who saw themselves as critics of existing society and as the vanguard of a socialist counter-culture to be realised after a proletarian revolution. Their writings attacked contemporary patterns of exploitation and deprivation and aimed to prepare the path for the construction of a new industrial order and culture which relied on the creative energies of the 'masses'.

Whatever the underlying differences in the perception of the human predicament, intellectual life in Weimar Germany was extremely rich and wide-ranging in terms of the ideas expressed. Speculating about the future of art and society became a favourite pastime. Artistic and literary activities were complemented by simultaneous great advances in the sciences. Göttingen University became one of the centres of modern physics where the famous of the world gathered in the 1920s. Philosophy and social science research likewise blossomed at Frankfurt, Berlin, Heidelberg and other institutions of higher learning. Apart from its intellectual intensity and innovative power, this activity in all fields, whether carried on in studios, coffee-houses, seminar rooms or research laboratories, was characterised by its cosmopolitanism and its elitism. Even men like Bertolt Brecht, who consciously tried to create forms of dramatic art with which, he hoped, the working class would identify, found their works more often discussed by fellow-intellectuals and seen on stage by educated and enlightened middle-class audiences. The connections between high culture and popular culture, however hard some artists worked to establish them, remained tenuous. This does not mean that the latter was less flourishing, but it took different forms and was less spontaneous and individualistic. Above all, it retained its basic prewar division into a middle-class and lower-middle-class culture on the one hand, and a working-class culture on the other. Thus the Weimar Republic saw the revival of clubs and associations which had dominated the life of millions of members outside the urban industrial centres. During the Wilhelmine period these organisations had been loyal supporters of the status quo against the rising SPD. Now they tended to look back to this period with nostalgia and subtly to nourish feelings of anti-Republican patriotism. This kind of popular culture with its manifold traditions existed side by side, as under the monarchy, with a working-class culture whose organisational scope was even wider than during the pre-1914 period.

One of the major reasons for this organisational expansion is that much of the cultural activity of the 'masses' took place after 1918 within the framework of two antagonistic working-class movements. The Revolution had led to an irreconcilable split between the extreme Left and the SPD, both vying for the support of the working class. This competition reinforced the attempts to create an authentic 'proletarian' culture. Consequently both working-class parties, the Communists and the Social Democrats, threw themselves into a wide range of cultural activities to which they recruited literally hundreds of thousands of members. The largest organisations were those which mobilised workers for sports activities. The *Arbeiter-Turn- und Sport-Bund* (ATB), whose roots went back to the 1890s, was the most successful among them, uniting under its umbrella over half a million people in over 6,000 clubs. Originally devoted to sports like soccer, cycling and gymnastics and rejecting 'bourgeois sport', the ATB introduced new activities like tennis, ice hockey, sailing and chess after 1918. As physical and mental recreation were seen as inseparable, both working-class movements also expanded the pre-1914 network of cultural and educational organisations. The range of evening classes widened and there was even a Proletarian University at Remscheid in the Ruhr area. Music and singing were other activities which aimed at the direct involvement of members. At the same time efforts were made to widen the appreciation of the arts. The *Volksbühne* movement continued to offer reduced theatre and concert tickets on a subscription basis.

It was, of course, no secret that the ideas behind the wide-ranging cultural activities of the two working-class movements and their affiliates were inspired by Marxist cultural theory and they were hence not without a political purpose. Politics also entered more explicitly through lectures and agitprop sessions on topical issues as well as on broader social questions which were built into the recreational and cultural programmes. Culture was not presented as *l'art pour l'art*, but given a specific meaning. It was to enhance the understanding, in a Marxist sense, of the socioeconomic mechanisms of existing society and to anticipate the cultural life of a socialist future. We have already touched upon the problem of how novel this proletarian culture could possibly be as long as it continued to operate within the world of bourgeois culture.

There was the related question of how to finance the raising of the cultural consciousness of the 'masses'. The organisers and theoreticians of a proletarian counter-culture were painfully aware that much of their effort was partially undermined by the daily exposure of the working class to 'bourgeois' ideas and habits. As before 1914, this influence was particularly strong with respect to reading matter. Although both the Communists and the Social Democrats published their own daily newspapers, circulation rates showed that the majority of the working population read either a national 'bourgeois' paper or a local paper which was linked with a larger network of syndicated news services and leader columns. One of the most successful of these enterprises was the one founded by Alfred Hugenberg during the First World War. Yet the figure of Hugenberg, a former Pan-German, director of Krupp and from 1928 leader of the DNVP, illustrates the nature of the problem confronting the two working-class movements. The journalism of the Hugenberg press was very skilfully done and responded to as well as reinforced popular tastes for scandal, crime and sensation. At the same time it increasingly purveyed in its columns the ideas of the right-wing opposition to the Weimar Republic.

If the impact which these papers were bound to make on the minds of their readers was to be counteracted, the Left had to create a profitable mass circulation press which copied many of the features of the bourgeois tabloids, but also infused its own ideological slant into the political and economic commentaries. Various attempts were made to build up this kind of press; yet only Willi Münzenberg, a Communist, developed the entrepreneurial skill and journalistic 'feel' for a readable political propaganda to establish a concern which ultimately owned papers with a circulation of several hundred thousand copies. However, these figures did little to modify the overall balance between newpapers of the two working-class movements on the one hand, and the *bürgerliche* press on the other. This does not mean that the Weimar press can be squeezed into a straight right–left dichotomy. Just as the party-political spectrum of the Wilhelmine period had been more fragmented than the systems of Britain or the United States, Weimar politics inherited the old divisions within the larger blocks of classes. The press reflected this fragmentation. Although there were a number of independent dailies and weeklies, many papers openly professed to be 'near' one of the many ideological positions.

Party politics and the problem of parliamentary government

What contributed perhaps more than anything else to the large variety of political parties was the principle of proportional representation on which the electoral law was based. This gave smaller parties an opportunity of winning seats in Parliament, but did little to bring about the formation of clear majorities or stable coalitions. Indeed, never throughout the Weimar period was there a party which succeeded in gaining over 50 per cent of the vote and hence in forming a government without help from other parties. This, in turn, necessitated the conclusion of elaborate coalition compromises which accommodated the diverse demands of a number of parties. Given the confused state of German society after the end of the First World War, parties appealing to particular ideological positions and economic interests mushroomed and won enough votes to sap the potential strength of the larger parties. Even more debilitating was the fact that some of these parties promoted political ideas which could only be realised outside the existing constitutional framework. They were not available for the formation of government coalitions.

We have seen that the original Weimar parties polled a mere 45 per cent in the elections of June 1920 (Table 42). Their decline posed a fundamental threat to the functioning of the parliamentary system. In fact, the system remained viable after the election shock of 1920 only because the DVP, originally a party of 'National Opposition', became available as a coalition partner and because President Ebert, during the extreme crisis of 1923, was prepared to use his emergency powers under Article 48 of the Constitution to save the Republic. The weakness of early Weimar parliamentarism is also manifested in the fact that the country was governed by a succession of no less than ten cabinets between 1919 and 1923. Nevertheless, there was a pattern to these governments to the extent that, following the resignation of Scheidemann from the Chancellorship in June 1919 in connection with the signing of the Versailles Treaty, none of these cabinets was chaired by a politician from the largest party in the Reichstag, the SPD. More than that, with the exception of an eighteen months' interlude between 1928 and 1930, the Social Democrats were never again to be the dominant party in the government until 1969, when Willy Brandt became Chancellor of the Federal Republic – a statement which says much about the balance of political power in Germany. The SPD's hegemonic position in Prussia until its overthrow by the Papen government in July 1932 provided some counterweight to the decisive influence of the *bürgerliche* parties in the Reich. On the other hand, the fathers of the Weimar Constitution had considerably weakened the federal element, and the Social Democratic position was certainly not to be compared with that of the Prussian Conservatives in the Imperial period.

Even though these realities did not prevent many people from believing or falsely arguing that the Republic was run by 'the socialists', the pattern of *bürgerliche* governments could not have established itself without the metamorphosis of the DVP. This party had been very much the creation of Gustav Stresemann, a former leader of the National Liberals who, partly because of his extreme annexationism during the First World War, had been unacceptable to the DDP in November 1918. Backed by powerful economic interest groups, notably from the Ruhr area, Stresemann decided to found his own party which adopted the black–white–red colours of the Hohenzollern Empire and a vociferously anti-Republican programme. On foreign policy matters, the DVP was staunchly revisionist and at home it campaigned under the slogan 'Alone the DVP will from Red chains set us free'.

The success of such appeals is reflected in the results of the 1920 elections, when the DVP gained 14 per cent of the vote and 65 seats in the Reichstag. In view of the new overall balance of parliamentary power, Stresemann had suddenly become an attractive coalition partner for the other middle-class parties. However, it was not merely the lure of power-sharing that caused him to change course. With the economic situation steadily worsening and the resistance against Versailles and the Western Allies getting nowhere, the DVP leadership came to recognise that a mindless anti-Republican obstructionism would merely accelerate the plunge into total chaos. Stresemann was an economist by training. A former National Liberal MP he had also been a leading functionary of the *Bund der Industriellen* (BdI), the pre-1918 lobby of manufacturing and export-orientated industry. The deterioration of Germany's position in the early 1920s had a decidedly sobering effect on Stresemann. By 1923, he and some of the industrial interests behind him had become so worried about the consequences of German economic brinkmanship that he agreed to accept the Chancellorship following the collapse of the Cuno Cabinet in September of that year. The confusion of that autumn made it impossible for him to initiate without delay a decisive change of direction. The survival of the Republic depended in the end on Ebert's use of his presidential emergency powers. Parliamentary government was temporarily suspended. But once the radical anti-Republicans had been dealt with and hyperinflation had been brought under control, the return to parliamentarism began. A new *bürgerliche* coalition was formed in which Stresemann took over the Foreign Ministry, a post which he held continuously until his death in October 1929.

To be sure, he had not become a Republican from inner conviction; he was one rather by reason. He saw that after the extreme crisis of 1923, the situation began to stabilise. To return to the anti-Republican opposition would have been both irresponsible and against the self-interest of the DVP. Henceforth Stresemann became one of the key figures in Weimar politics during the mid-1920s without whose support Reich Chancellors could do little. Any coalition compromise had to take account of the policies of the DVP; a withdrawal of the party from the Cabinet would lead to a major political crisis. Among the aims of the DVP was the containment of the working-class movement and the reconstruction of a liberal–capitalist economy which the regimentation of the war and the postwar crisis had done much to undermine. At home it was not merely the fight against the KPD with its demand for a revolutionary restructuring of the existing order which preoccupied Stresemann, but also the structural–reformist aspirations of the Social Democrat Left which, he thought, aimed at 'socialism through the backdoor' (*Sozialismus auf kaltem Wege*). On the other hand, he was not totally averse to collaboration with the SPD, unlike some of his backers in heavy industry with whom he found himself in frequent conflict over this question. Basically he believed in broad consensus politics, and it is telling of him that he felt an admiration for the way in which the British Conservatives had brought the Labour Movement into the parliamentary political process. His strategy neatly complemented the Centre Party's approach to domestic politics; for the Catholics formed the second pillar of the *bürgerliche* coalitions of the mid-1920s, and it is significant that one of the leaders, Heinrich Brauns, enjoyed a long term of office until 1929 at the Reich Labour Ministry. In these circumstances, the struggle over whether the working-class movement would gain a greater say in the policy-making of the Republic or might be pushed back on a whole range of socioeconomic and political issues remained the central problem of domestic politics.

Compared with the situation that had obtained under the monarchy, the Constitution and the post-revolutionary balance of political forces had made the confrontation between the SPD and the other parties as well as between the unions and the employers more complicated. Conflict had occurred on numerous occasions in the early 1920s and it continued to do so in different arenas of politics and economics. In the circumstances there was no more effective way of blocking the SPD, the largest party in the Reichstag, from exerting its full political weight than to exclude it from the formation and conduct of government. It made certain that Social Democrat demands for legislation did not have to be included in a compromise between coalition parties. Nor would the working-class movement have a direct voice in the executive. It cannot be said that it was entirely easy to keep the SPD out during the four years after the crisis of 1923 as the elections of 1924 resulted in a worryingly precarious division of seats (Table 42).

Nevertheless, the desire to exclude the Social Democrats was strong. It made any coalition government vitally dependent not merely on the Catholic Centre and the DVP, but also on the DNVP, the mainstay of the early postwar 'National Opposition'. Founded in December 1918, the German Nationalists had become the rallying point for the political forces of the Wilhelmine Right. It was composed of former supporters of the agrarian Conservatives and the Free Conservatives and, as the elections of 1924 were to confirm, its main electoral base was the Protestant countryside, especially east of the river Elbe. The party was reinforced by some arch-conservative men of heavy industry and remnants of the ultra-nationalist middle-class movement, formerly assembled in the Fatherland Party and the Pan-German League. Finally, the DNVP also incorporated assorted right-wing splinter elements of the incipient *völkische* and anti-Semitic radicalism of the Wilhelmine period. Its dogmatic, ideological stance put it squarely outside any Weimar consensus, and its early programmes invariably blamed the Republic and the Allies for all of Germany's postwar problems. The radicalism of its rhetoric was but marginally affected by the departure, in 1922, of the putschist and *völkische* elements in its ranks which left to form the *Deutsch-Völkische Freiheitspartei* (DVFP) and its satellites. Nevertheless, the DNVP remained a heterogeneous movement and the experience of 1923, while hardening the attitudes of some members, led others to think of moderation. The resulting differences of opinion came to a head during the parliamentary debates on the Dawes Plan. This reparations agreement, drawn up with the help of American business and banking interests, provided for the first mutually agreed schedule of payments stipulated by the Versailles Treaty. It envisaged contributions to be phased over a number of years and adjusted to the estimated economic recovery potential of German industry.

The Dawes Plan was anathema to those elements in the DNVP which

90

represented the irredentist opposition because it was alleged to give recognition to the Versailles Settlement. On the other hand, there were more pragmatic elements to whom the Plan appeared to be the lesser of two evils. If the choice was between continued economic chaos and a reparations agreement as a precondition of American financial aid to secure economic recovery, they would opt for the latter. In particular, the representatives of certain industrial and commercial interests in the DNVP were prepared to take this line. As Hans-Erdmann von Lindeiner-Wildau, one of the key strategists, put it in 1924:

The Republic is beginning to stabilise itself and the German people is beginning to become reconciled to the status quo. Now is the moment when we must not hesitate. If we wish to retain and reinforce the DNVP as an influential and powerful movement of the Right, we must move to share power in the State.

It is symptomatic that Lindeiner-Wildau used the word 'State', as the DNVP continued to withhold recognition of the Republican system. In other words, the advocates of collaboration inside the Party had become *Vernunftrepublikaner* in an even more tenuous way than Stresemann. At heart they were still monarchists. Their rapprochement was purely tactical, partly because of the continued existence within the Party of a group of irreconcilables, partly because the collaborationists were ruthlessly determined to rejoin the anti-Republican opposition if their own interests dictated this. It is against this background that the appearance, in November 1924, of DNVP ministers in the Reich Cabinet must be seen. They had been sent there not because the DNVP had accepted the legitimacy of the Republic, but rather because it had been lured by the prospect of power-sharing and the desire of all the *bürgerliche* parties to keep the Social Democrats out when it came to distributing, inter alia, the economic burdens of the reparations settlement on to the shoulders of divergent social groups.

The coalition arrangement with the DNVP lasted until October 1925 when the government collapsed, not over a domestic political issue, but over the ratification of the Locarno Treaties. This international agreement between Germany, France and Belgium and underwritten by Britain and Italy envisaged the recognition of the territorial status quo along Germany's western frontier. The implied acceptance, under the Treaty, of the Versailles Settlement was too much for the irredentists in the DNVP. They forced the withdrawal from the Cabinet of the DNVP ministers who had given their lukewarm support for the Locarno Pact, as negotiated by Stresemann. The retreat from government responsibility did not, however, put the DNVP at a great disadvantage. The other *bürgerliche* parties, keen to remain in power, but still unprepared to bring in the SPD, formed a minority cabinet of DVP, Centre Party and DDP. For legislation on domestic issues, they relied on *ad hoc* compromises with the DNVP which, of course, never promised its support cheaply. Once the Locarno Pact had been ratified and the fuss about it had died down, and with a number of important issues of social, fiscal and educational policy coming up for decision, pressures built up once more from inside and outside the DNVP to rejoin the Cabinet. At the beginning of 1927 the former alliance was renewed. The SPD upon whose commitment to international reconciliation the Cabinet had relied during the ratification of the Locarno Treaties, again found itself excluded from shaping government policy.

The constitution of another majority coalition did not mean that the DNVP ministers or the party's leadership which had supported the compromise had an easy passage. Criticism by the right wing of their own party remained unrelenting and venomous. Grappling with a growing anti-Republican dogmatism, the DNVP chairman, Count Kuno Westarp, outlined his objectives for the present session pragmatically: 'I want to maintain the coalition for as long as possible; next aim: School Bill; ultimate aim: Prussia. If the break comes [it must not be us] who will be held responsible for it.'

Whatever plans Westarp may have had with regard to Prussia, where an SPD-led government remained in power until its illegal removal by the Reich government in July 1932, the exploitation of coalition advantages without anything like a firm commitment to the existing parliamentary system obviously did not bode well for the future of the Weimar Republic. No less serious was the anti-parliamentarism which flourished around President Paul von Hindenburg, who had been elected Ebert's successor in 1925 at the age of 78. For the old Field Marshal and monarchist hero of the First World War to be chosen by a narrow majority of some 14.6 million votes as against 13.7 million for the Centre Party leader Wilhelm Marx and 1.9 million for the KPD's Ernst Thälmann was in itself a development which his predecessor Ebert would hardly have thought possible in 1918/19. Clearly, the conservative anti-Republican forces in Germany had made a good recovery. Although Hindenburg willingly swore an oath to the Constitution on his inauguration, in his heart he remained unattached to the political system of Weimar. Realising the Field Marshal's predilections for authoritarian government, one of his most influential advisers, State Secretary Otto Meissner, began to develop three options when Hindenburg became involved in reconstituting a government after the fall of the minority cabinet of Wilhelm Marx in the winter of 1926/7. The first alternative envisaged the renewed inclusion of the DNVP. This solution was eventually adopted when the German Nationalists abandoned their earlier opposition.

Meissner also ventilated the possibility of another minority government to which he gave a lower preference, however, than to the third idea. This was the concept of a 'government of personalities' which was to rule without parliamentary backing. He knew that this alternative was feasible only if the

Reich President dissolved the Reichstag and propped up 'this government [of personalities] with special measures which would then have to be taken'. These measures would be based on the use of Article 48 of the Constitution which endowed the President with legislative emergency powers, should the Reichstag prove incapable of providing majorities for legislative and Cabinet action. The original intention of this clause was to have a mechanism by which government could continue to function during a temporary political or economic crisis. It was in this sense that Ebert had used Article 48 in the autumn of 1923 when the Cabinet was paralysed and executive powers were needed to resolve the twin problems of putschism and inflation. Accordingly, presidential government by decree came to an end as soon as a coalition of parties had put together a majority capable of ending parliamentary paralysis and of constituting a government.

However, it is not difficult to see that Article 48 could equally well be invoked under the pretence of an emergency to establish a presidential dictatorship. And once this had been done, the emergency could be prolonged with the aim of thwarting the eventual return to parliamentary government. The point is that Meissner had this possibility clearly in mind when drawing up his scenarios in 1926/7. The third option therefore toyed with the idea of pushing the Weimar system in an authoritarian direction. Further evidence of how little acceptance parliamentarism had gained among the German bureaucracy and, ranged behind them, the political and economic elites on the Right is provided by the activities of a key department in the Reichswehr Ministry headed by Colonel Kurt von Schleicher. He got engaged in theoretical exercises similar to Meissner's and, oddly enough, at the same time. However, the opportunity of putting these anti-parliamentary plans into practice did not arise for the moment. At the beginning of 1927, a majority government was found which remained in office until the end of the session.

Fresh elections were held in May 1928 which resulted in a major leftward shift (Table 42). The newly won strength of the Social Democrats made their inclusion in the new Cabinet unavoidable. For the first time since 1919 the largest party in the Reichstag provided the Chancellor, but not for long. The Müller Cabinet soon had to grapple with dangerously divisive social and economic problems. Disagreements between the coalition partners – SPD, Centre, DVP and DDP – mounted and were further exacerbated when the Great Slump began to hit Germany in the winter of 1929/30. The government fell ultimately over the issue of increased unemployment contributions, but the wrangles in the spring of 1930 demonstrated how strained relations between the middle-class parties and the SPD had become. Hindenburg asked the Centre Party politician Heinrich Brüning to form a new Cabinet which, as neither the Social Democrats nor the DNVP were available for a coalition compromise, was initially a minority government. At the same time, the new

Chancellor announced that he would have to introduce tough and unpopular measures to cope with growing economic problems, irrespective of whether he possessed parliamentary backing.

Worried about the implied threat to the maintenance of parliamentary government, the SPD offered to co-operate and help the Chancellor find *ad hoc* majorities in the Reichstag. But, having introduced a stringent financial package, Brüning would not allow it to be whittled down in return for Social Democrat support. On 16 July 1930, his proposals were rejected by the majority in Parliament. Unprepared to change his mind, he now implemented the package as an emergency decree signed by Hindenburg under the provisions of Article 48. When the Reichstag voted for the abrogation of this legislation under the provisions of paragraph 2 of the Article, Brüning proclaimed the dissolution of Parliament and continued to govern with the backing of the President's emergency powers. In the elections of 14 September 1930, it was the National Socialist Workers' Party (NSDAP) which won a resounding victory whose causes will be examined later (Table 42).

The immediate significance of the 1930 elections was that parliamentary government had become impossible. The parties of the extreme Right (including the DNVP) and of the extreme Left were not available for co-operation, but bent on destroying the Weimar 'system'. A minority Cabinet would have faced an immediate vote of no-confidence and dismissal, if it had tried to rely on the Reichstag. Nor were the parties of the centre and the SPD, with their diminished majorities, able to agree on a compromise. Brüning fell back on the President and ruled with the help of emergency degrees. The Reichstag had been put out of action, and thenceforth the Reich Chancellor's legislative and executive authority derived from the constitutional prerogative of one man: the old Field Marshal and monarchist Hindenburg. So long as the parties were unable to present their own majority coalition, he could also nominate and dismiss the Chancellor.

Brüning was sustained by Hindenburg in this way until May 1932, 'tolerated' by the SPD which accepted Brüning as the lesser evil to another vote of no-confidence followed by further elections and a possible further landslide in favour of the extreme anti-Republican parties. This meant that political decision-making in Germany had become the domain of a small group of politicians huddling around the President and relying on his powers under Article 48. The Weimar Republic had, for all practical purposes, been transformed into a presidential dictatorship. The unwavering determination with which the Brüning solution was implemented in 1930 has since given rise to suspicions that Hindenburg had ulterior motives when he invoked Article 48. Might it be that he and his advisers were hoping to use the economic crisis in order to entrench an authoritarian regime so deeply that a return to parliamentarism became impossible once the crisis was over? Brüning's memoirs, published in 1970, have done much to strengthen this hypothesis. We have already mentioned the scenarios which had been drawn up around Hindenburg in 1926/7. At the beginning of 1929, long before anyone dreamed of the Great Depression, Schleicher was once more ventilating plans for removing the Social Democrats permanently from the government and for erecting a presidential regime. Schleicher did so believing that the President was aware of 'the danger that the entire domestic and foreign policy will end up in a *"débâcle"'*. Allegedly the old Field Marshal was determined to put order into affairs 'together with the Reichswehr and younger forces in Parliament before he died'. When Schleicher was asked if Hindenburg proposed to act 'with or without Parliament', he replied that the President would never violate the Constitution; but he would 'send the Reichstag home for a while and put the matter right with the help of Article 48 in the meantime'.

It appears that throughout the summer of 1929 Hindenburg continued to waver between the notion of 'following Ebert's tracks and of governing by himself' or of forming a right-wing Cabinet in the normal way by winning back the DNVP. However, the German Nationalists had long burned their bridges and abandoned their tactical rapprochement of the mid-1920s. In the autumn of 1928, Hugenberg had assumed the chairmanship of this party and steered it on to a course of radical opposition to the Republic. He absolutely refused to take on government responsibility and began to engage in demagogic extra-parliamentary propaganda against the signing of the Young Plan, a revised reparations agreement negotiated by Stresemann in 1929. His campaign against the 'war guilt lie' and the alleged 'enslavement of the German people' resulted in a first shaky alliance with the Nazis and an unsuccessful plebiscite designed to initiate a rejection of the Young Plan. These political activities of Hugenberg's, which greatly pained the President, ruled out the creation of a broadly based right-wing coalition. The only other way to oust the SPD from the Cabinet and to engineer a shift away from parliamentarism was the solution adopted under Brüning's Chancellorship in the spring and summer of 1930. However, before discussing the developments of the early 1930s in more detail, we shall have to move back in time to consider the broad outlines of Weimar foreign policy during Stresemann's time as well as certain major trends in the social and economic sphere prior to 1930. And, secondly, what was it that led Schleicher to believe the 'entire domestic and foreign policy' might 'end up in a *"débâcle"'*?

Weimar foreign policy

It is in the field of international relations that the continuities of German history across the divide of 1918 are distinctly more pronounced than in domestic politics, where the Revolution had resulted in a tangible change in the balance of political power in favour of the 'masses'. The defeat by the Allies halted German expansionism, but it could not stop influential political, economic and academic elites from continuing to harbour ideas of future empire. Wilhelmine imperialist feeling was too deeply ingrained and the consciousness of Germany's industrial and military power potential too strongly felt for the old designs to be abandoned merely because Wilhelm II, who had embodied them so authentically, had disappeared. However, there was one lesson which the elites, in adhering to these older Wilhelmine ambitions, had learned fairly well: in trying to account for the evident failure of German *Weltpolitik*, they came to believe that the country had overstretched its resources by antagonising too many foreign powers at a time.

As early as 1915, as Admiral Alfred von Tirpitz noted, 'many circles in the Army and other right-wing forces' in the country had reached the conclusion that, 'although Germany should have conducted power politics, it [should have been] a continental policy. First defeat the enemies on the continent for which purpose everything [was] to be invested in the Army. . . . *Weltpolitik* and naval armaments had been initiated too soon. We have bitten off too much with the Navy.' Four years later, in May 1919, Groener offered a very similar analysis when he remarked confidentially that 'we have unconsciously aimed at world domination . . . before we had secured our continental position'. There is also an important memorandum by Colonel Joachim von Stülpnagel, dated 6 March 1926, which was sent, with Seeckt's approval, to the German Foreign Office and which contained the following assessment of the Reich's foreign policy objectives:

The immediate aim of German policy must be the regaining of full sovereignty over the area retained by Germany, the firm acquisition of those areas at present separated from her and the reacquisition of those areas essential to the German economy. That is to say: (1) the liberation of the Rhineland and the Saar area; (2) the abolition of the Corridor and the regaining of Polish Upper Silesia; (3) the Anschluss of German Austria; (4) the abolition of the Demilitarised Zone. . . . The above exposition of Germany's political aims . . . clearly shows that the problem for Germany in the next stages of her political development can only be the re-establishment of her position in Europe, and that the regaining of her world position will be a task for the distant future. . . . It is certainly to be assumed that a reborn Germany will eventually come into conflict with the American–English powers in the struggle for raw materials and markets, and that she will then need adequate maritime forces. But this conflict will be fought out on the basis of a firm European position, after a new solution of the Franco-German problem has been achieved through either peace or war.

It is noteworthy that these views originated in military circles, although there is little doubt that they were shared by many right-wing politicians. It is also significant that these statements toy, implicitly or explicitly, with the notion of armed conflict and territorial annexation. They demonstrated a preparedness to base diplomacy on armed conflict and displayed an astonishing failure to comprehend the possibilities of peaceful economic penetration and informal empire. Direct occupation remained the yardstick of Reichswehr foreign policy. The idea of creating dependency without a military presence was more widespread in some industrial and commercial circles. Although the methods differed, there was a far-reaching consensus among influential groups that Germany must first re-establish herself as a continental power before overseas ambitions could be pursued. However, the difference in method did create an important divergence of opinion between those who thought in terms of straight military categories of physical possession and those who preferred an economic approach. Whereas they all refused to accept the Peace Settlement as final and were in this sense all revisionists, some could think of undoing the results of the war only by means of hardline resistance to the stipulations of the Versailles Treaty and of preparing for an early revanchist confrontation with France and her Eastern European allies. They rejected compliance with the territorial clauses of the Treaty; they furthered secret rearmament; they refused to pay reparations, no matter how much these policies contributed to the undermining not only of the Republic, but also of the economic and political basis from which this revisionism was to be launched.

The other group of revisionists, on the other hand, was painfully conscious of the precariously weak domestic platform from which German foreign policy was forced to operate in the 1920s. Their alternative solution was therefore to restabilise and strengthen the German economy not merely as a means of preventing chaos and a left-wing revolution at home, but also as a lever for obtaining modifications of the Versailles Treaty and of regaining a powerful voice in international politics. This was, in their view, a more viable strategy to achieve a restoration of Germany's former world position – the aim over which there was little disagreement – and to preserve the existing distribution of economic power at home. In this sense a strong interconnection may be seen to have existed between Stresemann's foreign policy and his key position in the formulation of domestic policy up to his death in 1929. Up to the spring of 1922, this moderate strategy was able to hold its own against the hardline revisionism of the Right, partly because it enjoyed the support of the SPD which advocated its own version of fulfilment and international reconciliation, partly because it matched up with plans which the British Prime Minister David Lloyd George was promoting. He had devised a comprehensive scheme of economic co-operation in Europe which would have included Germany and allowed her to regain her economic strength.

However, the potential benefits of a collaborative approach as a means of revisionism continued to be undermined by the hardliners to whom co-operation with the Western Allies represented an unacceptable recognition of the Peace Settlement, just as they refused to work with the SPD. In their view,

Versailles could only be destroyed by force from the outside, not by negotiation from within. In examining this internal conflict over German foreign policy, we must also take account of the deeply suspicious French, whose hegemony on the continent could only be maintained for as long as Germany remained militarily and economically weak. Opposition to the long-term power-political implications of fulfilment therefore created a tacit alliance between the hardline revisionists in the Reich and France which, for a period of about two years between 1922 and 1924, succeeded in outmanoeuvering the alternative of revisionism by fulfilment.

The Rapallo Treaty with Russia of April 1922 is the first clear evidence of such a shift in the balance of forces. Seeckt had been building up the Soviet connection for some time as one of the pillars of his uncompromising anti-Versailles policy. The Chief of the Army was not alone, but had many allies. Among them was Ago von Maltzan at the Foreign Ministry who had been worrying for some time that fulfilment might be too successful. There were also a number of powerful industrialists who had long been aware of the potentialities of the Russian market and who hoped to combat the economic crisis at home by obtaining export orders from the Bolshevik government. It is against this background of a keen interest in an Eastern orientation of German trade policy, especially in heavy industry and electrical engineering, that the rise of Walther Rathenau to the position of Foreign Minister must be seen. Although he had also played a prominent and conciliatory role at the reparations conferences of London, Paris and Cannes and was not a hardliner, he appreciated the importance of economic factors in modern international politics and had been looking East for some time.

By the beginning of 1922, strong pressures were building up to add the government's seal of approval to the growing trading relationship between Russia and Germany, the two countries which were in the position of outsiders in international politics. The Western Allies were bound to be displeased by this rapprochement. Rathenau probably did not wish to put the Reich's relationship with the Entente powers, and with Britain in particular, under serious strain. Unlike some of his anti-Versailles fellow-industrialists and Foreign Office bureaucrats, he also saw market opportunities in the West. During the crucial days before the conclusion of the Rapallo Agreement on 16 April 1922 there was a good deal of manoeuvering in which Maltzan was prominently involved. Yet, in the end Rathenau went along with the accord and, in so doing, strengthened the hands of the uncompromising revisionists in the Army, the Civil Service, in industry and on the Right of the party-political spectrum. Lloyd George's strategy had been wrecked. Rapallo was grist to the mills of those politicians in France who believed that Germany understood only the language of force and had to be compelled to fulfil the Versailles Treaty. Relations between Berlin and Paris deteriorated rapidly, culminating in the occupation of the Ruhr in January 1923. What looked like a victory for the hardliners in Germany turned out to be a national disaster as the year wore on. The passive resistance in the Ruhr area had to be abandoned, and by the spring of 1924 the developments of the previous year had decisively weakened rigid revisionism. Nor did those who had supported the formalisation of the Eastern link as a means of rebuilding Germany's economic position outside the Western orbit find their predictions justified by events. As it turned out, the Russian market was too underdeveloped to permit a rapid absorption of German industrial goods. Moreover, the Russo-German relationship had been complicated by the fact that, while economic collaboration was going on, Soviet-financed officials of the Communist International tried to exploit the upheavals of 1923 to stir up left-wing revolutionary activity in the Reich.

These experiences resulted in a relative weakening of the anti-Western position and a fundamental reassessment of Germany's foreign policy methods when Gustav Stresemann assumed office at the end of 1923. For his conversion from an anti-Republican to a *Vernunftrepublikaner* in respect of his domestic politics was complemented by his metamorphosis from a militant annexationist of the First World War to an advocate of a softline revisionism based on co-operation with the Western capitalist countries. As he put it on one occasion: 'A revision of the Versailles Treaty will not be achieved by the force of arms, but by the forces of the world-economic community of interests of the nations.' In November 1924 he added that 'economic power is the only respect in which we are still a great power, and it is only through it that we can conduct foreign policy'. These statements implied that to Stresemann, the trained economist who believed that German foreign policy and the country's reacceptance and participation in the world market were inseparable, Russia was not the main reference point. Yet his turn towards the West was even more radical than this. Neither France nor Britain was central to his diplomatic strategy. The key position was allocated rather to the United States, the country which he knew had emerged as the decisive economic power in the world after 1918. What was more logical therefore than to try to draw American capital into Europe and German industry in particular and to rebuild the German position abroad with the help of the United States? Britain was to play an important role in this scheme: as a mediator to mollify the French. Indeed, if Stresemann's policy was to work, France had to be reassured and to be convinced that, following the ruinous war and the catastrophic Ruhr occupation which had forced France into a devaluation of the franc, she too stood to benefit from an American economic engagement in Europe. Of course, it was also clear that the advantages of Stresemann's strategy to Germany would be even greater.

There can be little doubt that this design, which was revisionist at heart, won the German Foreign Minister impressive successes. It led to the withdrawal of the French and Belgian occupation troops from the Ruhr. The Locarno Treaty of 1925, so bitterly resented by the anti-Republican opposition, guaranteed not merely the eastern frontiers of France and Belgium against Germany, but conversely blocked another French incursion into the industrial heart of Germany, which could now be revitalised with American money. With reference to some of the other restrictions imposed on the Reich by the Versailles Treaty, Stresemann was able to negotiate the dissolution of the Inter-Allied Military Control Commission which had attempted to supervise the disarmament clauses of the Peace. In September 1926, Germany became a member of the League of Nations and, in recognition of her great power status, was given a permanent seat on the august Council of that international organisation. Stresemann finally succeeded in obtaining the premature withdrawal of Allied troops from the west bank of the Rhine in 1930, five years before the date originally set.

His most important achievement was to smooth the path for a reparations settlement. The Dawes Plan was the first step, followed in 1929 by the Young Plan which put a time-limit on Germany's payments and reduced the overall figure to 112 milliard dollars, to be paid by means of loans raised on the international money markets. But it was the Dawes Plan that first paved the way for enormous sums of American capital to flow into Germany. Between 1924 and 1930, there were 135 long-term issues amounting to 1,430 million dollars, of which 1,293 million dollars were raised in the United States. A further 1,560 million dollars came in as short-term loans. American firms also invested directly to the tune of 217 million dollars. By 1930 some 79 of them, including such giant corporations as General Electric, General Motors and Dupont, had established factories. The Weimar economy became a 'penetrated system' (W. Link), dependent on the United States.

While these investments greatly stimulated the country's recovery after 1924, there were several serious dangers in this lending policy. To begin with, the loans facilitated the relatively painless transfer of reparations payments. Moreover, much of the capital was taken up by central government and even more by local authorities as an easy alternative to the imposition of higher taxes. Many local politicians found it tempting to build a public swimming-pool with foreign money and even more tempting to run up further debts as a way of repaying earlier loans. Nor was American investment which was taken up by private industry always used to increase productivity. Some firms borrowed abroad in order to solve their cash-flow problems on the assumption that further funds would be available. Short-term loans were invested in long-term capital projects. Yet what if the bubble burst, if speculators panicked and if the loans were suddenly recalled? It is not difficult to see how bankruptcy, economic collapse and mass unemployment would then be virtually unavoidable.

For the time being, however, such nightmares were overridden by the fact that the German economy with its highly skilled workforce was poised to increase its output and was starved of capital (Tables 7 and 8). The world market was picking up. German industry merely had to mobilise its latent potential to reappear on the stage as a major trading nation (Table 10). The Russian connection, far from being the cornerstone, became a useful link in the German commercial network. Furthermore, the threat to expand the Rapallo deal remained a card which Stresemann would play skilfully both at home and in the Western capitals.

The ascendancy of the flexible revisionism from 1924 onwards did not, of course, silence the hardliners. On the nationalist Right both inside and outside Parliament the Dawes Plan, the Locarno Pact and Stresemann's policies in general met with vigorous opposition by those who kept on demanding the tearing-up of the Versailles Treaty. Unreconstructed revisionists also continued to operate within the government machinery. The Army in particular was still thinking in terms of a future conflict and of violent solutions to the territorial question. Its claim to a leading position in political decision-making was confidently upheld. The irony was that Stresemann's economic diplomacy did nothing to weaken such ambitions. On the contrary, the renewed mobilisation of the Reich's industrial power indirectly also increased the country's military power. Slowly but surely, the balance of power in Europe underwent a shift, and nothing illustrated it better than France's decision to build and to retreat behind the Maginot Line. It implicitly recognised that Germany's industrial recovery was tantamount to destroying the military hegemony which Paris had been able to maintain in the early postwar years, when the Reich was weak and torn by domestic crises. The German Foreign Minister was painfully aware of the sensibilities which this awakened and tried to reassure the French. He was much less forthcoming on the idea of an eastern Locarno, that is, a German recognition of the territorial status quo in the East. Here he tended to agree with the hardliners, even if there is no evidence which shows that he also subscribed to the views of the military as expounded in the Stülpnagel memorandum (see above p. 96).

By 1926, he and his civilian colleagues in the Cabinet were strong enough to curb the most blatant military revanchism with which Seeckt was identified. When the Chief of the Reichswehr invited the Crown Prince to attend a manoeuvre, he was swiftly dismissed by the Defence Minister. His departure led to the rise of a younger and more flexible generation of officers. They were prepared to align military policy with diplomatic and economic strategy as devised by the Cabinet. They were therefore also willing to cut the Army's ties with the anti-Republican paramilitary associations with which Seeckt had been collaborating within the context of his secret rearmament programme. Instead of wasting time training ill-equipped private armies, they were devoted to building a technologically advanced professional force which would enjoy the benevolent support of the civilian bureaucracy and the parliamentary parties of the centre and the Right. The armaments industry which drew considerable benefit from the new concept both in the form of orders for mechanised equipment and of subsidies for building projects and research were happy to co-operate. In this respect, Stülpnagel and Schleicher embodied a more modern type of officer who was anxious to apply the lessons of the 'industrialisation of warfare' during the First World War. Although Schleicher's above-mentioned anti-parliamentarism left some people to wonder whether this modernised Reichswehr might not become the instrument of a more aggressive foreign policy in the hands of an autocratic politician who was unhampered by parliamentary constraints, an open discussion of the long-term purposes of Germany's growing military power did not take place.

Schleicher and Groener, who became Defence Minister in 1928, were no doubt happy to leave it at that. Above all, as long as Stresemann's softline revisionism bore fruit, the Army would not need to provide more than a power-political back-up to the establishment of German economic hegemony on the European continent. Military power remained covert, even if its deployment in support of an aggressive revisionism, should it ever be adopted, remained a perfectly possible alternative. It is important to bear this ambiguity in mind for the discussion of the period when the diplomatic strategy of the 1920s came to be replaced, first by a harder and more combative line under Brüning and Papen and finally by Hitler's violent expansionism.

Economic tensions and the rise of the Nazis

Apart from these ambiguities and potentialities in the field of military policy, the period 1924–9 also left a number of domestic developments in precarious balance. One of these concerned the whole problem of industrial relations and welfare. The steadiest support for Stresemann's foreign policy came from those export-oriented and expansive manufacturing industries which stood to benefit very directly from the reintegration of the German economy into the world market. However, with the deprivations of war and of the postwar crisis behind them, there were also other groups which wanted a share in the wealth created during the stabilisation period, and it is not surprising that the working class should be prominent among them. As the economic position improved, the trade unions, whose constitutional status had been strengthened by the Revolution of 1918, began to push for higher wages and better conditions. Their efforts were not without success. For, although the two pillars of the *bürgerliche* coalitions of the mid-1920s, the DVP and Centre Party, were loath to take the SPD into the Cabinet, they were prepared to pursue compensatory strategies in the field of social policy in an attempt to establish a consensus in the industrial sphere at a time when Germany tried to re-establish her position in the world market. It was with the help of the Reich government that improvements were legislated in the areas of health, disability, public housing, unemployment insurance and labour law. And most of the time Stresemann and Brauns could rely on the support of important sections of industry who favoured this kind of tripartism.

It was especially the industries of the Second Industrial Revolution which were inclined to make concessions. They had been the main supporters of the ZAG before it collapsed under the strains of the 1923 crisis; they favoured a flexible collaborative approach to industrial relations as the best way of maintaining and increasing production. In January 1925, Carl Duisberg, a prominent spokesman of the chemical industries and 'Welfare Professor', became leader of the *Reichsverband der Deutschen Industrie* (RDI), supported at the head office by moderates like Ludwig Kastl and his two assistants Hermann Bücher of General Electric (AEG) and Jacob Herle, secretary of the BdI of the Imperial days. The reduction of class tensions which this approach was intended to promote was made more difficult, however, by the attitude of the coal and steel industries. Here the patriarchal views of the *Herr-im-Hause* which had prevailed during the Wilhelmine period continued to hold sway. Nor did the plunge into the world market fill the Ruhr managers with quite the same enthusiasm, partly because they were less dependent on exports. Thus the protectionist tradition of the Wilhelmine period was slow to die. The spokesmen of heavy industry were prone to view international politics and economics in terms of large powerful blocks and formal empires. Moreover, up to 1923 and beyond, many of them had been strictly opposed to fulfilment and gave Stresemann a hard time. Their attitude towards domestic issues was no less obstructionist.

The type of capitalism which they adhered to was authoritarian, anti-Western and, as far as the existing political system was concerned, openly or covertly anti-Republican. With regard to the domestic market, they favoured cartels which laid down production quotas, divided up the market and fixed prices at the expense of the consumer. By the late 1920s, Germany was probably the most highly cartellised country in the world. As many of these industries, apart from being rigidly organised and stagnant, were also labour-intensive, the temptation to revive the former tough line on wage bargaining was considerable. They wanted wage reductions and high prices secured by cartels. Their longstanding hostility to the working-class movement and their immediate economic interests almost impelled them to adopt a collision course. Nor were industrial relations eased by the fact that they turned into particularly ardent protagonists of rationalisation and automation – as imported from the United States – without subscribing to the American idea that the introduction of mass production would reduce prices and thus

103

also benefit the mass of the population. Cartels saw to it that prices stayed up and the trade unions, whose initial attitudes towards 'Fordism' had been ambivalent, were quickly disappointed. Soon heavy industry and the working-class movement were locked in their old irreconcilable battles. Below the surface of Weimar stability there existed considerable economic and social tensions, fed by the strengthened post-revolutionary position of the Social Democrats and the trade unions on the one hand, and by the tendency of powerful branches of industry to take a tough line with them on the other.

Heavy industry was in the forefront of this conflict, but could also rely on the backing of the *mittelständische* manufacturing industries whose views on industrial relations were a good way to the right of liberal employers like Robert Bosch. Typically the Boschs were in electrical engineering—to this day a famous firm. At the other end of the spectrum were not merely the Communists who agitated for the overthrow of capitalism, but also the internal critics of those more moderate SPD and trade union leaders who wished to negotiate improvements rather than fight the employers. Thus the beginnings of a triangular co-operative relationship between employers, trade unions and ministerial bureaucracies with the aim of reducing industrial conflict was being powerfully counteracted by confrontationist forces on the Right of industry and on the left wing of the working-class movement. As in the arena of parliamentary politics, the prospects of a more stable consensus emerging in the industrial sphere were constantly undermined by the existence of forces which were suspicious of compromise solutions. In fact, developments in the Reichstag and in industrial relations tended to reinforce each other.

We have noted how parts of the DNVP engaged in rabid propaganda campaigns against the Dawes Plan, the Locarno Pact and Germany's admission to the League of Nations in 1926. Worse was to come during the debate of the Young Plan. What made this opposition ultimately ineffective in the Stresemann period was that he was able to rely on the support of many Social Democrat deputies to get these policies ratified in the Reichstag. But we have also seen that when it came to the domestic issue of how the burdens of reparations were to be distributed on to the shoulders of different groups of taxpayers and, more generally, how revenue was to be collected and redistributed into society, the SPD found itself excluded from the decision-making process. It was the *bürgerliche* parties, at least up to 1928, that commanded the majority and used it in furtherance of their political and economic programmes.

The strategies of exclusion were not lost on the SPD leadership and only served to embitter them and their followers. While the Right, and the DNVP in particular, scorned international co-operation and fulfilment and derided the Republic as socialist, Social Democrats gained the impression that they were being shunted off into the political sidelines. Such feelings did little to enhance identification with the Republic. It is also important that the moderate Left was constantly confronted with the anti-Republican agitation of the KPD with its 45 deputies which called for outright struggle against the 'bourgeois–capitalist' Republic of Weimar. Although the moderates disagreed with Communist strategy and also did not like their Bolshevik blueprint for the establishment of a socialist society, there was clearly some truth in the KPD's analysis of the existing power structure.

All this was bound to leave a deep mark on the Social Democrats. Old feelings of alienation and frustration continued to simmer and resulted in a shift which was discernible at the Heidelberg Party Congress of 1925. This meeting reiterated the time-honoured principle that socialism was still something worth fighting for. At the same time the Party revived the idea that the political democracy which had been established in 1918 must be complemented by economic democracy (*Wirtschaftsdemokratie*). The aim was to obtain further rights for the shop-floor and a greater say for workers and their representatives in the management of company affairs beyond the Works' Councils legislation of 1920. A neat summary of these demands and the considerations behind them appeared in a programmatic statement on economic democracy published in 1928 by the *Allgemeiner Deutscher Gewerkschaftsbund* (ADGB) in an attempt to leave its defensive position. Although a clear product of Social Democrat reformism and an expression of the belief that the institutions of a parliamentary democracy provided legitimate channels for enhancing the status of the working class, *Wirtschaftsdemokratie* greatly rattled the employers. They discovered in it a design by which socialism was to be achieved not by revolution, but through the backdoor. To them it proved that the 'power-hungry' Social Democratic movement had ulterior motives which must be fought tooth and nail. Clearly, this was not a movement with which to conclude compromises on other issues.

Liberal industrialists, while also suspicious of the concept of economic democracy, thought it wrong to combat *Wirtschaftsdemokratie* tendencies by embarking upon a collision course. They remembered the initial successes of the ZAG and also acknowledged the benefits to be derived from limited forms of industrial participation, as enshrined in the Works' Councils Law. Other employers, particularly the managers of the Ruhr, had never become reconciled to these fruits of the 1918 compromise between industry and trade unions. Nor did they accept the elaborate machinery of arbitration for industrial disputes which had been set up in the form of a tribunal system. Thus, side by side with the conflicts over the formation of governments, there also existed, in this period of relative stability during the mid-1920s, tensions involving fundamental issues of the organisation of German industry and the distribution of economic power. If these tensions increased towards 1927/8, this was largely due to the success with which heavy industry had once more begun to consolidate its position as a group strong enough to veto all compromises.

At the same time as these problems strained industrial relations, there were the more mundane concerns of the mass of the working population: their living standards and conditions of service. The trade unions saw it as their natural task to negotiate improvements for their members. What complicated the collective bargaining process was that the working class continued to be represented by three movements and although the ADGB was by far the largest organisation, its members had to compete among workers with the Catholic Christian Unions and the 'liberal' *Hirsch-Dunckerschen Gewerkschaften* (Table 46). The latter two rejected Marxism and generally tended to disagree with the Social Democrat-related ADGB over major issues such as economic democracy. Nevertheless, despite these differences, the overall impact of trade unionism was much more marked than in the Wilhelmine period. After 1924, some 13 million employees were covered by collective wage agreements, which the Reich Labour Ministry had the power to extend, at the request of both sides of industry, to all employees in a particular branch, as not all workers were unionised. After the disaster of the inflation of 1923, real wages were rising again and white-collar employees experienced similar improvements, even if these changes must be kept in perspective (Table 23 and 25). It was only in 1928 that the real wage levels of 1913/14 were surpassed again. Evaluating a sample of some 584 questionnaires on the economic and political situation of German employees and workers, Erich Fromm found that 19 per cent of them earned around 600 marks a year and that 28 per cent of the households did not have a bed for every family member to sleep in. On the other hand, some 90 per cent of those questioned possessed essential items of furniture and a majority even called a bookshelf their own. Some 57 per cent had meat up to five times per week.

A related issue which also generated a considerable amount of argument was the eight-hour working day, which had been introduced as part of the bargain struck between the trade unions and the employers in the revolutionary days of 1918. However, many industrialists were never genuinely committed to this agreement. Arguing that productivity levels and the generally depressed state of the postwar economy could not bear the costs of such a reduction, they soon began to press for modifications. The crisis of 1923 provided a welcome opportunity to abolish the eight-hour work rule, reflecting at the same time the changing balance of power between the two sides of industry. But from 1924, the trade unions renewed their demand for a reduction which, though varying in different branches of industry, eventually met with some success. Whereas manufacturing industry worked an average of 50.5 hours per week in 1925, the figure had come down to 46.0 hours per week two years later and to 44.0 hours in 1930 (Table 31).

A further thorn in the flesh of the employers, and of heavy industry in particular, was the system of compulsory arbitration whereby an arbitrating judge could impose a wage settlement. Although statistics are notoriously unreliable in this field, the number of strikes and lock-outs which had reached a peak in 1922 declined rapidly thereafter to reach an all-time low in 1926 (Table 44). The number of workers involved likewise slumped dramatically. This was not merely because the mid-1920s were years of relative industrial peace, but also reflected the success of arbitration through which many disputes were resolved. Yet, far from being happy with the workings of this machinery, many industrialists, especially in the Ruhr, were convinced that the system was biased against them, quite apart from the question of its objectionable revolutionary origins. They therefore thought of ways of undermining the viability of the arbitration procedures, and the 1928 conflict with the metal workers appeared to be the appropriate moment for this. In November of that year, they organised a lock-out of 250,000 workers in the iron and steel industry as a result of which more workdays were lost than in any other dispute during this period. The origins of the *Ruhreisenstreit* and its high costs show that it was more than an ordinary labour conflict. As recent research has shown, the employers certainly achieved some of their more far-reaching political objectives in the course of this deliberately escalated confrontation. Above all the system of arbitration had been weakened and with it trade union influence. Nor did it help to consolidate the Cabinet of Hermann Müller which had taken office after the SPD's victory at the polls in May 1928.

There was finally the wide area of social insurance and welfare policy in which the working-class movement continued to be active, again much to the annoyance of the employers. One issue was who should bear the major share of higher national insurance and pension contributions. The greater prosperity of the mid-1920s notwithstanding, unemployment remained high (Table 18). In fact it jumped from a low 682,000 in 1925 to over 2 million in the following year and hovered around the 1.3 million mark in 1927 and 1928. Although the percentage of unemployed union members fluctuated, reaching a peak of 18 per cent only during the year of very high unemployment in 1926, the working-class movement understandably took a direct interest in the levels of social security benefits. When the SPD gained a dominant influence in the Müller Cabinet of 1928, its representatives, together with the Centre Party and its Labour Minister Brauns, were in a strategic position to expand the social policy by compensation of the previous governments. On the other hand, the renewed pressure in the field of social policy merely reinforced the determination of many industrialists to dislodge the Social Democrats from the Reich government and, if possible, for good. For beyond their perfectly legitimate resistance to the economic and social demands of the trade unions, there lurked a much more fundamental objection not merely to increased state intervention, but to the politics of Weimar as a whole. The above-mentioned plans drawn up in the President's office and in the Army therefore coincided with a growing movement among the industrial elites of the country to support a constitutional 'reformism towards the Right' (J. O. Spiller) and to modify the existing political structures of the Republic in an authoritarian direction. The advocates of co-operation and of the creation of consensus politics in the sense of a tripartism of State, trade unions and employers slowly lost out. Industry began to move away from the Republic even before the Great Slump hit Germany and before many people had heard about Adolf Hitler.

If any one group had never become reconciled to the outcome of the 1918 Revolution, it was the agrarian elites. Their strong political position under the Wilhelmine monarchy had brought them many tangible economic benefits in the form of subsidies and protective tariffs. They had, largely successfully, resisted changes in the tax system that might have imposed higher levels on their property. As a result, their decline which the changeover from an agricultural to an industrial economy had made inevitable, had been success- fully delayed in the pre-1914 period. The First World War had propped up their economic position when the Allied blockade and food shortages had upvalued the importance of agriculture. Demand had increased food prices despite rationing and price controls, not to mention the bonus of the black market. All in all, large-scale agriculture had not fared too badly during this period of crisis when bread and potatoes became the staple diet.

The collapse of the monarchy and the Revolution of 1918 changed this drastically. The political positions lost within those weeks and months were never recovered, not even during the Papen government of 1932 which was openly pro-agrarian. The manifold channels of informal influence which the Prussian landowners in particular had used so effectively at Court and in the bureaucracy during the Wilhelmine period to bolster their economic position were blocked. In the mid-1920s, when the DNVP joined the Cabinet, they succeeded in wringing a few concessions from the Reich government in respect of agricultural tariffs and property taxes. Yet these gains were merely a drop in the ocean as interest rates rose following the end of the inflation. Rural indebtedness increased by between 20 and 35 per cent. Worse, from 1928 onwards, agriculture was hit by another worldwide crisis of overproduction which sharpened existing problems. The price of wheat, rye and feedstuffs which had been around 250 marks per metric ton in 1927 slumped to around 160 marks by 1930. The price of cattle was also badly affected. Accordingly agricultural income declined from 9.5 per cent of the national income in 1925 to 7.4 per cent in 1930. Between 1928 and 1932 it took a further plunge of 40 per cent. Also by the late 1920s, per capita income in agriculture was 44 per cent below the national average, reflecting the economic decline not merely of the estates, but also of the peasants and small-holders. Cereal yields per hectare likewise shrank markedly, confirming the general picture of inefficiency (Tables 6 and 19). The great trek to the cities continued (Tables 3, 15 and 16).

It was, of course, another matter to acknowledge the actual causes of these problems and easier to blame the plight of agriculture on the Weimar Republic. Given their monarchist background and their overt anti-Republicanism which dated back to 1918, most Protestant farmers had quickly found their ideological home in the DNVP where they remained entrenched on the Party's irreconcil-able Right up to the late 1920s. Nor did it help them to overcome their deep sense of alienation that most of them lived in Prussia, the 'bastion of Republicanism', guarded by the Social Democrats and the Centre Party under Otto Braun's premiership. The *Junker* were particularly bitter that, on top of their economic decline, came the erosion of their legal position when the Prussian government finally won the long-drawn-out battle over the manorial districts (*Gutsbezirke*). Some 13,000 of these districts, which formed the local political power base of many *Junker* from pre-constitutional days, had remained independent ruling bodies side by side with the *Landgemeinden* (rural councils) even after 1918. As a result, some 36 per cent of the people of Pomerania, 28 per cent of Posen and 20 per cent of Prussia did not enjoy any rights of local self-government. Instead the *Gutsherren* continued to be in charge of the concerns of some 1.2 million people until, against the vigorous opposition of the DNVP, a bill abolishing this system reached the statute books on 27 December 1927. Communal elections were held in these districts for the first time in the following spring.

After this the estate owners were more than ever convinced that only the destruction of the Weimar Republic would bring about an amelioration of their position. To their ideological rejection of the Republican Constitution was added their total opposition to the emphasis on industrial policy and, relatedly, to Stresemann's export-orientated foreign policy. Participation in an international multilateral economy was anathema to them and they were also not to be mollified when the Reich government, prodded by Hindenburg, reverted to agricultural subsidies within the framework of the *Osthilfe* programme to help East Elbian farming. Instead, ideas of continental empire and autarky based on a strong, state-subsidised agrarian sector continued to enjoy strong support. Blood-and-soil slogans were as popular as talk of the damaging influence of the 'Red' and 'Golden' Internationals. It was also in this quarter that an aggressive territorial revisionism prevailed. Next to the traditional arch-enemy France, Poland became the object of their hatred and they never recognised the existence of the newly created Polish State.

By 1928, the opposition by the agrarian section in the DNVP had become so vociferous that the decisive push which moved the Party in the direction of a radical obstructionism became possible. Hugenberg became the hardline chairman. However, the DNVP had since the beginning had a broader base in the Protestant countryside than electoral support from the *Junker*. The farming community as a whole was threatened economically and in 1925 89.4 per cent of the 2 million farmers worked small units of up to 20 hectares. The Catholics among them would predominantly vote for the Centre Party or the BVP, as they had always done. In the 1928 elections, the DNVP had for the first time encountered a competitor, however, which had polled between 4 and 8.1 per cent in certain Protestant areas (Table 42). This party was the NSDAP, led by Hitler. Given its name and later prominence, a lively debate has arisen among historians concerning the nature of its electoral support.

The early membership lists of the National Socialist Workers' Party and its precursors indicate that it was a largely petty bourgeois splinter group in Munich which, thanks to the fanatical oratory and devotion of Hitler, succeeded in gaining some support in Lower Bavaria during the confused years of 1922 and 1923. It had attached to it the SA which, as we have seen, was a paramilitary association composed of young desperados of similar social background. Hitler and his SA were behind the attempt to push Kahr into the much-vaunted march on Berlin in November 1923. The putsch failed, but it helped Hitler to national notoriety when he appeared, together with Luden-dorff, at the subsequent trial. The ten months of imprisonment that followed gave Hitler time to think about the lessons to be learned from his abortive putschist activity and to commit his political ideas to paper. They were published in 1925 under the title *Mein Kampf*.

His conclusion was that he could only hope to seize power in Germany by constitutional means and with the help of the ballot-box. Whereas Hitler's broader views on world history and his visions of the future of human society will be examined later, the question here is: with whose support did he hope to gain power and who were the people who actually voted for him? In surveying the potential electorate, any Weimar politician who aimed at winning a majority as a prerequisite of taking over the government of the country was bound to be impressed by the sheer numerical strength of the working class. To obtain its support at the polls would obviously be a major step on the road to seizing power by legitimate constitutional means. The adoption of the terms 'Socialist' and 'Worker' as part of the NSDAP's name was, however, more than a tactical ploy. The term socialism, although it had nothing in common with Marxism, did have a meaning to Hitler and his early advisers which they thought would be understood by the working class. It was the 'socialism' which millions of workers were presumed to have experienced in the trenches of the First World War. Hitler had been a front soldier and was convinced that he had undergone this experience, which was said to have been 'socialist' in the sense that it had torn down class distinctions and class barriers. It was *'national* socialist' because it had created a solidarity against an opponent who was not an international class enemy in the Marxian sense, but one who tried to prevent, by military means, the self-assertion of the Germanic nation.

It is important to differentiate here between belief and historical reality. It has been mentioned that, although nationalism doubtlessly acted as an integrating force at the front, the experience of inter-class solidarity during the First World War was probably much less harmonious than Hitler and other nationalists made out. Yet, this did not prevent them from insisting that the society of the trenches had been classless and that it was the task of the former front soldiers to transmit this memory to peacetime society and to work for its implementation in a new 'national socialist' order. It was encouraging that these reinterpretations of the war experience by politicians of the so-called 'front generation' struck a responsive chord in many ex-servicemen who had been traumatised by the horrors of trench warfare and defeat. To them it was a way of 'digesting' this experience because it was turned into something majestic and politically worthwhile.

The problem was, however, that the 'national socialism' touted by the Right in general and the NSDAP in particular did not appeal to the working class. As the Nazis were to discover during the years 1926 to 1929, it was not that all workers were totally immune to their propaganda, but that most of the addressees in the urban and industrial centres of the Reich where Hitler's agitators appeared in this period were too strongly attached to the SPD or KPD, and these two parties had rather different interpretations of the character of the First World War and its lessons. On the other hand, the NSDAP met with a much greater positive response in the rural areas of northern and north-eastern Germany. Yet, here it was not so much their peculiar brand of 'socialism' and their visions of a future *Volksgemeinschaft* (folk community) which caused people to nod approvingly at Nazi arguments, but rather their demagogic whipping-up of deep-seated resentments against the 'November Republic' and all the social, economic and political evils it had come to represent in the eyes of the anti-Republican Right since the Revolution of 1918. In this respect, years of propaganda by the DNVP and some smaller splinter parties as well as that of various extraparliamentary pressure groups, such as the *Reichslandbund*, had prepared the ground well.

When it tried to establish itself in Lower Saxony, Hesse, Schleswig-Holstein, Palatinate, Franconia and East Elbia in the late 1920s, the NSDAP articulated these anti-Republican resentments merely more blatantly. Indeed, the keynote of this agitation – and this is the crucial point – was its 'anti' character: anti-Republican, anti-socialist, anti-Communist, anti-Versailles, anti-Semitic and anti-capitalist. It was an anti-capitalism which did not reject the principle of private property. Rather it was opposed to large-scale industrial capitalism of the type which had also emerged in Germany since the late nineteenth century and which, as we have seen, had hit the economic fortunes of the farming community as well as undermined the livelihood of artisans, shopkeepers and the provincial middle classes. Even before 1914, these groups had been easy prey to politicians who simplified the complexities of agricultural decline under the impact of industrialisation into slogans in which scapegoats played a prominent role. It was the moneylenders, the Jews, the socialists, the far-away government, Germany's foreign enemies who were interchangeably made responsible. The bewildering upheavals of the First World War, the defeat and Revolution of 1918, the effects of inflation and civil war had greatly reinforced the propensity of provincial Germany to accept even the most hare-brained conspiratorial theories to explain the country's fate since the turn of the century. It had begun to drift towards increasingly radical right-wing positions well before 1930.

The discovery of this potential of supporters disappointed the 'left-wingers' in the NSDAP. But Hitler, the 'Führer' in Munich, did not much care where his support came from. His first aim was to gain power by legal means, and if the mass of his voters were to be got, not among the industrial working class, but elsewhere, his programme was vague and flexible enough to accommodate a shift. Nor was it difficult to adjust his anti-Republican propaganda to incite the resentments of the Protestant bourgeoisie. The Reichstag elections of May 1928 provided Hitler with an encouraging lesson. Although the NSDAP did not win more than 12 seats, the Party achieved its greatest successes in the non-industrial provincial areas of the Reich. Its 810,000 supporters came from the radicalised lower middle classes and farmers (Table 42). The greatest gains were made in the areas listed in the following table:

Nazi support in 1928 Reichstag elections (%)

Thuringia	3.7	Lower Bavaria	3.5
Schleswig-Holstein	4.0	Franconia	8.1
Weser-Ems	5.2	Palatinate	5.6
Hanover South/Brunswick	4.4	Chemnitz-Zwickau	4.3
Upper Bavaria/Suebia	6.2		

The experiences gathered in the 1928 elections formed the basis of Hitler's election campaign in 1930. In the meantime he had made himself better known nationally when he joined the anti-Young Plan plebiscite of 1929 which was spearheaded and financed by Hugenberg in conjunction with a number of extraparliamentary associations. The results of the Reichstag poll of September 1930 in which the Nazis gained 6.4 million votes and 107 seats stunned contemporary observers at home and abroad and represented a watershed in the development of the Weimar Republic (Table 42). Historians and social scientists have understandably been intrigued to find out where those millions of Nazi voters came from. The factors which complicated a detailed calculation were that some 1.7 million first-time voters had been added to the electoral rolls since 1928 and that the percentage of those who actually went to the polling stations went up from 74.6 in 1928 to 81.4 in 1930. This meant that some 4.2 million additional voters have to be taken into account, and there can be little doubt that most of these people were mobilised because of the growing politicisation of the population under the impact of the Great Slump which had begun to hit Germany with full force, pushing the unemployment figure up from 1,899,000 in 1929 to 3,076,000 in 1930. Some 14 per cent of the working population were without a job (Table 18).

And yet it was not the unemployed who had flocked to the Nazis in large numbers. Most of the 6.4 million voters came from a pool of previous non-voters, young first-time voters and people who had defected from other right-wing parties, notably the DNVP and the DVP. Less than two years later, in July 1932, further Reichstag elections were held, to be followed by polls in November 1932 and finally in March 1933. In the meantime the number of unemployed had risen to 5.6 million (Table 18). The voting figures for the four elections to be investigated here are indicated in the table.

Reichstag election results, 1930–1933 (%)

	September 1930	July 1932	November 1932	March 1933
Electorate (000s)	42,958	44,211	44,374	44,665
Turnout (000s)	34,971 (81.4)	36,882 (83.4)	35,471 (79.9)	39,343 (88.1)
KPD	13.1 (10.7)[1]	14.3 (11.9)	16.6 (13.5)	12.3 (10.9)
SPD	24.6 (20.0)	21.6 (18.0)	20.4 (16.3)	18.3 (16.1)
Centre/BVP	14.8 (12.1)	15.7 (13.1)	15.0 (12.0)	14.0 (12.3)
Conservatives[2]	13.8 (11.2)	7.4 (6.2)	9.8 (7.8)	8.9 (7.9)
Liberals[3]	12.2 (9.9)	2.6 (2.2)	3.1 (2.5)	1.9 (1.7)
Regional parties	3.3 (2.6)	1.1 (0.9)	1.7 (1.4)	0.6 (0.6)
NSDAP	18.3 (14.9)	37.3 (31.1)	33.1 (26.5)	43.9 (38.7)

Notes: [1] as a percentage of turnout and, in brackets, of electorate.
[2] DNVP, Conservative People's Party, *Landbund, Landvolkpartei*
[3] DVP, DDP (since 1930: *Staatspartei*), *Wirtschaftspartei*

This table allows us to explore the question of Nazi support a little further. The first interesting point emerges from a glance at the performance of the two Catholic parties (Centre and BVP) which held their overall percentage remarkably well. The same applies to the two working-class parties taken together, where it must be remembered that the Communists were banned before the March 1933 elections and that the Social Democrats laboured under serious handicaps and persecution by the Hitler government which had come to power at the end of January 1933. As far as the three earlier elections are concerned, it is safe to assume that some former SPD voters moved to the KPD, reflecting the renewed radicalisation of politics in the early 1930s. However, few of them switched to the radical Right and taken together the Left held on to the percentage which it had obtained in 1930 (see also Table 42).

The above table also demonstrates how the parties of the Right and centre Right were reduced to splinter groups. Whereas there is a good deal of force in the argument, based on regional analyses, that the Nazis captured the Protestant rural and small-town voter, mainly of petty bourgeois background, in 1930, two years later, other middle-class groups had turned to the Nazis. Some of these voters probably experienced their radicalisation via an intermediate stage which led them from the centre Right to the DNVP and finally to the NSDAP. Other Nazi voters were erstwhile abstainers who became mobilised in July 1932, dropped out again in November, only to push up the Nazi vote again in March 1933, when no less than 3.9 million more people went to the polls than four months earlier. From the various electoral analyses which have been undertaken, it is therefore possible to say fairly reliably that, with exceptions mainly outside the urban centres, Hitler's National Socialist German Workers' Party did not attract the vote of the industrial working class. Nor did it succeed in winning over masses of the unemployed, most of whom were workers and remained loyal to SPD or KPD. Given the steadiness of the Catholic vote, it was the Protestant middle classes who voted predominantly for Hitler.

It should also be obvious that these middle-class supporters were not 'the Germans'. They were not even the majority. To begin with, however hard they tried, the Nazis failed to activate some 15 per cent of the population who continued to abstain altogether. And from among those who did go to the polling station, the potential maximum of Nazi support would appear to have been hovering around the 40 per cent mark, as some 45 per cent of the voters remained tied to parties which were rooted either in Catholicism or Marxism. It is useful to bear these figures in mind in view of what some authors have said about 'the Germans'' enthusiasm for Hitler. However, this should not lead us to overlook another important point: the election results for 1932 also demonstrate that a majority of Germans no longer wished to live under the Weimar 'system'. They had different ideas about what kind of political system they did want. Thus the Communists talked of establishing a Bolshevik dictatorship of the proletariat. The Nazis, at the other extreme, propounded a 'national revolution' and the creation of a 'Führer' state. The 3.0 million DNVP voters similarly advocated anti-parliamentary and authoritarian solutions, and even many Social Democrats and Catholics had lost confidence in the viability of the existing constitutional order.

In view of this, the fall of the Weimar Republic cannot be said to have been entirely unexpected, if one agrees that no political system, except a ruthless dictatorship, can survive for any length of time once the majority of the population refuses to identify with it and with the principles on which it is built. As our account of the upheavals of the early 1920s and even of the years of relative stability between 1924 and 1929 has shown, those who gave their unconditional and unequivocal support to the Republic remained in the minority. Then came the onslaught of the Great Depression. Other countries like Britain were also badly affected by this severe economic crisis, but what helped their parliamentary systems to survive was that they enjoyed a greater degree of legitimacy among the population and a greater public confidence that the troubles were manageable within the existing political framework; fewer voters than in Germany looked for solutions outside it. Any examination of the downfall of the Weimar Republic in the early 1930s must therefore consider the more long-term socioeconomic and political conflicts in German society since the late nineteenth century and certainly since 1915. However, we must also analyse the impact of the immediate policies pursued by successive Reich governments between 1930 and 1933.

From Brüning to Hitler

The immediate task of the Brüning Cabinet was to mitigate and resolve the economic crisis which was worsening at an alarming pace, even if the deeper considerations behind the establishment of the presidential regime in 1930 would appear to have been more sinister. The sudden recall of large sums of American money had quickly caused the collapse of the loan-induced prosperity of the late 1920s (Tables 7, 8 and 10). The victory of the Nazis in September 1930, which alarmed many foreign investors, accelerated this process. Since many German banks and industrial enterprises had used short-term credit to finance long-term investment programmes, the withdrawal of loans quickly caused a cash-flow crisis. Soon holders of German accounts also rushed to their bank to take out their money. Some institutions were forced into bankruptcy and the international banking system was in complete disarray. In their attempt to stave off disaster, many firms began to shed parts of their workforce. Those who were unable to solve their liquidity problems in this way and who found demand collapsing around them were forced into liquidation, thus throwing more people out of work (Table 18).

Brüning believed that the best way of combatting economic collapse was to adopt a policy of deflation. Above all, the budget had to be balanced. If state revenue declined, state expenditure had to be cut. If social security contributions fell because of unemployment, benefits had to be reduced. Civil servants and teachers who held tenured positions and could not be dismissed had their salaries cut (Table 23). No doubt this was preferable to redundancy, but it was a bitter pill, nonetheless. A petty bureaucrat, who had earned 260 marks per months in 1927, saw his income slashed by 58 marks by December 1932. In short, Brüning imposed an unprecedented austerity programme on the country which could claim to have merely one advantage: it enabled Germany to protest insolvency *vis-à-vis* the Allies and hence effectively ended reparations payments which had been one of the whipping-boys of German nationalists throughout the 1920s. The Hoover Moratorium of 1 July 1931 was accordingly celebrated as a great victory for Hindenburg's stand against Allied policy. It was not the only indication that German foreign policy, perhaps also to appease the increasingly influential Right at home, was becoming more assertive and hostile to international negotiations and co-operation. Issues like the idea of an Austro-German Customs Union were tackled very differently by Brüning from the way Stresemann had conducted his diplomacy. The change in tone and method was even more noticeable and ominous during the Geneva disarmament talks in 1932. Clearly, the politicians of force and the hardline revisionists were regaining the upper hand.

If the moratorium on reparations payments brought some relief, the other results of Brüning's deflation were nothing less than catastrophic. This did not prevent his successor, Franz von Papen, from continuing along this path. His policies can only be called unashamedly reactionary, and he was even more deaf than his predecessor to various alternative economic strategies which were being mooted at this time. One of these alternatives involved the introduction of demand management policies of the kind which the Keynesians later came to promote in Britain and America. Their remedy was to revive demand and production with the help of increased public expenditure instead of cutting it. The basic idea may have seemed plausible enough. The problem was that it took some time for it to be cast into a detailed programme. In fact it was only in 1932 that a group of trade unionists and economists came forward with a concrete scheme of anticyclical demand management and job creation. And when Schleicher, Papen's successor, developed an interest in these ideas in December of that year, his position with Hindenburg was already becoming precarious. A few weeks later he had lost the Chancellorship.

Knut Borchardt has argued that, owing to the economic policies adopted by his predecessors, Brüning was left with little room for manoeuvre and that alternative proposals, had they been available, would have come too late to be of any help. Yet the question remains as to whether the recipes applied after 1930 took the forms they did because they were inseparably connected with certain non-economic objectives. These were in the case of Brüning: the transformation of the Weimar Constitution to a point where a return to parliamentarism would be impossible; Papen's 'New State' concept leaves even less doubt about its anti-parliamentary design. It was not merely blatantly authoritarian, but also aimed at a permanent weakening of the working-class movement in the industrial sphere. Such purposes were incompatible with the democratic assumptions underlying demand management.

However, the SPD and the unions also bear their share of responsibility in the death of the Republic. Their burden, to be sure, is far lighter than that of the Right and of the Communists who, effectively Stalinised during the 1920s, refused, on Moscow's orders, to enter into an alliance with the Social Democrats against the Nazis. Instead they fought the moderate Left even harder than the extreme Right, allegedly in furtherance of the socialist revolution. And yet, their divisive tactics notwithstanding, the Communists were not alone within the broad working-class movement to hold that the Great Slump represented the final crisis of capitalism which would lead to the emergence of socialism. The question was merely whether it was possible and desirable to accelerate the downfall of the 'bourgeois–capitalist Republic', even at the price of collaborating with Weimar's extreme right-wing enemies (as the Communists argued) or whether it was preferable to take the attentist view of many Social Democrats who believed themselves to be sitting beside the 'sickbed of capitalism' and witnessing its terminal agonies with awe and apprehension.

No doubt it was also this fatalistic analysis of the crisis which helped to weaken the SPD's willingness to resist the activists on the extreme Right and Left who were bent on smashing the existing order. In view of these attitudes, often reinforced by the feeling of helplessness in the face of the unknown and by the demoralising effect of unemployment, proto-Keynesianism remained a minority position. Brüning and Papen continued to have the powerful backing of the President, who stoically signed the decrees which prescribed more of the deflationary medicine. The most the Reich government was prepared to contemplate was a small-scale public works programme, promoted by Schleicher and his mentor Groener, who in addition to the Defence Ministry had taken over the Ministry of the Interior in October 1931. However, the initial impetus behind this idea was apparently not the recognition that an active interventionist economic policy was needed, but rather the preoccupation of the military with the number of unemployed who joined the private armies of the Right and Left and challenged the Reichswehr's arms monopoly. It was only towards the end of 1932 that Schleicher became more seriously interested in the economics of a public works programme when he succeeded Papen as Reich Chancellor and was casting round for new ideas to overcome the continuing crisis. He failed like his predecessors before him and it was left to Hitler, employing his own peculiar methods of crisis management, to turn the depression into a boom.

The overall material effect of the orthodox economic policies of the Brüning government between 1930 and 1932 was therefore to deepen the recession. The index of industrial production fell from 100 points in 1929 to 87 in 1930 and to a mere 58 in 1932 (Table 7). The production of consumer goods was less badly affected than the manufacture of capital goods, which slumped from 102 points in 1929 to 47 in 1932 (Tables 7 and 8). The value of exports and imports was halved (Table 10). Consequently, the largest number of the 4–5 million unemployed were industrial workers. At a time when poverty and deprivation resulting from redundancy were exacerbated by a drastic trimming of the social security 'net', the suffering of the unemployed and their families was no doubt worst. There was simply not enough money to maintain the level of benefits. Those who kept their jobs saw a gradual fall in their real income from 102 points in 1929 to 86 in 1932, owing to wage freezes and short-time working. On 8 December 1932 all wages based on collective agreements were lowered by decree to the level of January 1927. Decrees were also issued on higher insurance contributions, indirect taxes and other areas affecting living standards. By 1932 some 260,000 people were on short time. No less serious was their fear of unemployment which strengthened the hand of the employers and weakened trade unionism. Strike figures declined markedly, but the days of industrial consensus politics were over (Table 44). The hardliners of heavy industry increasingly set the tone and submitted their proposals on economic policy to Brüning.

However, with few exceptions, other social groups suffered also, even if they had savings to fall back on. Like the civil servants and teachers, white-collar employees in commerce and industry received lower salaries, although not all of them saw their real incomes declining (Table 25). This was partly because the retail price index slumped by a quarter for food and by a third for clothing. Yet the drastic cutting of profit-margins by producers and retailers, which was largely responsible for this fall, was merely a reflection of the predicament of the self-employed. For many of them the main aim was to survive, not to make money out of their businesses. Bankruptcies and liquidations trebled from 9,300 in 1927 to 27,900 in 1931. Investors likewise had a bad time as the share index dropped from 101 points in 1928 to 41 in 1932 and dividends from 8.3 to 2.8 per cent (Table 21). Yields on capital disappeared (Table 20). Finally there was agriculture whose viability was likewise seriously affected although, as we have seen, there were also more long-term structural factors which, despite *Osthilfe*, undermined its profitability (Table 19).

These economic realities and their demoralising effect on millions of people have to be borne in mind when we now come to take a further look at the German political landscape during the fateful years of 1931 and 1932. Of course, Brüning was not the type of politician who enjoyed inflicting great hardship on his fellow-countrymen. Yet he was convinced that the deflation-ary medicine which he had administered was the right policy and that the 'self-healing forces of the market' would eventually assert themselves. Shielded against parliamentary opposition by President Hindenburg and Article 48, and with the hardliners in industry and in agriculture urging him to be tough, he was prepared to be unpopular. There was nothing charismatic about his rule. He did not try to persuade, but implemented his policies with bureaucratic stubbornness. Once or twice he considered giving his govern-ment a broader base of support by opening up towards the Right and towards Hitler who appeared to be the only right-wing politician commanding a mass base. However, these plans never got very far, partly because of Brüning's and Hindenburg's reluctance to take the radical and uncouth Nazis into the Cabinet, partly because Hitler, elated by the growing popularity of his movement, increased the price of his co-operation. By the spring of 1932 nothing short of gaining the Chancellorship for himself would have satisfied him. Brüning was understandably loath to agree and was able to ignore the political pressures exerted by Hitler's mass party so long as he possessed the President's confidence.

Being denied access to the executive, Hitler, in the spring of 1932, made a major effort to conquer the power centre of the constitutional dictatorship into which the political system of Weimar had degenerated since 1930: the Presidency itself. Hindenburg's seven-year term came to an end in March 1932. The President was elected in a plebiscitary fashion and the 'Führer' had hopes of winning a majority of the popular vote. Faced with this possibility, the 85-year-old Hindenburg was persuaded to stand for a second term. The first ballot, held on 13 March 1932, was inconclusive. Hindenburg gained 18.6 million votes as against Hitler's 11.3 million, with some 7.5 million votes cast for Thälmann, the Communist candidate, and Theodor Duesterberg, one of the leaders of the right-wing *Stahlhelm* association. This outcome necessitated a second ballot on 10 April which turned into a contest between Hindenburg, Hitler and Thälmann. This time the old Field Marshal obtained the absolute majority (53%) but Hitler won a triumphant 13 million votes (36.8%). Thälmann fell back from 13.2 to 10.2 per cent. More than ever before Hindenburg was now the gatekeeper to a Chancellorship by the leader of the NSDAP, whose party became the largest in the Reichstag after the national elections of July 1932, attracting over 13.7 million votes and winning 230 seats.

In these circumstances, the peculiarities of the presidential regime which had been established in 1930 are of the utmost importance for an understand-ing of the turbulent months before and after Hitler's eventual appointment as Chancellor in January 1933. What made these months so confusing was not merely the rapid succession of governments and elections, but the massive politicisation of the population. Politicians of all parties were almost permanently on the campaign trail. Hardly a day passed without rallies, demonstrations or marches being held by one or more groups in the major cities and smaller towns of Germany. Whereas most ordinary citizens acted as onlookers and audiences, the members of the large political organisations urged and cajoled the public to demonstrate their commitment to a particular political cause. By the early 1930s there were literally dozens of parties, many of which had also created affiliated associations to mobilise the young, the women, the elderly and, above all, the able-bodied activists. Indeed, one of the most striking developments of this period was the massive growth of extraparliamentary and paramilitary organisations, some of them pretending to be politically neutral. In effect most of them represented the combat arm of the various movements on the Right or Left.

Politics became more polarised, dogmatic and brutalised as ideological passions rose. Political arguments, whether conducted in the market-place or at the dinner table, escalated into shouting matches. Irrationality triumphed. Families split over their political differences. Violence increased and by 1932 several hundred people had died and thousands had been injured in clashes between political opponents. Nothing expressed this development more visibly and contributed to the poisoning of the political climate more obviously than the rise of the party armies which were sent out into the streets to protect rallies, beat up political enemies and generally display the putative power of a particular political movement. At the two ends of the political spectrum were to be found the most radical elements: predominantly young men who were prepared to kill and maim.

Various attempts have been made to explain this upsurge of paramilitarism and political violence. No doubt the associations also attracted criminal elements who had been involved in non-political violence before the crisis started. There were also the demoralising experiences of the 'war generation' to be considered: total war, defeat and civil war, the ideological trench warfare of the 1920s which never quite subsided and last, but not least, the impact of the Great Slump, engendering despair and hopelessness. Indeed, some authors who analysed the age structure of the movement at the two extremes of the political spectrum have concluded that the collapse of Weimar was in large measure also due to a rebellion of the younger generation. By 1932, open civil war had broken out in Germany for a second time within a decade and there were still enough ruthless fighters around who were prepared to settle political differences with bicycle chains, knives and fists. A sizeable number of such people were organised and trained in the SA, Hitler's party army. For the moment they were fighting for the victory of National Socialism in the squares and assembly halls. After the seizure of power they would beat up and kill political opponents in the police cells and concentration camps.

The tense atmosphere of perpetual conflict had a tremendous effect on the ordinary citizen who voted, but remained unorganised. Cowed by the sight of strong-arm battalions in the streets and battered by a constant barrage of party-political propaganda, he became convinced that the authorities had lost control and that a coup or a revolution was imminent. In this sense, Brüning's austerity programme was even more catastrophic for its political and psychological effect on the electorate than it was on the economy. It undermined such confidence as still existed that the authorities were capable of preserving law and order and increased the fear that one or the other of the radical movements might seize power. With the benefit of hindsight, it is probably more accurate to say that the divergent political forces were milling about quite aimlessly without being able to effect a decisive shift in any direction. Indeed, this is possibly the most curious aspect of the history of the year 1932: masses of people being mobilised; they longed for a 'solution', for their salvation, but their vote, their demands and their relentless activism did not directly influence the political decision-making at the top. They could not oust Hindenburg during his new seven-year term of office, even if his nomination of the reactionary Papen government in May 1932 had bitterly disappointed those millions of Social Democrats, Catholics and Liberals who had voted for the Field Marshal in the presidential elections a few weeks earlier. Nor could the 'masses' determine, through their elected representatives, what kind of policies should be adopted or what legislation should be approved. Impotently organised in large, cumbersome and internally divided blocks, they formed at most a latent asset when 'successful' politicians like Hitler began to bargain with those who had the constitutional power to make crucial decisions. The actual centre of political power was constituted by the President and those strategic cliques which had his ear. The months following the summer of 1932 were the months, not of the 'masses' and certainly not of the working class, but of the Schleichers and Meissners and, behind them, of the military, agrarian and industrial elites who were also moving about in search of an acceptable solution. Their power and influence was fragmented and disintegrating, but it had not been completely lost.

What united them was their desire to end parliamentarism for good and to dismantle the battered remnants of trade union and Social Democratic power. It must be said that they had made good progress in respect of these negative aims. Although their emotional attachment to the Republic had increased under the impact of the Great Slump and the threat of a right-wing dictatorship, many SPD leaders appeared to have lost the will to fight. Fatalism and fatigue had set in, which was clearly demonstrated in the response to Papen's coup against the Prussian government on 20 July 1932. The coup was clearly illegal, but Otto Braun and his colleagues offered no resistance to their removal, partly because they were afflicted by a mood of resignation, partly because they did not wish to unleash a civil war which they dreaded. The *Reichsbanner* men and other activists who would probably have been prepared to fight were ordered to stay at home. Thus the SPD surrendered Prussia, the traditional stronghold of Republicanism, to its enemies in the Reich government and to the elite groups supporting it. These groups toyed with ideas of an authoritarian regime which would, directly or indirectly, draw its popular legitimacy from an inclusion of the NSDAP, but would continue to rely on the powers of the President under Article 48. The question was what price they were prepared to pay, and on this issue two factions had begun to crystallise towards the end of 1932. There were those who were prepared to offer the Nazis a number of seats in the Cabinet, though not the Chancellorship; others were willing to let the 'Führer' lead the government, provided he was surrounded by conservatives who would strait-jacket him and moderate his radicalism. One of the main protagonists of the former strategy was Schleicher. He had been instrumental in the dismissal of Brüning in May which illustrated, if not for the first time, at least quite drastically, how far crucial decisions had come to hinge on the President and his entourage and how certain individuals were able to wield great informal influence.

Schleicher became Defence Minister in Papen's 'Cabinet of the Barons' which, significantly enough, was installed without possessing the support of any of the major political forces in the Reichstag. Being even more unpopular than Brüning, who had at least been 'tolerated' by the SPD and the Centre Party, Papen soon came to realise that he needed some popular legitimation for his reactionary programme. Accordingly, an attempt was made on 13 August 1932 to entice Hitler to join the Cabinet; but the audience with Hindenburg ended in failure. Hitler asked for the Chancellorship; Hindenburg was not prepared to entrust it to the 'Bohemian lance corporal'. A second conversation likewise came to nothing. Schleicher, by now the grey eminence of German politics, had by this time begun to pursue a different plan to obtain the support of those parts of the Nazi movement that were becoming increasingly critical of the 'Führer's' refusal to compromise. He made contact with Gregor Strasser, the chief of the Nazi party organisation, who was believed to be in favour of creating an 'axis of associations' stretching from the 'left wing' of the NSDAP across to the trade unions. From what little is known of Schleicher, he appears to have aimed at a consumer-oriented economic policy, at a 'dirigiste social dictatorship supported by anticapitalist masses' (David Abraham). It was possibly in order to smooth this path that he revoked many of the anti-labour measures of his predecessor. Yet negotiations never got beyond preliminaries and Strasser quickly found himself in trouble with his own party, leading to his resignation from his influential post.

In the meantime, Schleicher had replaced Papen as Chancellor, thinking that only he could save the situation. By then his role as string-puller and backstage politician was too well known and few politicians, whatever their persuasion, were prepared to trust him. Above all, he never gained the confidence of the agrarians and of heavy industry. And the more he himself was reaching the end of the road, the more obsessed he became with the notion that Hitler must at all cost be barred from becoming his successor. He sensed that the nomination of the leader of the NSDAP to this position was precisely the option which Papen had increasingly come to contemplate. His dismissal from the Chancellorship, which Schleicher was supposed to have engineered, added an element of personal vendetta to Papen's moves during the weeks before the appointment of Hitler on 30 January 1933. When one looks at the various manoeuvres by Papen and his group, it seems that they tried all kinds of combinations and names of potential ministers on Hindenburg, the man on whose constitutional powers all future action depended. The common denominator of their proposals was an inclusion of the Nazis. Schleicher, while still not totally averse to a Nazi presence in the government, increasingly came to favour a dissolution of the Reichstag, but wanted to avoid the holding of fresh elections within the mandatory period of 60 days. In other words, he thought of silencing the political opposition in Parliament which had become ever more scathingly critical of his government by asking Hindenburg to commit a breach of the Constitution. The old Field Marshal was prepared to engage in all kinds of moves, but did not wish openly to violate his oath. It also became clear that Schleicher did not have the support of the Reichswehr officer corps which was supposed to underwrite the plan. Nor had he succeeded in providing the popular backing for a presidential regime without which government had become more and more difficult. Finally, what helped Papen in his moves was that Hitler was growing rather desperate about what looked to him like successive plots to bar him from executive power. It was also worrying to him that his party had lost some 2 million votes and 34 seats in the elections of November 1932 (Table 42). Could it be that National Socialism had passed its peak?

Although many of the manoeuvres by various people remain obscure, it appears that with the shock of November in his bones, Hitler may have been prepared to accept the position of Reichswehr Minister in a revamped Cabinet. Clearly his nerves were very taut and his movement in deep trouble. He was only too glad to respond to Papen's overtures, since he was known to have good contacts in the President's office and to be pushing for a completely new 'Cabinet of National Concentration', to include Hugenberg and Hitler. The re-emergence of Hugenberg, who had been continuing his campaign of 'National Opposition' and whose DNVP had made modest gains in November 1932, is significant in that it demonstrated how far the country had progressed down the road of authoritarianism. Whether Hitler became Chancellor or not, the DNVP leader hoped to assume dictatorial responsibility for the economy in the proposed new Cabinet. Slowly the 'Hitler Solution' began to take shape after Meissner and Hindenburg's son Oskar had been brought in to talk to Hitler and to be given reassurances by the 'Führer' which could be used to sway the President. Although the exact composition of the government remained open literally up to the last minute and disagreements continued in the lobby outside Hindenburg's office before the swearing-in ceremony, Papen, Hugenberg and his colleagues were agreed on the principle that any Nazi ministers would remain in the minority surrounded by influential conservatives. Furthermore, if Hitler was to be Chancellor, he was to have placed at his side a Vice-Chancellor with equal rights of access to the President. Papen had a sufficiently high opinion of himself to earmark this post for himself.

It might be argued that it looked all very safe and that, when Hitler was nominated Chancellor on 30 January 1933, the much-feared radicalism and 'irresponsibility' of the Nazi movement appeared to have been effectively contained. It is a reflection on the hectic political activity of the Papen group that, on the one hand, negotiations were speeded up by rumours of an impending Reichswehr putsch by the pro-Schleicher faction in the officer corps and that, on the other hand, Hugenberg could only be persuaded to abandon a last-minute squabble with Hitler when he was reminded that the Field Marshal must not be kept waiting any longer to sign the documents relating to the appointment of the Hitler Cabinet. In the evening of that 30 January, jubilant supporters of the 'Führer' marched past him and the Nazis celebrated the seizure of power (*Machtergreifung*) all over the country.

Still the torch-parades should not distract us from the fact that Hitler had been brought to power by the intrigues and machinations of a small clique of politicians who, after ventilating various alternatives, had ended up with a solution which gave them both decisive executive control and legitimation by the largest right-wing movement. The events of January 1933 also make it difficult to maintain that Hitler had come to power as a result of the *direct* actions and influence of powerful elite groups. The confusions and manoeuvering of the previous weeks and months rather seem to suggest that their capacity to work concertedly towards a *specific* solution had also been thrown into disarray. Yet, while few of these groups had actively promoted a 'Hitler Solution', they certainly did nothing to block it and, tacitly at least, were prepared to give it a chance. This verdict would seem to apply particularly to two key groups, the officer corps and the front bench of German industry. Only the agrarians, who had always hated the Republic, appear to have played a more prominent part behind the scenes in working for a 'Hitler Solution'.

As far as the Reichswehr was concerned, sympathy with major aspects of Nazi doctrine had been steadily rising since 1930. Above all, it was the assertive nationalism, the anti-Republicanism and anti-socialism as well as the extolling of military virtues and the demand for rapid rearmament which were registered with much approval. Although many officers remained critical of what they considered the Hitler movement's radicalism and 'indiscipline', they came to regard the above demands on foreign and domestic policy as the 'good core' of National Socialism. Schleicher's response to these tendencies, about which he grew increasingly doubtful, but which he could not control, had been to uphold, outwardly at least, the political neutrality of the Army. It was to remain the bastion against a violent attempt to overthrow the existing order. However, while there was little doubt that the Reichswehr could be and would be deployed against the Left, should a civil war ever be unleashed from that quarter, by the end of 1932 it had also become clear that it would be useless if it were ordered to impose and supervise a ban of the extreme Right. More and more officers had become convinced that the Nazis must not be destroyed, but be taken into government responsibility. By January 1933, Schleicher's policies in effect enjoyed very little support among his comrades-in-arms. The political attitudes of men like Werner von Blomberg reflected Reichswehr feeling much more accurately and, although he was abroad when Papen negotiated the deal with Hitler and Hugenberg, his nomination to the post of Reichswehr Minister in the Hitler Cabinet did not come as a complete surprise to the officer corps. They now had the government which they believed to be inevitable in the circumstances. In it the Reichswehr had a spokesman and watchdog who represented their views, especially on rearmament and revisionism, more closely than the wayward Schleicher.

Nor has much conclusive evidence come to light to show that Germany's industrialists and in particular the main representatives of heavy industry had a hand in the negotiations of the Papen Circle. On the other hand, they too did nothing to prevent the installation of the Hitler Cabinet. The reasons for their attitudes are not difficult to pinpoint. We have already seen earlier in this chapter how the powerful managers of the Ruhr industries continued to perceive industrial relations in confrontationist terms even during the period of relative stability. They also had serious reservations about parliamentarism and the Republic in general. To them the main threat had always come, and continued to come, from the Left. By the middle of the Great Depression they had regained the upper hand against their more moderate colleagues in the RDI. An authoritarian government which promised to weaken or even destroy the power of the working-class movement was therefore preferable to the Weimar system of tripartist compromises. Most of them were correspondingly well disposed towards various moves designed to strengthen a presidential regime under Article 48. Later opinions diverged not so much over the economic and political effects of Brüning's and Papen's policies on the working-class movement, but over how to treat the right-wing opposition.

There were a few prominent industrialists who promoted the inclusion of

Hitler into the government as early as 1930. Yet, on the whole, they met with little enthusiasm from their colleagues, partly because certain 'socialist' clauses in the Nazi programme and the radical anti-capitalist propaganda of the movement worried them. Big business therefore did not *'pay* Hitler' in the sense that it provided the bulk of the funds for the Nazi election campaigns. Most of the party's finance appears to have come from the ordinary members and from smaller businessmen who, in 1931/2, thought it wise to take out a 'rain-check' in case the Nazis came to power. However, the pro-Hitler faction in heavy industry managed to channel some industrial donations into the NSDAP's coffers, much of it handed to 'moderate' Nazi leaders in the hope that it would strengthen their hands and prevent a further radicalisation of the movement. Moreover, in the course of 1932 pro-Nazi elements helped to organise a number of meetings with Hitler and other top functionaries to give them a chance to clarify their positions on various issues, in particular on economic policy, in front of the sceptics among the industrialists.

A number of exceptions always conceded, it is therefore fairly certain that by the second half of 1932 most industrialists supported not merely the blatantly reactionary social policies of the Papen government, but had also come to accept the notion that Hitler might be 'tamed' by giving him and his top collaborators posts in the Cabinet. Their attitudes of the 1920s and the developments on the economic and political front had drastically narrowed their options and were pushing them towards a Nazi experiment. Other legacies now proved overwhelmingly strong. Although few of them appear to have spoken up for the 'Führer's' nomination as *Chancellor* either in January 1933 or earlier, they all made their peace with the Hitler Cabinet with embarrassing haste when its emergence had finally been engineered. On 20 February a crucial meeting took place between the new Chancellor and the RDI at which Gustav Krupp, its new president, pledged the support of industry's peak association for the government. Subsequently, three million marks were donated with which Hitler and his allies financed their campaign for the elections of March 1933. A mutually beneficial relationship had been forged.

The decision to hold these elections was made, against the opposition of Hugenberg, at the first session of the Hitler Cabinet on 2 February 1933. The 'Führer' had good reasons for pressing to hold yet another poll. Favoured by his newly acquired power position, and with better access to private and public funds, he was confident of gaining further popular support, perhaps even an absolute majority. For it was only with the help of a governmental majority in the Reichstag, won single-handedly by his Party or in conjunction with his coalition partners, that he could hope to emancipate himself from the grip of the President. For the moment he remained very vulnerable, surrounded, as he was, by conservative watchdogs who might always use their influence and convince Hindenburg that the Chancellor should be dismissed. After all, his three predecessors had all fallen from power in this way. But there were, apart from Article 48, the other provisions of the Weimar Constitution which Hitler hoped to exploit to his advantage. The best way of doing this was to reconstruct the parliamentary pillar of the Weimar system which had supported the Cabinets after 1924. Only when it collapsed in 1930 had the presidential regime been established. A Hitler government, commanding a parliamentary majority which Brüning, Papen and Schleicher had lacked, could initiate legislation through the Reichstag and did not have to come begging to the President to sign an emergency decree. And there was one piece of legislation which Hitler was particularly keen to get adopted by Parliament: the government could be authorised to assume dictatorial powers, if a two-thirds parliamentary majority granted it an enabling act. In other words, it was possible under the Weimar Constitution for the Reichstag to ratify a bill empowering the Cabinet to enact laws without their having passed through the normal processes of parliamentary debate. Instead the Reichstag would give the government blanket approval in advance to promulgate whatever laws it considered necessary for the running of the country.

It should now be clear why Hitler was pressing so hard for early elections and why Hugenberg wished to avoid them: a victory at the polls would provide Hitler with an opportunity to end his dependence on the President and enable him briefly to revive parliamentary government, in order to destroy it by means of an enabling act (Table 42). Herein lies the great significance of the vote by the Reichstag of 23 March 1933 when the 'Führer' was empowered, with the support of the remaining *bürgerliche* parties and against the SPD, to govern without prior Reichstag consent for the next four years. Endowed with these powers, Hitler no longer required Hindenburg's signature when he proceeded to establish a dictatorial regime of his own which obliterated, step by step, all constitutional and organisational obstacles in the way of such a dictatorship. And all these dictatorial policies could be implemented without touching the façade of legality which the Nazis had been so careful to maintain since the abortive coup of 1923. The Enabling Act of March 1933 formed the basis for the subsequent ban on the trade unions, the dissolution of all non-Nazi parties, the destruction of the federal structure of the Reich, the purge of the Civil Service and a host of other measures which came to constitute the *Gleichschaltung* (synchronisation).

Thus the political landscape of Germany was completely transformed within the following 15 months, and a regime was established which remained without parallel as far as its all-pervasive brutality and ruthlessness are concerned. When Hindenburg finally died at the age of 87 on 2 August 1934, Hitler, without fear of being removed, was strong enough to combine the offices of Chancellor and President and to proclaim himself 'Führer and Reich Chancellor' of Germany. The move was the logical conclusion to the process of

127

Machtergreifung and 'synchronisation'. However, it would be wrong to assume that this process was greeted with overwhelming enthusiasm and met with little opposition. On the contrary, on closer inspection the Nazi seizure of power was unable to preserve its façade of legality from the moment of Hitler's nomination; for it was accompanied by unprecedented levels of violence against individuals and entire social and ethnic groups which were either actively opposed to the regime or presumed to be its enemies. It is to these illegal aspects of early Nazi rule that we shall have to turn at the beginning of the next chapter.

4 The Third Reich, 1933–1945

The face of the Nazi dictatorship

The first point to be made about the Nazi dictatorship is that it was much worse in human terms than can ever be expressed in words. One can merely try to analyse some of its more salient structural and developmental features. The second point is that the attitudes and experiences of those Germans who lived through the Third Reich differed widely and depended to a considerable extent on a person's socioeconomic position. Just as it is untenable to say that 'the Germans' brought Hitler to power, sociological accuracy also helps us to understand who fared well and who fared badly after 1933 and hence to illuminate the basic character of the regime.

As to the proclaimed enemies of the new regime, the Nazis had never made a secret of their uncompromising and fundamental hostility to Communism and Social Democracy. Both had been built up into a major threat to law and order and the NSDAP had always promised to those frightened Germans who had voted for the Party that this 'threat' would be dealt with as soon as power had been achieved. Having taken control of both the Reich Ministry of the Interior and the Prussian Interior Ministry in January 1933 – a move which in itself demonstrated a shrewd appreciation of which posts were important and more important than possessing an overall majority of Cabinet seats – known left-wingers of the Weimar days were among the first to be rounded up. At the same time the SA was let loose throughout the country to settle accounts with old political enemies. And the Nazis' memories were long. People were beaten up and taken into 'protective custody'; buildings were occupied and ransacked; shopwindows were smashed. Of course, the SA rowdies should have been prosecuted for these activities. Yet few charges were brought against them, partly because the victims feared reprisals, but more importantly perhaps because in Prussia, the largest State of Germany, the SA had been turned into an 'auxiliary police'. This enabled Nazi activists to go on the rampage under the guise of officially hunting down 'subversive' elements. They called it the 'restoration of law and order'. If anyone complained about their brutalities, the next police station might take the details, but no further action would follow. The complainant, with his name and address known, might subsequently receive a night-time visit from a gang of SA men.

The violence of the first weeks worsened after 28 February when Hitler got Hindenburg to sign an emergency decree which abolished basic rights of association, assembly and press freedom and enabled the regime to persecute opponents and Communists in particular by legislative fiat. The pretext for this far-reaching decree was provided by a fire which had gutted the Reichstag building on the previous evening and for which the Communists were immediately held responsible after a young Dutchman with extreme left-wing affiliations had been caught clambering down the walls of the burning building. There is still a debate among historians as to whether the spectacle had actually been staged by the Nazis themselves. The Reichstag Fire certainly presented them with a golden opportunity to exploit the incident just in time for the elections on 5 March 1933.

The results of these elections, which can hardly be considered to have been free and in which the KPD and the SPD were virtually prevented from campaigning, have been analysed in the previous chapter. Yet even under these favourable circumstances, the NSDAP achieved a majority only in conjunction with its conservative coalition partners who had participated under the name of *Kampffront Schwarz-Weiß-Rot*. However, enough deputies of the other *bürgerliche* parties voted for the enabling bill which provided the (pseudo-) legal basis of Hitler's dictatorship. Without breaching the form of the Constitution, he could move on to the proscription of other oppositional organisations. By the summer of 1933, this task had been successfully achieved. Leading the list was the working-class movement, which had been completely wiped out. The most activist members in the KPD, SPD and such smaller splinter groups as the *Sozialistische Arbeiterpartei* (SAP) had never had any illusions about the Nazis' ruthless determination. If they had not been arrested or forced into exile, they tried to set up underground networks. Yet most of them found they lacked resources and experience, with the exception perhaps of those Communists who had memories of illegal activities during the Weimar days. There were also many calls for unity in the fight against fascism. But co-operation was bedevilled by old animosities which were rooted in the great schism of the working-class movement in the Revolution of 1918 and had been revived during the bitter ideological battles of the early 1930s. In the long run nothing was more devasting to the anti-Nazi underground resistance than the growing efficiency of the political police.

Couriers may have succeeded for a while in smuggling anti-Nazi leaflets and messages across the border from Czechoslovakia, France, Scandinavia or Switzerland; sooner or later most of them would be caught with propaganda material in their bicycle tubes. Primitive illegal printing presses may have successfully churned out news-sheets, run off in cellars and garden sheds; sooner or later the security service would raid the premises and take away the machine, operators and all. Young activists may have managed to daub walls and fences with anti-Nazi slogans; sooner or later men in long black leather coats would be on their heels. By 1935, the authorities had broken up most underground organisations of this kind. Up to the beginning of the Second World War some 225,000 men and women were tried and convicted by the ordinary courts in connection with political 'crimes'. Hundreds of thousands of ordinary Germans were held without trial and sent to concentration camps for shorter or longer periods. According to a report by the political police of 10 April 1939 the number of those imprisoned for their beliefs, on that day, was 162,734 people in 'protective custody', 27,369 awaiting trial and 112,432 convicted for their opposition to the regime.

With their number decimated, the remaining activists found that the technical and psychological obstacles to resistance were becoming insuperable. Tim Mason has argued that by the late 1930s the working class had developed indirect forms of opposition. However, direct resistance activity which had at least some chance of weakening the regime was now barely conceivable outside the Army, which commanded the necessary technical means and was more immune to penetration by the political police.

The Jews were the other group to become the victims of brutal persecution by the Nazis. An anti-Semitism based on religious or social and economic prejudice had existed in Germany well before the founding of the NSDAP. Towards the end of the nineteenth century a biological argument had been added to the arsenal of anti-Semitic diatribes. The Jews were not only alleged to have an economically and culturally harmful influence, but were also said to pose a biological threat to the genetic purity of the 'Aryan race'. Even in retrospect it is quite astonishing to see how race theorists converted and twisted discoveries in the natural sciences to manufacture political ammunition from them. No argument about the role of Jewry in history was too abstruse not to find some faithfuls who fervently believed in it, including the theory that an elaborate plot had been hatched by the Jews to undermine the genetic substance of the 'Aryans' as part of a long-term plan to dominate the world.

Hitler and many of his early followers who picked up these ideas came to be absolutely convinced of the reality of this Jewish conspiracy. Whatever the deeper psychological sources which fed Hitler's anti-Semitism there is no doubt that he developed a consuming hatred of Jews. Even if his biological arguments, mixed as they were with a strong dose of Social Darwinism, did not appeal to more than a few crackpots, his vociferous anti-Semitic propaganda struck a responsive chord among many of his listeners who were themselves in search of scapegoats to explain to themselves the disasters that had afflicted Germany since the turn of the century. Blaming the country's predicament and one's own misery on a small identifiable minority was obviously an easy way out. However, for the Nazis anti-Semitism had a more fundamental significance, and some historians have even gone so far as to argue that it represented the real essence of their ideology. Hitler was certainly convinced that the Germans were engaged in a racial struggle with the Jews from which only one side could emerge victorious. It was such dogma of a life-and-death confrontation upon whose outcome the entire future of mankind was supposed to rest that pointed, tendentially at least, to the wholesale physical extermination of the Jewish minority. To the racist anti-Semites they were a poison, dangerous misfits against whom all 'defensive' means were justified. Men who talk about genocide are never far from actually committing it.

From the start Nazi anti-Semitism was therefore marked by a radicalism and by pathological hatreds which were bound to affect the life of the Jews once Hitler had come to power and had the large executive machinery of the State available to him. Spurred by him and other rabid anti-Semites, some of his supporters had been involved in isolated pogroms before 1933. In the spring of 1933, a massive wave of violence hit the Jewish communities throughout the Reich. Boycotts were organised against Jewish shops; stores were raided, windows smashed. Jews were beaten up in the streets or carted off into 'protective custody'. When this wave subsided, many of the victims hoped that life would return to 'normalcy' again. Then, on 7 April 1933, public servants of Jewish descent suddenly found themselves without a livelihood when the 'Law for the Restitution of the Professional Civil Service' was promulgated. Apart from providing for the dismissal of civil servants deemed politically undesirable, the Law also decreed the removal of persons of 'non-Aryan descent', with the exception of those who had been members before 1 August 1914 or had fought in the First World War as front soldiers.

Further decrees ordered the exclusion of Jewish barristers from the courts; doctors were taken off the public health insurance register; careers in higher education were blocked. Those who feared for their own and their family's safety or who were convinced that this was merely the beginning left the country. It did not take long for the radical anti-Semites in the NSDAP to push for further discrimination, this time in the economic and political sphere. But foreign policy considerations and the fear that a forcible removal of Jews from economic life would prove too disruptive resulted in any such plans being shelved for the moment. They were revived in 1934/5 when Goebbels's *Der Angriff* and Julius Streicher's *Der Stürmer* stepped up their demands for a disfranchisement of the Jews.

It is against this background of renewed agitation and persecution that the drafting of the so-called Nuremberg Laws of September 1935 must be seen.

Jews were henceforth to be classified according to their ancestry and their percentage of 'Jewish blood' as a preliminary to withdrawing their citizens' rights. The registration of persons of 'non-Aryan' descent paved the way for further discrimination. Except for a brief respite, imposed during the 1936 Olympic Games at Berlin, the system of anti-Semitic measures was progressively refined. Jews had their access to public education and their freedom of occupational choice curtailed. In 1937/8 they began to be physically segregated in spa resorts; in the parks, benches were marked with 'Germans only' labels.

Above all, Jews were now excluded from the economy. Pressure mounted on firms to dismiss their 'non-Aryan' employees. They were ordered to register their assets and had their driving licences withdrawn. The Night of Broken Glass on 7/8 November 1938 was taken by many Jews as the final warning sign for them to leave if they could. Although the pogrom was advertised as a spontaneous outburst of popular wrath after the killing of a German diplomat at the Embassy in Paris by a young Jew, it must be seen as part of a more calculated escalation process. Accordingly, further restrictions were introduced, for example on the freedom of movement, the education of Jewish children and the use of hotels. And yet, despite the growth of segregationism, historians analysing Nazi anti-Semitic policies have found it difficult to discover a co-ordinated purpose behind them. Numerous agencies were involved and it seems that only in Heinrich Himmler's police and SS empire were there a number of planners who developed something like a programme of 'emigration'. The war changed all this. But before going further down *The Twisted Road to Auschwitz* (K. Schleunes), we shall have to turn to the religiously motivated enemies of the Nazi regime.

Although the leadership of the Protestant and Catholic Churches sought accommodation with the Hitler government and sought a *modus vivendi* which safeguarded their established rights in the fields of religious observance, education and welfare, the dynamic of the Nazi movement with its totalitarian aspirations time and again caused serious conflict at the regional and local level. Many a minister or lay-member openly protested against the repeated assaults of the Party upon church institutions and individuals. Catholics were particularly outraged by anti-religious agitation and interference by local Party leaders, and more than once did their opposition reach the threshold of revolt. Nor did the regime ever quite succeed in silencing more covert criticism from the pulpit. However, the tough Nazi response to the religious opposition never assumed the proportions of the thorough-going swoops by the police and the SS against the Left or the Jews.

In the final analysis, the relationship between the regime and the Churches remained ambivalent. The Nazi leadership appreciated the great authority which the Churches continued to hold over large numbers of Germans and, for the sake of its own survival, avoided an all-out conflict. Hence repression and surveillance at grass-roots level was balanced by accommodation at the top. Conversely, the Churches knew that they posed a great threat to the NSDAP if they wished to use it. Yet at the beginning they refrained from doing so. Much of the criticism by the Church hierarchy was confined to religious matters and rarely amounted to a total rejection of the regime and its policies. On political questions the religious authorities tried to observe neutrality or even took a sympathetic view of the government's conduct. This was particularly strong at the beginning of the Third Reich. The Protestants even managed to create a supportive institutional framework, led by a Nazi-approved Reich Bishop. What facilitated their collaboration was their deeply ingrained nationalism which the First World War, the defeat of 1918 and the Weimar experience had done much to foster. Both Churches had also long been haunted by the spectre of social revolution and rejected 'godless' Marxism. Consequently both Hitler's nationalistic revisionism and his determined anti-Communism met with much approval in Church circles and undermined the opposition of those who believed that the 'negative' aspects of Nazism far outweighed its 'achievements'. Nevertheless, the regime knew only too well that it had many religious opponents and some of them, like the Jehovah's Witnesses, were considered dangerous (and few) enough collectively to be put into concentration camps. In short, the extent of systematic physical and psychological violence by which the Third Reich was characterised can hardly be overestimated; but it was always administered in doses which prevented a large-scale revolt.

At the other end of the political spectrum there were those Germans on whose loyal support the Hitler government could count. Some among them were so-called Old Fighters who had joined the Nazi movement from conviction before 1933. Although it is difficult to quantify the number of confirmed and fanatical members, the figures grew throughout the 1930s largely because the regime succeeded in winning over millions of young people, whereas many adults in the public services and later in private industry had it put to them that it would be better for them to join the Party or one of its affiliated associations. Membership in the *Jungvolk* and Hitler Youth (for boys) as well as *Jungmädelbund* and *Bund Deutscher Mädel* (BDM) was voluntary until the ratification of the Hitler Youth Law of 1 December 1936. In the three years to the end of 1939, recruitment of the 10–18-year-olds increased from 2.29 million to 3.94 million. No doubt a romantic appeal to a spirit of friendship and community, to sacrifice and to the ideal of a well-ordered society together with their acceptance of charismatic leadership met strong emotional needs among young people. There was also an element of rebellion against parents and teachers. So they went off, in Boy Scout fashion, to weekend camps or hikes, listening starry-eyed to the persuasive speeches of their leaders or joining in naively idealistic discussions about Germany's great future and about how much depended on their devotion to the Third Reich and its 'Führer'. It is not surprising that so many teenagers of both sexes should succumb to the sloganeering at the fireside. The Nazification of the educational system and of the school curricula merely reinforced this impact. The reverse side of the coin was a marked decline in the standards of knowledge, which is also reflected in the fall of the number of university students (Table 38). On the other hand, it is noteworthy that almost a quarter of the youth had not joined by 1939 in spite of the December 1936 Law and major recruitment drives by the Party. The Hitler Youth increased its membership from 1.2 million to 1.7 million during the years of compulsion, 1937–9.

Such figures would seem to invite sociological differentiation. It is safe to assume that the social and political milieu of an hierarchically organised class society (which, the wonderful propaganda of *Volksgemeinschaft* notwithstanding, Germany did not cease to be after 1933) also moulded the attitudes of the younger generation. Some fanatical Hitler Youths, to be sure, came from working-class families which had rejected the Nazis before 1933 and continued to do so, if not in public, then in private at the supper table. But it appears that critical attitudes towards the regime were more often than not transmitted to the next generation by their parents or other relatives, together with memories of pre-1933 working-class organisations, their fight against Nazism and an anticipation of the eventual 'inevitable' downfall of Hitler. Such influences were particularly strong in the former *Hochburgen* of the socialist movement like Mannheim, Hamburg, Essen, Leipzig or Berlin. If they were weakened by the mid-1930s it was more because of the successes of the political police in arresting opponents than because of the NSDAP's gaining the support of the industrial working class. Nor did a strict religious upbringing of the young work in the Party's favour. There were hence wide regional variations in the size of Nazi youth organisation membership and also in the degree of enthusiasm with which activities were pursued.

Although our knowledge of how pervasively German boys and girls were indoctrinated and where they came from remains sketchy, it seems that the majority of them had parents who were either committed champions of the Nazi cause or had made their peace with the new regime. Among them were those large numbers of adults who would keep quiet altogether. Others would weigh up the 'negative' manifestations of Nazi reality against the government's 'achievements', often more imaginary than real, and invariably come up with a positive balance sheet. The extent of passive acquiescence and opportunism is most massively reflected in the large number of applications for membership which the NSDAP received in the spring of 1933. In January 1933 the Party had had some 850,000 members. During the weeks following the seizure of power some 1.5 million people applied to join. Most of them were men and about 20 per cent worked as civil servants, evidently anxious to protect themselves against dismissal. The flood of applications was so large that a temporary moratorium had to be imposed on 1 May. Restrictions were relaxed again in 1935 and lifted altogether between May 1939 and February 1942, resulting in an increase from a total of 2.5 million in 1935 to 6.5 million in 1943. In percentage terms this meant that in 1935 some 10.2 per cent of the male population were card-carrying members; in 1943 the figure was 23 per cent.

It was also in the late 1930s that the Party and private employers began to apply more direct pressure on people who had not yet shown a formal commitment to the movement. This practice resulted in a further shift in the balance between blue-collar workers (who already in 1935 had been under-represented), on the one hand, and white-collar employees, civil servants, professional people and the self-employed (all of whom were over-represented in 1935), on the other. Given that Nazi Germany was by then anything but a liberal democracy, the inclination to take an opportunist view of one's career must have been strong. The fear of retribution against non-joiners caused many a fence-sitter to change his mind. The rapid growth of numerous Nazi-affiliated organisations is probably best seen in this context. Joining a professional association or even the National Socialist People's Welfare (NSV) or the Air Raid Protection Society gave, if nothing else, at least a semblance of 'reliability'. In 1937, for example, there was a recruiting drive among civil servants for the League of Large Families.

However, there were many others whose willingness to state their support for the regime was also influenced by ideological preferences and perceptions of socioeconomic interest. We have seen that the pre-1933 appeal of the NSDAP was directed particularly towards the large and heterogeneous middle class. The Party's propaganda had been specifically designed to mobilise the dissatisfaction of these groups with the Weimar Republic and to offer something to everyone. Accordingly millions of Germans from these social groups had voted for Hitler in 1932 and March 1933 and, although they were attracted by different and often contradictory parts of the programme, Hitler could count on their good-will and support, once he had assumed power. After all he had promised actively to tackle the country's manifold and manifest problems, and was he not making a good start with his fight against the hated and fear-inspiring Left?

In the vanguard of the joiners of 1933 marched the professional classes: doctors, lawyers, teachers. The universities witnessed many depressing scenes as some academics could not move fast enough to oust their colleagues with a Jewish background or an anti-Nazi record. Inevitably, schools came under similar pressures. By 1936, some 32 per cent of Germany's school teachers were members of the NSDAP. But by far the highest percentage proportionally was achieved by the medical profession, of which 45 per cent joined, and not merely because they expected greater material benefits from the Nazis. The seizure of power rather 'signified for the doctors also the restitution of social differences, the redefinition of lost power positions in their relationship with patients, greater room for political manoeuvre near the power centre without the detour of parliamentarism' (W. Wuttke-Groneberg). The editor of the *Deutsche Ärzteblatt* formulated accurately the resentments and hopes of this particular elite group. The Weimar 'party state', he complained, had never 'given the doctor what is his due'. But now 'the times of dishonour and corruption are over'. No one would be allowed to trample under foot again 'the patriotic virtues' of the people and the 'ethical values which are sacred to the German nation'.

Hitler's voters therefore welcomed the formation of this government, and with high expectations. He knew well that scoring successes was vital for the stability of his regime. And successes he scored in subsequent years – in his own way and, as we shall see, with astonishing recklessness. What we shall have to look at first, though, is how policies which deliberately and inevitably were to lead to war were put across to the population and how they were received. For it is important to remember that the Third Reich was not merely a dictatorship reliant on police terror and fear. From the early beginnings, the Nazis had also discovered the power of propaganda and agitation and had had more than a decade to experiment with techniques of mass communication. Prior to 1933, the appeal to resentments harboured against the existing order had formed a major plank of their campaigns against the Weimar Republic. These campaigns against the alleged destroyers of Germany – Jews, Republicans, Social Democrats, Communists and the Western Allies – continued after the seizure of power, if only in order to justify the violence and aggression which was unleashed after January 1933. However, it was clear that the regime could not rely on extolling its *tabula rasa* 'achievements' alone. It was in order to help advertise the 'constructive' work of the new government that the Ministry of Popular Enlightenment and Propaganda was created in March 1933. Joseph Goebbels, one of the most cunning manipulators of facts and opinions and a major figure behind the mobilisation of voters for the Nazi cause, was given this ministerial post. He started off with a relatively small staff of 350 people, which almost trebled by 1939. At the same time, other government departments and Party agencies expanded their own press and propaganda apparatuses. Thus the propaganda unit at the NSDAP's head-quarters in Munich had about 14,000 people on its pay-roll by 1934.

Once the press, the broadcasting services and the film companies of the Weimar period had been 'synchronised', the regime provided a more or less uniform interpretation of its objectives and of what had allegedly been achieved. The annual Nuremberg Party rallies must also be seen in this context as a major device not merely to unite the faithful, but also to publicise the irresistible and 'constructive' dynamic of the movement. Walter Benjamin and others have seen in the bombastic self-representation of Nazism, particularly at huge circus-like rallies with endless marching columns, floodlight displays, torch-parades and rabble-rousing speeches, another key feature of fascism. These displays gave the participants a feeling of involvement and elation which was proffered as a substitute for democratic participation; but all this was no more than an elaborate façade, erected to conceal an authoritarian power structure which effectively disfranchised the so-called masses. And indeed there is also no doubt that Hitler and his chief propagandists, for all their ideological dogmatism, took a totally cynical view of their techniques. As an American critic put it in the mid-1930s, in discussing their attitudes towards their audiences: 'According to the Nazis, the mass of the people are dumb. They are unintelligent, childlike and inarticulate. They will accept without serious question whatever they hear or are told. They believe everything they read. They do not bother to think; they feel. Their lives are not pivoted on logic, but on emotion.'

Although there is some truth in Kurt Schumacher's dictum of February 1932 that Nazism, 'for the first time in German politics achieved the complete mobilisation of the politically dumb', Richard Bessel has rightly wondered whether the Nazi views of the mass of the population represented 'an accurate description of political behaviour'. Thus, while many people were doubtless hypnotised by the splendid façade which the propaganda machine erected, the question arises how far people could be deluded if the day-to-day reality of their lives conflicted too sharply with Goebbels's slogans. An examination of the development of the economy and social structure under the Third Reich might help to elucidate this problem.

Economic conditions and mobilisation for war

Apart from proclaiming an active struggle against the 'injustices of Versailles' and, somewhat incongruously perhaps, protesting its entirely peaceful intentions, the new Hitler government promised a major attack on unemployment. This attack was very successful, and although any historical analysis of the gradual bottoming out of the Great Slump in 1933/4 would have to take many other factors into consideration, Nazi propaganda almost exclusively credited the 'Führer' with the reduction of unemployment. When he came to power, some 6.04 million people and possibly even more were on the dole. Twelve months later the figure had dropped to 3.7 million, followed by further reductions to 2.5 million (January 1936), 1.8 million (January 1937), 1.05 million (January 1938) and 300,000 (January 1939) (Table 18). For all practical purposes full employment had been achieved by the summer of 1937, and by 1939 there developed an acute shortage of labour, with a mere 34,000 people out of work in the summer of 1939 and industry desperately looking for no less than one million workers. In short, by the late 1930s, German industry was booming and the majority of the population was benefiting from it; but not equally, as a few further figures will demonstrate.

Although Nazi propaganda made a major effort to convince the workers that they were the real beneficiaries of the boom, their main gain was to be provided, albeit slowly, with regular employment and, as far as the skilled labour force in heavy and manufacturing industry was concerned, a slight rise in their living standards. However, they had to pay for this not merely with the loss of their rights to organise and bargain, but also with harder work and longer hours (Table 31). One factor that eroded rising nominal wages was inflation. Owing to the growing shortage of labour, but above all because of the emphasis on capital goods and armaments production (and the way these were financed), the Nazi economy soon developed inflationary tendencies. In an attempt to curb these dangerous developments, the government imposed pay and price controls. When workers tried to beat these restrictions by changing jobs, the regime intervened to curtail their freedom of movement. After the political emasculation of the working class there followed its economic regimentation.

In view of these complicating factors, it is not easy to pick one's way through the maze of statistics. The figures show that the index for weekly nominal wages, while starting at a lower point on the scale, saw a faster rise than hourly wages. As the minimum wage per hour for skilled as well as unskilled workers remained legally fixed at virtually the same amount between 1933 and 1938, the main way of achieving a higher income was to work longer hours. And indeed, the average weekly working time increased from 42.9 hours in 1933 to 47.0 hours in the first half of 1939 (Table 31). However, the weekly wage packet has to be set in relation to the cost-of-living index. Taking the official figures, real wages, calculated on the basis of the cost-of-living index, rose from 91 points in 1933 to 97 in 1936 and to 101 in 1937 (Table 25). In other words, it was only in 1938 that real wages were once more slightly above what they had been in 1929. The rewards for harder work would seem to be even less impressive if the above-average rate of inflation for food and clothing is considered. As half the weekly budget of a working-class household was spent on these items, a rise from 113.5 points (1933) to 122.8 (1939) for food and from 106.7 (1933) to 133.3 (1939) for clothing was very tangible for low-income families. Worse, there is strong evidence that the cost-of-living figures were deliberately rigged by the authorities and were about 6–7 per cent higher in 1935/6 than the statistics suggested. If this assumption is correct, real wages were trailing behind the official figure for 1935/6 by 2 points.

A further indication of material pressures influencing the economic behaviour of the industrial workforce is that women began to go back into the factories. As in other industrialised countries, the number of female labourers had grown in the 1920s until they, too, became victims of the Great Slump. On the other hand, as in other industrial societies, millions of women continued to work, and in some branches of the economy their contribution was absolutely indispensable. At the end of the Weimar period, one-third of the total labour force was female. On coming to power, the Nazis launched a major campaign to keep women at home or to induce them to give up work. Incentives were offered, partly in order to reduce the overloading of the job market, partly in order to implement Nazi ideas on family policy. The place of the woman was said to be not in the political and economic life of the nation, but in the home. Their 'natural' task was to bear and rear children to propagate and strengthen the 'Aryan race'.

A more detailed study of how the female half of the population was seen by Nazi ideology and the position which was to be accorded to women in the future society would tell us a good deal about how Hitler and his supporters were hoping to 'reorder' Germany and later the whole of Europe. It is also clear that the notion of the 'Beautiful Woman' who looked after her husband and children exerted a considerable influence on young girls and members of Nazi women's organisations, among whom most of the activists were middle class. Indeed various other associations had propagandised similar ideas about women and the family, albeit less candidly, until they were 'synchronised' in 1933. In particular, the BDF of Wilhelmine days had continued its drift towards the Right throughout the Weimar period. Comprising more than 750,000 members, it had campaigned against the laxity of morals and Republican politics in general. However, the experience of Weimar appears to have contributed in yet another and contradictory way to a preparedness on the part of many women to heed the Nazi call. The 1920s had seen a great expansion of the female workforce. In 1925, one in three women was employed, 35 per cent more than in 1907. The Revolution of 1918 and the Weimar Constitution had also given women the vote and declared that 'men and women have basically the same rights and duties'. Under Article 128, Civil Service positions were theoretically open to women. In practice, however, little was done to bring legal codes and policies into line with the Constitution. All parties, with the exception of KPD and SPD, remained wedded to the status quo.

This meant that increased female employment had little to do with a change in the role and position of women in society. To begin with, more than two-thirds of all married working women and over a third of all female employees were helping, without pay, on farms and in family businesses. Most of the remaining workforce were either manual workers, domestic servants or white-collar employees in industry, commerce, medical and public services, including teaching. Many of these jobs were boring and poorly paid. Prospects for promotion to positions of responsibility remained slim. Since most working women were unmarried, employment was not seen as a career, but as a stage between leaving school and marriage. Seen against the background of these experiences and of the Great Depression, being a housewife in Nazi Germany did not seem all that objectionable to many women. The economic realities of life in low-income groups, on the other hand, left a sizeable section of the female population with little time to ponder the virtues of Nazi family ideals. Although wages continued to be between 30 and 35 per cent below the rates for their male counterparts, women began to return to the factories in larger numbers from the mid-1930s, thus supplementing family income. By 1939, the available reserve of volunteers had been exhausted (Table 32).

Meanwhile workers were pressed to enter the German Labour Front (DAF), a Nazi-directed trade union ersatz founded in May 1933 and led by Robert Ley. The DAF became an important barometer of shop-floor feeling as its appointed representatives tried to monitor attitudes. They often found the workforce lacking the enthusiasm and support for the Third Reich which Hitler expected of a working class for whom he was allegedly doing so much. As to fundamental policy issues such as wage and price levels, taxation and production priorities, the influence of the DAF on top-level policy-making was, however, quite limited. Decisions on such matters tended to be guided by higher priorities which will be discussed in a moment. What Ley could do was to push for improvements elsewhere in the factory to provide compensations and to help boost the regime's popularity by means of noisily advertised recreational schemes.

Thus at the end of 1933, the DAF built up an organisation which was first named 'After Work', but soon given the more characteristic title 'Strength Through Joy' (KdF). As we have seen, the German working-class movement had been very active in the field of culture and sports before 1933. With the destruction of these associations by the Nazis, there existed an obvious need to try to organise the leisure activities of the 'masses', this time on a state-controlled basis. However, the KdF was also conceived as a means of winning over the working population by being seen to be doing something tangible for it. Accordingly, the DAF arranged KdF visits to concerts, theatres, films and exhibitions or organised courses in gymnastics, games and athletics. It also sponsored hikes and vacation schemes, cruises and day trips in which over nine million people participated in 1938. The DAF/KdF furthermore proclaimed the 'Beauty of Labour' scheme. It was used to exert pressure on employers to improve the work environment and the recreational facilities in their factories. Buildings were inspected and suggestions made for the provision of better ventilation, washing facilities, canteens and sports grounds. KdF enjoyed considerable popularity and, as far as can be gauged, did make an impact. Yet frills must not be confused with more far-reaching purposes. In effect, apart from surveillance, DAF work and its glorification

141

by the Nazi propaganda machine had the specific function of stabilising a precariously balanced political system and of gearing the economy of the country to a war of expansion and exploitation.

It was not easy for the average person to see through the complexities of the economic situation, and many were taken in by Goebbels. This is particularly true of those who on the whole did better under Hitler than the industrial labour force. Among them were the white-collar employees whose real monthly salary index climbed from 127.6 points in 1933 to 137.7 in 1936 and 158.3 in 1939. Investors also saw their fortunes rise again. The share index improved from 41 points in 1932 to 82 points in 1939, with dividends also moving up from an average of 2.83 per cent at the end of 1932 to 6.40 per cent at the end of 1938 (Tables 20 and 21). The beneficial effects of these figures are reflected in the overall growth of the income of the self-employed. Although unevenly distributed, it increased on average from 2,500 marks in 1933 to 5,750 marks in 1939, compared to 1,520 marks in 1933 and 2,260 marks in 1939 for employees. Since, as we have seen, industrial workers did not participate in this prosperity anywhere near proportionally, it would seem that other social groups made handsome gains from the boom of German industry. It was these groups which were also more prone to succumb to Goebbels's assertion that the government was tremendously successful. Of course, their ideological predilections merely reinforced their view of events in the 1930s. For working-class groups, on the other hand, there was a sufficiently large gap between their own day-to-day experiences and what was said by the Nazis for them to remain sceptical and in many cases even to become alienated from the regime. Nor did their pre-1933 ideological conditioning easily absorb the clap-trap about the Germanic folk community and the importance of looking at the course of world history in racial terms. To them, class continued to be a more plausible concept than race for interpreting the structure and reality of the Third Reich.

Brief mention must finally be made of the farming community which found itself in a peculiar position in the 1930s. At least the Protestants among the farmers had been among the first to flock to the Nazis who had promised economic help and had buttressed their agricultural programme by a mythical blood-and-soil ideology. Theoreticians like R. Walther Darré had celebrated in his writings the great role of those who tilled the land and assigned to them a central position in the future 'Aryan' racial community. All this had been very encouraging for the farmers and had bolstered their faltering self-esteem. Yet soon after the introduction of the Reich Inherited Farm Law in September 1933, if not before, they were to discover the double-edgedness of Nazi agrarian ideology. This law, while giving protection against foreclosure, drastically restricted the small farmer's ability to dispose of his property or to distribute it among his heirs. It also adversely affected his ability to obtain credit. Soon

Darré's Reich Food Estate was imposing new quality tests and intervening in the marketing of agricultural produce. Consequently, although Darré managed to get some price increases approved, dissatisfaction was growing, exacerbated by the fact that initial expectations had been particularly high in this section of the population (Tables 6 and 19). The farmers' predicament was further worsened by the large-scale drift of male rural labourers into the cities when after 1936 industry began to cry out for workers. Within a short period, some 400,000 of them disappeared, and the resulting acute shortages – which not only made the maintenance of the farms more difficult, but also increased pressure for higher wage rates – were the last straw (Tables 3 and 15). By the late 1930s, the population was in a rebellious mood in some parts of the Reich as production and income declined.

The fate of the farming community also shows that it is wise to differentiate between the blood-and-soil ideology of Nazism which promised enhanced prestige and social status to some groups and the social change that actually occurred after 1933. This caveat applies equally to other groups lower down the social scale whose position was supposed to be upvalued in that much-vaunted folk community of all Germans, as the small retailers and many craftsmen found to their dismay. However, we have already seen with reference to the Wilhelmine period that rapid economic growth and technological change do not necessarily result in an increased upward social mobility. Similar considerations are raised by the case of Nazi Germany. The process of industrialisation continued in this period, as is evidenced by the further growth of production units (Table 17), the use of rationalisation techniques and improved technology or the mobilisation methods of the labour market, and the effect on the Old *Mittelstand* remained the same as before. The 'revolution' of the socioeconomic structure which is supposed to have accompanied the establishment of Nazism, on the other hand, is to be viewed with caution.

To begin with, the industrial working class had made little direct contribution to the rise of the NSDAP, and Hitler's seizure of power did little to increase *inter*-class mobility. He was, after all, not a spokesman for that section of the population. The persecution of the Left which led to most working-class leaders being put into camps or driven into exile is one aspect of this. Inasmuch as the Great Depression had caused a proletarianisation of the middle classes and the petty bourgeoisie in particular (to which these groups had responded with a turn to the extreme *Right*), the emergence of Hitler's coalition government in January 1933 was likely to lead to attempts to widen once again the social distance between the working class and the social groups above it. The example of the medical profession certainly indicates that these were the hopes of many doctors when they greeted the *Machtergreifung*. Quite a few of those who scampered after Party membership and honorary positions

143

therefore did so in the expectation of arresting those 'levelling' tendencies which they associated with the 'socialist' Republic of Weimar, and doctors were merely one group among them. Not all groups, it is true, saw their expectations fulfilled as far as their income was concerned. Thus not only farmers, but also civil servants had a hard time. On the other hand, there are non-income aspects to stratification and in this respect the regime, its *Volksgemeinschaft* propaganda notwithstanding, revived traditional hierarchies.

By contrast, the advent of Hitler appears to have brought with it some *intra*-class mobility. A fairly large number of Old Fighters of lower-middle-class background succeeded in moving upwards as members of the new Party and administrative elite. However, much of this mobility was produced – and no doubt deliberately so – by the political purges of 1933 and the gaps created by anti-Semitic discrimination. Yet the tensions and arguments which soon arose between Party functionaries and the traditional bureaucracy also point to the limits of this upward movement. Thus it did not take the Civil Service long to try to build up barriers against 'unqualified' Nazis who were pushing hard to establish themselves in the higher echelons of the bureaucracy. The best researched example of the limits to social mobility in the Third Reich is the case of the SA. Among the many Nazi organisations it was probably the one with the largest petty bourgeois element. Its members had been useful in the spring of 1933 when they had 'sorted out' the Left. But soon Röhm's men began to talk about a 'Second Revolution' in which the existing social structure would be genuinely ploughed up. Furthermore, Röhm began to challenge the position of the conservative officer corps and the Army as the sole bearer of arms when he put forward a militia model of Germany's military power in which his men were to be the key factor. Although he may never have intended this, Röhm's radical language about removing the 'reactionaries' worried not merely the professional military, but also appeared to threaten Hitler's leadership and the wisdom of his policies. At a meeting with the *Reichsstatthalter* at the end of September 1933 the 'Führer' had argued for a need to scale back the revolutionary tendencies in the Party in order to achieve greater administrative stability. By the spring of 1934 the generals had become so concerned about Röhm's aim to undermine the Army's arms monopoly and generally to radicalise the regime that they coalesced with Hitler. With their help, the SA was emasculated in the bloody purge of 30 June 1934. The danger of a 'Second Revolution' whether imagined or real, had been removed.

Among the elite groups which succeeded best in keeping men of the 'wrong' background at bay were the managers of German industry; the high degree of self-recruitment from the upper middle class which had been the traditional pattern in industry barely changed, if compared with earlier periods. But even the SS, which claimed to epitomise a new Nazi elite, did not live up to its image, if looked at in sociological terms. As quantitative analyses of the SS leadership corps have shown, Himmler increasingly came to rely on members of the educated middle classes. Significantly enough, the promotions policy which was deliberately adopted at the suggestion of Reinhard Heydrich, son of the founder of the First Hallean Conservatorium of Music and an ex-naval officer, created a good deal of resentment among the Old Fighters of humble background who were left behind.

Sociologically speaking the overall effect of the Hitler regime after 1933 was therefore to generate some initial mobility within the broad confines of the middle class, which slowed down once the impact of the political upheaval of the spring of 1933 had subsided. Nevertheless, the reverberations of lower-middle-class ambitions after the Great Depression and the appearance of a Nazi 'elite' bursting into the established state apparatus were sufficiently serious to create tensions and rivalries. They expressed themselves in political terms in tough infighting, the extent of which has amazed those who thought the Third Reich to have been a tightly run 'Führer' State. What exacerbated the huge power struggles behind this monolithic façade were the coalition character of the Hitler government in its early stages and the attitudes which the Nazi leadership had developed towards the wielding of political power before 1933.

Although claiming to be governed by the autocratic 'Führer' principle, the NSDAP of the 1920s had seen a great deal of jockeying for influential positions within the Party hierarchy. Repeatedly, Hitler had to intervene in disputes between his sub-leaders, all of whom regarded themselves as 'little Führer', with their own autonomous powers and competences and surrounded by an entourage of loyal retainers. To some extent, the rights and privileges which they constantly arrogated to themselves or their underlings, only to find them disputed by other functionaries, were a reflection of the Social Darwinist world view of the Nazi movement. If life was said to be a lethal struggle for survival between races, nations or individuals, it was not surprising that the leading propagandists of these ideas should also practise them within their own realms. Even the 'Führer' and final arbiter Hitler was not exempt from criticism and challenges to his authority, no matter how hard Nazi propaganda tried to erect a myth of genius and infallibility around him.

As might be expected, the bickerings and wrangles over competences did not stop in 1933. Rather they became worse when the Nazi 'elite' suddenly got a taste of real power, but, apart from old rivals in the Party, had to contend with the traditional Civil Service, the officer corps, industrialists and other established groups. As was seen in the previous chapter, Hitler and his supporters did not come to power as the sole dictators of Germany but as a result of a precarious and elaborate compromise. While the belief that Hitler had been effectively 'boxed in' turned out to be a gross underestimation of the dynamism of the Nazi movement in the long run, for the moment the 'Führer' remained dependent on the support and co-operation of the conservative elites of Germany. Not all of them may have been as keen to get Hitler nominated to the Chancellorship as Papen and his associates had been; but once Hindenburg had somewhat totteringly made his decision they signalled their willingness to join in. This certainly applied to the captains of industry who wanted political action against the economic crisis and who needed the thrust and popular base of Hitler just as much as he needed them, if he was to implement his pledge to resolve the unemployment problem. For the industrialists, job creation meant getting production going again, preferably unhampered by the complicating factor of free trade unions and the political power of working-class parties. Hostility against unionisation among the bulk of Germany's entrepreneurs and managers had been profound and long standing. When Hitler began his clamp-down against the organised working class he therefore met with little objection and much approval. Once the industrial relations sphere had been cleared by violent means, concentration on production would be markedly easier.

One way of measuring the extent to which industrial production revived is to look at the decline of unemployment figures again. Another gauge is the index of industrial production (Table 7) which, by comparison with its 1928 base line of 100 points, rose as follows between 1933 and 1939:

1933	1934	1935	1936	1937	1938	1939
66	83	96	107	117	125	132

This impressive increase was facilitated by the State which, under the guidance of Hjalmar Schacht, banker and financial wizard, made massive credits available on easiest terms. Yet the hectic economic activity of the 1930s immediately raises the question of what kind of goods were being produced and who, if only a smaller portion of the credit was given by private investors, would pay for the huge debts incurred by the State.

On the first point, economic historians assumed for a long time that the initial boom was largely in goods for civilian use and that the switch to a fully fledged rearmament programme came only in the mid-1930s. However, more recent research has shown that Germany experienced an armaments-led boom from the start of 1933 and that the country's economic policy had little to do with Keynesianism and demand management. In fact, while Keynes's arguments were discussed among German experts in the mid-1930s, it is typical that they were rejected as inapplicable to the German case.

The alternative strategy to be followed had been outlined by Hitler before his ministers as early as 8 February 1933 when he linked the need to reduce unemployment directly with the need to rearm rather than to produce consumer goods. He added that the entire transport network would have to be put in order and expanded. Moreover, one would also have to develop the material and technological underpinnings upon which the proposed increase in military strength was to be based. It is against the background of these remarks that the Nazi building programme of the 1930s has to be viewed, among which the construction of the motorway network was the most conspicuous measure. As a job creation scheme, the autobahns were, however, much less significant than propaganda made out. Much more important was that the armed forces began to place orders for military equipment with those 2,800 firms which they had identified as *Rüstungs-betriebe*. The advantage of this system from the regime's point of view was that the purpose of this production could be camouflaged at a time when Hitler was anxious to appear as a Chancellor of peace, both at home and abroad. The trick worked fairly well.

Thus it happened that the *Auto-Union* motor manufacturers produced lorries which were in fact military vehicles. Krupp's 'agricultural tractor programme' was the initial code name for the production of tanks, banned under the Versailles Treaty, but started in July 1933. The explosives manufacturers *Pulverfabrik Rheinsdorf* increased its workforce from 2,000 to 5,200 in the first half of 1933. Meanwhile the Navy began to order 70 million marks' worth of new ships. By 1934, 840 of the 1,968 aeroplanes produced were for military purposes, also prohibited by the Versailles Peace Settlement.

The emphasis on the production of capital goods and heavy machinery led to an enormous demand for raw materials and precipitated a first shortage in 1934. It could only be solved if priorities were laid down for the allocation of raw materials, and the choice was between the continued manufacture of military equipment and a major shift towards the provision of consumer goods. In the event, the former solution was adopted, accompanied by stricter controls on foreign trade and foreign exchange without which vital raw materials could not be purchased abroad. There was a drive to increase German exports in order to earn more foreign currency. Yet with the German armed forces being a keen and regular customer, there was really not much that industry was able to offer to its traditional trading partners in the developed world (Table 49). Furthermore, the Third Reich's anti-Semitic policies which fuelled anti-German sentiments in other Western countries merely worsened an already tense international position.

In the long run, these developments strengthened the hand of those Nazi economists and German industrialists who had been arguing against the re-establishment of a multilateral world trading network and thought in terms of a large autarkic and German-dominated bloc. For the moment, the crisis pushed Germany in the direction of establishing bilateral and exclusivist trading links with less industrialised countries as purveyors of raw materials on a barter basis. Apart from Scandinavia, South-eastern Europe became a major area of German commercial activity. Finally the crisis resulted in the scouring of the German countryside for raw materials. Plans were drawn up to extract and smelt iron ore even at costs which were commercially totally unviable. The Salzgitter steel-making complex eventually became the most ambitious project to use low grade iron ore and to boost German steel output regardless of financial losses. At the same time experiments by the chemical industry were stepped up to develop synthetic rubber and to refine petrol from coal, the only raw material which the Third Reich had in large quantities.

But whatever was being done to help armaments production, industry's appetite for raw materials could not be satisfied. Stocks were running dangerously low; the fulfilment of targets was being threatened. A new and comprehensive plan had to be devised. It took the shape of the Four Year Plan of 1936, whose intricacies can be ignored here. What is more important is that it fixed both the ultimate objective of all this hectic rearmament activity, namely a war in four years' time, and pointed to the inexorability of national bankruptcy unless the military expenditure of the 1930s was recouped in such a war. It was clear that the debts which the government had incurred when ordering weapons and increasing the size of the armed forces would one day have to be paid. Raising a large part of the money by imposing higher taxes would have been, theoretically at least, one possibility. But an austerity programme of this kind would have cost Hitler what popularity he had gained.

We have seen that the main benefit of the armaments boom to the mass of the industrial workers had been to give them their jobs back. For quite a few of them this was already an achievement in itself and they were hence prepared to credit the man who was supposed to be responsible for this feat. But many other workers did not share such feelings of gratitude. They may have regained their jobs, but otherwise they had been able to participate in the economic upswing primarily by working longer hours. Nor was it encouraging that increased production had not resulted in the more plentiful availability of consumer goods. Most of the increased productivity had gone into guns and tanks which, even if there had been a demand for them, were not to be bought in shops. In a sense, the manufacturing priorities of the regime were already imposing a mild austerity programme on the country. Realising this and the damaging political effects it had on the stability of his government, Hitler was therefore loath to depress living standards further. Higher taxes were hence also out of the question. In short, there were social limits to both the speed and size of his rearmament programme and to his ability to recoup the public debts incurred. Even if he had wanted to rearm in depth, the stability problems of the Nazi regime induced the 'Führer' to acquire a military machine which was capable of no more than short lightning wars. The same stability problems, reinforced by his Social Darwinist view of international relations, also led him to a solution of his financial dilemma which was breathtakingly simple: the

Wehrmacht was to force the Reich's neighbours to foot the rearmament bill.

Looking back on his economic policies of the 1930s, Hitler made the following observation to his entourage on 25 March 1943:

Since the reintroduction of conscription, our armaments have swallowed fantastic sums which are still completely uncovered. There are only two ways: either these debts will be put on the shoulders of the *Volksgenossen* in the Reich in the shape of taxes or they will be paid for by the potential profits from the occupied eastern territories. The latter ought to be self-evident.

The rearmament programme which was begun in 1933 amounted therefore to nothing less than a deliberate unhinging of the national economy with the intention of recovering the financial losses by exploiting other national economies of Europe within the confines of a German-dominated empire conquered by force (Tables 35 and 36). The creation of jobs was merely a by-product of these reckless economic policies. The wars of expansion and looting which began in 1939, on the other hand, were the main purpose and had a certain inevitability about them.

Nazi foreign policy and war aims

This is not to minimise the fact that Hitler also always wanted these wars and considered them 'necessary' for reasons which set him on to his rearmament programme in the first place. These considerations stemmed from his ideas on human history which viewed the world in terms of an age-old struggle between the races for living space. Up to the twentieth century, the evolutionary process of history had seen the coming and going of great empires. In the twentieth century itself, this process would reach its culmination point in the struggle of the 'Aryans', with the Jews as their most dangerous enemies, either to establish themselves as the dominant race and to secure their dominance permanently or to perish. Of course, led by a determined 'Führer' (who saw these alternatives so clearly) and well-prepared militarily for the great conflict, the Germans were assumed to be in a good position to give permanency to their empire. It was to be secured by virtue of their racial superiority, upheld by careful breeding, biological isolation from the 'inferior races' and the brutal exploitation of the latter.

However inhuman and fantastic this utopia may appear to us today, it had a certain consistency to it, if viewed in terms of its own inner logic. This is particularly true of its power-political aspects. For in attempting to establish this Germanic empire, Hitler always knew that he would sooner or later and step by step find himself locked in military conflict with all other major powers. They would be bound to try to resist the overthrow of the international status quo and the proposed reordering of the map. There is now a striking congruity between Hitler's assessment of the problems posed by this international hostility and the conclusions which various conservative circles had come to during and after the First World War. Just as they had argued that the mistake of Wilhelmine foreign policy had been to take on too many great powers at a time, Hitler voiced similar criticisms of the Kaiser in his *Mein Kampf* and, like other revisionists, formulated a lesson to be learned from the Wilhelmine experience: Germany's next bid for empire had to be made successively and less impatiently. Accordingly, the 'Führer's' major writings and speeches on foreign policy time and again reveal an expansionist 'programme' to be achieved in two stages. The first stage was to involve the establishment of a German power position on the European continent stretching far to the east and including the vast agricultural areas of Russia for food production and the provision of raw materials. A further advantage of an eastward move was that it would enable him to stamp out Bolshevism and conquer Moscow, one of the putative citadels of 'world Jewry'.

If Hitler's imperialism thus coincided neatly with his racism, he also believed that he could not succeed with the acquisition of 'living space' if he found himself, like the Kaiser, engaged in a simultaneous conflict with the Western powers, above all Britain and the United States. For only after Germany's continental position had been broadened and consolidated would she be strong enough to face the sea powers. It remains a disputed question as to whether the second stage of his 'programme', involving a further deliberate attack on Britain and the United States, was already firmly built into Hitler's foreign policy design or whether the later global struggle for domination would be the culmination of an inexorable drift into a confrontation between a German-dominated European bloc and the Anglo-Saxon powers. The important point is that the assumption of eventual conflict with the United States was part and parcel of the 'Führer's' pre-1933 visions of the power politics of the future. The other point to bear in mind is that he was decidedly not a politician who was prepared to abandon basic beliefs once he was in power. His conservative partners of 1933 succumbed to this fallacy when they thought that giving Hitler government responsibility would force him to abandon his dogmatism and extremism. It was also the misconception of the 'appeasers' in Britain and elsewhere who believed that they were dealing with a conventional politician who was 'reasonable' and prepared to accept as permanent international settlements negotiated on the basis of compromise. Hitler, it is true, was prepared to be opportunist, but always in a cynical fashion and only for as long as compromise did not interfere with what he saw as the long-term necessities and inevitabilities of policies derived from his Social Darwinist and racist world view.

In view of this, the Nazi seizure of power did not only have, as we have already demonstrated, far-reaching implications for the country's domestic development, but also for its foreign policy. Inevitably there has been much research into this question and it appears that, if one cuts through the tangle of diplomatic minutiae to be found in the files, a pattern becomes discernible which tallies with Hitler's writings of the 1920s. Throughout the 1930s, he kept his eyes firmly fixed on the acquisition of 'living space' in the east, while trying to woo Britain into an alliance on the basis of a simple tit-for-tat: London was to acquiesce in Germany's violent expansion on the European continent in return for the Third Reich's co-operation in maintaining the British imperial position overseas. By 1937 it became clear that Britain was not prepared to make a deal with Germany on these terms. Yet this did not cause Hitler to abandon his European plans. Rather he began to pursue them without British approval. And when in 1939 he found himself, much against his will, embroiled in a war against Britain and hence in a conflict of Wilhelmine dimensions, he manoeuvred long to get out of it again.

This impression of a basic pattern underlying Hitler's diplomacy is re-inforced by changes in the German rearmament programme which was in itself a manifestation of his dogmatic approach to politics. If a German continental position was to be established as a first priority, it made sense to build up the land forces. However, in November 1937, the 'Führer' made a speech before his top military and political advisers of which a summary has survived, written by one of the participants, Colonel Friedrich Hossbach. According to this 'Protocol' Hitler, to begin with, identified two stages of military conflict, first on the continent and later with the Western powers. But largely because of the 'Führer's' revised assessment of British policy which had rejected his alliance overtures, the historical time-scale had become compressed. He now took the view that continental expansion would have to be completed by 1943/5 without British acquiescence and probably even in the face of British opposition. This meant that the Third Reich would, from that date onwards, have to be prepared for conflict in the West which required adequate naval forces. That this speech was not just idle talk is corroborated by the fact that detailed preparations for the construction of a *Weltmachtflotte* were initiated in 1938. A shift in rearmament priorities took place.

What has complicated the task of retrieving these basic outlines of Nazi foreign policy from the documents was not merely that Hitler received conflicting advice at every point of decision throughout the 1930s, but more importantly that there existed alternative concepts which were promoted by representatives of other power centres inside the regime. The most important option among them was propounded by Schacht and Hugenberg, but also by Joachim von Ribbentrop from inside the NSDAP and by the naval officer corps. They all cared little for the agricultural areas of Eastern Europe and looked towards colonies and markets for German industry. Unavoidably their strategy was distinctly more anti-British than Hitler's; worse, they were not prepared to hide this. Contemporary foreign observers were, not surprisingly, confused by these divergent tendencies. Certainly, if the two options were conflated, Nazi foreign policy appeared to be no more than a re-run of the Kaiser's. Moreover, it was difficult to know who was in day-to-day control of German diplomacy: the 'Führer' or the host of other people who made speeches on foreign policy issues?

The force of this question has been strengthened in recent years by work on the peculiarities of the internal power structure of the Nazi dictatorship. It was a system which was racked by fierce struggles and an extensive 'office Darwinism' (R. Bollmus) at all levels of government. Some historians have therefore come to believe that 'chaos' was the key feature of the regime: there were no consistent policies or programmes. Not even Hitler knew where he was going. He found it difficult to make decisions, constantly vacillated between different factions and was prone to side with the stronger battalions. E.N. Peterson has even gone so far as to call him 'a man who does not decide'. The implications of this view are not too difficult to discern. The regime is seen as a highly labile system which was constantly in danger of collapse under its own internal contradictions. However, the supporters of this view have been less interested in the possible deeper socioeconomic *roots* of the infighting over policies than they have been in the *consequences* of this political instability. To them it would seem to explain the truly breathtaking dynamic of the Nazi dictatorship. They see it as a badly listing and leaky racing boat, riddled with holes, which could be kept afloat only if its many captains increased the speed with which it zig-zagged towards ever more extreme objectives.

There is a good deal of plausibility in this interpretation of German fascism and its incomparable radicalism. Nevertheless, this should not lead us to underestimate another important source of its dynamism. Throughout the 1930s and early 1940s the regime was also kept going by the collaborative effort of those who believed themselves to be part of a gigantic enterprise of building an allegedly 'greater' and 'better' Germany. Many of them belonged to the political, military, economic and academic elites of the country and, whereas they may not have been fanatical Old Fighters, they nonetheless approved of Hitler's 'achievements' and were prepared to push on. This is particularly true of their views on the need for an anti-democratic order and discipline at home and for a greatly expanded power base abroad. The terms and parameters of these plans and expectations varied and, indeed, even power-political alternatives continued to be advocated. Yet gradually some proposals for the solution of the Reich's problems, as perceived by other Nazis *and* non-Nazis of power and influence, asserted themselves over others and these were usually the strategies which harmonised most closely with Hitler's. To call the Third Reich a chaotic political system therefore misses this central point.

An illustration of this is provided by an examination of the policies and attitudes of the entrepreneurial and managerial elites who, after all, had a major share in generating the boom of the Nazi economy and in supplying the Wehrmacht with tanks, ships and planes. It was not merely that the representatives of the powerful and all-important heavy industries 'very quickly and without any qualms established a business relationship' with the Nazis and that 'for a long time they did not fare badly' (D. Petzina). In the event, good business prospects and ideological affinities went hand in hand. Some industrialists like Bosch, who had hoped to build good industrial relations in co-operation with the trade unions, felt very uneasy about the destruction of the trade unions. But he found himself in a minority *vis-à-vis* the *Herr-im-Hause* hardliners who were quite happy to witness the proscription of the working-class movement.

There were also some industrialists who believed that even after the shock of the Great Slump and the economic nationalism it produced Germany's place was among the other industrial nations in a multilateral trading network and open world market. Yet they found themselves outmanoeuvred by those who favoured the establishment of an autarkic bloc on the European continent, a *Grossraumwirtschaft* to be taken out of the world economy. They were the same men who promoted the further cartellisation of the domestic market into a highly ordered system of production and regimented marketing which they also presumed to be sufficiently superior to Anglo-Saxon models of market organisation to be worth extending on a *Grossraum* basis. It is true that the congruity of aims between Hitler and his conservative allies was not total. For the 'Führer', the idea of 'living space' always had racist connotations, whereas the advocates of *Grossraumwirtschaft* in industry were more inclined to view a future German empire as an economic proposition and scoffed at the blood-and-soil dreams of Darré and Himmler.

The same may be said about the Wehrmacht elites, who tended to perceive the country's international position in power-political and military terms. Like the dynamic men of industry, they had little time for the Party's more extreme *völkische* ideas. Nevertheless, just as the dominant branches of German industry rejected, with Hitler, the notion of helping to rebuild the international economic structure which had been shattered in the early 1930s, the German generals and admirals turned against the concept of international political co-operation and the pacific settlement of disputes outside or within the League of Nations. Up to 1932, Weimar's military policy had still been based on the premise of international negotiation, in the same way as Stresemann had worked to reintegrate the German industrial system into the world economy and thereby to regain the country's influence as a major power. It was in this spirit that Groener had participated in the efforts to limit armaments.

The balance between the forces around Stresemann and the outright opponents of their efforts had always remained delicate, however. Just as Stresemann's international economic policies, in particular his reparations plans, had been viewed with scepticism by heavy industry, powerful sections of the officer corps continued to follow the disarmament negotiations with suspicion and disdain. In fact any co-operation within the framework of the League of Nations was incompatible with their long-nourished hardline revisionism. Hitler, that ruthless civilian revisionist who was also dreaming of establishing Germany's world power position, if necessary by force, therefore did not have to worry about the Reichswehr too much when pulling Germany out of the Lausanne Disarmament Conference and the League of Nations in October 1933. The rejection of *multilateral disarmament* by the officer corps was merely the reverse side of the simultaneous decision of 1933 to go for *unilateral rearmament*. The greatly strengthened Wehrmacht was to be the lever with which the Versailles order could be unhinged and an imperial position be regained. Although there existed divergent conceptions of the geographical boundaries of a future German empire, with the admirals throwing further megalomaniac ideas into the debate, few considered the frontiers of 1914 to be sufficient.

It was only consistent with their attitude towards the use of military force that the generals not merely willingly co-operated in the rearmament programme of the Hitler government, but also were among the protagonists of the early changeover from what was at first still a defensive rearmament programme to the establishment of an offensive and highly mechanised force. Nor could the leading military claim to have been ignorant of the effects which the vigorous mobilisation of German industry for the creation of a modern offensive military instrument was having upon the national economy. They had never been sentimental about the burdens which rearmament imposed on the mass of the population. If the choice was between military power or raising the level of civilian consumption and better welfare provision, the officer corps would opt for austerity. If this created unrest, it was up to Himmler's police and Goebbels's propaganda machine to contain it. This is why the German generals, absorbed by the preparation for foreign war, were so pleased to see the Nazis establishing 'law and order' and to be able to forget about their domestic function, except for rare occasions such as the Röhm Affair (see above, p. 144).

Nevertheless, their immersion in professional matters, their drawing up of organisational charts and of coping with the influx of masses of recruits after the introduction of universal military service in March 1935, did not prevent their pondering on the consequences of rapid rearmament which was beginning to unhinge the entire national economy. The most telling contribution to the recognition of this problem came in August 1936 from General Erich Fromm, the head of the General Army Office. He confronted his military superiors with a few simple calculations of the recurrent costs of the offensive instrument which was being created. Theoretically, he argued, it would be possible to establish and supply this instrument. However, at the end of the build-up period the choice would be between using the Wehrmacht or finding a way of reducing the astronomical costs of rearmament. Fromm therefore asked for clarification as to whether or not it was intended to deploy the Wehrmacht at a specific and predetermined point. He never appears to have received a straightforward answer, not because his superiors rejected war and the full-steam preparation for it as a matter of principle. On the contrary, while they may have felt a disdain for Hitler's pontifications on a future racial New Order in Europe, most of them had no fundamental objections to his power-political objectives. It was also welcome to them that rearmament had not merely increased their importance as a functional elite, but also enhanced their political power well beyond Weimar levels.

Where the generals differed and hence repeatedly found themselves at loggerheads with the 'Führer' and Supreme Commander was their persistently pessimistic assessment of the sufficiency of German military power and the lack of 'in-depth' rearmament. In their view the First World War had been lost because the country had been inadequately prepared for it. They were anxious to avoid that 'mistake' the next time and aimed for more total preparation. However, the adoption of such a strategy would have required an unprecedented austerity programme and this Hitler, fearful of the collapse of popular morale, was unwilling to do. His decision to provide guns *and* butter in preference to the generals' guns-only policy pointed to a fundamental contradiction in his regime. But it also forced him to take greater risks. He could not wait for his military experts to proclaim that victory was certain; he had to pull them along by demonstrating that military preparedness is a relative concept and depends on the potential opponent's capacity and his determination to use it. As was demonstrated by the remilitarisation of the Rhineland in March 1936, the annexation of Austria in March 1938 and the destruction of Czechoslovakia a year later, the 'Führer's' risk-taking paid off militarily, as did his daring lightning wars in 1939/40. It was these 'splendid victories' which time and again made his pessimistic generals look rather foolish and undermined their power position. They had been proven wrong about the achievability of territorial goals which they themselves had subscribed to. All they could do was either press on, rather helplessly, with their preparations for war or resign. The Chief of the General Staff, Ludwig Beck, took the latter course of action, but significantly enough not because he fundamentally disagreed with the regime's foreign policy objectives, but because he was opposed to a high-risk expansionism.

What added to Hitler's determination to push ahead was an inkling that, if the crisis of the German rearmament economy was to be avoided, the plunder of other national economies had to begin. The way Austria and Czechoslovakia were 'integrated' economically was a harbinger of the pressures to come.

Further resources to fill the gap which had opened up in the Reich's ability to finance the huge military expenditures could only be found beyond the annexations of 1938/9 (Tables 35 and 36). Poland was the next target on the list and ultimately (as Hitler explained to Carl Burckhardt, the League of Nations Commissioner for Danzig) Russia. Detailed preparations for the destruction of Poland started in April 1939, leading to war six months later. There is no doubt that Hitler wanted this war against the Polish neighbour; but he did not want the world war which began when Britain and France refused to abandon their eastern ally. A war in the west would put him precisely into the Wilhelmine position which he had been so keen to avoid.

The trouble was that since the destruction of Czechoslovakia it had become more difficult to prevent a British and French military involvement in a German–Polish conflict. Hitler was still manoeuvering to achieve his diplomatic objective when the golden opportunity presented itself in the shape of a prospective pact between Germany and Russia. In August Stalin, worried about his own military security and convinced that the capitalist West was bent on directing fascist Germany towards an invasion of the Soviet Union, dropped his negotiations with Britain and signed a non-aggression pact with the Third Reich. Although the 'Führer' had to overcome considerable ideological inhibitions when he linked up with the Bolsheviks, the immediate advantages of the agreement were so obvious that he was even prepared to hand the eastern parts of Poland to the Russians. Economically the pact provided him with Russian deliveries of food and desperately needed raw materials. Strategically it offered him a glacis from which an attack on the Soviet Union could be launched once the accord had fulfilled its usefulness. Politically it seemed to deal so shattering a blow to the Western position that Britain and France would sit tight while Nazi Germany made her next move east.

It was against the background of these calculations that Hitler's 'generous offer' of an Anglo-German alliance was made three days after the signing of the Nazi–Soviet Pact on 22 August 1939. The hope of keeping the Western powers out also formed the basis of his subsequent moves to put the onus for the breakdown of last-minute negotiations with Warsaw on the shoulders of the allegedly obstinate Poles. At the same time the Nazi press tried to whip up feelings at home against Polish treatment of the German minority in the country's western provinces. But the mood in the Reich was different from that in August 1914, and not even the Gleiwitz Radio Station incident,* carefully staged to give the appearance of a defensive response by the Hitler government to Polish 'aggression', changed the decidedly glum reaction of all too

---

* To justify the German attack, Nazi propaganda alleged that the Poles had opened hostilities by attempting to seize the radio station at Gleiwitz in Silesia.

many Germans. Two days after Hitler's march into Poland, the Western allies, having unsuccessfully demanded Germany's withdrawal, declared war on Berlin. The 'Führer' found himself embroiled in a conflict in the west which he had not wanted, at least not at this stage. Fortunately for him there was little military activity on the western front. Nor was it totally inconceivable that peace in the west might be restored once Poland had been defeated in a lightning attack.

From the evidence available, there appears to be little doubt that the idea of further eastward expansion to establish a continental empire continued to preoccupy Hitler throughout the autumn and winter of 1939. Yet he also appreciated that a future invasion of Russia could be contemplated only if he had his back free in the west. The problem there was not so much France and even less the smaller Western European neighbours, but Britain. It was unlikely that she would be inclined to make peace as long as British soldiers, together with their Allies, were undefeated and entrenched along Germany's western frontier. The prospect of peace might brighten up, however, if they were swept off the European mainland. Such military–strategic and political considerations apart, the establishment of a German position on the Atlantic and Channel coasts would also provide the Reich with an opportunity of incorporating the sizeable industrial complexes of France and Belgium into a German-dominated European economy. There were hence several reasons for not signing a peace with France before she had been militarily defeated. Britain, on the other hand, was, in Hitler's eyes, a different matter. He might wish to humiliate her, but did not want to crush her.

The Polish campaign was not yet over when, in pursuit of these calculations, the Wehrmacht began to make tentative preparations for the invasion of Belgium, Holland, Luxemburg and France. Six months later the swift destruction of these nations had been achieved. The campaign in the west was delayed for a few weeks by the equally successful occupation of Denmark and Norway in April 1940. It was a move which was initiated partly in response to the demands of the Navy to gain a direct access to the North Atlantic, partly in anticipation of a British landing in Norway. The lightning victories in the west boosted Hitler's prestige and self-confidence tremendously, but they did not lead him to abandon his coolly calculating approach towards Britain. Surely, now that she was completely on her own, she would enter into armistice negotiations?

Accordingly Germany put out various feelers towards the stubborn power across the Channel in an attempt to entice her into a ceasefire. These overtures reached their peak during and immediately after the end of the French campaign. Thus, less than a fortnight after the beginning of the war against France General Franz Halder, the Army Chief of Staff, recorded in his diary on 21 May 1940: 'We seek contact with Britain on the basis of a division of the world.' It seems that Hitler was still looking east and hoped that Britain could still be brought to agree to a grand tit-for-tat. Two days after the defeat of France on 19 June 1940, Ribbentrop, since 1938 German Foreign Minister, remarked to Count Galeazzo Ciano, his Italian counterpart:

> The 'Führer' does not desire the destruction of the British Empire. He asks that England renounce some of her possessions and recognise the fait accompli [on the Continent]. On these conditions Hitler would be prepared to come to an agreement. England has already been informed of the above through the confidential channels of the Swedish legation. After the armistice with France, the decisions of the future will be taken. If England chooses war, it will again be total war, pitiless, decisive until the destruction of England and the Empire. If England chooses peace, the 'Führer' will be happy to collaborate in the reconstruction of a Europe in which order and peace will be assured for the time-space of some generations.

At the same time as the Swedish contacts were mobilised, the German ambassador to Washington twice sought a meeting with his British colleague, Lord Lothian. Hitler, so Lothian telegraphed to London, had no desire to attack Britain. He would like to preserve the British Empire and wanted peace in the west. Winston Churchill, who had meanwhile replaced Neville Chamberlain as Prime Minister, was in no mood to conclude such a deal. For him there was no alternative to fighting on until the complete destruction of the Third Reich, which both in terms of what it had already done and what it proposed to do posed a fundamental challenge to the British Empire and the existing international order. Consequently, the 'Führer' also found the 'peace offer' which he made in his speech before the Reichstag on 19 July 1940 flatly rejected.

Unable to bring the war in the west to an end, some of his advisers now urged him to attack the British Isles, and plans for Operation Sea Lion were in fact drawn up. However, unlike some other decision-makers, Hitler never seriously considered a cross-Channel attack, and with his prestige and power as a military leader and politician now at its height, his views remained decisive. The outcome of the Battle of Britain by September 1940 merely strengthened his resolve to turn against Stalin and, as so many times before, even those who had some qualms about this particular leap into the dark went along with the 'Führer'. By November 1940 military preparations for Operation Barbarossa were in full swing. The calculations behind the invasion of Russia, which most people around him expected to succumb quickly, emerged once more during a conference between Hitler and his top military advisers on 9 January 1941.

> The gigantic Russian territory [he argued] harbours immense riches. Germany should dominate this space economically and politically, but not incorporate it. She would then possess all the prerequisites for conducting the struggle also against [other] continents; no one will be able to defeat her then.

Whereas this statement reiterated the exploitative intentions of German imperialism, it is not absolutely clear whether Hitler was looking for a pause in the fighting to consolidate his conquests or whether he wanted to take up the struggle against the Anglo-Saxon powers straightaway.

If consolidation was his aim, the subsequent extension of the war in North Africa and inclusion of the United States would appear to be the consequence of Germany's inability to defeat the Soviet Union in a lightning war and to establish a German-dominated autarkic bloc in Europe and Russia. In other words, global warfare became a desperate move to achieve final victory, although the overstretching of the country's military capacities merely led to this victory slipping inexorably from Hitler's hands. He was forced to escalate the war because the decisive breakthrough in the east never came. The dynamic of the world struggle which began in 1941 slowly devoured those who had unleashed it. However, there are other documents which point to a more deliberate planning for global war even before the disastrous outcome of the Russian campaign was known. Thus, as early as February 1941, four months before the beginning of Operation Barbarossa, plans were drawn up on the 'Führer's' orders 'for operations against Afghanistan and India'. Other pre-Barbarossa preparations include an operations plan for the occupation of the Azores for trans-Atlantic bomber warfare against the United States. Detailed plans were also made at this time for the establishment and training of a colonial service to administer a future German empire in Africa. Obviously, all these preparations, which went as far as the compilation of dictionaries in African languages, remained on paper as the Russian campaign got bogged down. The German 'dream of empire' (W. W. Schmokel) is nonetheless of considerable interest because in it became amalgamated the various ideas of Germany's world power position which had been mooted for many years. Nor is there any doubt that the blueprints were serious even if they lacked precision and detail. In 1940/1 quite a few people in various offices were, from their Central European vantage-point, greedily scanning different parts of the globe in search of territories which would have made the projected German empire very expansive indeed. Above all, it was not a small circle of Nazis who allowed their imagination to wheel freely, as a host of publications by economists on *Grossraumwirtschaft* and world empire confirm.

This was the period when the self-confidence of those who had engineered and managed the impressive military feats barely knew limitations. Most officers, industrialists, bureaucrats and intellectuals had been swept off their feet. Thus a team of architects under Albert Speer was beavering away at scale models for a rebuilt centre of Berlin. There was to be an avenue, four miles long and 130 yards across along which all major ministries would be housed. At the centre, a railway station was to be erected which was to be larger than Grand Central Station in New York, with a huge square in front around which the arms of the defeated nations were to be put on display. A model was also made of an Arc de Triomphe, 130 yards high, and through the gap was to be seen, three miles away, the largest assembly hall in the world, with a seating capacity of 180,000. The rally grounds at Nuremberg were to be rebuilt in a grand style, and plans have also survived for an extension of Trondheim harbour in Norway which was to serve as a base for a *Weltmachtflotte* about whose mission the admirals wrote long memoranda.

The point is that these were, on the whole, fairly intelligent people who cannot be written off as belonging to the lunatic fringe of the Nazi movement. Nor was it that they merely did their duty. Most of them saw their work as a contribution, however small, to a vast national effort. Meanwhile military bureaucrats and civilian administrators went out to the occupied territories to help to reshape the political and economic structures of the conquered nations of Europe. Among them were also many managers of industry who came as representatives of their firms and business empires. Although it is difficult to reconstruct the general climate of opinion among the professionals in the armed forces, the economy and bureaucracy, it would seem that the superiority complex proved infectious. The ordinary soldier sitting in a pavement café on the Champs Elysées and the corporal who advanced along a dirt road in Yugoslavia both began to suffer from it. Even people like the historian Friedrich Meinecke, himself by no means a Nazi, got carried away by the defeat of France.

Although it will probably never be possible to quantify this enthusiastic support, it is clear that there existed a positive determination to succeed in 1940/1 which might well have carried Hitler to victory over the Soviet Union. It is a matter of conjecture what the course of modern history would have been had Russia collapsed in the autumn of 1941. Yet, though designed as another lightning war, the invasion which began on 22 June 1941 turned out to be a different campaign from the earlier ones. Literally hundreds of thousands of Red Army soldiers were captured in huge encirclement battles; thousands of miles were covered by the rapidly advancing Wehrmacht, and still the Russians continued to fight hard; the German lines became over-extended; the logistical support failed to keep up with demand for ammunition, petrol, spares and food. The rainy season came and the German mechanised units got stuck in the mud of an underdeveloped road network. The wet autumn was followed by an unusually harsh winter with temperatures so low that the lubricants began to freeze. Nor was the ordinary foot-soldier equipped to cope with such adverse conditions.

In the spring of 1942, the Wehrmacht made another gigantic effort to throw the Soviet Union out of the war. However, the thrust of this offensive in a south-eastern direction towards the Ukraine and the Caucasus with their vast resources also provided a clue to the crisis which had begun to hit the Third

Reich in 1941/2. This was not the war which the country had been prepared for or had the capacity to sustain. Following the Japanese attack on Pearl Harbor on 7/8 December 1941, the United States, already a supplier of military equipment to the Allies, had finally been brought into the war. Three days later Germany declared war on the Americans. It was a decision which would appear to defy rational explanation, if seen in connection with a remark by Hitler during a general assessment of the military situation in November 1941 that his chances of winning the war were slim. Although he may have made his move against the United States in the hope of scuttling for good the possibility of an early peace in the Far East and hence of keeping America pinned down in the Pacific, basically his decision to declare war on the United States merely revealed the 'Führer's' helplessness in the face of the developments which he could no longer control.

With the United States, a power had entered the global struggle whose industrial capacity, once fully mobilised, far outstripped Germany's. It was such economic factors that counted henceforth, now that the original German strategy of lightning wars had failed. By the summer of 1942, American material superiority began to push the Japanese on to the defensive. The 'Führer' Headquarters witnessed a brief spell of renewed optimism when the German offensive in southern Russia made rapid territorial gains and Erwin Rommel swept through North Africa. Yet when, by September 1942, victory was still out of sight, Hitler finally admitted that he would not be able to win a protracted war of the kind which had now developed. Although the grand ambitions of empire which had been debated and prepared inside and outside the Party in 1940/1 were not shelved overnight, thenceforth they turned into airy castles. And yet the plans provide an insight into the state of mind and mentalities not merely of the Nazi leadership, but also of the various elite groups which, in writing about the future or through their leading activities, participated in the great wars of looting and exploitation.

Occupation, exploitation and extermination

However, the early 1940s are of interest not only for the study of Germany's war aims. We must also examine the forms which the Second World War took, if we want to understand its character and hence the *telos* of the regime that had declared it. When, by the end of 1939, the Third Reich occupied the western and central parts of Poland up to the dividing-line agreed with Stalin under the terms of the Nazi–Soviet Pact, a brutal regime was immediately imposed on the native population. In fact, what happened in Poland provides a good illustration of how a German-dominated continental empire was to be reorganised demographically and economically. The Polish case is particularly interesting because German policies towards the Poles were not adopted in the period when the Nazi regime was, as later on in the war, under additional pressure to be brutal in the face of its own military failure. The only pressure that existed in 1939 was the need to mobilise the Polish economy in order to give support to the German national economy, overstrained, as it was to the point of breakdown by the policies adopted between 1933 and 1939. In addition there was the dogmatism of the Nazi ideologues and Pan-German resettlement politicians who wanted to use Slavonic Poland as an experimental ground for their racist theories.

Hitler explained the general approach to the OKW chief Wilhelm Keitel when he remarked that the Third Reich was not interested in retaining a Polish intelligentsia. As to the mass of the Polish population, he envisaged it to be provided with no more than a low standard of living. 'We want', he concluded, 'nothing but labourers from there.' The most effective way of achieving this objective was to concentrate all Poles in one area which could act as a pool of forced labour. Accordingly the General Government was established as an administrative unit in southern Poland. At the same time, tens of thousands of Poles were removed from their houses and farms in the rest of German-occupied Poland, herded into freight cars and sent to the General Government areas. As a directive by the *Reichssicherheitshauptamt* (RSHA), the SS office in overall control of these operations, decreed, each expellee was allowed to take no more than a small suitcase, a light blanket, food for two weeks and 20 zlotys in cash. Savings, valuables, shares and foreign exchange all had to be left behind. Effectively expropriated, these people were rehoused in southern Poland in conditions which defy description. If they did not die on the way, they were threatened by starvation and epidemics once they had arrived in the General Government area. While the suffering and misery for most was appalling, some of the most able-bodied Poles were deported to the Reich, mainly to work in German industry. In 1940 they numbered some 312,000.

Polish Jews were singled out for a different treatment which augured ill for their future. On 21 September 1939, only three weeks after the war had begun, the RSHA issued a circular to the effect that 'the Jews are to be concentrated in ghettoes in order to secure better means of control and to remove them at a later date'. However, on the way to these ghettoes the first mass killings began. Death was also the fate of the Polish intelligentsia, nobility and clergy. Behind the advancing Wehrmacht there appeared special commandos of the SS (*Einsatzgruppen*) who simply 'liquidated' thousands of people. The earlier statements by Hitler and other Nazi leaders about the fate of the Poles thus became a gruesome reality. While these murderous activities were going on, an ambitious resettlement programme was launched for so-called ethnic Germans in those parts of the country from which the native population had been forcibly removed. Some 70,000 of these people were shipped in from the Baltic States, others arrived from Galicia and Transylvania. The 700,000 Polish citizens of German extraction were neatly classified into activists in the 'ethnic struggle' before 1939, those who had preserved their Germandom, those who still possessed a 'German consciousness' and 'polonised' Germans at the bottom of the scale.

All these measures and bureaucratic exercises took place under the formal authority of the Army whose commander-in-chief had published a declaration to the Polish population on the day of the German attack. He reassured the Poles that international law would be fully observed, but added that active or passive resistance would be dealt with 'by all the means' available to the occupation authorities. Although this formula left plenty of scope for interpretation, it was only a week later, on 8 September 1939, that Hitler as supreme commander issued more specific 'guidelines for the establishment of a military administration in the occupied eastern territory'. The circular affirmed that executive power in Poland would be in the hands of the Commander-in-Chief East (*Oberost*) and his subordinate regional commanders. However, their powers were to be limited to the extent that a civilian administrative staff was created at their side, composed of committed Nazis. More importantly, the SS liquidation squads, though formally under the command of the Wehrmacht, were to be directed by the RSHA in respect of their 'police' functions.

It cannot be said that the Army High Command was blissfully ignorant of what these functions were to be. Negotiations between the military leadership and the RSHA chief Heydrich left no doubt that he proposed to execute without trial not merely suspected Polish *franc tireurs*, but also expected to use the opportunity to murder, as one of the Army delegates, Admiral Wilhelm Canaris, reported, 'nobility, priests and Jews'. As no objections to these plans had been voiced by the generals, the regional commanders on the Polish front soon saw themselves confronted with the news of SS units being engaged in summary executions and large-scale butchery in their own rear areas. Not realising at first that these activities enjoyed highest approval or acquiescence, they believed them to be outgrowths of poor discipline and excessive zeal by some SS fanatics. Being formally responsible for these activities, a number of commanders tried to stop the killings, only to be told by the SS that they had no authority to do so. Some officers quickly washed their hands of these occurrences altogether, like the commander of the 18th Army who instructed his subordinates to refrain from criticism of 'the ethnic struggle in the General Government'. He justified his call for abstinence as follows: 'In order to find its final *völkische* resolution, the ethnic struggle which has been raging along the eastern frontier for centuries required unprecedented and firmly executed measures.' Therefore, 'certain units of Party and State had been charged with implementing this ethnic struggle'.

There was however no uniform reaction and many other officers protested.

They argued that SS occupation policies besmirched the name of the Army and of the German nation. By October 1939, these protests had become so vociferous that *Oberost* General Johannes Blaskowitz submitted a memorandum to Hitler at the beginning of November in which he warned against the negative effects which shootings and arrests were having on military discipline. If executions were unavoidable, they should take place after proper trials had been conducted. Hitler was furious when he saw this *Denkschrift* and asked for Blaskowitz to be removed. War, he added, could not be waged with 'Salvation Army methods'. In the end, neither these nor later protests bore any fruit, not because the top military decision-makers were particularly afraid of Hitler's wrath, but because most of them had come to agree with his verdict long ago. As Michael Geyer concluded in his study of the notions of warfare held in the interwar period, 'total and terroristic warfare . . . without regard for the population or – more generally – for the social costs of war did not just represent the horrific image of a war of annihilation conducted by the SS, but reflected the "normal" image of war of the Reichswehr.'

In view of this and also of the brutalities inside Germany after 1933, it is not surprising that a determined attempt to stop the 'ethnic struggle' in Poland never occurred. Although there were some officers who began to think of overthrowing the regime, the key people in the High Command decided to let the SS do the 'dirty work', even if it became more and more difficult to keep regular troops out of mass shootings and 'cleansing operations' as the war wore on. When Hitler later ordered that executive authority in Poland be taken out of the hands of the military there was but a faint attempt to resist this move, as if their silence absolved the generals of their historical co-responsibility for the methods of Nazi imperialism. In the spring of 1940, public attention was conveniently fixed on Western Europe and Germany's campaigns against Denmark, Norway, Holland, Belgium, Luxemburg and France. This left the new civilian administrators and the SS police bureaucrats in Poland plenty of scope to implement their racial policies.

Nine months later, by early 1941, planning for the invasion of the Soviet Union was proceeding at full speed, and this included preparations for treating the native populations. After what had already happened in Poland in 1939/40, German rule in Russia was different only in scale, not in quality – with the possible exception of the treatment meted out to Red Army soldiers. Here a widespread German prejudice concerning the 'inferiority' of the Slavs was sharpened by a virulent anti-Communism. Consequently, the war which the Third Reich started in June 1941 was not merely a war of plunder against the Eastern *'Untermensch'*, but at the same time a crusade against Bolshevism whose representatives were to meet the same fate as the Polish intelligentsia. The first Bolsheviks which the Wehrmacht expected to encounter were the political commissars of the Red Army. The Commissar Order, issued a fortnight before the invasion, demanded that prisoners of war of political status be shot without further ado. The Wehrmacht had been deeply involved in the drafting of this Order and, together with the SS, it participated in its execution.

The SS liquidation squads frequently reported on the great support which they received from such top army leaders as Karl-Heinrich von Stülpnagel, Erich Hoepner, Gerd von Rundstedt, Walther von Reichenau and others. More significantly, it was not blind obedience or lack of courage which prevented the generals from objecting to this criminal decree. Their co-operation was rather based on 'a considerable measure of agreement with the views of Hitler' (H. Krausnick) who had told them more than once what forms he expected the war in the east to assume. The decrees which field marshals like Reichenau or Erich von Manstein issued in connection with the German crusade against the 'Asiatic-Jewish danger' make positively awful reading. Only when it became clear that the implementation of the Commissar Order increased the Red Army's determination to resist, did various front-line officers voice serious qualms—on military rather than legal or humanitarian grounds.

While thousands of Russians thus met their end before the firing squads, ordinary POWs who were never removed from the authority of the Wehrmacht cannot be said to have fared much better. According to German records, some 3 million of them died in detention up to 1 May 1944. The figure is almost certainly too low and was probably closer to 3.5 million. They died from starvation, illness and exhaustion. Those soldiers who collapsed on the long trek to the camps were usually shot on the spot. Those who got to the camps had their chances of survival drastically cut by the principles of custody on which the system was based. For it was less bureaucratic chaos and German inability to cope with such large numbers which caused millions of Russian POWs to perish than the deliberate decision to maintain them at starvation levels.

At the same time as these men were marched off to the rear areas and the fittest among them sent to the Reich to work as slave labourers, Nazi functionaries, engineers, railway experts, bureaucrats, managers of industry and (from 1942) representatives of Fritz Sauckel's labour recruitment enterprise moved in to remobilise the Russian economy for the Reich. Foodstuffs and raw materials were desperately needed. Soon large numbers of foreign workers were also required to replace those Germans who were being called up by the armed forces now that the war had become a protracted global struggle. In the course of four so-called Sauckel Actions some five million men and women from all over Europe were brought into the Reich; some volunteered, most of them came under compulsion (Table 32). Their pay was at most half of what a German worker received before automatic deductions for food and accommodation. Another source of labour were the thousands of concentration camp inmates. It may be possible to calculate the economic costs of these operations and also to tot up the material gains made during the looting of the occupied territories. But it would be a futile exercise to do the same for the human costs. If the millions of slave labourers were not worked to death, many of them had their physical and mental health wrecked and their careers destroyed.

All this did not prevent those responsible for the organisation of the European economy from deeming the system an efficient and rational way of mobilising resources. It was only later, when the military situation deteriorated and rising numbers of partisans succeeded in blowing up goods trains and sabotaging factories, that disillusionment set in. For the moment, armies of technicians swarmed out not only to solve immediate problems of production and supply in the occupied territories, but also to draw up plans for the long-term restructuring of the respective national economies in Norway, France or Eastern Europe. Although there was not much time to initiate these plans, the contours of the New Economic Order did become visible. As Alan Milward concluded with reference to the Nazi occupation of Norway:

Ultimately the intention was to exploit the country in Germany's interests while arresting, in the name of the fascist revolution, its future economic growth or changing the purposes for which such growth was normally fostered.... Norway's role in the *Grossraumwirtschaft* was, like that of all of the peripheral states, to be that of a primary producer.... The New Order's economic objectives were best served by retraining Norwegian labour in these sectors of employment [fishing and agriculture], and their retention there also strengthened the barriers to social change in the new society.

In economic terms, the new German empire, had it ever been established, would have been a large-scale structure organised for, and run on, the principles of a colonialism of the crudest kind. To the same end, the societies of the occupied countries would also have been adapted – nations of helots led by their German 'masters' and their racially acceptable collaborators from Western and Northern Europe. The east in particular repeatedly fired Hitler's imagination, as on 9 August 1941 when he developed the following vistas in front of his entourage:

The German colonist ought to live on handsome, spacious farms. The German services will be lodged in marvellous buildings, the governors in palaces. Beneath the shelter of the administrative services, we shall gradually organise all that is indispensable to the maintenance of a certain standard of living. Around the city, to a depth of thirty or forty kilometres, we shall have a belt of handsome villages connected by the best roads. What exists beyond that will be another world in which we mean to let the Russians live as they like. It is merely necessary that we should rule them. In the event of a revolution, we shall only have to drop a few bombs on their cities and the affair will be liquidated. Once a year we shall lead a troop of Kirghizes through the capital of the Reich in order to strike their imagination with the size of our monuments.

Meanwhile Himmler's offices were drawing up resettlement plans, and Martin Bormann, the chief of the Party Chancellery, urged that public whipping be reintroduced as a penalty. Yet even if the peoples of Europe were to be forced to toil for the benefit of the Germans with their living standards severely depressed, at least they were allowed to survive. The Jews, together with the gypsies, were to be denied a place in the New Europe altogether.

Earlier in this chapter we traced the steady deterioration of the position of the Jews in Germany, culminating in the Night of Broken Glass in November 1938. It has also been mentioned that not only Hitler and some of his closest advisers, but also many Nazis in the lower ranks of the movement were afflicted by a pathological hatred of the Jews. They saw the Jews as both the perpetrators of a world-wide conspiracy against the 'Aryans' and the biological carriers of disease and decay. If the language of the rabid anti-Semites who openly talked of a 'Jewish vermin' and of 'extermination' was to be taken literally, the Jews had good reason to fear not merely for their property or citizens' rights, but also for their lives.

This is not to imply that the inventors of the 'Final Solution' had a clear idea before 1939 of how to solve the 'Jewish Question'. The connections are more tortuous. As we have seen, the only organisation to take a systematic approach to this 'question' was the SS and it came up with an 'emigration' programme. A revised version of the programme re-emerged in 1940/1 in the shape of a plan to ship all Jews to Madagascar for resettlement. Heydrich called this idea, ominously, the 'territorial final solution'. However, the outbreak of war and its subsequent escalation into total war seriously worsened the Jews' chances of survival for a number of reasons. To begin with, the military victories in east and west suddenly added several million Jews to the decimated number of those Jews who had been unable to leave the Reich before September 1939. Any 'resettlement' plans had now become a major logistical and bureaucratic operation, the size of which helped to tip the scales in favour of physical annihilation.

However, before this possibility could be seriously contemplated, there were also various psychological barriers to be removed. The systematic murder of millions of people was bound to run up against considerable moral scruples, not among those who gave the orders, but among those who were supposed to undertake the actual killing. The *Einsatzgruppen*, during their first actions in Poland in 1939/40, had managed to shoot thousands of allegedly 'subversive elements', Jewish and non-Jewish. But in the course of these executions it was also found that the members of the commandos were able to carry on only after generous rations of schnaps. Others had nervous breakdowns and had to be transferred, and the problem was likely to become worse where women and children were among the victims. Nor had it been possible to stop the news of these mass killings from spreading to the Wehrmacht and back to the Reich,

167

resulting in some indignation and protests. So, it was clear that other methods had to be applied to the wholesale murder of millions of people and that the 'Jewish Question' had to be solved in the greatest possible secrecy.

It was at this point that Hitler could draw upon another experience which, launched by offices which operated outside the traditional bureaucratic machinery of the State, paved the road to the death camps both psychologically and technologically. This was the gassing of mentally and physically handicapped Germans which started in 1939 and had two intellectual roots. On the one hand, it was an outgrowth of a Nazi obsession with heredity and racial purity; on the other, it represented the practical application of ideas which had been debated long before 1933 among doctors, theologians and intellectuals all over Europe concerning the forcible sterilisation of the handicapped and, in the case of serious mental disease, euthanasia. In restrospect, it seems all too obvious what terribly dangerous ground these discussions among 'experts' were treading. But in Germany this did not prevent the protagonists of 'genetic hygiene' from lending their pens and surgical skills to its promotion when the 'race-conscious' Nazi government came to power. Involuntary sterilisation began in January 1934 to which some 15,300 women and many more men fell victims. Meanwhile the discussion on 'mercy killing' of the incurably ill was gathering momentum, leading to the killing of a child at the Leipzig Central Hospital on the authority of the 'Führer'.

The outbreak of war facilitated the expansion of these early beginnings into a fully fledged programme of euthanasia. With the help of Karl Brandt, Hitler's personal doctor, and Victor Brack of the Party Chancellery, a team of some fifty doctors and technicians was put together. The doctors were to certify that a particular patient had forfeited his or her life. Chemists at the Reich Criminal Investigation Office had developed techniques using carbon monoxide, and in the course of the 'T4' Action which ensued, some 70,000 mentally and physically handicapped persons were killed at remote institutions in Hesse, Lower Austria, Württemberg and Saxony. The programme was interrupted in August 1941 in the face of mounting protest from relatives and most effectively the Churches, but was soon resumed in secret.

Consequently the methods of 'bloodless' and industrial mass murder had been successfully tried out and were in principle available. If any moral barriers still existed against employing them, racist dogma and the first two years of the war had lowered them appreciably. It appears from what little documentary evidence has survived about the origins of the 'Final Solution' that resettlement plans were still being discussed as late as the spring of 1941, but dropped shortly thereafter. In October of that year former 'T4' personnel were transferred to the east and in December the first gassings of Jews took place at Chelmno. The infamous Wannsee Conference of January 1942 therefore merely gave retroactive sanction to policies which had already been adopted.

At Wannsee, the Reich bureaucracy, the Reichsbahn and other agencies became accessories to what was to be known in the camouflage language of the Third Reich as 'The Final Solution of the Jewish Question'. The story of the freight trains from all over Europe to the death camps in Poland, of the arrival of the Jews on the ramps and of the gas chambers has been told many times in its gruesome details. Most of the victims went to their death too stunned and terrorised to say or do anything when they were shoved forward and shouted at by the 'selectors'. Some gestured their defiance and cursed the Germans; others resisted actively or, if they had been singled out as 'work-Jews', plotted breakouts and uprisings.

It is not too difficult to comprehend the reactions of the victims to the hell they faced. The behaviour of their guards and tormentors, on the other hand, would appear to elude rational historical explanation. Yet although there was a deviant element among the staff of the camps, it would be all too easy to regard them all as sadists and psychopaths. Most of them knew that they were violating traditional norms, but their conscience became partially or totally suspended by ideology and the assurance that they were not engaged in criminal activity. Even Himmler, one of the key organisers of the 'Final Solution', vomited when he witnessed the operation of a gas chamber. Yet he never tired of reminding his subordinates that they were fulfilling an historical mission. The power of prejudice clearly acted as a further motivating force, the more so as it had been cast into a more or less coherent framework of anti-Semitic rationalisation, sanctioned by the authority of the 'Führer'.

Those who stood on the ramps and guarded the camps appreciated that they were involved in 'extra-normative' activities, but they had been told and had convinced themselves, that mass murder had to be committed for the sake of a supposedly higher good. Some of the guards had gained their first experience in the concentration camps before the war or had been involved in the 'T4' operation. The brutality and racism of warfare in Poland and Russia between 1939 and 1941 seemed to lend plausibility to the argument, however sick, that Germany was engaged in a struggle in which the use of all methods was permitted. Some importance will also have to be attached to the fact that the murderers were taken outside their peacetime social environment and into the secrecy of an operation with its own mechanisms of social control and criminal group solidarity. Finally, there is the general and, perhaps, most frightening point which has been raised by R. Rubenstein when he wrote:

It is tempting to portray the Nazis as demons or perverts, for such a view protects our illusions about ourselves. To see the Nazis as more or less ordinary men is neither to excuse their deeds nor minimise the threat they pose. On the contrary, it is to recognise how fragile are the bonds of civility and decency that keep any kind of human community from utter collapse.

This statement leads on to the broader question of how many Germans knew about the 'Final Solution' apart from those who were directly involved in its implementation. The answer would seem to be that more people knew in the sense that they had been told indirectly, and that the higher up in the political, administrative, military and economic hierarchy they were, the more they were in a position to suspect. Thus Hitler explained to a full house of high-ranking officers in May 1944 by reference to one of his earlier speeches:

The Jew has drawn up a programme to exterminate the German people. I have declared in the German Reichstag on 1 September 1939: if anybody believes that he can exterminate the German nation in such a world war, he is mistaken; if Jewry should really instigate this, then it will be Jewry which will be exterminated.

The stenographer recorded 'vivid applause' when these words had been uttered. In view of this it is barely plausible that those present did not know what was meant, especially when they had seen the reality of Nazi *Ausrottungspolitik* in the eastern occupied territories against the population there. What they did not know, to the extent that they had not witnessed it, was the greater efficiency of the gas chambers. Other men at the top like Albert Speer knew about the 'Final Solution' in the sense that they received information which they chose not to follow up. For it was his friend Karl Hanke, the Gauleiter of Lower Silesia, who had advised him 'never to accept an invitation to inspect a concentration camp in Upper Silesia. Never, under any circumstances. He had seen something there which he was not permitted to describe and moreover could not describe.' And accordingly Speer 'did not query him. I did not query Himmler, I did not query Hitler, I did not speak with personal friends. I did not investigate – for I did not want to know what was happening there.' The same reaction might have been found in the Reichsbahn official in charge of timetabling at Budapest or the bureaucrat who received masses of clothes and personal belongings from certain obscure places in central Poland.

As to the mass of the German population which was not in a similarly privileged position for having access to secret information, it is safe to assume that more was suspected than was admitted after 1945. Soldiers on leave from the front, especially from the east, did not fail to report how the natives or the POWs were being treated. Many of those in the occupied west had also seen Belgian, Dutch or French Jews being rounded up. And then there were also those German Jews next door who, forced to wear a Star of David, had suddenly disappeared with their families. Nevertheless, few people, it seems, put all the different bits of information together to arrive at the conclusion that the Jews of Europe were being systematically murdered. Basically, the reality of Auschwitz was beyond their imagination because, as Walter Laqueur has convincingly argued, that reality was outside the realm of their human experience. Their experience of political violence of the 1920s and 1930s notwithstanding, they continued to see themselves as members of a civilised country and hence just would not believe that the 'bonds of civility and decency' had been broken in an orgy of organised crime and finally genocide. It was an illusion to which even many German Jews fell prey when they refused to leave before 1939. Later, they were more prone to make the connection between deportation and death, as is evidenced by the large number of suicides. There are also those Jews who went into hiding. An estimated 4,000 Jews survived the war in this way in the city of Berlin alone, and as most of them were sheltered by 'Aryan' friends, such a figure would again appear to make it advisable to differentiate when one looks at 'the Germans' and their attitude towards the Nazi regime, this time during the Second World War.

Resistance and collaboration during the final years

Judging from the incomplete statistics of executions of civilians, opposition to the regime continued despite increased police vigilance and harsher wartime penalties. For example, the records of the Brandenburg penitentiary list a total of 2,042 executions between 1940 and 1945, of which 1,807 were for politically or religiously motivated 'crimes'. A table compiled by the Reich Ministry of Justice refers to a total of 16,300 executions for the period 1940–4. It is estimated that some 20,000 soldiers were condemned to death by military courts. No less interesting is the sociological breakdown of the above figures, provided in the Brandenburg files. Of the 1,807 men and women executed, 775 were workers and craftsmen, 363 technicians, engineers, builders and architects, 234 employees and civil servants, 97 entrepreneurs, industrialists and commercial people, 79 farmers and gardeners, 51 scholars and academics, including university professors, doctors and school teachers, 49 artists, 35 professional soldiers, 38 higher civil servants and former politicians, 21 clergymen, 22 students and pupils and 12 journalists. These were the people who were caught by the traditional judicial machinery in just one region of Germany. There were no precise figures for those who perished in the concentration camps which were part of a separate system of Nazi 'justice' – another peculiarity of the regime in which the established courts and prisons administered the Criminal Code side by side with an 'extra-normative' camp bureaucracy which was subject to its own rules.

The lawyers who ran the German court system under the supervision of the Reich Justice Ministry represent, like the doctors, another group which made a significant contribution to the maintenance of the Third Reich. Although their independence from the State was guaranteed under the *Gerichtsverfassungsgesetz*, judges, as civil servants, were obviously more exposed to political pressures from above than the medical profession. Time and again, the government offered 'guidance' on how specific clauses of the Reich Criminal

Code of 1871, which had never been abolished, or Nazi laws were to be applied, such as the 'Law against the Propagation of Hereditary Diseases' of July 1933, the 'Law for the Protection of German Blood and Honour' of September 1935 or the *Volksschädling* Decree of November 1938. Nevertheless, judges continued to have some scope not merely with reference to the weighing of evidence, but also as regards the penalty to be imposed. And in these respects the Reich Justice Ministry by and large did not have to feel dissatisfied with the way in which the courts responded to 'guidance'. Many judges did not have to be pushed very hard to interpret certain paragraphs extensively and to apply harsh penalties. The right-wing political views which the majority of the legal profession had adhered to long before 1933 and which it continued to hold during the Third Reich, predisposed it to meting out justice in line with what was deemed to be the 'healthy sentiment of the people' (*gesundes Volksempfinden*). Indeed, it is very instructive to read some of the verdicts that were handed down. If the penalties became increasingly harsher during the war, this trend is partly a reflection of the growing crisis of the regime and the belief, shared by many judges, that there was a deterrent value in draconian verdicts. In 1942, 3,393 executions took place, ten times the figure of 1940. By 1943 and 1944, the figures had risen to 5,684 and 5,764 respectively.

However, these figures are to some extent also a gauge of the growth of an opposition to the regime which the courts felt obliged to stamp out. 1940 was, of course, the year when the Wehrmacht was winning its astonishing victories and when the home front was well provided for. Great care had been taken that families whose breadwinner had been drafted into the armed forces were paid generous allowances. The government tried very hard to give the impression that the war did not mean austerity. There was also little fresh recruitment of women into the factories (Table 51). On this point pragmatic considerations happily coincided with the ideological postulates of Nazi family policy of keeping the female population at home. However, the issue also throws an interesting light on the realities of social stratification in the Third Reich. Working-class women, as we have seen, had of course been in employment long before the outbreak of the war and the numbers employed did not decline thereafter. The beneficiaries of Nazi policy were therefore middle-class women who were under no economic pressure to find a job. Not surprisingly, their attitudes created a good deal of resentment and social tension.

All in all, the policies adopted for the benefit of the home front provide an interesting comment upon the latent instability of the regime. Never quite assured of a solid and steady popular backing, Hitler continued to rely on the carrot-and-stick approach adopted in the 1930s. Nor did he fail to realise that popular morale was, in the final analysis, most directly related to the development of the military situation. We have already seen that the chances of a German victory receded into the distance after the Russian winter of 1941/2. The psychological effect of the Wehrmacht's failure to achieve a breakthrough in the east did not take long to emerge. The first to be overcome by lasting doubts and depression were those Germans on the eastern front who experienced the realities of total war most directly and who encountered a Russian soldier very different from the one portrayed in Nazi propaganda. He proved to be a tough and resourceful fighter, not the demoralised '*Untermensch*' who would be beaten in a matter of a few months.

The feelings of unease and despair were exacerbated by the sight of the monotonously rolling hills and wide plains of western Russia which never seemed to end. Clearly, this was a different country from Poland, Holland or Denmark. Hence the nagging question of whether this war would ever come to a victorious conclusion. Back in the Reich, similar questions were being asked by the civilians whenever they cared to look at a map or were able to talk to a soldier on leave. All these changing moods were carefully recorded by the *SD-Inland-Nachrichtendienst* of the RSHA whose local representatives reported daily from September 1939 on the situation. Their *Berichte zur innenpolitischen Lage* provide an intriguing picture of public opinion under Nazism. It was in the summer of 1942 that the SS Security Service monitored the last upsurge of optimism. Thenceforth defeatism spread relentlessly, leading ultimately to the cessation of the SD Reports in July 1944 because they had, in the view of Bormann and Goebbels, become counterproductively gloomy.

The irony is that the tenor of Goebbels's propaganda itself grew into a reliable indicator that the war was going badly, and the more defeat was approaching the more frantically did he try to whip up fears and defensive instincts. The Propaganda Minister had been warning as early as 1941 against an unwarranted optimism. He favoured a Churchillian sweat-and-tears strategy in order to maintain popular morale. But he met, significantly, with much opposition in the upper echelons of the Nazi hierarchy, in particular from the powerful Gauleiter. It was only in 1942 that he finally succeeded in getting his way. His overall strategy is probably best echoed by the words which he uttered during a rally at the Berlin *Sportpalast* on 18 February 1943. Having received an enthusiastic response from a carefully selected audience of Party faithfuls, he shouted: 'Do you want total war? If necessary more total and radical than we could ever imagine at this moment?'

While the psychological mobilisation of the population for this type of war was gathering momentum, the mobilisation of the country's material resources was already in full swing. With the Wehrmacht's failure to defeat Russia in a lightning war, a shift in German rearmament strategy had to be made. The first preparations for it began in the autumn of 1941 on Hitler's order and after pressure from both General Georg Thomas, one of the key figures in Germany's armaments policy on the Wehrmacht side, and Fritz Todt, the Minister for Armaments and Munitions. Following Todt's death in a plane crash in February 1942, his post was taken over by Albert Speer who built on his predecessor's plans and succeeded in boosting German heavy goods production from 149 index points to 180 points between 1941 and 1943 (Table 7). The mobilisation of the country's industrial capacity for war production had inevitable repercussions on the civilian sector. The production index for consumer goods, which had actually risen by two points between 1940 and 1941, slumped by 11 points in 1942. Even more serious was the growing scarcity of food. Shortages of fertiliser and spare parts were partly responsible for a decline in agricultural production. Some 1.7 million farmers and labourers had been conscripted into the armed forces and slave labour was a poor substitute. Finally, under the impact of Allied bombing, distribution became more and more difficult. And yet for most of the time and in most places the situation never got quite so bad as in the final stages of the First World War. One reason for this would seem to have been the greater ruthlessness with which the regime enforced its decrees and economic policies. This also applies to industrial production. By 1943, little of the earlier optimism was left. What motivated people and partly explains the remarkable increase in armaments production was not only the grip of the Nazi police state, but also the fear that only an all-out effort would stave off defeat and something much worse that would follow.

Yet, however impressive the growth rates which the Speer programme achieved, they were no match for the output on the Allied side. In 1943, the United States alone produced military goods which were worth almost three times as much as those manufactured by the Third Reich. The overall balance between America, Britain and Russia, on the one hand, and Germany and Japan, on the other, was 62.5:18.3 milliard dollars in 1943. This meant that Hitler had no hope of winning a war which by this time had become less dependent on 'will-power' and military intuition than on the availability of hardware.

All too soon this point was driven home to the mass of the German population when Allied bombers appeared in large numbers over their cities. By 1944, there were few major towns which had not been severely damaged by Allied bombing. The Wehrmacht was on the defensive in the east since the Battle of Stalingrad and in the west since June 1944 when the second front was successfully established in northern France. In the south, Rommel and the Italians had been pushed out of North Africa and Allied forces were slowly moving up the Italian Peninsula. After the cessation of the SD reports, the Army continued to monitor public morale, and if the surveys that have survived are a reliable guide, support for the regime was rapidly dwindling. The last straw, proffered by Goebbels's propaganda machine which people were apparently prepared to cling to for a while, was the 'doodle-bug' campaign of the summer and autumn of 1944. But it was more a desperate belief in a last-minute miracle to be achieved with the help of rockets than a willingness to fight to the hilt or a commitment to National Socialism which inspired this short-lived optimism. It might be argued that disaffection with the Third Reich came rather late in the day. Indeed, a sizeable number of people who never supported the regime notwithstanding, there were millions of Germans who had put their faith in Hitler. They were reluctant to abandon now the hopes and expectations they had placed in him. Instead, they floundered about, emotionalised by Goebbels's nightmarish pictures of what would happen to a defeated Germany and disorientated by the growing chaos around them. Above all, they became increasingly preoccupied with the problems of day-to-day survival: queuing for food, sitting in air-raid shelters, worrying about the family.

Chances of organising something like a resistance movement had remained greatest in the Army throughout the war. Plans to remove Hitler had been ventilated by a small band of military opponents of Hitler as early as 1938. But although the Army was the only institution to possess the technical means for successful rebellion, plotting never moved beyond a preliminary stage. Nor could individual officers who had access to Hitler ever bring themselves to forget about organised conspiracy and simply kill the 'Führer'. After the beginning of the war and with the information of atrocities pouring into the Army High Command, Halder appears to have contemplated shooting 'Emil' on a number of occasions. Yet, in the end, he too pulled back and, like so many other generals, bureaucrats and economists, stayed on, professedly to prevent worse from happening although they knew or suspected that the worst was already occurring.

It was only after 1942 that the military resistance was gathering momentum. Its members, most of whom had been anti-Republicans and had welcomed the *Machtergreifung*, were moved by a genuine and deeply felt revulsion against what the regime was doing in the name of a country which they loved. By the beginning of 1944, a small circle of officers was determined to abandon their former scruples and to attempt to overthrow Hitler. However, even now they were not without illusions about Germany's position in the world. They found it difficult to accept that unconditional surrender and Allied occupation might be preferable to prolonging the life of the existing regime by a single day. Colonel Claus Schenk von Stauffenberg, one of the most principled and courageous conspirators, hoped to push the Allies out of Normandy after a successful coup before starting peace negotiations. Consequently, long discussions took place in various circles in an effort to evolve a framework within which a future German society and its place in the postwar world might be reconstituted. What characterised most of the proposals that were made with reference to the country's post-Hitler political and social structures or to its place in the community of nations is the patent inability of the conspirators to emancipate themselves from their old perceptions of the world. It was a backward-looking conservatism which has led historians like Hans Mommsen to conclude that the programmes of the military resistance were barely suitable as models upon which a postwar Germany might have been rebuilt.

However, this does not detract from their sacrifice on 20 July 1944 when they decided to remove Hitler and when, after the failure of the coup, they accepted their death sentences with courage and dignity. For it was in connection with the apprehension and trial of the plotters that Hitler and his entourage displayed once more the brutality and criminal potential which had been the hallmark of the regime since 1933. The July 1944 conspiracy also symbolised the final collapse of the alliance between the Nazi movement and the conservative elites of Germany which had facilitated the 'Führer's' rise to power in the first place. Thenceforth repression and fear became almost the exclusive method by which the regime tried to survive until the total defeat in May 1945. There is something terrifyingly logical about this end to a system whose dogmatic adherence to its proclaimed goals had caused the death of some 50 million people and left a trail of unprecedented destruction. Until his suicide on 30 April 1945, Hitler refused to shorten the agony. Sitting in his bunker in Berlin, he ordered the remnants of the Wehrmacht, supplemented by teenage Hitler Youths and old men, to fight on. When Russian tanks were already moving towards the centre of the ruined capital, he wrote his 'testament' in which he blamed 'international Jewry and its helpers' for the death of those millions and asserted that the Germans had let him down in his heroic struggle. Extinction would therefore be their deserved fate.

Finally, he appointed Admiral Karl Doenitz as President of the Reich and Supreme Commander of the Armed Forces. Doenitz loyally accepted the position, but realised from his outpost in Schleswig-Holstein that further resistance was senseless. On 8 May he empowered General Field Marshal Wilhelm Keitel, General Admiral Hans von Friedeburg and Colonel General Hans-Jürgen Stumpff to sign the document of unconditional surrender at Berlin. The Third Reich had at last been destroyed. An orgy of unprecedented violence had come to an end.

5 Occupation and division, 1945–1960

Economic and political life in the Western Zones of Occupation

When the Second World War finally ended at the beginning of May 1945, the nations of Europe began to take stock of five years of unprecedented bloodshed and destruction. As far as the Germans were concerned, the balance-sheet, though not as catastrophic as that of some of their neighbours, above all Poland and Russia, was depressing enough. An estimated seven million of them had been killed, or were presumed dead, of whom 3.2 millions were civilians. Some of the soldiers who had been reported missing later re-emerged from POW camps, many of them after ten years. But as late as 1962, the Red Cross and other agencies were still trying to clear up the fate of some 1.3 million former soldiers. At least one million ex-servicemen had suffered severe injuries and were disabled. Civilian health was also badly shaken.

Large parts of the country's major cities had been reduced to piles of rubble. Overall, some 3.4 million flats and houses out of a total of 17.1 million had been completely destroyed. A further 30 per cent had been severely damaged. Where possible those who had been bombed-out had built make-shift shelters in which they lived like cavemen. Others had been rehoused in undamaged accommodation, often five or six people to a room. The desperate shortage of housing was worsened by the influx of some 10 million refugees and expellees from the eastern parts of the former Reich and the German-occupied territories. Most of them had fled before the advancing Red Army. The rest were people of 'ethnic German' origin who were expelled from Eastern Europe under the terms of the Potsdam Agreement. It was only after 1947 that this flood of people abated, if one ignores for the moment the stream of refugees who began to leave East Germany from the late 1940s onwards up to the building of the Wall in August 1961. Many of these millions of the first phase were moved to the rural areas and given accommodation on farms and in the small villages of Bavaria, Schleswig-Holstein, Lower Saxony and Hesse. Others were put into camps which had either been hastily set up or, as in the

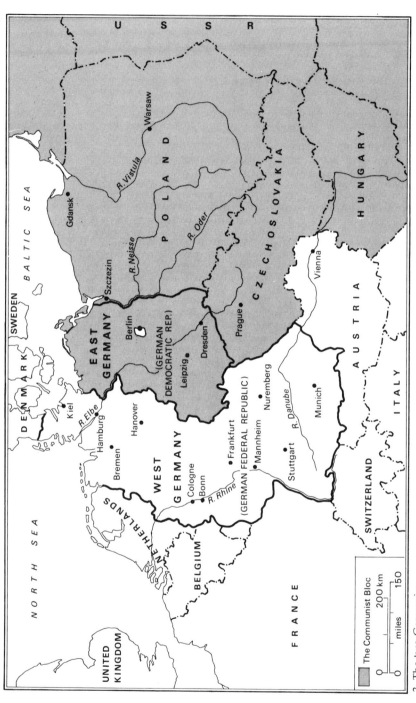

3. The two Germanies.

case of Dachau near Munich, had been converted from a former concentration camp. There were also in the spring of 1945 scores of evacuees from the cities who were trying to make their way home. At the same time several million soldiers were on the road in search of their families. Finally there were the Displaced Persons (DPs), former slave labourers or inmates of concentration camps from all over Europe waiting to be repatriated or to be given an immigration permit to start a new life overseas. According to Allied estimates there were at least 1.5 million Russian DPs, 1.2 million Frenchmen, 600,000 Poles, 350,000 Italians, 400,000 Dutch and Belgians, 100,000 Yugoslavs and thousands of nationals from other countries. All in all, probably some 25 million people were away from their former residences (Table 4).

The social and economic problems raised by the existence of these millions of destitute and homeless Germans and non-Germans had fallen into the lap of the Allied occupation authorities after Unconditional Surrender. For a number of years Britain, Russia and the United States had been holding top-level discussions among themselves in an attempt to agree on the principles according to which a defeated Germany was to be treated. It had been relatively easy to establish a consensus on certain 'negative' aims. Thus there was no question that Germany must be demilitarised and her war industries destroyed. Those primarily responsible for unleashing the Second World War and for perpetrating war crimes were to be brought to justice. All other Germans were to be de-Nazified. The Allies also agreed that Austria, Poland and Czechoslovakia were to be reconstituted as sovereign states.

It had been more difficult at the various wartime conferences between Roosevelt, Churchill and Stalin to formulate conclusive plans concerning the future of Germany. One of the main bones of contention was whether the Reich should be dismembered or treated as a unit. As no consensus had been reached on this issue, the Allies fell back on the accord of the Yalta Conference of February 1945 which had finalised the division of the country into zones of occupation, with the question of a Peace Treaty and of the future territorial shape to be decided at a later date. In the end France was to take charge of the south-west and Palatinate; the United States of Bavaria, Württemberg-Baden and Hesse; Britain of northern Germany and the Rhineland, except for an American enclave around Bremen and Bremerhaven; and the Soviet Union of the eastern provinces of the Reich between the rivers Elbe and Werra in the west and the rivers Oder and Neisse in the east. Berlin became divided into sectors and was administered jointly by an Inter-Allied authority chaired by the Allied military commanders there. As an Allied Declaration of 5 June 1945 reiterated, the four powers assumed supreme government authority in Germany, though without intending to annex German territory. The supreme military commanders of the four Allied contingents were to administer their respective zones in accordance with the instructions received from their governments. They were to deal jointly with all matters relating to the country as a whole. It was for this purpose that an Inter-Allied Control Council was set up, supported by an administrative infrastructure, to look after military matters, transport, finance, economic affairs, reparations, justice, prisoners of war, communications, law and order, as well as political affairs.

Detailed provisions were also published for the arrest of leading Nazis (the most prominent of whom would soon be tried and sentenced by a Tribunal at Nuremberg), the disarmament of the Wehrmacht and the internment of German soldiers. Further arrangements emerged at the end of July 1945 during the Potsdam Conference of the Big Three (America, Russia, Great Britain), at which the demilitarisation and de-Nazification policies were confirmed. Administratively the country was to be decentralised and all concentrations of economic power in industry demolished. Local self-government was to be permitted and the establishment of political parties and other organisations granted on application. Finally, the issue of reparations was raised again. The Russians, especially, whose industry had been badly affected by Nazi occupation, were keen to put forward their claims. Although no precise sum was fixed, it was agreed that the Germans should be left with sufficient resources after the extraction of reparations to enable them to survive economically without outside help.

For the moment, there was no hope of the population being able to do this. Something had to be done to help those millions who were either living in appalling squalor and deprivation or were moving aimlessly around the country in search of food and shelter. As late as August 1945 some 25,000 to 30,000 refugees were drifting through Berlin every day. Further south, in Bavaria, the daily influx of German Nationals from Eastern Europe was 3,500. Most fellow-Germans were themselves in no position to help the refugees and, if they were, they often showed little sense of human solidarity. Initial feelings of pity were soon displaced by hostility. It was a measure of the demoralising impact of Nazism and the total collapse of the social fabric of German society that tensions between refugees and the indigenous population, especially in the rural areas, repeatedly reached boiling point. So, only the military authorities were in a position to help effectively. It was left to them to organise relief and, supported by an embryonic local German administration, to stop starvation and chaos. When the Supreme Headquarters Allied Expeditionary Forces in Europe (SHAEF) took stock of food supplies in the Western Zones of Occupation at the end of May 1945, it was found that they would last for a maximum of 60 days. The main problem was to distribute a minimum daily ration to the population. The British Military Governor laid down a ration of 1,500 calories per day; yet by July the average had slumped to between 950 and 1,150 calories.

With the agricultural East lost and the Russians unable (or unwilling) to help, the importation of foodstuffs became unavoidable, and in subsequent weeks some 600,000 tons of wheat were shipped to Germany, together with further quantities of seed grain. This was only the beginning of a major relief operation. Food, fertiliser, fuel and medical supplies soon reached the Western zones under the auspices of the GARIOA programme. At the same time a host of private organisations in the United States, Switzerland and Sweden began to send food and clothes, while the DPs, many of whom were either mental or physical wrecks or both, were looked after by the Relief and Rehabilitation Administration of the newly created United Nations Organisation.

However, it was clear that millions of people could not be maintained like this for any length of time. Agricultural and industrial production had to be got going again in the Western zones. The occupation authorities made a major effort to achieve this and with considerable success. By 1946/7 non-meat food production reached 89 per cent of its totals in the years before the war. There was a slight drop in the following year, which the Western Allies compensated for by stepping up food imports. With these measures and the continuation of rationing, all of which required a considerable organisational effort, it was possible to avoid large-scale famine despite a simultaneous worldwide food shortage. Of course, Germany had long been a major industrial country and, if the economy was to support its population again, industry had to be revived. The potential still existed and it was merely a matter of deciding what to do with it. During the war, American planning in particular had been vacillating as regards German industry and for a while a number of politicians had gained an influential voice in Washington who wanted to reduce the level of German industrialisation quite drastically.

However, when confronted with the practical realities of the postwar situation in Central Europe, the British and American military authorities quickly began to build up a zonal machinery for economic administration to encourage the reopening of the factories for the provision of consumer goods. There was also the Western and increasingly American-dominated vision of a postwar international order which soon was to prove incompatible with Soviet policy. Although the Allies had resolved to treat Germany as a single economic unit, the remobilisation of industrial production took place on a zonal level, at least until the East–West conflict became more tense and the British–American Bi-Zone was created on 1 January 1947. There was an abundance of labour and skilled people who were eager to work. It has even been suggested that the skill levels of the working population increased as a result of the intensive industrial war effort. On the other hand, there were limiting factors. Above all, the losses of young men as a result of the war had changed the age structure. For the same reason the female population had also grown disproportionately. As late as 1950 the female population exceeded the male population by 3 million (53.1% : 46.9%). Many women were looking for employment, often because they were the only breadwinner in the family. However, as long as production levels remained low, employers were able to pick and choose from the large pool of unemployed. The unlucky ones continued to rely on poverty relief or could be seen travelling with their rucksacks far into the countryside to knock on farmers' doors begging for food. Those who were temporarily barred from their profession because of Allied de-Nazification procedures and who possessed valuables suitable for barter got their pound of butter or bucketful of coal on the black market.

It also turned out that the extent of the damage done to industry by bombing was deceptive. Repairs could be carried out relatively quickly and many entrepreneurs, especially the smaller ones, found it easy to switch back from military to civilian production. Naturally, much of the machinery was badly worn by round-the-clock use during the war and spare parts were difficult to come by. But for the moment inefficient production was better than none and there was no capital for a major modernisation programme. This was implemented only later and paid its dividends in the 1950s when high-quality German goods reappeared on the world market. A special effort was made with regard to coal mining which both Allied and German authorities came to see as the 'key to increasing industrial production' (W. Abelshauser). Whereas a bare 60,000 tons had been dug by July 1945, output rose to 173,000 tons by the end of the year. During the following twelve months there were only slight monthly increases on this figure, but by the end of 1947 monthly output stood at 235,000 tons. Because of the heavy work and special skills required, miners were actually in short supply in this period. However, better wage rates and special food rations, suitably publicised, soon attracted younger untrained men into the profession. The index of overall industrial production reflects a rather less impressive performance than that of coal mining. Nevertheless, Werner Abelshauser's point remains that the upward trend of the Bizonal industrial economy had set in before the financial aid of the famous American Marshall Plan began to pour into the Western Zones of Occupation and before the Currency Reform of June 1948 had been enacted. Both these policies created the conditions of further and more rapid growth from a fairly high plateau which had already been reached by the beginning of 1948.

On the other hand, the temporary slump in industrial production which occurred in the first quarter of 1947 revealed the precarious position in which the economy of the Western zones continued to find itself, even if it has been shown that the recession was primarily due to a breakdown of the transport and distribution system. Railways, roads and waterways had also been badly affected by the war and reconstruction proved difficult. In this field, as in all other areas, Allied help therefore remained indispensable. Although the humanitarian impulse behind Western aid must be emphasised, support was not given for entirely altruistic reasons. In particular, the political and economic elites of the United States – the country which had emerged from the war as the strongest power – had, well before 1945, developed a vision of how the postwar world should ideally be structured. What in their view had caused the breakdown of international relations and of the world economy in the 1930s and had ultimately led to world war was economic nationalism. This nationalism was to be replaced once and for all by a multilateral world trading system based on the principle of the Open Door. The Americans were determined that the postwar network of international relations should be reconstructed as a 'One World' system in which nations would exchange their goods peacefully and freely. Although few American politicians and businessmen would admit it, it was clear that this One World would be dominated by the powerful United States. There was also no question that a liberal representative constitution was deemed to be the political system most compatible with the Open Door.

Whereas these ideas were firmly established in American thinking by the early 1940s, it took somewhat longer for those politicians and businessmen who wished to give the Germans an equal place within this New Economic Order to assert themselves. But the logic of their argument was too compelling and by 1944 it was, as the Executive Committee of Economic Foreign Policy of the US stated, a 'major objective' of American policy to achieve German reintegration at the appropriate time. What accelerated this development was the deterioration in the relations between the Western Allies and the Soviet Union after the end of the war. The origins of the Cold War have been the subject of a lively debate between those historians who have made the westward expansionism of Russia responsible for the confrontation and those who identified the dynamic of America's One World vision as the decisive factor. Without wanting to go into the details of this particular controversy, there can be little doubt that the divergent concepts for shaping the postwar world held in Moscow and Washington made the East–West conflict virtually inevitable.

The leaders of the new superpower across the Atlantic self-confidently aspired to a world order which would be based on the principles of a competitive American-style capitalism. The Russians, on the other hand, wanted to consolidate the gains made as a result of the Second World War and may for a while even have hoped to extend their own system beyond the sphere of influence which the defeat of Germany had put under their control. Certainly, there were many statements by Soviet leaders which indicated that they, too, cherished notions of a One World, although it was to be structured very differently from the US model. And as the two systems were so patently incompatible with each other, it was to be expected that sooner or later one side would try to seal its own sphere of influence off from the other. The One World, whether of the Soviet or of the American variety, became a 'half-world'

(M. Balfour) organised as blocs within which East and West began to revamp the existing socioeconomic and political structures and harmonise them with their own institutional arrangements. The division of Europe along the line established at the end of the war slowly took shape.

As this line ran through the middle of Germany, the cutting in two of that country was a direct function of the escalating Cold War crisis. The re-integration of Germany into the community of nations thus came to mean reintegration of the Western Zones of Occupation into the Western world and of the Russian Zone into the Soviet world. We shall analyse below how the Russians went about this task. For the moment the aim is to look at how the process worked on the Western side and in particular how it was effected in the economic field. It has already been mentioned that, while the French continued to keep apart, collaboration between the British and American occupation authorities in the face of the sharpening East–West conflict grew close enough to create a Bizonal administration. In April 1949, this arrange-ment was expanded into the Trizone to include the French which further facilitated a co-ordinated economic policy. More and more the Americans took the lead, pressing both the German administrators, whose offices had been moved to Frankfurt, and their Allies to adopt their economic recipes. Above all they were concerned to construct the preconditions of the integration of the Western Zones of Occupation into the world market. Decartellisation provides a good illustration of what the problems were in the American view. We have seen above how the German economy had become dominated by cartels and syndicates at all levels and how the principle of competition in the market-place had virtually been abolished by a thorough-going regulation of the production and marketing of goods. The cartel tradition was very deeply rooted in German industry, but it was dysfunctional to the type of competitive world economy, free from nationalist protectionism and market regulation, which the Americans envisaged. Hence cartels had to be destroyed and German industrial practice had to be adjusted.

The idea of restoring an open and dynamic capitalism corresponded broadly with the views of a group of influential German economists who became known as the neo-liberals. They, too, stressed the wealth producing force of a modern industrial capitalism. Like many American politicians and businessmen, they believed 'that a systematically developed competitive system' not only mobilised the productive energies of society most effectively, but also provided for increased purchasing power of the masses permitting even 'the weakest members of society to lead a worthwhile life befitting a human being' (C. Watrin). Although some of them took a greater interest than the Americans in problems of wealth distribution (hence the term: 'social market economy''), protagonists of the neo-liberal model agreed that the mistakes of the interwar period must not be repeated. Protective tariffs, cartels, centralised planning and nationalism were elements of a German type of industrial capitalism whose remnants had to be removed.

However, it was not just a matter of creating compatible structures in the Western Zones of Occupation to make economic reintegration possible; there was also the political question of how the German population might be convinced of its advantages. One way of achieving this was to extol the blessings of a mass production economy which would secure a rise in living standards for everyone. On the other hand, most Germans in the late 1940s living, as they did, under conditions of extreme austerity, found it difficult to visualise a successful market economy of plenty. Worse, capitalism had become discredited in the eyes of many who associated it with the disaster of the Great Slump, the rise of Hitler and the subsequent catastrophes of German history. The mood in all four occupation zones was distinctly 'socialist' in the early years after the war. If they cared at all, many people talked of a need to search for new solutions and were often prepared to support radical alternatives to capitalism. Yet it was not merely the economic predicament of millions of Germans and the dissatisfaction this generated among them which made them accessible to anti-capitalist arguments. With the general economic situation improving but slowly, it was of course convenient to blame the miseries of postwar life on the Western Allies.

Economic resentments which undermined official attempts to convince the Germans of the viability of American economic strategy were reinforced by a growing political opposition to the West's interpretation of modern German history and the handling of de-Nazification. It may be questioned whether the Germans as a nation would ever have been capable of facing their recent past squarely and without resort to myths and apologies. As the philosopher Karl Jaspers put it disapprovingly at the time: 'One simply does not want to suffer any more. One wants to escape the misery [and] to live, but does not wish to ponder. The mood is as if one expects to be compensated after the terrible suffering or at least to be comforted; but one does not want to be burdened with guilt.' Clearly the general climate for a hard look back at German history was most unfavourable. Self-pity was widespread. However, the Western notion of collective guilt made a genuine reappraisal even more difficult. This is not to deny that, viewed from their perspective, the Allies had good reason to be wanting to pursue de-Nazification. It is also certain that awkward dilemmas would have arisen whatever policy they decided to adopt. The Americans especially were convinced that Nazism had been deeply ingrained in German society and that their aim of reintegrating the Western Zones of Occupation into the community of nations would be doomed to failure unless there was a thorough purge followed by a re-education programme in 'liberal democracy'. In their view, a liberal market economy which they were pre-paring to establish in what was to become West Germany would not work, if it was not complemented by compatible political institutions and attitudes. Hence Nazi mentalities and institutions had to be eradicated. The men and women who had played an important part in maintaining them were to be removed. Only after this process had been completed would the introduction of a Western-type political system possess a solid foundation; a relapse into old habits would be impossible.

These were the broader assumptions behind the American decision to require all Germans over 18 years of age to fill in a questionnaire about their past political activities and commitments. On the basis of this document they were then categorised according to their presumed or proven degree of involvement with the Third Reich. As the system developed, five categories were established: major offenders, offenders, lesser offenders, followers and exonerated. Whatever else one may think of this system, those responsible for promulgating it certainly totally underestimated the bureaucratic complexities of the operation which got slowly underway from 1945 onwards. At first the security officers of the occupation forces tried to process the questionnaires. People who had been put into one of the first three categories lost their jobs, had their pensions withdrawn, their property confiscated, were fined, imprisoned or had their civic rights removed. But by the end of 1945 there was a growing backlog of cases and mounting criticism of the whole procedure. In March 1946, the Americans therefore induced the German *Länder* governments which had meanwhile been constituted in their occupation zone to take charge of the operation. The British and French authorities similarly began to rely on the Germans to execute the programme under Allied supervision.

Unfortunately the handling of de-Nazification by German administrators and tribunals which were set up did little to expedite matters. Nor did it introduce greater uniformity with regard to the standards of justice applied. Considerable differences continued to obtain in the application of the rules between the French, British and American zones. Thus persons of similar record could find themselves classified in different categories depending on whether they lived in Munich, Freiburg or Hamburg (Table 47). Inequalities also arose because the whole process was taking so long and could ultimately only be abbreviated by general amnesties and stroke-of-the-pen decisions. Consequently those who, by good luck or design, came later in the queue would get away more lightly than those whose past was scrutinised in 1945/6. In the end, the whole programme petered out. Up to early 1950, the tribunals heard more than six million cases, two-thirds of which were dealt with summarily through amnesties, for example for those who were born after 1 January 1919. Some 1,700 persons were identified as major offenders, 23,000 as offenders, 150,500 as lesser offenders, 1 million as followers and 1.2 million as exonerated. In the American Zone alone some 13 million people had returned their questionnaires of whom three-quarters were not even chargeable under the de-Nazification criteria.

Looking back on the whole programme, the Western Allies clearly found themselves in a great quandary. It was obviously unthinkable for prominent Nazis or people who had been closely involved with the regime not to be made accountable for their activities. Yet, could the sheep ever be separated from the goats? The task was further complicated by the fact that German friends, colleagues and relatives of defendants were prepared to provide mitigating evidence and 'laundering certificates' (*Persilscheine*). The role of the Catholic and Protestant Churches is also of considerable importance here. With their moral authority enhanced by their (often exaggerated) anti-Nazi record and their power and informal influence tangibly increased, a testimony by a member of the Church hierarchy was bound to count heavily. If necessary, a large network of international contacts could also be mobilised against an overharsh, primitive policy by the Allied de-Nazification bureaucracy. All these different witnesses were prone to argue that the defendant had tacitly or openly resisted the Nazi regime or had saved some other person from the clutches of the SS. Since an entire nation had been put in the dock and hence on the defensive, the general tendency was to portray everyone as an opponent of the Third Reich. This was evidently just as untenable as the American view that almost everyone had been a Nazi. We have already attempted to be somewhat more sophisticated when dealing with this question. A look at the social background of those who appeared before the tribunals and those whose questionnaires were merely filed away would seem to confirm our earlier findings about 'the Germans' and Nazism.

It is at this point that a fundamental contradiction between the realities of de-Nazification and the broader aims of the Western Allies opened up. A de-Nazification policy which would have taken to task those individuals who made a major contribution to sustaining the Hitler regime would have touched the social and economic power structures of the Western zones much more radically than the Allies were prepared to permit. Neither the kind of economic system nor the society which they were hoping to reconstruct could exist without the expertise of the administrative, managerial and technical elites which had collaborated with Hitler. The beginning of the Cold War caused this contradiction to come to the surface, and once it had been recognised that it was impossible to do both, it was only logical for the tribunals to be wound up. For the developing confrontation with Russia meant 'that the conservative fear of Communism gradually replaced the liberal fear of fascism' (E. N. Peterson).

Nor did de-Nazification and 'collective guilt' assumptions square too well with the policy of permitting some people to found parties and other political organisations. On the other hand, from the point of view of integration it made sense to hold elections, first at local and later at regional level, to encourage political activity and to allow the constitution of *Länder* governments on the basis of parliamentary majorities. Thus, less than a year after the end of the war, there emerged a range of political parties in the Western zones. They began to canvas popular support and to put out programmatic statements which they thought would appeal to potential voters. It is as documents of prevalent ideologies and aspirations that these statements are of interest here. Most of the men and women who applied for licence to organise politically had been prominent in Weimar politics. The first steps were usually taken at the local level. But like-minded people soon established contact with each other beyond the locality. Their parties became active on a regional and zonal and finally on an inter-zonal level.

This is certainly how various Liberal groups sprang up in all three zones before forming the Free Democratic Party (FDP) in December 1948. What characterised the early proclamations of the Liberals is the woolliness of their demands. Little attempt was made to present an interpretation of National Socialism. Instead there was a strong emphasis on the Reich as a centralised, though democratically structured German State. As to the organisation of the economy, a certain amount of planning was widely deemed to be unavoidable although personal initiative, free competition and private ownership were seen as essentials. Social policy was advocated 'as a major instrument of alleviating material need and for securing social peace. The Liberals also revived their traditional demand of secular education. Most programmatic statements finally contained broadsides against clerical, nationalist or socialist panaceas for Germany's problems. Otherwise, they presented hazy notions of a future *Volksstaat* which meant all things to all people. Nevertheless, compared with the other major parties, the FDP stood on the right of the political spectrum and some of its regional groups championed an unashamed nationalism.

Intellectually more substantial were the ideas advanced by a number of political groups which finally merged to constitute the Christian Democratic Union (CDU). Catholics who had been associated with the Centre Party in the Weimar Republic, together with a number of theologians, were among the prime movers behind this party. But both the groups in the Rhineland and the circle which emerged in Frankfurt agreed that it would be a mistake to re-establish a purely denominational organisation. This time Protestants and Catholics were to be united under one roof. Most of the early proclamations had brief but strong words of rejection for the Nazi experience and stressed the persecution of the Churches. As to future policy, the CDU, under the strong influence of the Rhenish regional organisation, promoted the teachings of Catholic social theory. The early statements urged the adoption of Christian

Social ideas as an antidote to Marxist influences on the Left. Not surprisingly, great importance was also attached to religious instruction in state schools and to the right to run denominationally based private schools. The Protestant factions in the CDU, especially those from northern Germany, lacked a similarly coherent social policy and, as many of its representatives had formerly been associated with the DNVP or DVP of the Weimar days, they tended to counterbalance the more left-wing Christian Socialism of the Rhineland with more conservative ideas about the future shape of State and society. There was an attempt by a number of Catholic politicians to refound the Centre Party (Table 43); but the unification of Protestants and Catholics under the banner of a Christian Democratic front against Communism and Social Democracy proved more viable this time.

The CDU's left-wing achieved its greatest success in February 1947 when the Party adopted the so-called Ahlen Programme. Openly denouncing private as well as 'state capitalism', it rejected the concentration of economic power and favoured an extended participation of the workforce in managerial matters. However, as Wolf-Dieter Narr and others have argued, the Ahlen Programme represented at the same time the high-water mark of Christian Socialism in the CDU. Although this wing retained considerable influence, mainstream Christian Democracy came under the spell of the advocates of a neo-liberal market economy like Ludwig Erhard. Ideologically and sociologically the Party remained a heterogeneous and in many ways opportunist movement which, apart from middle-class professionals, industrialists, businessmen and farmers, also retained a working-class membership. On the other hand, the *bürgerliche* groups increasingly came to dominate the political orientation of the CDU. This was even more true of the Christian Social Union (CSU), the Bavarian branch of Christian Democracy.

The third large political party to emerge in the Western Zones of Occupation was the SPD. Ideologically much less flexible than the CDU, Social Democracy was a 'moralistic' party which tried to appeal to the politically and historically educated and thoughtful person as well as its old working-class clientele. Its ethos was possibly best embodied in the personality of its leader, Kurt Schumacher, who had emerged from eleven years in a Nazi concentration camp an even more unbending politician than he had been in the Weimar period: passionate, at times demagogic, but equally devoted to rational argument and backed by the moral authority of his anti-Nazi record. Like Schumacher in his speeches, the SPD's early programmatic declarations minced no words about the past. As the Guidelines of May 1946 put it:

During the interwar period the forces of high capitalism and reaction have tried everywhere to escape the socialist consequences of democracy. They succeeded in Germany because of the country's special economic, historical and intellectual predicament. With the coming of the 'Third Reich' democracy had been put out of action after the destruction of the political force of the working class, and the preconditions of a European catastrophe were created owing to the absence of democratic opinion formation and control. What constitutes the share of historical guilt of the German people is the failure of the German bourgeoisie and of those Communist parts of the working-class movement which did not recognise the value of democracy.

The lesson to be learned from the experience of fascism was to build up a *democratic* socialism. Political democracy was to be complemented by a nationalisation of large-scale private enterprise, with the coal and steel industries at the top of the list. Estate owners were similarly to be expropriated and land distributed to the small farmers. Another marked feature of the SPD's programme was its distinct nationalism and anti-Communism. A pronounced identification with the Reich and the nation had, of course, deep roots among some sections of the German working-class movement. But what contributed to an anti-Allied nationalism becoming a major plank in SPD propaganda was the belief, held by many of the leaders, that the Party's failure to retain its initial electoral support after the First World War was related to its successful stigmatisation by the Right as a stooge of the Allies and of fulfilment. In the same way the Social Democrats' anti-Communism was a response to the past experience of bitter conflict between the two working-class parties. They also suggested that, its protestations to the contrary notwithstanding, the emergent Communist Party (KPD), strongly influenced by Stalinists as it soon was, merely paid lip-service to the postulated inseparability of socialism and democracy.

The programmes of the major parties which emerged in the Western Zones of Occupation are of interest both as statements by those who became active in postwar German politics and as reflections of what they considered to be the popular mood. In this latter respect it is interesting to see how they tried to appeal to ideological positions which had traditionally been held by specific social groups in the class society of pre-1933 Germany. Materially, millions of Germans were living in conditions of utmost deprivation after 1945. But as a glance not only at the spectrum of parties, but also at some election results will show, this did not mean that the voters had become an ideologically undifferentiated mass which would vote for one and the same party. De facto proletarianisation did not create a uniform proletarian consciousness. The Americans were the first of the three Western Allies to permit local elections in their zone, in January 1946, followed by elections to Constituent Assemblies in the *Länder* of Hesse, Bavaria and Württemberg-Baden later in that year. In September the first local elections were held in the British and French zones of occupation, with *Land* elections taking place a few months later. The proportions of votes for the parties in various *Land* elections in 1946/7 are shown in the accompanying table.

Land election results in the Western Zones, 1946–1947

	KPD	SPD	CDU (CSU)	Liberals	Splinter groups
			%		
Schleswig-Holstein (20.4.1947)	4.7	43.8	34.1	5.0	12.5
Hamburg (13.10.1946)	10.4	43.1	26.7	18.2	1.6
Lower Saxony (20.4.1947)	5.6	43.4	19.9	8.8	22.3
Bremen (20.10.1947)	8.8	41.7	22.0	5.5	22.0
Northrhine-Westphalia (20.4.1947)	14.0	32.0	37.6	5.9	10.6
Palatinate (18.5.1947)	8.7	34.3	47.2	9.8	—
Württ.-Baden (24.11.1946)	10.2	31.9	38.4	19.5	—
Hesse (1.12.1946)	10.7	42.7	30.9	15.7	—
Bavaria (18.5.1947)	6.1	28.6	52.3	5.6	7.4
Baden (18.5.1947)	7.4	22.4	55.9	14.3	—
Württ.-Hohenzollern (18.5.1947)	7.3	20.8	54.2	17.7	—

An averaging of voting figures provides a rough guide as to relative strength of the different parties in the three Western zones, even if it must be remembered that the elections were held over a time-span of several months. Nevertheless, it is significant that the CDU/CSU managed to become the largest party (37.6%), followed by the SPD (35.0%), the KPD (9.4%), the Liberals (9.3%) and various right-wing or regional parties (8.7%). Although all the large parties presented themselves as omnibus parties, a comparison with the Weimar period reveals that traditional allegiances had not been obliterated. Many voters evidently recognised certain fundamental programmatic positions and were strongly guided in their decisions by old affinities (Table 42). Religious affiliation once again emerges as a clearly recognisable factor, especially in the west and south. Nor had social origin and status lost its significance. The political spectrum, it is true, had seen a general shift towards the Left. Yet a major and lasting rebalancing of socioeconomic and political power would have been possible only if the underlying power structure had also been tackled; but such radical policies did not have the support of the Western Allies and of the Americans in particular. An early indication of their aversion to a fundamental change can be found in the treatment of the *Antifa* (Anti-Fascist) committees which sprang up in many industrial cities in 1945, but were quickly contained even where they were not dominated by Communists or emasculated politically as auxiliaries of the Allied de-Nazification machinery. Later the US authorities deleted a clause from the Hessian Constitution which would have allowed the SPD-led government there to experiment with public ownership. Nor did plans for workers' participation get very far. Integration of the Western zones into a US-dominated Western community of capitalist nations became the overriding concern once the Cold War had started.

In view of this, the proposals of the SPD were far too radical. As there was no overwhelming popular pressure for introducing them, the fresh beginning after 1945 consisted mainly in adjusting the socioeconomic and political structures of the three zones to fit in with Western parliamentarism and free enterprise capitalism. The concomitant re-education programme was designed to generate a favourable mental disposition towards the ideas on which representative democracy and liberal market economics were based. Nevertheless, it is unlikely that these basic policies would have asserted themselves so soon over those of the Social Democrats which aimed at more fundamental reform, had it not been for the Cold War. The rising fear of Communism strengthened the hand of the United States *vis-à-vis* both the French and the British, whose Labour Government was favourably disposed towards the more far-reaching aims of the Social Democrats. As we have seen, the fear had been deeply ingrained in large sections of the population since the turn of the century and had been reinforced by fifteen years of incessant Nazi propaganda. Towards the end of the war, personal experiences, second-hand accounts and rumours about Russian treatment of German refugees did nothing to reduce the abhorrence of socialism. After 1945 it was events and policies adopted in the Soviet Zone of Occupation that also destroyed the chances of the democratic socialists in the SPD to succeed with their reforms or ever to leave the 30–35 per cent 'ghetto'. What were these Soviet policies?

The Russian Zone of Occupation, 1945–1949

There is considerable doubt that Stalin and his advisers knew exactly what they wanted to achieve when they moved into Germany to assume control of the Zone allocated to them. At least they appear to have kept an open mind concerning the future of the Reich as a whole. But even with regard to their Zone it was by no means clear from the start that a Soviet-style economic and political system would be imposed by force. The Russian interpretation of National Socialism was to some extent responsible for this ambiguity. Stalin had always seen the Hitler regime more as an outgrowth of the crisis of 'monopoly capitalism' in Germany than as a movement of the 'masses'. What he wished to destroy therefore was the socioeconomic power structures which, he believed, had given birth to and maintained fascism. Accordingly, de-Nazification in the Russian style was not the ideological screening of millions of people; rather it was used to oust the economic and social elites from their pre-1945 positions. This policy, it was hoped, would also generate popular support among the rest of the population which was to be governed by a Soviet-backed, though not necessarily Sovietised, new leadership.

It was hence not sheer cynicism when, a mere four weeks after the armistice, the Soviet authorities cleared the way for the founding of political parties which, as the decree put it, 'have as their aim the final extermination of the remnants of fascism and the fostering of the foundation of democracy and civil liberties in Germany as well as the development of the initiative and the self-activity of the broad masses of the population'. The Communists were to be one of these parties. Since the end of April, a number of KPD exiles had been brought back to the Soviet zone to establish contact with former comrades who had returned from Britain, had worked underground or had been liberated from the concentration camps. One of the possibilities which they began to explore was the formation of a unified working-class party. There was a strong desire not to perpetuate the fatal split of the Weimar period. But the speed with which the KPD was refounded after the publication of the decree by the Soviet military authorities on 9 June 1945 put paid to the idea of unification. A few weeks later the Social Democrats constituted themselves in Berlin under the leadership of Otto Grotewohl. The East German CDU and a Liberal Party (LDPD) emerged shortly afterwards. But what surprised people even more than Soviet openness was the contents of the first KPD proclamation. It stressed that the situation was not suited to introducing a Soviet-type system in Germany. Instead of nationalisation, private enterprise and personal initiative were to be encouraged.

Whatever disagreements over long-term strategy may have existed in the Kremlin, it appears that the Russian government saw the revival of the zonal economy as one of its most urgent tasks. Starvation was even worse than in the Western zones and the Soviet Union was in no position to ship large amounts of supplies to their occupation zone. On the contrary, it was important to restart German production not only to enable the Germans to help themselves, but also to extract a contribution to the rebuilding of war-torn Russia. Stalin was keenly interested in reparations and by the end of 1946 the equipment of some 1,400 industrial enterprises in the Soviet Zone of Occupation had been wholly or partially transported to the East. In the following year a further 200 firms were converted into so-called Soviet Joint Stock Companies. As these companies produced about one quarter of the total output of the East German industrial economy, a tangible percentage of wealth was siphoned off from the zonal economy.

Whereas these policies depressed the living standards of the entire population more or less with equal harshness, Stalin also began to make structural changes in the East German economy which hit the propertied classes. One of the first of these measures was to expropriate without compensation some 7,000 estate owners who owned about 2.5 million hectares of land. A further 600,000 hectares were confiscated from people who had occupied prominent positions in the Third Reich. Two-thirds of this land (some 2.1 million hectares) were subsequently distributed to half a million land labourers, peasants and refugees from the East. The remaining third was administered by the local authorities. Although this large-scale redistribution of land did not always create viable agricultural entities, the effect was doubtless tremendous; it destroyed the economic power base of large-scale agriculture and no doubt helped to create a favourable disposition towards the Soviet authorities among the beneficiaries of the land reforms.

It is also indicative of the general popular mood that Soviet policies received the support of the major East German parties. Even the CDU favoured them in principle although it insisted on the payment of compensation. There was evidently also some groundswell for taking industrial enterprises into collective ownership. Thus, in 1945, workers in many places spontaneously formed committees to take over factories and organise the resumption of production. In the spring of 1946, a concerted attack on the industrial property structure was launched from above. It started in the State of Saxony and on 30 June 1946 a plebiscite was held to approve or reject the nationalisation of those 'firms and enterprises which profited from the war or are owned by Nazi criminals, active Nazis or war profiteers'. The proposal, cunningly worded as it was, received the support of over three-quarters of the electorate. Subsequently expropriations of industrial enterprises were initiated also in other parts of the Soviet zone.

In the meantime a purge of the judiciary had begun which led to the removal from office of the overwhelming majority of judges. The educational reforms abolished private schools and proclaimed open access to education irrespective of social background and status. It is not too difficult to see that these and other measures resulted in a ploughing-up of the previous distribution of wealth and influence. Many of those who were expropriated moved to the Western zones, swelling the ranks of embittered and virulently anti-Communist refugees. The beneficiaries of these radical policies, on the other hand, were, to say the least, not averse to the changes and few recognised their double-edgedness. Economic restructuring could of course form the basis of a democratic political system of the kind the Social Democrats envisaged; alternatively, the purge of the economic, administrative and professional elites could be used for the conquest of major power positions in order to build up a one-party dictatorship relying on a newly created intelligentsia.

The latter solution appeared to be relatively remote in 1945 when even the KPD proclaimed itself to be opposed to the introduction of this type of regime and openly competed with other parties for electoral support. Presumably the East German Communists and their Soviet backers hoped for a time that they would emerge as the strongest party. It was for the same reason that they resisted continuing pressures by Social Democrats to form a united working-class party. However, by the end of 1945 it was all too depressingly clear that a 'democratic' strategy would not result in absolute KPD majorities. Just as in the Western zones voting behaviour was guided by tradition and memories of the past, suspicions of the Communists were deeply ingrained and it was perfectly possible to vote for other parties. The Cold War was beginning in earnest. The Soviet position in the Eastern zone had to be consolidated by different means. The Social Democrats were the first to experience this change. Suddenly the SPD found itself pressed to negotiate a merger of the two working-class parties. When these negotiations were opened just before Christmas 1945, Grotewohl and his entourage evidently still hoped that the KPD could be persuaded to return to the path of democratic virtue. Yet this optimism was dwindling rapidly as blunt pressure was unashamedly applied on all sides. In the end, resistance seemed futile. The forced merger of the two movements into the Socialist Unity Party (SED) took place at a joint meeting on 21/22 April 1946.

What eased the way for the SPD leadership to enter into this shot-gun marriage was the simultaneous proclamation of a 'special German road towards socialism', different from the generally unpopular Stalinist path. Moreover, the executive of the new party was composed equally of representatives of the KPD and SPD. One reason for the creation of the SED was the impending local and regional elections. Prospects of a left-wing, though not a Communist, victory in the autumn of 1946 were deemed to be good. To be sure, the CDU and LDPD were formidable forces to be reckoned with. But there were ways of undermining their position, and throughout the summer the Soviet occupation authorities did their best to hamper the campaigns of these parties while granting privileged status to the SED. Tampering with newsprint allocations was one device. It did not help much. The SED gained 49 per cent of the vote in the Saxon elections, with the LDPD and CDU holding 22 and 21 per cent respectively. But what was particularly galling to the SED leadership was that the Left failed to gain the absolute majority in the cities. This pattern repeated itself in the local elections in Thuringia and Sachsen-Anhalt. The party's performance in the regional elections of October 1946 was even more disconcerting: the SED was denied the absolute majority in all five provinces. The final percentages of the vote in October 1946 are indicated in the table on page 196.

Having failed to win a popular mandate for a 'German road towards socialism', the SED, supported by the Soviet authorities, abandoned its earlier strategy altogether. The Cold War was by now in full swing and, just as the Western Allies had begun to stabilise their own zones of occupation, Stalin decided to integrate his zone into the emergent Soviet bloc. More and more the Stalinists in the SED leadership were coming to play a prominent role. The CDU and LDPD were 'synchronised' and forced to recognise the primacy of the SED. Those politicians who disagreed were unceremoniously ousted. The

Regional election results in Soviet Zone, October 1946

	SED	CDU	LDPD	Peasants' League
			%	
Mecklenburg	49.5	34.1	12.5	3.9
Thuringia	49.3	18.9	28.5	3.5
Saxony	49.1	23.3	24.7	2.7
Brandenburg	43.9	30.6	20.6	4.9
Sachsen-Anhalt	45.8	29.9	21.8	2.5

prison cells were filling up with men and women who resisted the conversion of the Eastern zone into a 'people's democracy'. In the political sphere, this process culminated in January 1949 when the SED was formally proclaimed to have been transformed into a 'new-type party' which adhered to the principles of Marxism-Leninism. In the industrial sphere, the experimentation with models of economic democracy which had started in the factories in 1945 was slowly throttled. By the end of 1948, the Works' Councils had been dissolved or put under the control of the SED-dominated centralised *Freier Deutscher Gewerkschaftsbund* (FDGB). The Soviet Zone of Occupation had effectively become a copy of the Stalin dictatorship.

Corresponding measures were taken on the economic policy front and the move towards a planned economy accelerated. A prerequisite of this was the further nationalisation of industry and commerce which had begun in 1946. Two years later the share of private industry in industrial production had shrunk to 39 per cent, with the Soviet Joint Stock Companies and the state-run companies sharing the rest. Also during 1948 the newly constituted German Economic Commission (DWK) established a state-owned trading organisation (HO) which competed against private retailers. As HO shops were often given first place in the queue for supplies, the system established another technique for squeezing out private business. In 1948 retailers still commanded 82 per cent of the trade, but it did not take long for HO shops to dominate the market. The intermediate trade fell almost completely into the hands of the state organisation even more quickly. The last sector of the economy to come under attack was agriculture. As we have seen, it had been decentralised only a few years before when some 500,000 new farms were created during the land reforms. Now these small farmers were pressed into collectives. Following the Soviet pattern, the first Machine Tractor Stations (MTS) were built up in March 1949, and by 1953 collectivisation was in full swing (Table 33).

The whole system of collectivised agricultural and industrial production came to be supervised and directed by a large bureaucracy which produced its first programme at the end of 1948: the Two-Year Plan for 1949–50. The targets were hopelessly unrealistic and envisaged an increase in production of 35 per cent and in productivity of 30 per cent. The only way of coming anywhere near these targets was to increase pressure on the population to work more for less money, with consequences which we shall have to examine later in this chapter.

The shaping of the Federal Republic of Germany, 1949–1960

The system of economic and political organisation which the SED introduced in the Soviet Zone of Occupation after 1946 was more or less an exact replica of the Stalinist regime in Russia. Certainly it was very different from the economic and political structures in the Western zones of occupation. There the Currency Reform of June 1948 had cleared the way for the evolution of a free-market economy, unhampered in principle by regimentation, even if it took some time for the bureaucratic vestiges of postwar austerity and rationing to disappear. Marshall Plan money came into the country. The Western Allies and their German administrators at Frankfurt went in the opposite direction from their Communist counterparts and unleashed the energies of a private enterprise economy. It was also after the Currency Reform that the consequences of Allied policy became clearer with regard to their decision not to upset the existing property structures in any fundamental way. Although all West Germans started with 40 marks in cash in their pockets, there were some who were more equal than others. In particular those who had assets in the shape of machines, land and factories could now freely mobilise their resources in order profitably to supply a market which was starved of investment goods as well as consumer goods. A tax system which encouraged reinvestment and modernisation furthered accumulation, and an unequal distribution of wealth was created.

In 1948/9, therefore, the Western zones of occupation took a big step in the direction of an American-style competitive market economy. And just as there was a correspondence between the principles of economic and political organisation in the East, the Western zones developed corresponding links between the type of economy that was emerging and what was presumed to be the ideally 'compatible' political system. At a time when the SED was changed into a 'new-style' party, German representatives in the Western zones of occupation began to draw up a constitutional document which established parliamentarism on an inter-zonal scale.

The drafters of the Basic Law (as it came to be called), while agreeing on the essentials of a parliamentary representative system, were time and again in their discussions preoccupied with the lessons to be learned from the Weimar experience, and it is instructive to compare the Weimar Constitution with the document which became the Constitution of the Federal Republic of Germany. Thus the position of the President, unlike that of Ebert and Hindenburg, became largely ceremonial. The Chancellor was the strong figure of the executive. It was also made considerably more difficult to topple an elected government. Under the Basic Law, a 'constructive vote of no-confidence' is required, that is, the opposition is obliged to present its own alternative chancellor to be voted into office on the occasion of the confidence vote. Federalism is another marked feature of the Basic Law, with the individual *Länder* possessing a considerable degree of autonomy, especially in educational and cultural affairs. They also have a direct say, through the Federal Council (*Bundesrat*), in the legislative process and in certain cases even command veto powers.

However, just as in earlier German constitutions, the Basic Law does not merely regulate the technicalities of the governmental process; it is also a document of the aims and compromises between divergent political forces, and these are best reflected in the first twenty articles of the Basic Law. This section contains first of all the catalogue of the classic civil liberties, such as freedom of assembly, freedom of speech, freedom of association and freedom of religious belief. The Churches, which had re-emerged from the Third Reich with their moral authority surprisingly unscathed and even enhanced and which operated as highly organised pressure groups in German politics well before the drafting of the Basic Law, made their views forcefully known. Their influence can be traced directly in the wording of Articles 6 and 7. The former clause refers to the special protection to be given to marriage and the family; the latter is concerned with the importance of religious instruction in state schools and with Church-endowed private education.

However, Articles 6 and 7 must also be seen as part of an elaborate compromise which the two main political forces behind the drafting of the Basic Law, the Christian Democrats and the Social Democrats, concluded during the constitutional debates. It has already been mentioned that, as far as the fundamental principles of economic organisation were concerned, the ideas of the CDU's Ahlen Programme gave way to the concepts of a neo-liberal market economy, as enshrined in the Düsseldorf Guidelines of April 1949. The western SPD and the trade unions close to it, by contrast, continued to promote their ideas of a democratic socialism which involved economic planning and the nationalisation of basic industries. The climate of public opinion, but also the direction of Allied and particularly American policy, had, of course, become very unfavourable to the realisation of economic reforms. However, in alliance with the Christian Socialist wing of the CDU, the Social Democrats were still strong enough in 1949 to force a *quid pro quo* upon the other parties in return for agreeing to Articles 6 and 7. It is against this background that the wording of Article 20 ('The Federal Republic is a democratic and social federal state') must be seen. This is one of the immutable clauses of the Basic Law. It means that there is no going back on the principles of democracy, social welfare and federalism, short of a breach of the constitution itself. More controversial and ratified only as part of the above-mentioned compromise on Articles 6 and 7 were Articles 14 and 15. The former clause, while guaranteeing private property, is designed as a constant reminder that property is not merely an individual right but also carries with it social obligations. Above all, it must not be misused. Finally, Article 14 legalises expropriation in the interest of the commonwealth, provided an appropriate parliamentary majority can be found and compensation is paid.

This clause is reinforced by Article 15. It stipulates that 'land, natural resources and means of production may be socialised and transformed into public ownership or other forms of nationalisation by a law which regulates the kind and extent of compensation'. The implication of this is that the fathers of the Basic Law, in concluding their compromise, agreed not to close the door for ever on changes to the existing socioeconomic order. They did so not only because they saw the Basic Law as a provisional constitution to be replaced by a new document, should a peace treaty ever be signed between the wartime enemies of the Reich and a reunified Germany; Articles 14 and 15 were also incorporated as a result of pressures not to block irreversibly the possibility of adopting an economic system other than the liberal-capitalist one that was beginning to emerge in the Western zones of occupation, should there be democratically elected legislative majorities in favour of such a change. As Gerhard Leibholz, an eminent judge at the Constitutional Court, put it in December 1970: 'In subscribing to the idea of a *Sozialstaat*, the fathers of the Basic Law did not opt for a specific economic system nor for a specific social order. . . . The existing economic order is rooted in a decision by the law-makers which may be replaced and reconstituted by another decision if it places a greater emphasis on social policy.'

The Basic Law was proclaimed with the approval of the Western Allies on 23 May 1949 and in August elections were held for the Federal Parliament (*Bundestag*). The results confirmed the trend of the previous years towards a system in which the Social Democrats and Communists would remain in a minority (Table 43). The two parties gained 29.2 and 5.7 per cent of the votes respectively. The CDU/CSU emerged as the largest party (31.0%), with the FDP obtaining a respectable 11.9 per cent. The fact that some 22 per cent of the electorate voted for splinter parties (among which the German Party [DP], the Bavaria Party [BP] and the Centre Party were the largest) indicated that, whereas the working-class movement was back in its Weimar ghetto, the other social groups were far from being united. By the arithmetic of the election result, the CDU/CSU, if it wanted to form the first government of the Federal Republic, was forced to enter into coalition not only with the FDP, but also with some of the splinter parties. On 15 September 1949, Konrad Adenauer, the chairman of the CDU, finally succeeded in cobbling such a coalition together and was voted into the office of Federal Chancellor by a majority of one.

The balance of forces in the first *Bundestag*, though precarious, made certain that more far-reaching reforms which some of the Social Democrat-led *Land* governments had begun to initiate on a regional basis would not be translated into national legislation. The tendency was now for a restoration, freed from the dilemma of Allied policy in the early years after the defeat. It was only now after 1949 that it became clear how much resentment had been generated by de-Nazification, deconcentration and a host of other measures, and not merely among those directly affected. By this time, the unwillingness and inability of Germans to face the past as well as the postwar world squarely had become so strong that they voted for parties which promoted quite unreconstructed arguments about Nazism and the occupation period. The most successful among the extreme right-wing movements was the German Reich Party (DRP) which polled 1.8 per cent of the vote at the first elections to the *Bundestag* and dispatched five deputies to Bonn, the new capital of the Federal Republic. It was not a large number, but it must be seen in conjunction with the nationalism of some of the other smaller parties and of the FDP.

As both the 'collective guilt' argument of the Western Allies and the Social Democrat interpretation of National Socialism had failed to gain wider acceptance, apologetic views of German history abounded. One of the more moderate interpretations which probably shaped German perceptions of their history most powerfully after 1949 was the *Betriebsunfall* (accident in the works) theory. According to this theory, Hitler had not been brought to power by specific political forces, but had arrived on the scene virtually out of the blue. He and his band of criminals had then terrorised the country for twelve years before disappearing again like a bad dream. What this interpretation did was to cut the Third Reich out of the mainstream of German history. The Nazi period was an aberration without deeper roots. The beauty of this theory was that it did not require any agonising self-questioning, whether at a personal or institutional level. It seemed only logical that pre-1933 habits, traditions and institutions should be revived. If the Nazis had tried to destroy them, this merely seemed to prove their undiminished value.

Consequently there were whole areas of social, political and cultural life in West Germany which experienced no institutional or attitudinal change. Thus education saw little rethinking of its organisation. While blatant Nazi ideas were excised from the curricula, there was little turnover of personnel. Some *Länder* tried to broaden educational opportunities, but to obtain a better education continued to be an expensive business. The system of teaching, examining and selecting made it difficult for pupils of lower-class background to obtain the *Abitur*, even if their parents could afford the fees.

Nor was there a system of grants for those who did receive the necessary qualifications for university study. Most university teachers had negotiated the collapse of the Third Reich remarkably well and resumed their duties within institutions which did not take a critical look at their status hierarchies, examination procedures or constitutions until the 1960s. The freedom of association also led to the restoration of university fraternities which soon began to revive their time-honoured traditions and to promote an unadulterated elitism. At the grass-roots level of society there re-emerged the *Schützen-*, *Kegel-* and other associations which proudly looked back upon a long history which made no reference to the Third Reich.

Perhaps it should not be surprising that so many middle-class West Germans, having overcome the worst early postwar poverty, should attempt to restore their social and cultural institutions. The trouble was that these institutions had been important agents of illiberal socialisation and that many of them could not be as neatly separated from Nazism as the *Betriebsunfall* theory suggested. If quite a few of these associations had not directly helped to prepare the ideological ground for the Third Reich, they had certainly been abused by the regime in the 1930s. By starting up again after the war as if nothing had happened, they contributed to the creation of a public atmosphere in which self-pity and nostalgia replaced self-scrutiny.

At the same time there were millions of West Germans who kept away from all organised life and also abstained during elections (Table 43). During the 1949 elections some 22 per cent of the voting population had stayed at home and at least 10 per cent of those who went to the polls opted for parties which had gone out of their way to attract the embittered and the resentful. These people, who took a 'count-me-out' (*ohne mich*) view of politics and society, were no less dangerous than radical activists as far as the stability of the newly founded West German Republic and its government was concerned. No one was more acutely aware of the problem posed by the uncommitted than Adenauer himself. With the memories of the Weimar Republic before him, the existence of a large percentage of citizens who felt no attachment to the parliamentary–republican order amounted to a grave threat to the viability of West Germany.

There were many leading politicians who came to believe that the social and political integration of millions of psychologically and materially uprooted people could succeed only on the basis of a prosperous economy. They were correct in the sense that nothing did more to consolidate the Federal Republic as a social and political entity and, as the *Bundestag* elections of 1953 and 1957 were to demonstrate, to strengthen the initially weak position of the Adenauer government than the prosperity of the 1950s. With the exception of agriculture, the index of production increased so rapidly in all branches of the economy that people began to speak of a 'miracle'. The overall index of production rose from 61 points in 1948 to 165 six years later (Tables 7 and 8). Within a few years West Germany became a major exporter of industrial goods which earned its living by its integration into a multilateral trading system of the West (Table 49). The success of Erhard's social market economy is also reflected in the real Gross National Product (GNP), which grew from 98 to 162 points between 1949 and 1954, and in high annual growth rates (Table 12).

Nevertheless, such averages can be misleading because they tell us nothing about how the newly created national wealth was distributed among the population. We have already noted that the neo-liberals around Erhard were concerned to unleash the productive energies of the country. Most of them had not worried too deeply about the distributive problems raised by a free enterprise economy. To provide incentives for an expansion of industry and capital formation were Erhard's major objectives. *Wohlstand für alle* would then follow more or less automatically. The boom no doubt achieved this objective, but it also resulted in a noticeably more rapid rise in the incomes of the self-employed engaged in non-agricultural enterprise than in the incomes of wage-earners (Tables 22 and 26). The unemployed and their families could barely be said to be participating in the 'Economic Miracle', as social security benefits remained meagre. Unemployment figures, fed by the constant influx of refugees from the East, remained relatively high, even if the overall decline was impressive (Table 18). Nor did war widows and old-age pensioners gain more than a marginal stake in the new prosperity. The economic imbalance between agriculture and industry, which is also reflected in the production figures and the employment structure, caused the farmers to lag behind in the incomes league table.

Former public employees, on the other hand, saw their material position greatly improved when legislation was introduced and ratified at great speed to comply with Article 131 of the Basic Law. This Article put an obligation on the politicians to regulate 'the legal status of persons . . . who were employed by the public service on 8 May 1945, left it for reasons other than those provided by the civil service rules and have since then not been employed or found employment in positions not commensurate to their status'(!). The bill which reached the statute book on 1 April 1951 restored the pension rights and the employment of civil servants and professional soldiers who had been caught by Allied de-Nazification policies, with the exception of members of the Gestapo and organisations declared as criminal at the Nuremberg Trials. The *131er-Gesetz* was a costly piece of legislation financially, but was seen as an important political step towards reconciling large numbers of *déclassé* and de-Nazified public employees to the Federal Republic and, one might add, towards restoring the economic and social position of sizeable sections of the middle class.

Similar political considerations also lay behind the Equalisation of Burdens Law (LAG), another piece of legislation which tried to grapple with the legacy of the Third Reich and the fact that millions of refugees had lost most of their property. They had thus paid very dearly for the last war, while their fellow-citizens in the Western parts of the Reich who had not been bombed out had retained their assets. The idea underlying the LAG was to distribute the economic losses more equally and to collect a contribution, amounting to half of the estimated assets value, but payable in instalments over thirty years, from those who owned property above a unit value of 5,000 marks. This money was to be allocated to those Germans who had suffered material losses. In the event the total levy came to 37 milliard marks, to be raised from some three million Germans who had agricultural, industrial or real estate assets. Compensation payments took the form of small monthly pensions, calculated on the basis of former income, and a lump sum for lost household property. A large sum was set aside, however, for reimbursements whose size depended on the value of the properties lost. In other words, those who had lost most and were able to document these losses absolutely, though not proportionally, got more under the terms of the main compensation scheme (*Hauptentschädigung*). Thus a person who had had assets of 5,000 marks would be compensated in full. A loss of 50,000 marks would fetch 19,000 marks in compensation. Documented assets of 2 million marks were compensated at a rate of 8 per cent. This may not have been much in proportional terms, but it provided a nice financial base for making a fresh start. Although the fact that large numbers of refugees benefited from the LAG in a small way was psychologically important and helped to stabilise the Republic, the distributive effect of the Law was by and large marginal. For the lower-income groups the compensation payments were too small to do more than confirm traditional income inequalities. And for those three million wealthy people who were affected by the levy, the instalments were not so sizeable as to hurt them seriously once the economy was booming.

In 1963, 83.9 per cent of all households owned 53 per cent of the national wealth, representing the employees and pensioners (Table 28). The self-employed, on the other hand, amounting to 10.7 per cent of all households, held 39 per cent of the national wealth. Otherwise the LAG merely demonstrated how far the outcome of the Second World War had destroyed the economic power base of the East Elbian landowners while leaving that of the industrialists largely intact. Marion Countess Dönhoff, having lost her estates in East Prussia, received 1.2 pfennigs per sq. metre of fertile land under the Equalisation of Burdens Law. The big names of German industry can barely be said to have shared her economic fate. The value of their assets rose quickly. The yield on their capital between 1950 and 1959 averaged out at over 12 per cent.

One would expect the German industrialists who presided over the reintegration of West Germany into the world economy and who gained so much from the 'Economic Miracle' to have had fewer problems in adjusting to the Republic and to Erhard's competitive capitalism. Yet this was by no means so, and the Economics Minister had great initial difficulty in convincing the older generation of managers and owners of the blessings of *Marktwirtschaft*. In particular he met with scepticism when he preached the principle of competition and moved to ban forever the traditional market-regulating mechanisms of German industry, the cartels and syndicates. It will be remembered that cartels had been one of the peculiar features of the German type of industrial capitalism of the interwar period. The Allies had destroyed the institutional structures of cartels but, as in other areas of West German politics where old attitudes lingered on, they had not been able to eradicate the cartel mentality. Too many industrialists, to quote Dietrich von Menges, a former GHH Chairman, were still around for whom 'a world collapsed when the syndicates were dissolved'.

Erhard's attempt to block a revival of the cartel tradition by legislation consequently met with fierce resistance led by the *Bundesverband der Deutschen Industrie* (BDI). A long-drawn-out battle over the *Kartellgesetz* ensued. As late as 1952, when the results of Erhard's free enterprise policies had clearly begun to show, one participant at a meeting of the *Rhein-Ruhr-Klub* which debated one of the early drafts of the anti-cartel bill, called the proposal a 'regulation dysfunctional' to the German national economy. The Economics Minister, on the other hand, became a travelling salesman trying to convince German industry of the dangers of market regulation. He pointed to the disasters of the past and extolled the advantages of free competition. It was only in 1957, after years of negotiation in Parliament and with the BDI, that a watered-down version of the anti-cartel bill was finally adopted.

German industrialists had even greater difficulty in coming to terms with the re-emergence of free trade unions. From the employers' point of view, the repression of the working-class movement by the Nazis had conveniently simplified industrial relations in Germany between 1933 and 1945. It took the Western occupation authorities several months to grant permission for the formation of trade unions. But once a licence had been issued, the unions experienced a rapid growth. By July 1946 the membership in the British zone had risen to 1.2 million. Five months later, a further 500,000 had been added and in July 1947 the figure for the British zone (which comprised the Ruhr industrial complex) reached 2.1 million. The Western Allies also accepted the industrial principle of union organisation so that no more than one union was represented in each enterprise. Finally a unitary structure largely overcame earlier historical divisions into 'free', Catholic and 'liberal' trade union movements. Inter-zonal co-operation was greatly enhanced by the founding of the *Deutscher Gewerkschaftsbund* (DGB, British Zone) at Bielefeld in March 1947.

However, it was not merely this newly found unity and the large membership which accounted for the thrust of the trade union movement. Many of the leaders had either been imprisoned or driven into exile by the Nazis. This political record and the general confusion into which the commercial and industrial middle classes had been thrown after the defeat of 1945 contributed to a marked shift in the balance of power between the two sides of industry. It was in this atmosphere that the trade unions revived their concepts of economic democracy of the Weimar days. Now, after the experience of National Socialism, which they believed could not have assumed power without the backing of industrialists, it seemed all the more important that political democracy was complemented by checks on managerial power, to be wielded by the unions as the representation of the workforce. Many union leaders moreover adhered to notions of economic planning which could also be found in the programme of the SPD. All this was obviously very menacing to management and owner prerogatives, and industrial relations in the late 1940s remained uneasy. The large enterprises were the ones in the firing line because of their past record; the occupation authorities had also to be reckoned with. While most of the smaller entrepreneurs concentrated on increasing their output, appealed to a pioneering spirit of reconstruction and took a wait-and-see attitude, a number of Ruhr industrialists responded constructively and preemptively, indicating that they were prepared to agree to a measure of workers' participation. It would seem plausible that they were partly motivated in their policy towards the trade unions by the hope of enlisting workers' support against a further deconcentration of industry by the Allies. But there was also opposition, and in the end the Ruhr had to be pushed into co-determination. With British support the German steel trustees agreed with the DGB (British Zone) to introduce equal representation for union officials on the supervisory boards of a number of steel companies and a 'worker director' on their management board. An expansion of this system of industrial relations to other branches seemed possible.

However, by 1949, the initial balance of power was slowly shifting against the unions. The adoption of the Erhardian market economy, the intensification of the Cold War, the hostility of the American authorities to 'socialist' experiments and the founding of the Federal Republic under the leadership of a *bürgerliche* coalition government all militated against notions of economic democracy. This shift was reflected in the history of Articles 14 and 15 of the Basic Law which, as we have seen, were incorporated into the Basic Law only as part of an elaborate compromise. It also affected the question of workers' participation. The majority of industrialists remained fundamentally opposed to an erosion of managerial power and in the changed circumstances of 1949/50 they were in a better position to assert themselves than before. Prospects of extending *Mitbestimmung* to other branches of industry waned. When a worried trade union leadership proposed to safeguard by law the co-determination system which had emerged in parts of the iron and steel industry, the employers – spearheaded by the BDI and the *Bundesvereinigung deutscher Arbeitgeberverbände* (BdA), the summit organisation concerned with wages and social policy – not only tried to block this legislation, but also aimed to undermine what had already been achieved. Faced with the possibility of a complete roll-back, the DGB began to apply counter-pressure against the Adenauer government, even threatening an all-out strike to make its point. The Chancellor, after some further prodding by the 'Christian Socialist' wing within the CDU, arranged for negotiations to be held between the two sides of industry. These talks ultimately paved the way for the adoption of a bill in the *Bundestag* which established the principle of co-determination in the coal and steel industry. Henceforth all enterprises in these industries with 1,000 or more employees were to have workers' representatives on the supervisory board. A worker director was to be nominated to sit on the board of directors of each of these firms, with an equal vote in management affairs.

Although the Co-determination Law of May 1951 fell short by a long way of the original ideas on economic democracy and 'equal participation of capital and labour' as enunciated in the early postwar years, it represented an innovation which demonstrated the limits of the restoration movement in West German society. In the industrial sphere important changes did survive and, although all too many spokesmen of industry and their foot-soldiers often refused to recognise this, have contributed to a relative absence of industrial strife in the Federal Republic. Compared with other European countries, strike figures remained very low in West Germany (Table 45). Of course, there were other important factors to account for this peace, such as the high growth rates in the economy which made a satisfactory compromise at the bargaining table possible in most branches of industry. There is also the most intangible point of the loss of self-confidence and solidarity of the German working class which had occurred as a result of the devastating and demoralising experience of fascism. Nevertheless, the framework which West Germany created to institutionalise industrial conflict no doubt helped to stabilise economic development and to avoid costly crises in industrial relations of the magnitude which had undermined the political stability of the Weimar Republic.

Brief reference must finally be made in this context to the *Betriebsverfassungsgesetz* (Works' Constitution Act) of October 1952. This law obliged all larger firms to establish a Works' Council which, although it did not possess decision-making powers and was expected to keep industrial peace, had to be informed and consulted about management plans relating to personnel and welfare policy. In effect, it curbed trade union influence in these areas; but this did not prevent many employers of the older generation from being haunted by nightmares of creeping socialism and an erosion of the efficiency and viability of industry. None of these claims were borne out by actual experience in subsequent years. It seems therefore that these fears were more the outgrowth of mentalities and leadership-styles which American scholars, who interviewed West German industrialists in the 1950s, found to be autocratic and very conservative. Nor, apparently, had the economic elite abandoned nationalism.

Western integration and the problem of reunification

While the slow process of structural and mental adjustment to the conditions of the post-Nazi era continued, West Germany's integration into the world market also progressed at the institutional level. Here Europe became a major focus of political and economic activity. The idea of a united and peacefully co-operating community of European nations was, of course, one about which various people had been dreaming for decades. Yet nationalist rivalries had time and again proved more potent. The Europeanists were hopelessly outnumbered. In the 1930s, then, the Nazis and their revisionist allies in Army, industry and bureaucracy made their bid to establish a New European Order which, although it masqueraded as a framework for uniting the nations of Europe under one roof, was never anything more than a particularly brutal version of German nationalist megalomania and imperialism. The experience of Nazism and occupation, however, gave a strong boost to a revived Europeanism which accepted all nations, large and small, as equals. Some Pan-Europeans even wished to move away from the nation-state system altogether and promoted the idea of complete union. It was a concept which was particularly popular among the younger generation, including those Germans in the Western zones of occupation who were looking for a fresh start.

Others were less sanguine about the feasibility or even desirability of total merger. They perceived European integration more as a means of containing German nationalism, which they did not believe to be dead. Above all, they feared the latent economic and military potential of a united Germany. Hence they pushed for a united Western Europe as a way of keeping Germany divided. Only the Western zones of occupation were to be integrated into this European community of nations. They were also more acutely aware of the difficulties which political union was likely to encounter, not only in France and the Benelux countries, but above all in West Germany, particularly among those who refused to abandon the idea of German reunification.

In this situation, so full of difficulties, ambiguities and contradictions, the pragmatists in the European movement gained the upper hand. They proposed partial integration which would include the emerging *West* Germany. It would start in a field less charged with ideological conflict and nationalist emotion: the economies of Western Europe and, more specifically, the basic industries. Accordingly, the European Coal and Steel Community (ECSC), which combined the heavy industrial sectors of France, West Germany, Italy and the Benelux countries in a common market under the supervision of a High Authority, was established in April 1951. It was an agreement designed to kill several birds with one stone. The ECSC represented the first step, however modest, towards a united Europe of the kind many Europeanists had been talking about. But, seen from the perspective of West Germany's neighbours, it also tied a key section of the German economy, which was deemed to have made a major contribution to the unleashing and prolongation of the Second World War, to a transnational supervisory machinery.

What persuaded the political and economic elites of the Federal Republic to respond positively to the Plan, first advanced in May 1950 by the French Foreign Minister Robert Schuman, was their hope that it would make their country's reacceptance by her neighbours easier and open up a larger market to German goods. The experiment of the ECSC proved sufficiently successful for the six members to decide in June 1955 that economic union should be expanded to other areas of industrial and commercial activity. Less than two years later, on 25 March 1957, the Rome Treaty which established the European Economic Community (EEC) was signed.

It was to be expected that the policies of economic union would run into opposition in the Federal Republic. If it was, on the whole, less strong than some Europeanists feared, a partial explanation may lie in the fact that economic integration was concerned with highly complex and technical arrangements. It was not altogether easy for the anti-unionists to translate these issues into popular slogans. Nor was the connection between the economic and the political problems of German unification immediately recognisable to all. However, it was a different matter when it came to the question of West Germany's military integration into the Western alliance, for at this point the implications for national unity became all too obvious.

Few other debates have aroused greater political passions in the early 1950s than that on German rearmament. What made the controversy so fierce was that several questions became compounded in it, making for a highly explosive political mixture. Considering that there existed high emotional obstacles to the re-establishment of a German army among the country's neighbours, it is not difficult to see why the West Germans themselves should be even less prepared to contemplate the idea of a military contribution. To be sure, the counter-pressures which were brought to bear on the German opposition to rearmament were tremendous and ultimately swung the balance in favour of those who thought a military contribution to be unavoidable. It was fear of Communism and of the Soviet Union which unleashed the debate in the first place. While, by 1947–8, the Western Allies and Stalin were busy consolidating their respective zones of occupation as integral parts of the two spheres of influence which had emerged as a result of the Second World War, Western leaders' perceptions of Soviet policy had become increasingly pessimistic. Soon the former Russian ally was viewed as an aggressive dictatorship which was bent on conquering the rest of Europe and on establishing Stalinist regimes in Western Europe. The Communist seizure of power in Czechoslovakia in February 1948 and the blockading of Berlin, which lasted from the summer of 1948 to May 1949, made a great psychological impact in the West and heightened East–West tensions. As Lucius D. Clay, the Military Governor in the American Zone and one of the main actors, put it during the Berlin Crisis: 'We have lost Czechoslovakia, Norway is threatened. We retreat from Berlin. When Berlin falls, Western Germany will be next. If we mean to hold Europe against Communism, we must not budge. . . . If we withdraw our position in Europe is threatened.'

The outbreak of the Korean War finally tipped the balance as far as Adenauer was concerned. Korea was another divided country whose non-Communist half appeared to be falling prey to Communist aggression. The Federal Chancellor decided formally to respond to American suggestions and to offer a West German military contribution to the defence of Western Europe. When these moves became public in September 1950, they started a major political row at home which went on unabated for several years. It was in 1957/8, after the establishment of the *Bundeswehr* had been approved by Parliament, that a campaign against nuclear weapons which mobilised thousands of West Germans on the Left of the political spectrum against government policy resulted in a fresh polarisation of political forces. With the benefit of hindsight, it can be said that this movement against 'atomic death' was less dangerous to the Adenauer government than the more broadly based resistance against the principle of rearmament between 1950 and 1955, although it is a fine point as to whether the creation of the *Bundeswehr* would have succeeded in 1955/6 had the debate of the principle become mixed up with the nuclear issue.

What lay behind the question of atomic rearmament was that Western defence efforts had been suffering from chronic manpower deficiencies. Time and again, the military on both sides of the Atlantic exhorted the members of the North Atlantic Treaty Organisation (NATO), which had been founded in April 1949, to call up more soldiers. Yet governments, worried about the extra expense, did not show any great urgency to remedy these weaknesses. However, it was not because they were banking on the West Germans to fill the gap that they remained passive. Rather, with the United States firmly committed through NATO to the defence of Europe, all members had come under the American nuclear umbrella, and this was thought to be protection enough.

Since the obliteration of Hiroshima and Nagasaki by atomic bombs in August 1945, American nuclear technology had developed in two directions. On the one hand, research had progressed to the construction of the hydrogen bomb whose destructive power was several thousand times that of the devices dropped on Japan. On the other hand, weapons developments had advanced in the direction of low-yield 'tactical' nuclear weapons, the first of which were tested in 1952, the year of the first explosion of the hydrogen bomb. At the same time missiles were being built which were capable of delivering these weapons at different ranges. The advantages of the smaller 'tactical' weapons were immediately obvious: they could plug NATO's firepower deficit without its members having to maintain large ground forces. Strategic planning was accordingly adjusted and in September 1953 the first 'atomic guns' appeared with American troops stationed in West Germany. The military significance of the emphasis on nuclear war was illustrated in the summer of 1955 during a NATO exercise, code-named *Carte Blanche*, in the course of which some 335 tactical devices were 'used' on the territory of the Federal Republic. The assumed death toll among the civilian population was 1.7 million, with 3.5 million 'injured'.

These were the assumptions of Western military planners at the time when the Adenauer government was preparing the introduction of its Conscription Bill. Yet statements by German ministers and their military advisers remained curiously vague whenever the atomic issue was raised. There is good reason to believe that the government played down the nuclear aspect of West German rearmament so long as the more fundamental question was being debated as to whether the Federal Republic should have a conventional army or none at all. Nevertheless, it would be wrong to suspect that the fathers of the *Bundeswehr* cynically deceived the West German public. It may have looked like this in the final stages of the debate, but it was not so at the beginning. In fact, the way in which the West German contribution was originally designed by the experts showed little awareness of the nuclear dimension of Western policy. Instead it was heavily influenced by the experiences which the planners, all of whom were ex-Wehrmacht officers, had had during the Second World War.

This emerges from the Himmerod Memorandum of October 1950 which grew out of a secret conference of experts whom Adenauer and his adviser on military matters, Gerhard Count von Schwerin, had invited to a Benedictine monastery near Wittlich. It is also reflected in the controversy which raged in the *Dienststelle Blank*, the embryonic West German Defence Ministry, in 1954/5 over the type of conventional army to be established. One group of officers advocated a conscript army of some 500,000 men. On the other hand, Colonel Bogislav von Bonin had drawn up a plan which envisaged so-called Blocking

Units to counter a Soviet offensive right along the Iron Curtain, (i.e. before the Red Army would be able to make large territorial gains). Bonin's plan took account of the crucial psychological aspect of West German rearmament which the ex-tank general Leo Geyr von Schweppenburg formulated as follows: 'They [the West Germans] want to be defended, not liberated.' But it also suffered from a fatal weakness in that it was based upon the idea of a professional long-service army of between 120,000 and 125,000 men. Political considerations and memories of the Reichswehr and its role in Weimar politics ultimately defeated Bonin's plan. The Federal Republic opted for a conventional 500,000-man conscript army. During the emotional debates concerning the shape of this force, the nuclear aspect became almost completely fudged.

Whereas the military and strategic dilemma of West German rearmament thus barely came into the open, the Adenauer Cabinet found itself locked in a fierce domestic battle against an odd alliance of pacifists and nationalists. On the one hand, there were those (many of whom were members of the younger generation) who were opposed to war and armaments on principle. They believed they had the experience of the Second World War as the most recent case to support their anti-rearmament stance. On the other hand, there were those who were not opposed to rearmament on moral or ideological grounds, but refused to support it so long as the 'defamation of the German soldier' continued. It has already been mentioned how much resentment Allied de-Nazification policies had generated among sections of the population. In this case it was the campaign against German militarism which had deeply upset the officer corps and many former soldiers. Their grievances, pent-up in the late 1940s, now surfaced during the rearmament debate, articulated by a welter of ex-servicemen's associations which began to mushroom in the early 1950s.

The Federal government had justified hopes of winning over the majority of these groups. Indeed, they had to be won over as they represented precisely those people on whose professional expertise the new West German armed forces would have to rely and, more generally speaking, whose electoral support was indispensable for the stability of the Adenauer coalition. What was worrying to Adenauer was not merely their anti-Westernism and their apologetic view of Germany's recent history, but also their visions of the country's future. Basically, they were all nationalists, and this seemed to make it all the more imperative to try to integrate them into the two main non-socialist parties. Otherwise they might drift into radical right-wing and anti-Republican positions. The trouble was that they were convinced that the military integration of the Federal Republic into the West would seal the division of the former Reich, and this they refused to accept.

Consequently, some of the ex-soldiers' leagues began to toy with neutralism and supported the idea of a unified, but 'disengaged' Germany between the two blocs. However, for the majority of the nationalists this solution was unacceptable because of their suspicion and rejection of Communism and the Left in general. This is where Adenauer and his alliance of *bürgerliche* parties came in. Anti-Communism began to provide a powerful glue which bridged the divide between the 'Christian occidentalist' advocates of a West German integration into the Western alliance and the non-neutralist nationalists. In fact, it is difficult to overestimate the extent to which the inner consolidation of the Federal Republic, achieved by its economic success, was complemented by the ideological cohesion created by a virulent Cold War anti-Communism. The intensity of this feeling lent plausibility to an argument which was in itself barely logical. This argument was that Germany's integration into the West actually enhanced the prospect of reunification. More than that, it would facilitate a policy of pushing the Soviet Union out of Central and Eastern Europe altogether, thereby opening up the prospect of regaining the former German territories east of the Oder–Neisse line. It was a persuasive dream for nationalists as well as for those millions of refugees and expellees in the Federal Republic who would be able to return to their homelands. In other words, German revisionism received a new lease of life although it must be remembered that the Americans abetted it by their crusading talk of 'rolling' the Russians back into Asia.

For Adenauer, on the other hand, of whom it has now been shown that he was more interested in creating a Christian Democratic Western European bloc than in German national unity, the linkage between rearmament and roll-back strategy was helpful in so far as it removed some of the political barriers between his government and the nationalist opposition on the Right. It also conveniently widened the political trenches between the *bürgerliche* parties and the SPD, the Chancellor's fiercest opposition at home, which, though strongly anti-Communist itself, could be tainted with the same red brush as the Russians and Ulbricht. 'All paths of Marxism', proclaimed a CDU poster in the 1953 Federal elections, 'lead to Moscow.' Many ex-officers and nationalists agreed. However, Adenauer did not gain the co-operation of these groups without moves to restore the 'honour of the German soldier'. The strength of feeling on this issue, which was shared by those moderates who were in principle prepared to help promote rearmament, emerges not merely from the publications of the nationalist lobby, but also from the Himmerod Memorandum. For the experts of the Military–Political Committee of the Himmerod group West German rearmament was predicated on the following conditions: (1) the granting of full political and economic sovereignty; (2) military equality, in particular if (1) could not be achieved quickly; (3) the rehabilitation of the German soldier of the Second World War through public declarations by the Western powers and the Federal government.

The first two demands are interesting for the way rearmament was to be used as a lever to remove Allied restrictions on the Republic's freedom of manoeuvre, a strategy which Adenauer employed with considerable success. What is noteworthy about the third point is that it envisaged not merely a declaration of honour on behalf of the Wehrmacht, but also a demand to release 'those Germans who have been imprisoned as "war criminals" in so far as they did no more than to execute an order and did not fall foul of former German laws'. It also meant 'dropping all defamatory statements against German ex-soldiers (including those Waffen-SS men who served within the framework of the Wehrmacht)'. In December 1952 Adenauer made a formal declaration in the *Bundestag* to the effect that 'all bearers of arms of our nation have fought honourably', a position which was hardly borne out by the historical evidence. However, the political advantages of this policy were clear: it eased the rapprochement between the government and the bulk of the former Wehrmacht officer corps and non-commissioned officer corps. Henceforth, the irreconcilable nationalists on the extreme Right and the pacifist opponents on the Left could be more safely ignored, the more so as more and more Social Democrat deputies recognised the inevitability of a West German defence contribution and merely wished to make certain that an army was created which would not grow into a 'state within the state'.

We have devoted some space to the rearmament issue and its wider ramifications because it provided a good illustration of some of the problems which beset the Federal Republic and its society in the early 1950s. The economy was booming; a parliamentary-representative system had been established. Yet behind the façade of prosperity and liberal-democratic respectability there lurked great tensions. They resulted in the final analysis from the desire to reconstruct a liberal-bourgeois society and the difficulties of those on whom Adenauer relied in making painful mental and psychological adjustments to the postwar world. Old attitudes and mentalities lingered on. It was not that West Germany, like the Weimar Republic, was in any immediate danger of becoming a Republic without Republicans. The balance of social and political forces was different from that of the 1920s. On the other hand, it cannot be said that the new constitutional order rested on a broad popular consensus. One of the main issues which impeded this consensus was the vexed problem of national unity. From the viewpoint of her neighbours, West Germany continued to be a revisionist power which, like its predecessors since the turn of the century, refused to recognise the territorial status quo in Europe. These tendencies frequently worried the Western Allies, who wondered just how far they could rely on the West Germans and what were the chances of a revival of old traditions.

Although the extreme Right always remained in the minority, it was difficult to overlook that by the early 1950s a number of parties and associations, most ex-servicemen's among them, had sprung up which propagated quite unreconstructed views of the past and peddled thinly veiled anti-democratic and illiberal blueprints of a future Reich. The most extreme of these movements, like the blatantly neo-Nazi *Sozialistische Reichspartei* (SRP), were eventually declared unconstitutional, just as the Communist Party was outlawed on grounds of its hostility to the existing order, in August 1956. On the other hand, there were quite a few people in politics and in the bureaucracy who professed to be democrats but whose activities in the Third Reich did not inspire much confidence. Finally, there was the problem of the major, solidly Republican parties becoming infiltrated by right-wing radicals and their unadulterated ideas. Viewing these parties' reactions to this threat, it was this latter possibility that the Allies took particularly seriously.

Under the Occupation Statute of 21 September 1949, and a number of subsequent agreements with the Federal government, the Allies had reserved certain powers of intervention into the internal affairs of the Republic. What emerged on the few occasions on which these powers were used is of interest to an understanding of West German domestic politics. Thus in January 1953 the British High Commissioner, Sir Ivone Kirkpatrick, decided to crack down on a group of former high-ranking Nazi officials around Werner Naumann, one of Goebbels's state secretaries. They were suspected of trying to subvert the FDP with the aim of moving it further to the Right. Although the large quantities of documents seized by the British were never made public, we are informed of the results of an investigation by the FDP national executive into the Naumann Affair. The committee was set up to determine whether and how far 'members of the executive board of the Northrhine-Westphalian FDP and executive secretaries maintained contact with right-wing radical circles . . . in full knowledge of their intentions to erect again an authoritarian and radically national socialist state'. The enquiries revealed that the political adviser of the *Land* organisation, Dr Ernst Achenbach, had not only been 'in continual contact with Naumann' during the previous years, but had also 'tried to launch Naumann politically'.

However, these and other embarrassing findings notwithstanding, the committee rejected the notion that the planned infiltration of the Party had been successful. Nor did the FDP members implicated in the affair suffer any damage to their subsequent political careers. And here lies the significance of this case: it was not so much that the views of the Naumann Circle were radical, but that leading politicians would enter into negotiations with men as compromised as Naumann and evidently found common ground with them. Two years later, another major row rocked Federal politics which demonstrated that the Northrhine-Westphalian FDP was not the only *Land* organisation with right-wing leanings. In May 1955 Leonard Schlüter was nominated as Minister of Education in the newly elected government of Lower Saxony.

Schlüter had been active on the extreme Right since the late 1940s before rising to prominence in the FDP. He had also built up a successful publishing house which disseminated nationalist literature. He himself was on record with statements such as 'National Socialism has been the healthiest movement in Germany since 1900' and 'We reject every form of parliamentary party democracy.' In a reference to the previous *Land* government which had been led by the Social Democrats he argued: 'What is the good of economic successes when the key positions of the state are occupied by disguised Communists who at the right moment will sell us to the Communists and to the trade unions?' What prevented Schlüter from assuming office was not his rejection by the CDU, the FDP's main coalition partner in Lower Saxony, but the opposition of professors and students at Göttingen University who refused to co-operate with him as the *Land* minister responsible for higher education. Schlüter was kept out.

These and other incidents would seem to reinforce our earlier observations on West Germany's precarious domestic stability. The legacies of the past were ubiquitous. The social problems were enormous and were overcome only gradually as the economy generated more tax revenue which could be used to increase social security provision and pensions. It helped that the worst material deprivation was over. But habits and attitudes did not change so quickly, if only because the older generation with vivid memories of the ideological battles of the interwar period was still around. As Kirkpatrick, looking back on his time as British High Commissioner, put it in his memoirs: 'Whenever I travelled, I ran into ghosts of Hitler's Reich, men who had occupied positions in the administration, in industry, or the society of the day. They were either living in retirement or were taking jobs in banks, commerce or industry.'

Certainly, few of these people were neo-Nazis. But, resentful of their treatment by the Allies in the late 1940s and frightened by Soviet power, they found it convenient to justify their politics in terms of a fundamental aversion to 'socialism' and of their belief in the unity of the Reich. This, they argued, was what the 1920s and 1930s had been about and these were the issues of the 1950s as well. Adenauer knew how to play on these beliefs. The Federal elections of March 1953 resulted in a large rise of the CDU/CSU's share to 45.2 per cent, while cutting that of the SPD and KPD to 31.0 per cent (Table 43). Nevertheless, the Chancellor continued to be dependent on the support of smaller parties on the far Right, both in the *Bundestag* and in a number of *Länder*. This required further accommodation to their views and, as the statements by Schlüter show, this reliance perpetuated nationalist, if not Nazi, notions of the past and a crude thinking in polarities which identified Social Democracy and unions with Communism. It was an old recipe for there was, in this period of Cold War and domestic divisions over major political and economic issues between the CDU/CSU and the SPD, no more effective way to weld *bürgerliche* coalitions together than to play on traditional middle-class nationalism and the fear of the Left.

Soviet Western policy and the consolidation of East Germany

No other foreign power, perhaps with the exception of France, was more alarmed by the continued force of German nationalism than the Russians and now, in the early 1950s, this force was to be underpinned by military power. It was not surprising that, faced with the prospect of West German rearmament, they should launch a diplomatic offensive to prevent it. Possibly the most important of these Soviet counter-moves was a proposal by Stalin of March 1952 in which he suggested that the wartime Allies consider 'without delay the question of a peace treaty with Germany'. His démarche was accompanied by a draft peace treaty, moving that the division of Germany be ended and that a reunified Germany be permitted to develop into a democratic country pledged to the maintenance of peace. The document further proposed that all foreign troops be withdrawn from German soil and that all policies to disturb the peace and to prepare for an expansionist war be declared unconstitutional. Nor was the reunified Germany to be allowed to join an alliance or military coalition directed against any of her wartime enemies. All she was to have were defensive forces.

Stalin's much-debated note of March 1952 was virtually rejected by the United States in their reply a fortnight later. The conclusion of a peace treaty, Washington submitted, preconditioned the formation of an all-German government. However, such a government could only emerge on the basis of free elections to be held in all four former zones of occupation. It was suggested that these elections be supervised by the United Nations. The Russians' response to this, while not opposing free elections as such, was to declare UN supervision unacceptable. Nothing came of the exchange; but it did unleash a long argument inside West Germany to the effect that Stalin's offer had not been taken seriously and should have been explored more fully. Many people believed that an opportunity had been missed to obtain a peace treaty and national unity. Others, and Adenauer in particular, were fearful of the proposed neutralisation of the country and refused to be distracted from their policy of integrating the Federal Republic into the Western alliance. Given the unconsolidated state of the Republic, it seemed better not to test the Russian offer if further debate threatened to rend the political system asunder. In May 1952 the government initialled a treaty document which committed West Germany to rearmament within the framework of a projected European Defence Community (EDC). Shortly afterwards, Adenauer opened negotiations with the Western Allies which, lasting until the autumn 1954, finally resulted in the Germany Treaty (*Deutschlandvertrag*) of 23 October 1954 and a number of supplementary agreements. Under Article 1 of the Treaty, the American, British and French governments formally ended their occupation and declared the Federal Republic a sovereign state, although they claimed to retain responsibility for Berlin and Germany as a whole should a peace treaty ever be concluded between the former Reich and its wartime opponents.

There was a brief revival of the debate on reunification after Stalin's death in March 1953. The Russian dictator was succeeded by a *troika* of Malenkov, Molotov and Beria, who began to toy once more with the possibility of free elections in the whole of Germany in return for the neutralisation of a reunified country. The Soviet leadership, and Beria in particular, apparently had some doubts about the continued value to Russia of the German Democratic Republic (GDR) which had been founded in October 1949, shortly after the establishment of the West German Federal Republic.

Politically, the SED under Ulbricht's leadership had indeed been Russia's faithful ally. Nor had the Soviet Union fared badly when it decided to extract resources and goods from the GDR and continued to do so until reparations were formally ended in August 1953. But the depressive effect of political autocracy and reparations was all too visible in the daily life of East Germany and merely exacerbated by the fact that capital goods production was given priority over the production of consumer goods. Basic items of consumption like fat, sugar and meat were still subject to rationing. Consumer durables remained extremely scarce and expensive. Prices in the state-owned HO shops were artificially high in order to generate revenue for industrial investment and, although wages increased, living standards of the mass of the population were very low. What probably rankled more than inadequate supplies was that, though the population were told they were living in a 'people's democracy', the structure of the SED regime did not give ordinary citizens a say even in matters of income and working conditions. Early postwar hopes of grass-roots democracy had been destroyed. By 1950 workers' representation had been 'synchronised' within the framework of the FDGB. There was no wage bargaining. Instead the regime, following the Soviet example, had introduced works' collective wage agreements (BKV) which were tailored to the requirements and objectives of the government's planning targets.

The introduction of these agreements in 1951 caused endless troubles on the shop-floor. Thus, literally hundreds of meetings were held at the Carl Zeiss Optical Works at Jena alone before the third draft of the firm's BKV was pushed through. It was no less galling that, together with the reintroduction of a managerial command structure, the supervisory staffs and the engineering personnel were given status privileges and special material advantages. At a time (in 1951) when metal workers would earn less than 300 marks per month, salaries of 4,000 marks, in some cases even 15,000 marks per month, were paid

217

to top managers. They were also given perks such as cheap mortgages and separate canteen facilities. Not surprisingly, dissatisfaction with and resistance to the blatantly inegalitarian policies of the regime never subsided. Preventing wage levels from rising was, of course, only one way of improving the performance of industry. Putting up work norms for wage labour was another and one which created even more unrest than the BKVs. Bitterness grew further when early in 1953 the government was forced to decree price increases for key items of consumption such as sugar and meat. The problem of food supplies was reaching crisis proportions and led to loud protests. Strikes broke out against a renewed increase of work norms in the spring of 1953. However, in this case it was not merely the problem of worker resistance which the SED had to cope with. The question of norms also provoked serious disagreements within the top leadership, which climaxed in the weeks and months after Stalin's death. The disputes in the Central Committee revolved around two issues which were seemingly unrelated, but linked, on closer inspection, by what might be called the problem of East German 'nationalism'.

On the one hand, the SED leadership was divided about the question of reunification following Winston Churchill's proposal of 11 May 1953 to hold a Four-Power Conference to discuss a German peace treaty and a positive response to this by the new Soviet leadership. The Ulbricht group in the Central Committee was opposed to any plan to undo the integration of the GDR into the East Bloc. Another faction led by Rudolf Herrnstadt and Wilhelm Zaisser had never been happy with the country's absolute dependence on the Soviet Union and – this was the other aspect of their criticism – the slavish copying of the Soviet model. They were therefore pressing for the adoption of a 'new course' which emancipated East Germany from direct Soviet interference both at home and in foreign policy matters. Above all, they hoped to free resources to improve the material position of the population and to contain the growth of the police state. At the beginning of June 1953, the Herrnstadt/ Zaisser faction won a curious victory. On 9 June, the Politbureau of the SED approved the promise of a number of political and economic reforms, though, as it turned out, the main beneficiaries were the self-employed, peasants and white-collar workers. This announcement came after a decision by the Ministerial Council of 28 May decreeing further increases in work norms.

If the crisis had by then not already reached boiling point, it was certainly stoked up in the middle of June when Herrnstadt published an article in *Neues Deutschland* criticising the increase in work norms. Two days later, a leading SED trade unionist, Otto Lehmann, put the opposite view in *Die Tribüne*. It was this article, as Otto Nuschke, the Deputy Prime Minister, later admitted, that 'unleashed the demonstrations of the building workers on Berlin's *Stalinallee*'. And indeed, while the SED leadership kept on squabbling, dissatisfaction with the regime was welling up from below. At the beginning of June, building workers in Berlin, having received their first wage packet based on the new norms and finding that their income had once again been reduced, had held spontaneous meetings and had formulated a resolution demanding the rescinding of the decision of 28 May. After the publication of Lehmann's piece, on 16 June, unrest escalated into demonstrations. These quickly attracted a crowd of some 10,000 people, who marched to the House of Ministries.

A meeting of the Politbureau was hastily called, which decided, a few hours later, that the norms should be reduced to their former levels. Confusion reigned. The news of the events in Berlin spread like wild-fire throughout the GDR. On the following day demonstrations and strikes took place in some 270 towns and cities mobilising some 300,000 to 400,000 people, most of them workers. This was grist to the mill of the Herrnstadt/Zaisser faction who charged Ulbricht and his followers with incompetence and demanded thorough-going reforms. They pointed to the fact that most of the demonstrators were workers from the industrial centres of East Germany. By lunchtime of 17 June, the situation was quickly running out of control. In Berlin clashes between demonstrators and the police became more and more violent. Shops were looted; SED functionaries were beaten up. It was at this point that the Russians intervened. The Soviet military commander proclaimed a state of siege and tanks moved into the centres of the cities. Faced with overwhelming military power, the rebels were soon forced to retreat. A night curfew was imposed and by midnight the situation in Berlin was calm again. Two days later, demonstrations in other parts of the country had also petered out.

The June Uprising had several consequences which were of crucial importance to the subsequent development of the East German Republic. To begin with, the leadership made a number of economic concessions which tangibly improved the material position of the population. On 21 June 1953 the Central Committee resolved to revert to the old norms which had been in force on 1 April of that year. It also introduced greatly reduced fares for commuters with incomes below 500 marks per month. There were improvements in social security and health care benefits as well as a 15 per cent increase in pensions. In October, prices were cut back by between 10 and 25 per cent for some 12,000 items of consumption, including basic foods, with the exception of sugar, bread and butter. Hire-purchase arrangements were also simplified to facilitate the acquisition of furniture, radios and motor cars.

Obviously, these concessions could not be effected without a revision of the 1951–5 Five Year Plan which had laid down the priorities for industrial production. The 15th meeting of the Central Committee of the SED, which took place only five weeks after the Uprising, at the end of July 1953, reduced the targets for heavy industry for 1953 by 1.4 milliard marks. Production of consumer goods and food, on the other hand, was to be stepped up by 950 million marks. The meeting also approved a significant shift in investment away from heavy industry to the provision of better housing, recreational facilities, nurseries and improved workplace conditions. Although rationing cards did not disappear completely until May 1958, there is little doubt that material conditions in East Germany saw a definite improvement. It was achieved not so much by wage rises as by considerable reductions of prices and the introduction of indirect benefits. Consumer durables, nonetheless, remained prohibitively expensive, partly because it took several years and another Five Year Plan for industry to be capable of providing them in larger quantities. The Second Five Year Plan also promised real wage increases of up to 30 per cent, the seven-hour workday and better housing.

If the main purpose of these policies was to win back the loyalty of the population and of the industrial workers in particular, the regime's new education programme pursued a similar objective. Reforms in the school and higher education system were designed to increase upward mobility and were based on the expectation that the beneficiaries would become the staunch supporters of the State which had made their advancement possible. We have seen earlier that the Soviet occupation authorities had started something like a social revolution by means of their de-Nazification and expropriation policies. By the early 1950s, those whose estates or businesses had been nationalised and who had not left the GDR to begin a new life in the West also found the careers of their children blocked as the SED set out systematically to disrupt old mechanisms of elite circulation. After the immediate postwar period when ideological reliability was considered more important than technical expertise to run an expropriated farm or a factory, the drawbacks of managing a complex economy with the help of old Communists who had been underground or who had returned to the Soviet zone to help in the 'building of socialism' had become apparent. It was too late to train them in the administrative or managerial skills needed to organise an industrial recovery. It was a different matter with their sons and daughters.

Many of them had been exposed since their primary school days in the late 1940s to the teachings of Marxism-Leninism. They had been members of the Communist youth organisation, FDJ, and they had learned to view the world in Communist terms. If the opportunity of occupational specialisation was added to this experience, the regime could hope to gain both a technical intelligentsia to run the East German economy and a new elite indebted to it. Education became the vehicle of this dual objective. It is against this background that the reform of the secondary school system during the 1950s must be seen. School fees and charges for books and teaching materials were abolished. A system of grants was introduced to support children of 'workers and peasants'. Between 1953 and 1954, some 25 new universities and polytechnics were added to the existing six universities and 15 institutes of technology. They were geared to training a rapidly increasing number of

220

young people. Between 1951 and 1954, the number of full-time students in the higher education sector more than doubled from 28,000 to 57,500, rising further to 66,000 in 1957. Further students took their degrees by correspondence courses. To the numbers of people in higher education must be added several thousand specially selected children from lower-class background who, without possessing the East German equivalent of A-levels, prepared themselves for university study at so-called Workers' and Peasants' Faculties. No less significantly, the system encouraged the study of applied sciences and technical skills, a development which, from 1956 onwards, also began to affect the curricula of secondary schools. This 'polytechnical instruction' in schools tried to combine traditional learning with a practical introduction to the day-to-day operations of industry and to techniques of industrial production and management.

Children of non-working-class background, on the other hand, faced increasing discrimination and limitations on their educational choices. If the father had once owned a factory or was a doctor, their political reliability would be under suspicion and their occupational opportunities curtailed. The net effect of these policies was that, side by side with the old party elite which continued to occupy strategic positions in the political and administrative machinery, there arose a new 'polytechnical' group of highly trained younger managers and technicians. While the fathers of this latter group concluded their life as semi-skilled workers in a factory or as farmers on a collective, they came to occupy white-collar positions with better pay and enhanced social prestige.

However, from the SED's point of view the expansion of education had the drawback that it promoted an awareness of broader social and political questions. The new intelligentsia was not necessarily prepared to accept official interpretations of events uncritically. However hard the leadership tried to insist on the acceptance of Party doctrine and methods of autocratic decision-making from the top, it proved difficult to suppress criticism. It is in this context that we must consider a further major consequence of the crisis of June 1953. Once the Uprising had collapsed before the Soviet tanks, the Ulbricht faction moved swiftly to restore party unity. The July meeting of the Central Committee ousted Herrnstadt and Zaisser from their positions. Other members of the anti-Ulbricht group were reprimanded. Subsequently, the adherents of the Herrnstadt/Zaisser wing were also purged lower down in the SED bureaucracy. Ideological indoctrination inside the Party received special attention and was tightened up. Relations between the SED and the other parties, notably the CDU and LDPD, were also reorganised. They were left practically without room for manoeuvre. Whoever was considered an undesirable politician by the dominant faction was unceremoniously dismissed and in some cases arrested. Thus, in June 1954, a trial was staged against leading

Christian Democrats at the end of which Georg Dertinger, the deputy leader of the CDU and a former Foreign Minister, was sentenced to 15 years' imprisonment.

Finally, the SED also assumed tighter control of the Council of Ministers, the official state government. After the national elections of October 1954, which gave the SED-led 'National Front' a somewhat suspect 99.3 per cent majority, the newly constituted government under the premiership of Grotewohl was dominated by SED ministers, all of whom occupied the key posts. At the same time the Party had succeeded in establishing its leading role in all areas of policy-making and hence indirectly in the economy, where the State had slowly become almost all-pervasive. After the founding of the GDR in 1949, the nationalisation and collectivisation programme continued at a steady pace. In 1955, 82.4 per cent of industrial production originated in the state sector. Heavy industry and large-scale retailing were almost completely nationalised. Private ownership persisted to a perceptible degree only in light industry and in food processing. The market share of the small retailers had been reduced to one-third of the total domestic trading volume. Only the collectivisation of agriculture proceeded more slowly, and as late as 1955 some 780,000 farmers worked their land independently (Table 33). In short, East Germany was well on its way to completing its gradual metmorphosis to a Soviet-style system and, as elsewhere in the Soviet Bloc, this transition was accompanied by coercion and the repression of dissent.

What prevented an overcrowding of prisons with 'enemies of the state' was the possibility of escaping to the Federal Republic, although this was made more difficult from 1952 when the frontier between the GDR and West Germany became closely guarded. However, provided the would-be refugee and his family travelled inconspicuously to East Berlin, it was not too difficult or dangerous to cross into the Western sectors of the city. Only the building of the Berlin Wall in August 1961 plugged this hole in the Iron Curtain. Most of the refugees tended to be people who disagreed with the overall development of the GDR, the lack of freedom of expression and the forced expropriations which destroyed their livelihood. On the other hand, criticism from within the ranks of the SED, which had contributed to unleashing the crisis of 1953, never died down completely. In fact it reached a new peak in 1956/7 when the events in Poland and Hungary began to have their effect on those East German Communists who, though they never dreamed of a return to capitalism, nevertheless continued to look for ways of developing more democratic forms of socialism and of gaining greater independence from the Soviet Union.

The search for new formulas of domestic political organisation and national variety within the East Bloc was particularly intensive among the academic intelligentsia. But the hardliners around Ulbricht, always sensitive to threats to their own position and to East Germany's exposed front-line situation *vis-à-vis* the Western alliance, were in no mood to tolerate debates on alternative policies. Consequently, the year 1957 saw a number of show trials against Wolfgang Harich and other prominent intellectuals. At the same time the FDJ youth organisation published a new action programme for higher education which demanded the creation of 'socialist universities and high schools'. As in 1953, the ferment in East German society at large and among the students in particular cannot be separated from disagreements among the leadership over how to deal with the 'thaw' and the question of de-Stalinisation which had surfaced in the wake of Nikita Khrushchev's famous speech before the 20th Congress of the Soviet Communist Party in February 1956. A group of functionaries around Karl Schirdewan and Ernst Wollweber was opposed to a continuation of Ulbricht's hardline policies. Again fierce power struggles resulted, until Ulbricht succeeded once more in silencing his opponents. By the end of 1957, he and his faction were in firm control of the SED and thus had also stamped out all discussion of reunification.

National unity had been the other issue that aroused the controversy in the early summer of 1953 in the wake of the Soviet diplomatic manoeuvres after Stalin's death. But the June Uprising decisively weakened the advocates of negotiations with the West and strengthened the hand of those who were profoundly suspicious of the idea of free all-German elections and a neutral reunified Germany. It also contributed to bringing to a head the power-struggle in the Kremlin over the shape of Soviet foreign and domestic policy in the post-Stalin era, and there the confrontation ended in the liquidation of the Beria faction. To the SED, the Uprising had demonstrated the unpopularity of the regime, and the lessons were clear: if it could be rescued from collapse only with the help of Soviet tanks, the holding of free elections for the whole of Germany would most likely mean the destruction of the paramount position of the German Communists east of the river Elbe. Ulbricht and his followers, backed by the victorious faction in Moscow, were henceforth in a strong position to torpedo the debate on reunification. Their recipe envisaged the opposite: the further integration of East Germany into the Soviet Bloc. They succeeded, just as Adenauer overcame his anti-integrationist critics in the Federal Republic. In March 1954, the Russians granted the rights of an 'equal people's democratic state' to the GDR, modified by a number of provisos. A year later, in May 1955, East Germany became a member of the Warsaw Treaty Organisation, the Eastern equivalent to NATO to which West Germany had been admitted in the previous month.

Attempts to unite East and West around the conference table to discuss the problem of German reunification were never completely abandoned between 1954 and 1957. Yet neither the overall political climate between the super-powers nor the balance of forces within the political establishments of East

223

and West Germany were ever such as to make a diplomatic breakthrough on this issue a realistic possibility. It may be interesting to trace the various debates and diplomatic moves that occurred. But it is more important to look at what was actually *done* by the two sides. The only tangible results that were achieved reinforced the economic, political and military integration of the two Germanies into the respective power blocs which deepened the division of the country. Basically all Allies of the Second World War were agreed that the integration of the two halves into East and West was more advantageous than reunification. It was unwise to say this in public. Especially in West Germany, the question remained so charged with emotion that even a tentative support for the status quo was considered a betrayal. Hence the stirring 'Sunday speeches' by Adenauer and his Cabinet colleagues, preferably before the Annual Congress of some refugee organisation, whose contents bore little relation to their day-to-day work for European integration at different levels. In the early 1950s it was the verbal blustering of roll-back and a 'policy of strength' which drew the applause. When this turned out to be illusory, it was replaced by such palliatives as the Hallstein Doctrine, according to which the Federal Republic would break off diplomatic relations with any foreign country that gave international recognition to East Germany. Ultimately the question of unity degenerated into upholding formalistic legal positions without political substance: the fiction of a German Reich within its 1937 frontiers.

Meanwhile the actual policies of the dominant groups worked in the direction of division and, inseparably connected with this, for the establishment of two divergent socioeconomic systems. For, as Schumacher perspicaciously emphasised, 'the controversy over foreign policy was basically a controversy over domestic policy and over the social contents of the political order'. Adenauer, if he had any political dreams at all, pursued the idea of a Christian Democratic anti-socialist Western European union within the framework of a bourgeois–capitalist economic order. Ulbricht pushed on with his concept of the construction of a Communist and anti-capitalist Eastern bloc within the framework of a state-owned economy. Seen in this light, it is not surprising that the policies of integration met with a good deal of opposition at home and that both leading politicians were frequently given a rough ride. However, by the late 1950s, it was not merely Ulbricht who had reconsolidated his own position. After the upheavals over rearmament in 1955/6, Adenauer likewise re-emerged strengthened, and the elections of 15 September 1957 gave him the absolute majority in the *Bundestag* (Table 43). The first postwar phase was over. Henceforth German history was the history of two Germanies which had risen from the turmoil of the first decade after the end of the war with distinctly different and basically irreconcilable socioeconomic and political systems and divergent, though curiously symmetrical, foreign policies. As Grotewohl put it in August 1957: 'The societal poles of the two German states are so far apart today that it would be an illusion to believe they could be bridged at the present time by means of the ballot paper.' The building of the Berlin Wall in August 1961 merely cemented the developments of the previous decade.

6 The two Germanies since the 1960s

If, as has been argued in the preceding chapter, Germany had effectively become divided into two separate countries with very different socioeconomic and political structures by the late 1950s, the question arises as to the most sensible way of covering the most recent period of Central European history. It was difficult enough to condense the gradual division of Germany and the development of the two emergent states into the space of the preceding chapter. Logically, the rest of this book should devote two chapters to the 1960s and 1970s – one to East Germany and the other to the Federal Republic. Lack of space prevents the addition of another one hundred or so pages, and there is room only for one chapter divided into five sections. The first two sections will deal with East Germany up to the early 1980s. Given the larger size and greater economic and political weight of the Federal Republic, it seemed justified to use the three sections remaining thereafter for a discussion of West German society in its economic and political context.

The development of the East German economy, 1960–1980

From the point of view of the East German government, the building of the Berlin Wall in August 1961 and the closing of the country's border with West Germany between Travemünde on the Baltic Sea and Hof in Upper Franconia were vital for the economy and, inseparable from this, for the political survival of the regime. Of course, officially the SED argued that the Wall was designed to stop the aggressive infiltration and political subversion of the GDR by Bonn's secret services and the American CIA. However, there can be little doubt that the refugee problem lay at the heart of the matter. The daily departure of ever larger numbers of East Germans to the West amounted to a blood-letting which fundamentally threatened the stability of the Ulbricht government. Up to the end of 1960, some 2.5 million people had abandoned all their belongings and absconded. In the eight months before August 1961 an estimated 160,000 had taken the train to East Berlin and thence the suburban train to one of the Western sectors of the city, or they had simply

226

walked across one of the many thinly patrolled sectoral border-lines. Thus by the spring of 1961 the stream had become a flood, with many of the male refugees being highly skilled workers or academically trained white-collar specialists. Whether they left for political or economic reasons or both, no industrial enterprise or agricultural collective could hope to maintain regular production if key personnel could no longer be relied upon to report for work the following morning. All the emotions it raised at the time notwithstanding, the building of the Berlin Wall was therefore not only a tacit recognition by the West of '16-year-old realities' (McGeorge Bundy), but also a measure which, as some authors have argued, constituted the actual founding of East Germany, twelve years after its formal establishment in 1949. The political and psychological significance of this 'second founding' will be dealt with later in this chapter. The question to be investigated in this section is what the decision of August 1961 meant in economic terms.

It seems quite safe to assume that the SED and the planners in the various economic agencies greeted the sealing of the borders with a sigh of relief. As is customary in socialist economies, they had for years been setting production targets about which there was an air of unreality typical of such exercises in Soviet bloc countries. But what had made a real mockery of all planning was the constant drain of personnel from the offices and factories. After 1961 at least one factor, if nothing else, could be calculated with some accuracy – manpower – and, it should be added, educational investments. We have seen in the preceding chapter how the broadening of higher education was designed to create new channels of upward mobility and generate feelings of gratitude and loyalty among its beneficiaries. But by the late 1950s it had become clear that educational planning and expenditure would bring future rewards to the regime only if there existed no alternative to building a successful career in the East. Up to 1961, such an alternative was available, and in the late 1950s a West German economist even tried to tot up what the westward migration had cost the GDR in terms of lost educational investments up to 1957: 22,500 million marks.

Four years and further losses in people and investments later, the escape route had been closed and it seemed possible to put the future economic development of the country on an even keel, with consequences for its overall stability which will be assessed in the next section. Taking a long-term economic perspective, it may be said that East Germany presents a success story which is in many ways no less startling than the West German 'Economic Miracle' of the 1950s. Although the agricultural sector of the economy, employing 12 per cent of the working population (Table 15), is larger than the West German one, the GDR rose to occupy eighth place among the world's industrial nations. Crises in the late 1960s and in the wake of the oil shocks notwithstanding, its manufacturing industry experienced on the whole impressive growth rates. They averaged out at 6.5 per cent between 1966 and 1970, dropping only slightly to 6.3 per cent during the period 1971–5. The rises in the cost of raw materials on the world market were also bound to have an adverse effect on a manufacturing country like East Germany; but tangible economic growth remained a strategic aim which was set at an average annual rate of no less than 5.8 per cent in the 1981 Five-Year Plan. Production increases were particularly large in the electronics, chemical and engineering industries, deliberately promoted by a government and Party which set great store in rationalisation and high technology. Accordingly, it was also manufacturing industry which contributed the lion's share to the Gross Domestic Product (GDP), with agriculture trailing far behind (Table 13). The national income increased from 73.6 milliard marks in 1960 to 142.4 milliard marks in 1975. In 1980 it totalled no less than 201.0 milliard marks.

Like the Federal Republic, the German Democratic Republic became an important trading nation, occupying fifteenth place in the world league table. In fact in 1975, the percentage of exports in terms of the GDP was about the same as that of West Germany. The main flow of trade was towards the East, however, in the opposite direction from that of the Federal Republic. In the 1960s, roughly 75 per cent of the GDR's trade was with other socialist countries. Later the percentage of imports declined somewhat to an average of 65 per cent, with exports continuing at over 70 per cent in the early 1970s. In 1983, the percentage was 62, a figure which must be seen against the background of an expansion of trade with the West and especially with the Federal Republic which occurred from the mid-1970s and is linked to the political 'normalisation' of relations with Bonn. In 1960, the GDR received goods worth 1,030 million marks from West Germany and delivered goods worth 1,007 million marks. These figures doubled in the following decade and doubled again by 1975. In 1983 receipts had risen to 7,681 million marks, with deliveries being worth 7,562 million marks, indicating that, through its relatively open and special trading links with West Germany, the GDR has become a kind of secret member of the European Economic Community (EEC). Some of the wealth generated by industrial and commercial activity was used to raise living standards and welfare provision, as will be seen in a moment. But resource allocations earmarked for reinvestment remained high and were particularly large in the 1960s, before there was a partial reversal of priorities.

One reason for the high rates of reinvestment during the 1960s is to be found in a fresh optimism and determination by which the ministerial and Party bureaucracy became infected after the building of the Berlin Wall. In principle, the SED had long been wedded to a programme of economic modernisation. This deeply ingrained belief received another boost when, after the successful launching of the Soviet *sputnik*, it looked as if it might be possible for the socialist countries to overtake the capitalist West. Nikita Khrushchev even went so far as to proclaim such ambitions in public. Yet up to August 1961, Ulbricht had been so preoccupied with maintaining his regime almost on a day-to-day basis and at tremendous cost that a forward-looking modernisation programme barely got beyond the drawing-board. Now, in the 1960s, it seemed all of a sudden as if only the sky was the limit. Efficiency and 'results' came to be considered more important than ideological purity. This was certainly the view of Erich Apel and Günter Mittag, two members of a younger generation of East German communists who emerged as the leading lights behind a programme aimed at expanding certain industries and at reorganising and rationalising management structures and chains of command in the economy.

Named New Economic System of Planning and Guidance (NÖSPL) and finally proclaimed in June 1963, East Germany's post-1961 economic policy was designed to fulfil four requirements: (a) to develop a long-term planning perspective which concentrated upon the leading branches of industry and was responsive to scientific and technological innovation; (b) to mobilise the workforce by means of material incentives; (c) to create a scientifically based management of industry, and (d) to draw upon the creativity and experience of the workers in the planning and direction of production at factory level. One of the most important consequences of NÖSPL was therefore to decentralise economic decision-making and, no less importantly, the disposition of profits. It is not surprising that this move away from a Stalinist command economy was welcomed by managers and workers alike. Thenceforth the Ulbricht government attempted to mobilise quite unashamedly what came to be called the 'material interestedness' of the working population. Science and technology were to provide, in almost Saint-Simonian fashion, a common bond which bound party functionaries, managers and the shop-floor together in the great task of building a better and more productive socioeconomic system. Thus it was not just the modernisation of the existing production apparatus which drove on men like Mittag, Apel or Willi Stoph, the GDR's first Defence Minister who was promoted president of the Ministerial Council from 1964 to 1973. Stoph in particular was fascinated by cybernetics and systems theory. It was thought possible in those optimistic 1960s to develop accurate projections for the East German economy for the next dozen years or more and to plan technological change and investment in the industries of the future accordingly. They were less explicit about the corollary that these policies would open up new opportunities for *social* engineering and move the country forward on the road towards a highly industrialised socialist society.

It was in this broad sense that the planning bureaucracy was to set the framework within which the individual *volkseigene* company was to produce and overproduce unhampered by considerations of demand and changing market conditions. Yet the greater freedom of the factories to decide their own production priorities and to distribute some of the gains to the employees in the shape of bonuses and incentives also generated serious problems. Inevitably perhaps, there developed a growing and increasingly counterproductive gulf between the macro-economic targets aimed at by the central bureaucracy and the planning of investment and production at local level. The tensions which arose over this difference in perception and interest were exacerbated by the limited participation granted to the shop-floor in determining bonuses and other material incentives as well as production priorities. In short, central planners, factory directors and workforces began to move in opposite directions. By the late 1960s, these contradictions, together with Soviet pressures in the wake of the Czech Crisis of 1968, had become serious enough that the regime decided to reassert its authority against the periphery and to resume greater control over output and the disposition of surpluses. If this nevertheless did not imply a return to Stalinist practices, it was due in part to the growing recognition that the future was not as predictable and malleable as had been assumed ten years earlier. A new realism set in and with it a sense that, from the point of view of the regime's stability and future viability, it was more important to offer butter now instead of diverting overlarge resources into 'futuristic' programmes deemed to be of long-term structural importance.

In explaining these developments of the 1970s, factors of personality and generation must also be taken into account. In 1970, Ulbricht, the man who had been central to the establishment and consolidation of the GDR and who, through guile and ruthlessness, had survived every crisis of the previous 25 years of communist rule, had reached the age of 77. Throughout the 1960s, he had retained command of SED politics, and NÖSPL could not have been started without his support. No doubt it also bore his stamp and that of an old-style authoritarian communism which he embodied in the sense that long-term socioeconomic change, as has been mentioned, continued to be given priority over short-term material concession in order to gain popularity. However, during this period a new generation was growing up not only in the economic planning bureaucracy, but also in the SED. Few people represented that generation better than Erich Honecker who, born in 1912, took over the leadership of the Party from Ulbricht in 1971, assuming the title of Secretary General of the Central Committee in May 1976.

It was under Honecker that the above-mentioned reassertion of greater central control over production and investment was accompanied by a shift away from preparing for a scientific-technological future towards the satisfaction of present-day needs and expectations of the population. As he put it at the SED Party Congress in East Berlin in June 1971: 'The economy is the means to an end for our society, a means for the ever improving satisfaction of the growing material and cultural needs of the working population.' Prognosticating a scientific revolution and waiting for 'miracles', he added, was to be abandoned. Sober calculation was to take its place. Henceforth the regime would 'weigh carefully where improvements were most needed and where, with the means available, it is possible to achieve advances which are particularly important to the working population'.

In line with such postulates, the 1971–5 Five-Year Plan gave priority to the production of consumer goods and better housing provision in an effort to bring about a 'further rise in the material and cultural living standards' of the East Germans. Honecker turned the country towards a 'consumer socialism' (D. Staritz) in the hope of obtaining, in return, a new and more stable support for his regime. Subsequently, more goods did become available in the shops, and people's wage packets grew sufficiently to be able to buy them. Thus nominal wages rose from 494 marks to 755 marks between 1960 and 1970, and there was a further increase to 1,021 marks by 1980. That people had more money in their pockets is also indicated by the fact that turnover in the high-street shops as well as savings accounts grew substantially during the 1970s. Nevertheless it is not easy to obtain a clear picture of living standards in East Germany. Although most experts agree that real income is lagging behind that of the West Germans, there is no consensus about the actual percentage. Some authors have assumed a gap of 30 per cent; others believe it to be nearer 50 per cent. These discrepancies have arisen because of the problem of quantifying the impact of the regime's economic and social policies. As the market is centrally regulated, prices for basic items of consumption such as bread, potatoes and vegetables as well as for services and transport have been kept at very low levels. Meat, milk and many other items of daily consumption are also much cheaper than in the Federal Republic, and prices have not been raised for over 20 years. On the other hand, butter, eggs, fruit, cocoa, coffee and imported foodstuffs in general are several times more expensive than in the West. Prices for mass-produced clothes are also held down by administrative fiat; deductions for national insurance and other benefits are lower than in the Federal Republic, though consumer durables and especially cars are priced very high. Nevertheless, many people have earned enough to be able to save up for such 'luxuries' or for holidays. The number of radios, television sets, refrigerators and washing-machines per 100 households is, no doubt, very impressive, even if cars, unlike motorcycles and mopeds, have remained beyond most people's reach (Table 30). Since 1972, more than half the adult population have been able to afford an annual holiday, and one in three of these holiday-makers has gone abroad, typically to other countries of the socialist bloc.

Low rents have been a major item keeping down the monthly expenditure of the average household. By 1975 the building programme announced four

231

years earlier of 500,000 units had been over-fulfilled by 20 per cent. In 1985, a further major modernisation programme was under way in East Berlin, aiming at the construction of 117,000 units. Rent levels were originally staggered according to income, although since 1981 a standard rate has been introduced for all newly-built apartment blocks. The East Germans are also well provided with crèches, play groups, schools and medical services. The pressures for a high-level school and pre-school provision were, it should be added, unusually strong: the GDR has one of the highest percentages of working women in the industrialised world. But it was not merely the desire to increase the family income which led to this development; it was also a consequence of the massive loss of manpower to the West prior to the building of the Berlin Wall and of the peculiar age structure. Up to 1961 many of the younger people had left; the older ones had stayed behind. Labour was, therefore, so scarce that most adults had a job, even beyond retirement age. Above all, the regime tried to lure women back into the offices and factories. These women may have achieved greater equality in pay by comparison with their counterparts in the West, but old hierarchies persist where positions of responsibility are concerned. The high percentage of working women has resulted in another peculiarity which has raised government concern about the future: the GDR has one of the lowest birth rates in the world, and during the 1970s resistance to having children even led to a decline of the population in absolute terms. The government has responded to these trends by introducing various benefits for working mothers, including increased paid maternity leave, shorter weekly working-time and extended holidays. Special marriage loans and child benefits are also being paid. These incentives have been successful in the sense that they have helped to reverse the earlier population decline.

All this means that the East Germans have two ways of measuring their living standard. If they switch on their TV set to watch (as they are no longer banned from doing) a West German programme, they will see and hear that they continue to be worse off than their friends and relatives in the Federal Republic. If, on the other hand, they travel to Rumania or to Poland, to Prague or the Black Sea, they will discover that they enjoy, perhaps next to Hungary, the highest living standard in Eastern Europe, and may also not be doing too badly in comparison with the Italians or the British.

Society and politics in contemporary East Germany

Yet men and women do not live by bread alone. Their cultural and intellectual needs must also be considered, and on this score we must return, as a first step, to the SED's educational policies. If the opening up of educational opportunities in the 1950s was ultimately intended to create technically qualified cadres to take over from the Old Guard, it should not be ignored that the policy also implied a commitment to greater social equality, albeit at the expense of free choice and liberty. Guided by the Leninist tradition of an anti-democratic socialism, the Party leadership pursued what R. Thomas has called a policy of 'calculated emancipation'. East Germany was turned into an *Erziehungsgesellschaft* in which the SED combined pragmatic considerations of survival with an attempt to create greater equality.

We have already examined the emergence of a ten-form polytechnical high school during the 1950s which created new channels of upward mobility. This system was greatly expanded in the 1960s and 1970s so that by the end of the last decade over 90 per cent of all pupils received a broadly based science-oriented education up to the age of 16. Moreover, since 1980 all school-leavers have been given some kind of vocational training. While the aim here is to build up a highly skilled workforce for industry, about 10 per cent of those who complete the final (tenth) year continue for a further two years to work for their *Abitur* certificate. A further 4 per cent obtain this certificate via an alternative route called 'professional training with *Abitur*' which takes a total of three years and provides the graduands with an additional diploma in a craft. The *Abitur* remains the main avenue to university. In 1977 some 162,500 students received further training at one of the 233 polytechnic-type *Fachhochschulen*. Among the students pursuing courses at *Hochschul* level in 1977, some 20 per cent were part-timers and some 47.5 per cent were women. The applied sciences continued to attract large numbers, and 85 per cent of the full-timers receive a state scholarship. After the experience of the 1950s when sons and daughters of working-class or peasant families were given preferential access to higher education over children of the old professional elite groups, social background became a less important criterion in the selection process. During the 1970s, however, there occurred a reduction in total student numbers by government fiat when it was discovered that tertiary qualifications could not always be rewarded with jobs commensurate with the graduate's expectations. So, it seemed better not to raise expectations in the first place and to try to promote the regime's ideological commitment to equality by other means.

What these educational policies have led to (in conjunction with a modernisation of the Civil Code, family legislation and welfare provision) is a surprisingly stable, but at the same time dynamic *leistungsorientierte Laufbahngesellschaft* (achievement-orientated career society), as Peter Christian Ludz, one of the foremost West German scholars on the GDR, has put it. Any further political emancipation of this society is tightly controlled and ultimately blocked by a cumbersome party apparatus, even if the methods of domination are no longer as heavy-handed as in the 1950s, but those of a consultative authoritarianism. Certainly there have been substantial changes in the top SED leadership owing to rejuvenation and the infusion of a pragmatic professionalism. To quote Ludz again: 'The Central Committee of the SED is no longer an organisational focal point for the "old guard" of Communist functionaries whose political mores were established in the struggles of the 1920s and 1930s and who were therefore frequently unable to adapt themselves to the reality of a highly mobile industrial society.' Instead there is a younger generation of which Honecker and Stoph are typical representatives. In the lower cadres, too, the thoroughly trained official and administrator has taken over from the unskilled political organiser.

The social and economic policies adopted by this new party elite have created a dynamism within the higher echelons of the SED itself which has acted as a 'limitation of control and thus of the monopoly enjoyed by the leadership' in earlier years, even if this dynamism has not been 'powerful enough to seize control of the hierarchical system away from the one-party rulers' (Ludz). Yet, these sociological shifts towards a meritocracy which have been particularly marked in the industrial sphere have not obliterated stratification. East Germany is no longer a class society like the Wilhelmine Reich. Nevertheless, positions higher up in the political or economic hierarchy continue to confer material privileges and social prestige. Rudolf Bahro, the dissident Communist who was able to gain an inside view of the East German system, has gone so far as to speak of a 'pyramid society'. However, whereas this pyramid is sharply pointed at the top as far as political power and influence are concerned, it is much flatter in respect of differences in wealth and income than that of West Germany. There are no people who might be called rich and very rich. On the other hand, all sections of the population survive fairly comfortably, and even the farmers on the collectives are no worse off than the urban population. They can afford holidays and many of them have gained a stake in the *Erziehungsgesellschaft*, having received a specialised training. A growing number at least have come to recognize that the regime's argricultural policies since the 1950s have not been disadvantageous to them. Levels of productivity, like those of industry, are the highest within the Soviet bloc. All in all, East Germany is therefore a more egalitarian society than that of the Federal Republic, but it is also more uniform than its Western counterpart.

This uniformity is most evident in the field of formal political and cultural organisation. Pressures are strong to join one or more of the movements and associations which enjoy SED support. The FDGB has over 7 million members, and 65 per cent of the young (1.7 million) are organised in the Free German Youth (FDJ). Uniforms – symbols of uniformity – are frequently to be seen, and some observers have even discovered a 'Red Prussianism' and commented on the persistent militarisation of life. A more detailed analysis of the political system would also reveal that, mass organisations of all descriptions notwithstanding, everything is geared to rulings from the top, and the leadership of the SED *vis-à-vis* the governmental machinery is secured.

The main mass organisation to fit very uneasily into this picture is the Protestant Church of East Germany. By force of circumstance, its leadership may have been all too accommodating towards the SED in its quest to preserve its organisational infrastructure and financial independence and to provide unfettered contact with ordinary members and their spiritual needs. In 1978 top-level discussions took place which put relations between Church and State on a more official and predictable footing, and in 1983 the two sides co-operated quite closely during the celebrations of the Luther Year. On the other hand, the Church's position between the two fronts of party centralism and pressures at the grass-roots became more ambiguous again during the early 1980s with the rise of an East German peace movement. Obviously, the hierarchy found it difficult to avoid giving a moral lead on such vital issues as nuclear war and disarmament, and to some extent the Honecker regime was presumably not even unhappy about the 'controlled' stirrings of a Christian peace movement. Yet, however welcome the condemnation of Reaganism and NATO strategy may have been to the SED, there always remained the danger that these arguments might spill over into a criticism of superpower politics in general and of the lack of democratic rights in Eastern Europe. As a result, the regime and its secret services have been watching with suspicion the activities of the Christian peace campaigners in their own backyard.

Like religious worship, cultural and artistic life was not allowed to stray too far from the party-line either. In the long run, it is true, the dogmatism of the early postwar years has mellowed, most strikingly perhaps in respect of attitudes towards modern German history and 'pre-socialist' culture. There was a time when the eighteenth and nineteenth centuries were interpreted within the framework of a most rigid orthodox Marxism-Leninism. More recently some remarkably sophisticated interpretations of that earlier period have appeared, and Ernst Engelberg's biography of Bismarck even aroused so much interest that it got onto the West German bestseller list! There was also a time when historic buildings and monuments were unceremoniously demolished as irrelevant or undesirable symbols of a bygone age. Meanwhile this policy has been completely reversed and many famous places in Berlin, Dresden, Potsdam and Weimar have been proudly restored and are open to the public.

Changes in government attitudes have also occurred in respect of writers and artists, even if the record is more contradictory and ultimately more disillusioning. East German literature started after 1945 with the return from exile of a number of very well-known authors, among them Brecht, Johannes R. Becher, Anna Seghers and Arnold Zweig. Not surprisingly perhaps, their main concern was with the experience of fascism. Coming to grips with this experience was, of course, something which the SED could only approve of. But soon the older generation of writers began to venture into the present. Thus Brecht's late poetry is written in a vein which combines an encouragement of the new socialist society with a criticism of certain of its manifestations. He quickly found that he was intellectually isolated and without political influence. Becher, who became minister for cultural affairs in 1954, was virtually the only one who could claim to have achieved a position in which he could move things forward. But even he soon found himself under attack and died a disappointed man in 1958.

It might be argued that this older generation, many of whose members were born in the late nineteenth century, was after years of exile in any case too out-of-touch with postwar German society ever to play a major role within it. It was, on the surface at least, a different matter with a younger generation of intellectuals which had grown up in East Germany and gained its first literary successes in the late 1950s and early 1960s. Some of them were not only deeply influenced by Brecht's drama, but also by the encouragement-criticism approach which he had developed in the 1950s. Slowly authors like Christa Wolf or Hermann Kant succeeded in emancipating themselves from the straitjacket of a 'socialist realism' in the Soviet literary tradition of the Stalinist period. The same is true of East German theatre where Peter Hacks and Heiner Müller developed 'a combination of socialist classicism and irreverent youthfulness' (F. Trommler). Predictably, these experiments did not go down well with Ulbricht and the Old Guard, and writers continued to be stifled while he remained in power.

However, government attitudes towards intellectuals became more flexible under Honecker, in the sense that what was permissible was never clearly defined; unfortunately, this also meant that official views were subject to sudden relapses into illiberalism. The first half of the 1970s saw the relaxation of censorship and the re-emergence of writers who had previously been literary un-persons. Poetry and drama once again became major vehicles of artistic expression, and their protagonists, like Günter Kunert, Wolf Biermann, Stefan Heym, Reiner Kunze, Ulrich Plenzdorf, Christa Wolf and Sarah Kirsch, attracted international attention. East German painters, hitherto nailed down to a strictly partisan choice of their themes and styles, were also permitted to display their works in larger exhibitions, and men like Willi Sitte and Wolfgang Mattheuer gained acclaim at home and abroad. Above all, literature really blossomed. Wolf achieved a status as a novelist which has made her work mandatory reading in many German Studies courses in the West. Müller had another most productive phase and wrote a number of plays which revolved around the traumatic course of modern German history and its collapse in death and destruction during the 1940s.

Yet poets, even if they are professed socialists in a socialist country, are dangerous people in any authoritarian system, and their subtle ambiguities and juggling with words and meanings soon aroused the suspicion of the authorities once more. The thaw of the early 1970s did not last long, and by 1975–6 East Germany's intellectual climate once again became quite inclement. Wolf Biermann, who had been a thorn in the flesh of the SED for more than a decade, was deprived of his citizenship in 1976 while on one of his visits to the Federal Republic. Some, like Kunert and Kirsch, followed him and emigrated to the West; others lapsed into silence or had their manuscripts rejected by their publishers and the censor. Nor was much scope ever allowed to Marxist philosophers to debate the present state and future development of Marxism, as Robert Havemann was reminded every day when he noticed the plain-clothes policemen patrolling in front of his house.

Such practices have reinforced the uniformity that pervades East German cultural life. It is not that there are no cinemas or theatres, but what is being offered on screen and stage, in the mass media and elsewhere provides an unexciting intellectual diet. So much of it is very conventional. Western visitors to the German Democratic Repulic may be struck most by the more limited choice of goods in the shops and the less colourful façades of the cities. Yet even more remarkable would seem to be the survival, behind this façade, of habits, traditions and life-styles which prevailed in northern and eastern Germany prior to the takeover by the Socialist Unity Party. Social intercourse takes place in a milieu which one tends to associate with the *Kleinbürgertum* of interwar Germany. The older generation at least has evidently been reluctant to abandon deeply held convictions about how best to organise social relationships – never mind your wife's science diploma and job. They acknowledge the 'achievements of socialism' in the economic and welfare sphere; they work in a modern technological environment, but their attitudes and consciousness have remained curiously *bieder* (proper). The younger generation may be different, more prepared to engage in experimentation. One can even see hippies and punkers, skinheads and new romantics. Yet, even if the young are more cosmopolitan and less stuffy than their elders, they are also more incongruous, as they sit on their mopeds in the streets of Merseburg or Kleinmachnow, wearing jeans and listening to American rock music blaring from their transistor radios.

If there are some young and equally some older people who feel alienated from the regime and socialism, there can be little doubt that the GDR's economic successes as well as the victories of its athletes at international competitions have helped to instil in the majority of the East German population a certain pride in their country. This in turn has had a stabilising effect on society and the political system as a whole, as the Party had hoped it would. Certainly East Germans appear to identify more strongly than ever before

237

with the State in which they live. Some observers believe that several hundred thousand people would leave if the frontiers to the West were ever opened again; but they have also detected a new East German national consciousness not unlike the patriotism felt by many West Germans for the Federal Republic. It is not surprising that the government in East Berlin should be actively encouraging these feelings and be promoting them through the state-controlled media and in the field of sport. The SED has always displayed a highly developed sense of self-preservation, and it would be naive to assume that all this was not quite consciously enacted in order to consolidate the GDR and to endow the regime with a greater legitimacy. In this it has evidently succeeded.

This may seem paradoxical in view of the fact that East Germany still bars its citizens from travelling outside the Soviet bloc. Only old-age pensioners are free to visit the West, and presumably the regime would even be glad to see them stay there for good. It seems no less paradoxical that the building of the Berlin Wall and the fortifications along the GDR's western frontier should have enhanced its *international* legitimacy. In understanding this contradiction it is worth remembering that early in 1961 the reputation of the Ulbricht government had reached a depressingly low point even among his fellow-leaders in the socialist camp. Although Ulbricht had been pressing them for some time to approve some kind of drastic action against the mass exodus from East Germany, they were reluctant to support him, arguing that the virtual imprisonment of the entire population behind concrete blocks and barbed wire fences was a poor advertisement for the presumed superiority of socialism. They soon changed their minds. Not only is the GDR a major economic power in the Soviet bloc today which fulfills specific production functions within the division of labour system established by COMECON, the economic union of the East European countries under Russian leadership; East Germany, the ultimate power of decision in the hands of the Soviet leadership notwithstanding, also has an important political voice and can currently boast greater prosperity and stability than all other socialist regimes with the possible exception of Hungary.

Gaining diplomatic recognition as a sovereign state in the rest of the world has been a more arduous process. For a long time West Germany and the power of the Hallstein Doctrine remained a major stumbling bloc which stipulated that Bonn would break off relations with any state that established diplomatic links with East Berlin. By the mid-1960s the Doctrine had for all practical purposes ceased to be an effective instrument of West German diplomacy. Recognising its erosion, the government of West Berlin under the leadership of Willy Brandt and his press secretary Egon Bahr had begun to make, at the local level, an attempt to leave 'the trenches of the Cold War' and to facilitate Christmas-time visits between families living in West and

East Berlin. Up to March 1966, four temporary agreements had been signed between the West Berlin Senate and the Ulbricht regime which enabled West Berliners to pay short visits to their relatives across the Wall and implied an official recognition of a country which in the eyes of many politicians in Bonn was still the 'Soviet Zone of Occupation'. At the end of 1966 Brandt became Foreign Minister in the newly-formed Grand Coalition government with the CDU/CSU, while the United States had begun to pursue their policy of dé-tente with the Soviet Union. Slowly but persistently Bonn now pursued a strategy of rapprochement in Central Europe which ended in a series of in-ternational treaties in the early 1970s and which we shall have to come back to in a moment. The important point here is that it was in this period that East Germany achieved full recognition under international law and became a member of the United Nations. As Honecker emphasised at the time, this ended the long-standing claim of the Federal Republic to represent and speak for all Germans in East and West. The *Abgrenzung* (demarcation) from West Germany had been achieved. Yet, paradoxically, it was precisely this *Abgren-zung* which opened up new possibilities of closer contact between the two Germanies. Once mutual official recognition was no longer the obstacle, an intensification of a one-way traffic across the Iron Curtain could be effected which has since then enabled millions of West Germans to visit their relatives in the East without endless bureaucratic formalities. The SED's old inferiority complex, never admitted but nevertheless real, disappeared. The dialectics of *Abgrenzung* have also resulted in a frequency of contacts at government level which was quite inconceivable in the 1960s and have led some foreign countries to wonder whether the Germans are preparing the unification of the two countries under a different guise. Such suspicions are hardly well-founded, if one considers the question of how a socioeconomic and political system like that of the GDR could ever be merged, with the negotiated agree-ment of the two sides, into a single entity with the Federal Republic.

West German capitalism and the international economy

Whatever the features of the socioeconomic order which the East German communists have been running during the last two decades – some of them distressing and repellent, others redeeming – it is necessary to return to the Federal Republic, the larger, more complex and more important of the two Germanies. For the past twenty years, visitors to the Federal Republic have been struck by its continued and very visible prosperity. There have been, it is true, periods of economic recession and gloom. But in retrospect and compared with what other countries experienced, much of the pessimism which accompanied temporary crises seems to have been exaggerated: in the long term, the expansion of the national economy continued. Thus, except for 1967, 1975, and 1981/2, West Germany's annual growth rates remained higher than those of most other industrialised countries, even if they were halved during the 1970s by comparison with the 1960s. Next to the United States and Japan, the Federal Republic held its place at the top of the Western economic league table. Of course, there were considerable variations in the size of the contribution to the national wealth made by different branches of the economy, with industry and commerce contributing roughly one-third of the total in 1975. Meanwhile the share of agriculture had dropped to a mere 2.7 per cent. The decline of agriculture is also reflected in the further reduction of the number of people it employed and of the number of farmsteads, which contracted to a quarter of the 1950 figure (Tables 2 and 15), even if the farmers, thanks to the peculiarities of the EEC's Common Agricultural Policy, continued to wield powers as a lobby which were totally out of proportion with their economic significance. Industry, in other words, was the dominant creator of wealth, and the index of total industrial production doubled in the fifteen years after 1960. Much of this production was for exports, whose value went up from 47,900 million marks in 1960 to 350,300 million marks in 1980, providing a surplus over imports until 1980 when, largely due to the high costs of fossil fuel and other forms of energy, the country's balance of payments slipped into the red (Table 11).

However, by 1983, the country had once again overcome these problems, not least because it had adopted an *export-led* growth strategy, in many ways similar to the one with the help of which the Germans had pulled themselves out of their 1966 recession (Table 49). There were a number of international and domestic factors which facilitated industry's success in those economically very difficult years, among them a strong dollar, a constant and high rate of technological modernisation, skillful managerial and marketing techniques, good industrial relations and increases in productivity. Complaints about a declining work morale notwithstanding, the West Germans also worked hard, and their output was boosted by the sweat and toil of foreign labour – the so-called guest workers – imported mainly from Spain, Italy, Yugoslavia, Greece and Turkey, whose number rose from 279,000 in 1960 to 2.5 million in the mid-1970s before falling back to below 2 million in the 1980s (Table 48). Calculated on a per-capita basis, all West Germans benefited from the prosperity of the 1960s and 1970s. Thus, the average income rose from 4,331 marks per annum in 1960 to 8,790 marks in 1970, reaching 16,281 marks in 1978. Throughout this period incomes also showed a real growth over inflation until the world recession and the economic policies of the 1980s brought an actual loss in average purchasing power (Table 50). Moreover, it must always be remembered that the newly created wealth remained unevenly distributed – a point to which we shall have to come back later in this section. What is important here is that virtually all groups in West German society received a growing slice of the national economic cake. Until the 1980s real wages kept ahead of price rises, while average weekly work-hours were consecutively reduced and fell below 40 in the early 1980s (Tables 50 and 31). The legal entitlement for holidays increased from an average of 16.7 days in 1960 to around 30 days in 1983. The changes in the patterns of family expenditure which occurred after 1957 confirm these developments. In the mid-1980s, less than a fifth of the average income was spent on basic food items, and well over 50 per cent could be set aside for leisure activities, travel and automobile expenses, or be put into a savings account (Table 29).

The implications of these figures and developments can hardly be over-emphasised if seen against the background of the country's economic performance in the first half of this century. For the first time in its history, Germany (or at least its Western parts) had evolved a Western-style industrial capitalism both with regard to its economic structures and the economic behaviour of the overwhelming majority of its citizens. As to the structures, the peculiarities of the 'German capitalism' which became most clearly discernible in the 1930s and which, as has been argued, were dysfunctional to a US-dominated liberal world economy as designed by the Americans in the 1940s, have for all practical purposes disappeared. Yet the reintegration and 're-education' process which began in the late 1940s simply took a while to be completed. By the 1960s the West German economic system had been largely 'Americanised'. Its structural features thenceforth evolved along lines similar to those of other capitalist countries. This means that the Federal Republic is firmly plugged into the global system of trading and banking. Its enterprises have seen a vast expansion of their economic power (Table 17); they are transnational and conduct their operations like their American, Japanese, French or British competitors within an international and increasingly concentrated world market. Thus, while direct investments by the United States in the West German economy doubled from $7,650 million in 1973 to $16,077 million in 1981, German total investments in the United States rose from $965 million to $7,067 million during the same period. Companies in key manufacturing sectors like Volkswagen Cars, Bayer Chemicals, Siemens Electrics or Thyssen Steel are to be found among the top ten in the league table of large multinationals. It is not that the protagonists of protectionism, cartellisation and economic nationalism as well as anti-unionism have retreated altogether. But the balance of forces has shifted decisively in favour of industries which had promoted their 'dynamic' concepts of economic policy-making and industrial relations during the 1920s, but proved too weak at the time. They were the industries of the Second Industrial Revolution, whose new importance is reflected both in the production indices and in their voice in politics. They fully supported 'Germany's return to the world market' (L. Erhard) and were also instrumental in building bridges towards the trade unions and in creating forms of tripartism which also emerged in other Western capitalist countries. They propagated economic management and consensus politics within the political framework of a parliamentary representative system. The Ruhr valley is no longer the power centre of West German industry; it has moved to the south and south-west.

Again these developments have to be seen as a slow process of evolution. Just as the employers and the ministerial bureaucracy took some time to learn to treat the unions as partners and indispensable pillars of the existing economic system, the latter did not abandon overnight their early postwar ideas about 'economic democracy' following the bitter conflicts with the employers over co-determination in the early 1950s. A change of attitude became more clearly discernible, however, from the mid-1950s onwards when the DGB began to pursue a policy designed to obtain a larger percentage of the newly-created industrial wealth for their members and the working population at large. This concentration on material improvement implied a recognition by the unions of the type of 'welfare tempered capitalism' (*sozial gedämpfter Kappitalismus*) which had emerged under Erhard, yielding impressive results in absolute terms and promoting a kind of consumerism and affluence which is so striking of West German high streets to this day.

On the other hand, as has already been mentioned, wealth remained quite unevenly distributed and it would to be wrong to be overimpressed by calculations according to which the average household in 1983 owned assets worth 230,000 marks or even 360,000 marks, if future pension rights are included. Closer inspection and a breakdown by social groups reveals that in 1970 only 0.1 per cent of the manual workers earned more than 1,800 marks per month, as against one third of all self-employed (Table 27). Returns on investment remained high (Table 22). The continued growth of the West German industrial economy and the fiscal incentives favouring capital formation made a deepening of economic inequalities almost inevitable. When, in the 1960s, economists began to look systematically at how the newly created wealth had become distributed among different social groups, they discovered that among the self-employed in agriculture, commerce and industry some 16 per cent of all households owned 47 per cent of the total private wealth. Working-class families, on the other hand, making up 33.7 per cent of all households, owned a mere 17 per cent. Such averages mask a further concentration of wealth at the top of the scale: as early as 1960, the number of households owning more than 100,000 marks was a mere 305,000. This means that 1.7 per cent of the population possessed 35 per cent of the private wealth. At the same time there were 14,000 families with more than 1 million marks: one-thousandth of the population which held 13 per cent of all privately owned assets in its hands. Although the total number of millionaires has grown since then, the overall imbalance has barely changed.

The above figures caused some alarm in the late 1960s when various politicians warned against the dangers of creating a society which was sharply divided into 'haves' and 'have-nots'. In response to this debate, fresh schemes were put forward to promote profit-sharing, employee participation and share-holding by ordinary citizens. Although a number of firms conducted individual experiments in this field, it proved impossible to introduce a systematic *Vermögensbildung* on a national scale which might have shifted the existing distribution of wealth in favour of the 'masses'. Nor were saving programmes, like the *624-Mark-Gesetz* for low-income taxpayers and the encouragement of the building society movement (*Bausparkassen*) anything more than drops in the ocean.

The rich live well in the Federal Republic, but they are not extravagant. They are reluctant to display their wealth and have ploughed large sums back into their enterprises. They and the top managers of industry have been acutely aware of the need to modernise their plants and to adopt the latest technologies to be able to compete in the world market. Considerable sums have also been spent on improving the factory environment and workplace facilities in an effort to increase productivity and motivation. The 1970s also saw a refinement of the constitutional framework within which employers and trade unions regulate their conflicts. In November 1971, the *Bundestag* ratified a revised version of the Works' Council Law of 1952 which extended the rights of the employee to be informed and consulted about issues of personnel management. More controversial was the extension of co-determination beyond the iron and coal industries; but in May 1976, after much chopping and changing, a modified form of *Mitbestimmung* became applicable to all joint stock companies with more than 2,000 employees. Although employers are loath to admit it, such schemes have helped to preserve industrial peace, as has the moderation of the trade unions. Strike figures remained low in the 1960s (Table 45). Their rise in the following decade reflected growing economic conflict, although the number of employees involved remained small by comparison with other European countries. Relations between the unions and employers also became strained when the latter went to the Constitutional Court in what was probably an attempt to block any future extension of co-determination.

In the eyes of the DGB the suit was tantamount to an attack on a key element of the Republic's constitution, and it pulled out of the *Konzertierte Aktion*, the tripartist consultative framework, which had been established in 1967. But the unions remained a factor to be reckoned with, and behind the scenes the co-operative relationship between the State and the two sides of industry continued in the interest of a co-ordinated economic strategy. The preservation of economic stability and future growth were also the considerations behind the huge investment programmes in which Bonn and the

Länder governments have been permanently engaged. They appreciated that a high-technology and export-orientated industry needs a modern infrastructure. Milliards of marks have been pumped into the railways and urban commuter systems. Large sums have also been channelled into basic research and education. There was much talk during the 1960s of an impending 'education catastrophe' unless the training of young people in schools, colleges of further education and universities was expanded and modernised. Subsequently great efforts were made to build new facilities and to revamp time-honoured practices of training and retraining. The wave of concentration, technological modernisation and infrastructural improvement has not by-passed West German agriculture. Behind the façade of timber-framed farmhouses many producers have succeeded in converting their properties into intensively mechanised and efficiently managed capitalist enterprises which are highly specialised. This trend is also reflected in the renewed fall in the number of people employed in agriculture and in an increased concentration of land-holding as small and less competitive farmers have sold up and moved to the cities (Table 15).

In physical appearance West Germany therefore presents a modern and successfully modernised industrial society. Western patterns of economic behaviour motivate the West German population, and it cannot be emphasised too strongly how much the 1960s and 1970s, with its political upheavals and Lib-Lab rule, accelerated this change. There are many manifestations of this in daily life. The choice of goods in shops and supermarkets is very wide; the 'hidden persuaders' in television commercials, newspaper advertisements and radio talks constantly urge the average consumers to spend their money. And these consumers fill up their trolleys; they eat in 'fast food' chains; they listen to and play rock; they wear blue jeans. Many West German managers speak good English – with an American accent – and hold diplomas from Anglo-Saxon business schools. They practise 'human relations' in their approach to their employees and negotiate skilfully when they meet union officials across the table to talk about wages and work conditions. The factories house advanced-design machinery; its marketing and retailing structures are adapted to a mass consumption economy. The high-speed intercity trains arrive on time; after years of digging and pile-driving, the urban underground systems are now operating smoothly and semi-automatically. Interest in higher educational qualifications has never been greater. German bureaucrats are no longer what they are reputed to be. Nor is the Federal Republic, for all its inequalities, an ungenerous society. The social security 'net' is fairly closely knit and universal. Between 1960 and 1980, the social security budget rose from 63 milliard marks (20.7% of the GNP) to 450 milliard marks (32% of the GNP). The hospitals are modern and medical provision is adequate, owing to the *Krankenkassen* system which covers about 90 per cent of the population, with the rest having private insurance. There have been constant improvements in the support of families and working mothers.

However, there are also the poor and the underprivileged. In 1975, there were some 2 million people whose monthly income was less than 600 marks. As 15 per cent of these low-income households were single old-age pensioners, it is clear that many elderly people suffer and live below the poverty line. Though 'dynamically' related and automatically adjusted to incomes and prices, state pensions at the lower end of the scale remain small unless supplemented by savings or retirement schemes. In 1980, 62 per cent of the female old-age pensioners and 10 per cent of the male pensioners had less than 500 marks per month. Another major social problem is posed by the foreign workers whose numbers rose to over 2 million in the 1970s. As Seyfi Ozgen, a representative of Turkish *Gastarbeiter* at the Workers' Welfare Federal Association in Bonn put it: 'The Germans wanted manpower, and human beings came'. Indeed on the surface it was a problem of low income levels, and the exploitation of foreign labour by West German employers often reached appalling proportions. There have been improvements, but most *Gastarbeiter*, economically and socially, continue to be at the bottom of the pile, and the implications of this will become clearer towards the end of this chapter.

Mention must finally be made of the unemployed who also tend to be left behind in the race for higher living standards. There was of course a period when unemployment and the economic and social problems it traditionally raises were negligible. In the 1960s and early 1970s, less than one per cent of the working population was without a job. In fact industry was crying out for labour and hence promoted the importation of foreign workers from the Mediterranean countries. A drastic change has set in in this respect since the mid-1970s. After the first oil shock, unemployment jumped to 1.1 million. Following the second crisis of the early 1980s, official statistics began to record hitherto unheard-of figures of around 2.5 million, over 9 per cent of the working population (Table 18). Worse, behind these figures lurks the problem of long-term and structural unemployment. If drawing an unemployment benefit already means a lowering of a person's living standard, his or her inability to find a job within a year leads to demotion to the unemployment *assistance* register. Changes in legislation have brought a further deterioration of the situation. Thus, since January 1983, those who have paid contributions for a minimum of two years prior to losing their job are given eight months' benefit instead of the previous twelve. Consequently people have had to rely on unemployment assistance earlier and, given its meagre levels, which have also been cut further in recent years, have been likely to be forced to apply for the stigmatised welfare support and to fall into a poverty trap which supposedly no longer existed in the Federal Republic.

However, it should be added that the authorities have not been sitting idly, the Federal states possibly even less so than the Bonn government. In fact, federalism has promoted a competition between the different regions of West Germany in terms of development programmes from which various retraining schemes have also benefited. It was no doubt helpful that these schemes could base themselves on an already existing infrastructure in the shape of vocational schools and similar institutions. They could be geared relatively quickly to a systematic training and retraining of school-leavers and other unemployed people. The gist of this section is therefore that, while it is difficult to make accurate predictions of the country's economic future during the late 1980s, technologically, organisationally, infrastructurally and in terms of the skills of the workforce, the Federal Republic appears to be quite well prepared for the Third Industrial Revolution.

Problems of political stability

Looking at the development of the political system, it is no exaggeration to say that the West Germans have, in their overwhelming majority, accepted parliamentarism. There are few voters today who would look for radical alternatives to the existing constitutional framework, as the powerful Right and Left had offered under the Weimar Republic. We have seen in the preceding chapter that the political picture was much less stable in the late 1940s and early 1950s. Given the distribution of votes, people wondered with some justification whether the parliamentary-representative system which came into being in 1949 was really secure. Apart from the fear of communism, one of the main factors to win over many initially disaffected and radicalised West Germans was no doubt the 'Economic Miracle' of the 1950s. By deliberately unleashing the latent energies of industry, Erhard made an important contribution also to the political stabilisation of the Federal Republic; but the dynamic developments of the economy also led to shifts and changes in the structure of industry. As it turned out, the initial economic recipes of his neo-liberalism were incapable of coping with these processes. An adjustment of existing economic policy instruments was required. Thus, while Erhard largely succeeded in destroying the cartel tradition whose revival would have undermined the objective of building a competitive market economy, he did not prevent (and probably did not mean to prevent) the re-emergence of big firms and concentrations of economic power large enough to affect the management of the West German *Marktwirtschaft* very directly (Table 17). Technological developments, automation and the organisational and financial requirements of very large production units were also bound to make an impact. Certainly, by the early 1960s the national economy, plugged into the world market as it was, had become infinitely more complex than it had been in

246

1949. It was no longer sufficient for the Economics Minister simply to set industry loose. Careful strategic planning, projection and tuning were necessary on a scale also practised by the giants of West German manufacturing industry. And this is what Erhard was increasingly unable to provide.

By 1965 his economic policies were in disarray. There was a crisis of public finance. The economy appeared to be running out of control. The time had come to scrap the remnants of neo-liberalism and to replace it by concepts of economic management which were inspired by Keynesianism. Karl Schiller, a professor of economics from Hamburg, became the embodiment of this change of course. It was under his guidance at the Economics Ministry that the Federal government engineered a textbook-style export-led *Aufschwung nach Mass* (controlled upswing) and formally established a framework of tripartite co-operation between unions, government and employers in the shape of the *Konzertierte Aktion*. Rational planning also restored sound financial conditions.

It is likely that this transformation, which took account of the more recent structural changes of West German capitalism, would, in any case, not have been possible without the removal of Erhard. What made his downfall in November 1966 virtually inevitable, though, was the growing discord between the CDU/CSU and the FDP in the coalition government. To some extent these disagreements were due to the above-mentioned crisis of the economy. However, there were political factors, too. One which clearly accelerated Erhard's demise in the long term was the major reorientation of Social Democrat policy, inaugurated by the Godesberg Programme of November 1959. What this Programme amounted to was nothing less than the abandonment by the SPD of its early postwar attempt to derive its aims from the theoretical positions of democratic socialism. Throughout the 1950s this stance had vitiated the Party's prospect of taking over the government in Bonn; conversely democratic socialism had been instrumental in welding together, on an anti-socialist platform, a dwindling number of *bürgerliche* parties which made up the Adenauer coalitions of 1949, 1953 and 1957. But in 1959 the ugly word 'socialism' had disappeared from the SPD's Godesberg Programme. The Social Democrats made themselves available as coalition partners. They recognised the 'special mission of the Churches'. Above all, as Fritz Erler, one of the protagonists of the metamorphosis from a working-class party to an 'omnibus party' (*Volkspartei*), put it at the time: 'We do not fight against the State, but wrestle to influence its development; it is not a struggle for a State of the distant future nor for a State within a reunified Germany, but specifically one for the State of the Federal Republic which we want to govern and shall govern.'

The constellation of 1966 which led to the formation of the Grand Coalition between CDU/CSU and SPD was thus slowly taking shape over half a decade.

247

Erhard, who had succeeded Adenauer as Chancellor on 16 October 1963, was foundering politically and economically. The 1965 recession was deepening. Tensions were mounting within the *bürgerliche* bloc. The SPD leadership, believing that it would never escape from the traditional electoral ghetto unless it demonstrated its Republican reliability as a government party, and frustrated by fifteen years in opposition, was keen to join the Cabinet. However, what provided the final impetus was the growth in 1966 of opposition movements on the extreme Right and Left which proffered solutions to the crisis which transcended the existing political order. The political and economic elites of the Federal Republic were familiar with the left-wing criticism of the postwar constitution. The SPD had contained and smothered this anticapitalist critique after 1959, but not extinguished it within its own ranks. There was also the Marxist analysis of the West German political economy advanced by the *Sozialistischer Deutscher Studentenbund* (SDS) which had been expelled from the SPD in 1960; the status quo was called into question by some of the more left-wing unions, like *IG Metall*.

What was new and much more alarming to the West German elites was the sudden rise of a radical right-wing anti-capitalism and anti-Republicanism organised in the *Nationaldemokratische Partei Deutschlands* (NPD). Although there had been waves of neo-Nazism before, the right-wing parties had virtually disappeared by the early 1960s. In the national elections of 1965, the NPD was the only splinter group of any significance (Table 43). It polled 664,000 votes and, with the 5 per cent Clause in operation, obtained no seats in the *Bundestag*. A year later, the National Democrats, by skilfully exploiting the political and economic crisis of 1966, saw their electoral fortunes dramatically improved after two *Land* elections. On 6 November, they won 7.9 per cent of the vote and 7 seats in the Diet of Hesse. Two weeks later, elections were held in Bavaria in which the NPD achieved 7.9 per cent and 15 seats. The politicians of the main parties in Bonn began to be haunted by the ghost of Weimar. Without delay CDU/CSU and SPD hammered out a coalition programme, and on 1 December Kurt-Georg Kiesinger was installed as Erhard's successor, with Brandt as his deputy and Foreign Minister.

The record of the Grand Coalition is ambiguous. On the one hand, it succeeded with remarkable speed in producing a renewed economic boom, in reassuring and appeasing the unions and in containing the threat from the Right. By 1969, the NPD had dropped back to 4.3 per cent and hence never obtained a seat in the *Bundestag* (Table 43). On the other hand, the entry of the Social Democrats into the Cabinet unleashed an opposition movement on the Left and particularly in the universities which, paradoxical as it may seem, stimulated reformist expectations among wider circles of the population. The SPD was the main beneficiary of this trend. In the elections of September 1969, the Social Democrats for the first time crashed through the

40 per cent barrier. The FDP, which had gained 9.5 per cent in 1965, had its share reduced to 5.8 per cent. However, in the meantime the Left-Liberals in this party had outmanoeuvred the hitherto powerful Right for whom the Christian Democrats had always been the only conceivable coalition partners. Led by Walter Scheel and Hans-Dietrich Genscher, the FDP forged a coalition with the SPD under the Chancellorship of Brandt.

In terms of domestic politics the Brandt Cabinet ended twenty years of Christian Democrat domination at Bonn and carried to the top of the executive a man of working-class background who had been a member of the anti-Nazi underground in 1933 before being driven into exile in Scandinavia. Given the transformations of the social and age structure of the Federal Republic as well as the changing political perceptions of a new generation of West Germans, it may be argued that an SPD-led government was bound to emerge some twenty-five years after the end of the Second World War. Yet, this still leaves us with the problem of how to assess the consequences of Lib-Lab rule on the development of the Federal Republic since 1969.

The rise of the SPD and of Brandt opened up two important developments, one relating to West German foreign policy, the other to domestic politics. It has been shown above how Adenauer was forced in the 1950s to walk a tightrope between the pursuit of Western integration, which he was deter-mined to achieve, and the demands of important sections of the population which pressed for a reunification of Germany within the frontiers of 1937. We have also analysed how the step-by-step scrapping of the Hallstein Doc-trine and the slow unfolding of the 'two-state' theory and of *Ostpolitik* ben-efited the stabilisation policy of the East German government. It had the same effect on the international position of the Federal Republic. For what Ad-enauer, his nationalist rhetoric notwithstanding, initiated and what Brandt completed with his foreign policy was to destroy, as Karl Kaiser has put it, 'the foundations of the classical German *Mitteleuropa* position that resulted in Germany's fatal *Schaukelpolitik* (see-saw policy) between East and West' after the First World War. It was a process which culminated, quite logically, in that series of treaties which 'normalised' relations with Eastern Europe, but also tangibly consolidated the Republic's position in Europe and in the rest of the world.

It is not necessary to go into the complexities of these treaties here and in particular the Berlin Agreement of September 1971 and the *Grundvertrag* be-tween the two Germanies which was signed in December of the following year. Seen in historical perspective, however, one of the crucial clauses in this latter agreement, as well as those concluded between the Federal Re-public and the Soviet Union in August 1970 and between Bonn and Warsaw in December 1970, related to the renunciation of force and the recognition of the territorial status quo. Article 1 of the accord with Poland declared that the Oder–Neisse line would henceforth constitute the western frontier of the Polish People's Republic. For the first time since the Wilhelmine period Germany formally recognised the distribution of territory in Europe. The Federal Republic ceased to be a revisionist power in the heart of Europe, which she had been in the 1950s, just as the Reich, whose successor state West Germany claimed to be, had challenged the status quo during the previous sixty years or so. To abandon the foreign policy hopes and aspirations of German nationalism was painful even in 1971/2. *Ostpolitik* sparked off tremendous political conflicts. Many secret documents were leaked to the opposition which was spearheaded by the CDU/CSU. The CSU leadership submitted the *Grundvertrag* to the Federal Constitutional Court, arguing that it violated the Basic Law of 1949. The Brandt Cabinet was almost toppled during a dramatic 'constructive vote of no-confidence' in which Rainer Barzel, the leader of the CDU, narrowly failed to obtain the requisite majority. Meanwhile the negotiators of the Eastern Treaties were publicly accused of treason and of selling West Germany out to Communism.

There was, indeed, a domestic dimension to the rows over *Ostpolitik* which will be dealt with later. However, looking for the moment at the forces behind the foreign policy options of the early 1970s, the important point is that the balance had shifted in favour of those for whom the Eastern Treaties represented the long-overdue break with the pre-1945 tradition of German power politics and the logical conclusion to the policies of reintegration of the 1950s. Brandt could base himself on a fairly broad popular support. Sections of the West German political and economic elites, on the other hand, had grave misgivings, but they lost out. It was fashionable in the Adenauer period to speculate which path the Federal Republic would take, and there were many observers who expected a relapse into the foreign policy postures of the first half of this century. Recently it has again been conjectured whether, in view of the disintegration of the American hegemonic position in the Western world, West Germany might revive the 'nationalist option', and it was David Calleo in particular who expanded these arguments into a book-length reconsideration of the 'German Problem'. The difficulty with such analyses, which are heavily inspired by geopolitics and diplomatic history, is that they underrate the weight of 'systemic' socioeconomic factors and structural arrangements by which both Germanies are now tied into the international political economy and which, reflecting a new balance of internal social forces, would seem to make a repetition of the 1920s and 1930s quite impossible. It is not that there have been no currents in West German society promoting a new nationalism. It is also interesting to note that the Federal government has continued to treat with great caution the question of whether there is something like a 'German nation' overarching the two Germanies. But it appears that such notions are being tossed about in a debate among politicians

of the older generation and have little support among the population, particularly the younger voters. As Gebhard Schweigler has demonstrated, a
West German national consciousness has developed which has formed the
underpinning of the Federal government's foreign policy in the 1970s. He
added that the 'most important achievement' of the two Republics was, if
nothing else, that 'through their existence they have ended the "German
menace"'.

This assessment does not mean to imply that no attempts will be made to
revive the 'German question'. In fact, Chancellor Helmut Kohl himself, partly
on the advice of historians in his entourage, did much to raise the issue again
when, in June 1985, he addressed the annual meeting of the Association of
Silesian Refugees at Hanover. The Bavarian Minister President Franz Josef
Strauß used the same occasion to send a telegram to the assembled Silesians
reaffirming his view that, in legal terms, the German Reich continued to exist
within its 1937 frontiers. The Eastern Treaties of the early 1970s, he added,
could not change this fact. It seems, however, that Kohl's advisers who, as
Bismarck experts, have studied the Iron Chancellor's manipulative approach
to politics closely, are more concerned to mobilise the presumed emotional
potential of a German nationalism not because they consider reunification a
realistic option, but because it appears to be an integrating device in domestic
politics.

In order to understand this strategy, it must be recalled just how profound
a shock the CDU/CSU suffered when it lost power in 1969 and the Lib-Lab
government of Willy Brandt embarked upon an ambitious programme of
economic and social reforms. This programme immediately generated bitter
hostility among the Christian Democrats. By 1972 this opposition had become
so widespread that the above-mentioned attempt was made by Barzel to un-
seat Brandt by means of a constructive vote of no-confidence in the *Bundestag*.
It was an unpopular move among large sections of the electorate, and after
its failure, Brandt turned the table on the CDU/CSU by calling fresh elections.
Held in November 1972, the contest ended in a resounding victory for the
Lib-Lab coalition. The SPD gained its highest ever share at 45.9 per cent of
the total vote, overtaking the share of the Christian Democrats for the first
time in the history of the Federal Republic (Table 43). Thereafter Brandt continued his legislative programme with renewed vigour in conjunction with
the much strengthened FDP.

It was the economic repercussions of this programme which the Conservatives, supported by West German industry, thought to be particularly worrying. They were fearful of a growing welfare budget, public borrowing and
increased burdens resulting from tax reforms and higher insurance payments.
The oil shock of 1973/4 put a first damper upon these expenditure plans. At
this point doubts also arose within the FDP and among the elders in the SPD

executive as to whether Brandt was the right man for piloting West Germany through the economically rough waters of the mid-1970s. The next elections were due to be held in the autumn of 1976. The unmasking in 1974 of Günter Guillaume, an East German spy in the immediate entourage of the Chancellor, provided Brandt's critics within his Party with an opportunity to replace him with Helmut Schmidt, a highly intelligent and popular pragmatist with a superior understanding of modern economics. Schmidt trimmed the reformist sails of the Lib-Lab coalition and subsequently also steered West Germany through the second oil shock of 1979/80.

However, as the results of the 1976 elections demonstrated, it was not just Brandt's public image that had suffered, but also that of the Social Democrats. Support dropped by 3.3 per cent to 42.6 per cent, while that of the CDU/CSU rose by 3.8 per cent to 48.6 per cent (Table 43). One factor which aroused popular fears and was suitably highlighted by the Opposition was inflation. Fuelled by the energy crisis, it moved up to 7.8 per cent in 1974, and although this and the lower rates of the late 1970s compared favourably with price rises in other Western countries, the figures reawakened deep-seated memories of the hyperinflation of 1923. Schmidt's subsequent economic policies which by 1979 succeeded in bringing inflation down to below three per cent may have helped his Cabinet in the national elections of October 1980. They resulted in tangible losses for the CDU/CSU, though only in marginal gains for the SPD. However, the main beneficiary was the FDP which increased its share from 7.9 per cent to 10.6 per cent of the total vote.

How are these shifts in political behaviour to be explained? One fruitful approach which tries to look, beyond the vagaries of day-to-day politics and election sloganeering, at interests and ideological predispositions is to examine changes in West Germany's social structure during the 1970s. Indeed, there occurred a number of notable shifts in the way society was stratified. Thus, there has been an appreciable fall not only in the number of self-employed people, but also of manual workers. On the other hand, the percentage of white-collar workers in industry and the public services has doubled, reflecting greater social mobility although circulation at the top remains relatively low as it has always been (Tables 14 and 39). The growth of the white-collar section of society has had important repercussions on party politics in that the three main political parties have increasingly been forced to compete for the 'middle ground'. Some of the traditional voting patterns have certainly proven very durable. Two-thirds of the unionised industrial workers support the Social Democrats, and in most cases trade union membership by one member of the family means that the rest of that family also vote SPD. Such behaviour would seem to indicate that it has not become completely meaningless to speak of a West German working class. Although little empirical work has been done on this question, the indications are that, income differentials apart, subjective perceptions of one's own group and of others persist. *Ihr da oben – wir da unten* is not just the flashy title of a book by B. Engelmann and G. Wallraff.

The CDU/CSU, by contrast, has attracted a growing proportion of the self-employed: 65 per cent of them in 1976. In the same year, 47 per cent of the white-collar workers showed an electoral preference for the CDU/CSU. The high percentage of 'workers' leaning towards the Christian Democrats (41%) would seem to indicate the continued importance of Christian Socialist ideas in determining the voting behaviour of Catholic industrial workers. The CDU/CSU's share is further boosted by those employed in handicrafts. In fact the number of this type of artisan without strong Social Democratic leanings has steadily risen from 3.31 million in 1950 to 4.23 million in 1980. Finally, the shift towards the middle ground has been most striking in the case of the FDP which, since 1972 at the latest, has become par excellence the party of employees and civil servants. Class background, however, provides but a partial explanation of this division, for it is also generational. Nowhere else in Western Europe is the conflict between the very young and the very old sharper than in the Federal Republic, with the problem of the Third Reich constituting the biggest single issue in it.

A glance at demographic developments shows why the division has been prolonged and is unlikely to disappear in the immediate future. On the one hand, West Germans live much longer today than a few decades ago. Around 1910, the average life expectancy was 46.6 years. By 1949/51 it had risen to 66.5 years, and the figure for the mid-1970s was not less than 71.3 years. Recent averages are even higher. Consequently, there are many more elderly people in West Germany today than ever before. Arrayed against them are the cohorts of three baby booms in the late 1930s, early 1950s and 1960s, all of which had no conscious experience of Nazism. Finally, the 1970s saw a sharp fall in the birth rate. For the first time since the war the total population of the Federal Republic actually declined absolutely.

It has emerged from the preceding chapter how strongly and persistently those who had lived through the Third Reich as politically conscious men and women refused to contemplate that period and its possible significance. Little change occurred in this respect in the 1960s and 1970s. The parents and grandparents, and in particular those coming from social groups which had supported Hitler, continued to remain silent or to resort to excuses and plain myths. A considerable proportion of them belonged to the political and economic elites of West Germany. Their children and grandchildren found it difficult enough to accept the silence, but they vigorously rejected the propagation of myths and legends. While the early postwar interpretations of Nazism, which have been outlined above, retained their popularity with the older generation, their offspring, many of whom started their university education in the restive 1960s, found the sociological and 'structural' explanations of the Third Reich more plausible. This difference, if nothing else, almost inevitably pushed the younger generation towards the Left. The conviction that too much had been restored and too little had changed became a major impulse behind the reform movement of the 1970s. Brandt and the SPD, the only party with a creditable anti-Nazi record, became the organisation to which many young voters attached their hope for change. The Christian Democrats, on the other hand, have increasingly become the party of the older generation, and at the time of the 1980 national elections the CDU/CSU attracted fewer younger voters than ever before.

However, the SPD did not succeed in keeping the younger generation solidly in its fold. Some of them believed that West Germany, the SPD/FDP coalition notwithstanding, was still governed by the same forces that had brought Hitler to power. They disagreed with the gradualism of the Social Democrats and advocated a radical destruction of the existing order. Some of these younger people quickly drifted into splinter groups on the extreme Left; others joined the environmentalist movements which have mushroomed in some parts of the country, particularly as a protest movement against the building of nuclear power stations. A small minority of the disaffected finally went underground to organise fire-bombings, kidnappings and political murders. Although they were numerically insignificant among the younger generation, it is difficult to exaggerate their impact on the recent political development of the Federal Republic. It was the uncompromising extremism of the urban terrorists which decisively weakened the initial thrust behind the optimistic reformism of the Brandt era and, even more decisively, bedevilled the Schmidt coalition in electoral terms. For it motivated a conservative older generation which had distrusted the 'socialists' throughout its life and an increasingly worried middle generation of well-to-do white-collar workers and civil servants to come out in favour, if not of the CDU/CSU, of the FDP. Meanwhile sections of the younger generation, though rejecting the violent tactics of the Red Army Faction (RAF) and other extreme left-wing groups, turned towards a new movement which had been boosted by two oil crises and the debate on the environment and the 'Limits to Growth'. The question as to whether industrialism offered a future had been put on the agenda of West German politics. In party-political terms the 'Greens' became the main organisational focus of this movement particularly among the younger generation.

Not least a product of the *Aufbruchstimmung* and the reformism of the early 1970s which in their view did not go far enough, the 'Greens' are no doubt a peculiar phenomenon in West German politics. They became strong enough to make it impossible for the established parties to ignore them and the issues which they propagated both inside and outside the parliamentary assemblies.

254

But the Party's most striking feature is its colourful heterogeneity. It combines young genuinely 'green' environmentalists and 'health freaks' with people who could be their grandparents and whose ideological roots are in the 'brown' anti-capitalist anti-industrialism of the Weimar right-wing youth movement and of the Nazi Party in particular. Finally, there is a 'red' element of partly hard-line communists, but also of anarchists and syndicalists of various persuasions.

It is unlikely that this conglomerate of very divergent ideological traditions would ever have made the electoral gains it achieved from 1980 onwards, had it not partly overlapped with, and partly complemented, the peace movement. And the rise of this latter movement, in turn, can only be understood against the background of the decision of the Reagan Administration to step up its nuclear rearmament programme. Mobilising fears about nuclear war and about the destruction of the environment by industry, the 'Greens', having decided to take the plunge into elections and parliamentarism, gained their most impressive successes, like the NPD in the 1960s, at first in the provinces. Then, in the national elections of March 1983, they were propelled into the *Bundestag* having obtained 5.6 per cent and 27 seats (Table 43).

This rise has brought them a great deal of media attention both at home and abroad and created plenty of bewilderment. As in the 1960s, when the threat of the NPD loomed large, pessimistic assessments have tended to predominate. It was anticipated that this movement would continue to grow and ultimately eat into the substance not only of the established parties, but also of the political system at large. As their stance on the merits of parliamentary democracy was highly critical, fears were expressed of a gradual erosion of the postwar political order.

These commentators, however, have probably overestimated the party's homogeneity, when in fact its cohesion and viability have been threatened from the start by disagreements over local, regional and national issues. Above all, no other aspect of the movement has done more to exacerbate such disagreements and to exhaust the possibilities for compromise than the proclaimed adherence of the 'Greens' to the principle of grass-roots democracy and a basically syndicalist model of popular politics. The decision to compete for seats within the established parliamentary representative system of the Federal Republic was bound to bring the dilemmas of a council-type decision-making structure to the surface. For a while it hoped to be able to overcome these dilemmas by introducing the principle of rotating representation. Yet, when it came to implementing this idea, some members refused to be replaced and have since continued as Independents, while those who did abide by the decisions of their constituents made room for deputies who had to start all over again trying to learn the rules of parliamentary procedures and of committee work.

There is a further and related constitutional issue that has widened the rift between the so-called *Realos* and the *Fundamentalos* in the movement and which also came to a head in the party's confrontation with political reality. This is the question of whether to collaborate with other parties, in particular with the SPD, in the hope of getting an environmentalist programme implemented or of whether to remain a radical opposition whose influence on actual decision-making would be nil. The development in Hesse, where the 'Greens' obtained 8.0 per cent in 1982, but were reduced to 5.9 per cent a year later, is a good case in point. In Hesse the environmentalists held the balance between the major parties, and the SPD-led government of H. Börner was forced to woo their support. Should they in these circumstances refuse to support the ratification of the State budget, as the *Fundamentalos* argued? Or should they vote for it knowing that in this way funds will be released which are vital for the implementation of environmentalist programmes which they are so keen to start at local level? In the end, they did join, and Joschka Fischer was appointed Hessian Minister for the Environment. He has been an incongruous figure who has alienated fundamentalists at the Party's grass-roots while struggling with industry's and bureaucracy's capacity to obstruct his programme.

The conclusion to be drawn from these seemingly unbridgeable contradictions is that, Chernobyl notwithstanding, the Green Party will remain below the 10 per cent mark at the national level. It is likely to remain strong in some constituencies, like West Berlin, with its sizeable fringe culture. However, if recent election results in the Saar, Northrhine-Westphalia and Lower Saxony provide any pointers, the majority of the population is sceptical about the movement. Sooner or later it is likely to split into *Realos* and *Fundamentalos*. The dividing-line between the two will be not merely a constitutional one but also one relating to substantive policy. On one side there will be those who see industrialism as the basic evil and therefore advocate a return to a non-industrial economy and decentralized communal system. On the other side will be found those 'Green' politicians who see no real alternative to retaining an industrial economy, but would like to use some of industry's wealth-creating potential for an improvement of the environment. Unlike the *Fundamentalos*, they will be available as coalition partners of the major parties, above all, of the SPD. Their dilemma after the schism will be that increasingly the Social Democrats, but also the CDU, will take on board many of their reformist demands and will hence ultimately steal a march on them. If this is the outcome, the main political function of the 'Greens' will have been to have raised certain serious problems which advanced industrial societies now face, while the solutions to the problems of an 'ecological modernisation of industrial society' (H.-J. Axt) will be worked out primarily within the existing constitutional framework of parliamentary politics.

This would moreover seem to imply that the prospects of a comprehensive 'Red-Green' alliance at national level are poor. Even if it came about, it would be rather a washed-out green, in the literal as well as the metaphorical sense. More plausible would be a scenario in which the SPD, while preserving a certain openness towards the more moderate environmentalist elements in the younger generation, would once again embark upon a search for middle-aged voters at the centre of the political spectrum in an attempt to win back those professional and other more highly qualified white-collar groups whom they lost to the CDU and FDP in the early 1980s. And indeed the strategy for the 1987 national elections strongly emphasised the appeal to the 'technical intelligentsia' (*technische Intelligenz*).

There is a good deal of plausibility in the argument that the impressive rise in FDP support in 1980 was meant to signal that the voters wished to retain the Schmidt coalition, but by opting for the Liberals rather than the Social Democrats also wanted to strengthen the Chancellor's hand against those in his own Party who aimed to keep the SPD open towards the 'Greens' and towards the critical younger generation. In effect, however, the growth of the FDP not only weakened the Chancellor's position within his own Party, but also reinforced the position of those who, like Otto Count Lambsdorff, the Economics Minister, had been contemplating for some time another realignment of political forces and a link-up with the CDU/CSU. Given the balance between the two major parties, such a switch had been on the cards since the oil shock of 1973/4. It must also be remembered that the German Liberals had always been a movement combining, in an uneasy alliance, left-liberal reformists and conservative National Liberals, and for much of the time since the Bismarckian era the scales had been tipped towards the latter. After the Second World War, as we have seen, the FDP at first turned towards the Right and wooed the disgruntled and the nationalists among the electorate. It was on this basis that it remained a coalition partner in the conservative Adenauer Cabinets.

The 1960s, then, saw the ascendancy of a group of Liberals which ultimately paved the way for the Lib-Lab pact of 1969. But faced with the political and economic upheavals of the following decade, the old fissures became more marked, and the inner-party balance of power began to shift back towards the National Liberals. In these circumstances chances of toppling the Schmidt government by means of a Liberal pull-out and of a constructive vote of no-confidence were much improved in comparison with the abortive attempt of 1972. On that earlier occasion, the CDU/CSU had been able to count on a few 'deserters' crossing the floor. The bulk of the Liberal deputies, on the other hand, remained loyal to the Cabinet. By the spring 1982 an FDP majority, in which men like Lambsdorff had begun to call the tune, inclined increasingly towards an alliance with the CDU/CSU. On 17 September,

257

Lambsdorff and three other FDP ministers resigned form the Cabinet. Two weeks later, on 1 October, Helmut Kohl, the CDU leader, having initiated a constructive vote of no-confidence, was elected Chancellor with 256 votes to 235. Some 30 FDP deputies decided to support a new Christian Democrat–Liberal coalition. With it began the 'great change of course' (*Tendenzwende*) for which Kohl sought a fresh mandate on 6 March 1983. In these national elections, reflecting the mood of the early 1980s, the CDU/CSU gained 48.8 per cent, while the SPD once again lapsed into its old 'ghetto' below the 40 per cent mark (Table 43). Before examining some of the political consequences of this change, however, it is necessary to deal with cultural and social life in the Federal Republic during the past two decades or so.

Culture and society in West Germany

If the analysis of 'culture' in the sense of remarkable intellectual and artistic creativity was left out of the chapter on the Third Reich in order to emphasise the character of that period of German history, dealing in this section with cultural life in West Germany is likewise not primarily motivated by a quest for comprehensiveness but is intended to make a point and to highlight features of contemporary German society. Although trying to establish links between artistic production and society at large is problematical, a survey of the main themes of literature, drama and the visual arts may nevertheless tell us something about the state of mind of the authors and of the audiences to which they wished to appeal.

First of all, however, an important preliminary point has to be reiterated: West Germany comprises 11 Federal states which possess a constitutionally guaranteed autonomy in cultural and educational affairs. Berlin may have been the cultural capital of the Weimar Republic; the contemporary situation is characterized by a marked polycentrism. This situation has made for a great variety of currents and tastes and for competition between the individual states and municipalities. Towns and cities throughout the Federal Republic take considerable pride in supporting a local theatre or orchestra or both. Major developments have also occurred in the field of museum work and art galleries. In marked contrast to Anglo-Saxon countries, there are hence no cultural 'provinces' and 'backwaters'. Excellent musicians or actors may be found in the most unexpected places. Although the public expenditure cuts of the past ten years have also hit the cultural budgets of the Federal states and communities, the size of the funds still available tends to arouse the envy of foreign artists. In the better days, around 1 per cent of State and local government budgets, equalling more than 50 milliard marks, was spent in support of cultural activities of various kinds.

A considerable portion of these funds is used for the maintenance of some

70 orchestras and more than 60 opera houses. Standards of performance tend to be high, even if popular tastes have remained as catholic as in other West European countries. The main repertory consists of the classic composers, while *avant-garde* composers of international repute, like Karl Heinz Stockhausen, have to this day never attracted more than a small band of *connaisseurs*. Nor have Hans Werner Henze's attempts during the late 1960s to incorporate topical political allusions in his work had much of an echo. By and large, orchestras have catered to those who attend a concert in search of elation or distraction. Meanwhile youth culture came to be deeply influenced by Anglo-Saxon forms of popular music. In the 1950s, it was jazz, mainly in its New Orleans and Dixieland varieties, which left a deep impression on the younger generation. Later it was the Beatles before they, too, were overtaken by new waves of experimental sounds and styles. Often these were decried by parents as imported trash, as young West Germans moved with the mainstream of Anglo-Saxon popular music. The tastes of the older generation, by contrast, remained surprisingly static. Certainly the basic ingredients of the sentimental German *Schlager* of the 1950s have not changed, and the old tunes can be heard not only from the bandstand of a local fair but also in expensively staged hit parades on television in prime evening time to delight the millions. South of the River Main, the Bavarian oompah-band continues to enjoy popularity at festivals and club functions.

Painting, on the other hand, has long been devoted to experimentation in Germany, except for the Nazi period, when Expressionism and other genres were declared 'degenerate'. The immediate postwar period saw the re-emergence of Munich and Frankfurt as centres, where painters began their work in the abstract tradition. Later the focus of attention moved towards Düsseldorf and Cologne. For a while kinetic art aroused considerable interest, whereas American 'pop art', at least in its pure form, never made a major impact in the Federal Republic. There was, however, a 'return to figuration' (K. Thomas). In the 1970s, then, Joseph Beuys's 'action art' caused a considerable uproar, as did his insistence on a democratic notion of art which assumed an innate creativity in all human beings and dispensed with traditional criteria of admission to the Düsseldorf Academy of Art. Not surprisingly, perhaps, the cultural bureaucracy of Northrhine-Westphalia tried to resist such unorthodox experiments.

Scandals have time and again also racked West German theatre. Catering to some 3.5 million regular theatre-goers, the Federal Republic, according to Ingo Seidler, has, statistically speaking, the 'greatest density of theatre anywhere in the world'. Only some 60 of the country's 300 theatres are private and do not rely on public subsidies, which totalled around 1.5 milliard marks in 1980. The crucial significance of these subsidies may also be gauged from the fact that entrance fees cover no more than 16 per cent of the annual budget of the average theatre. The relative absence of economic pressures led directors to mix in plays which they knew would generate political controversy. Early postwar theatre, still under the influence of Heinz Hilpert and Gustav Gründgens, had typically revived classic drama and the pre-Nazi repertory. No less significantly, it presented these plays true to their original design, appreciating that West Germans were tired of open politicisation. But soon the rebellion against the *Werktreue* approach began. By the 1960s, theatre and contemporary issues were once more being quite directly linked, resulting in provocative presentations of Shakespeare by Peter Zadek or Hans Günther Heyme's modernised productions of classic theatre. Increasingly, postwar authors were shown, some of whom wrote in an openly political vein. Rolf Hochhuth's *Representative*, which raised the problem of Pope Pius XII's attitude towards the Third Reich and anti-Semitism, was first produced in West Berlin in 1963 by Erwin Piscator, a returnee, opponent of Gründgens and 'grand old man of German political theatre of the 1920s' (E. Bahr). Heinar Kipphardt's *Brother Eichmann* became the most frequently staged play, whereas the drama which attracted the largest audiences in the early 1980s was Friedrich Dürrenmatt's *Physicists*, concerned with the nuclear question. Although there has been a 15 per cent drop in the total number of theatregoers since the early 1970s, the figure for 1981/2 (7.6 million) may still be regarded as high by any standards.

Much of this drop in attendance was, of course, due to the rise of television, which also had a profound effect on the German cinema culture. During the 1920s and 1930s, millions had visited the cinema every week. However, while the famous and disturbing films by Fritz Lang and others tend to be held up as examples of the Weimar tradition, most of the ordinary viewers saw those Hollywood spectacles which flooded the European market during the interwar period and which Goebbels tried to counter with his own, mainly escapist productions during the 1930s. In a curious way, this tradition of unpolitical soap-operas on the screen continued well into the 1950s. Next to Hollywood it was fed by a re-emerging indigenous film industry, whose products, like *Green Is the Heath*, *Black Forest Maiden* or *Sissi*, pandered to a popular longing for a world untouched by the ravages of war. Hans Hellmut Kirst's *0815* novels depicting the experiences of the front-soldier were turned into highly successful visual accounts of the honest German fighter who never gave a damn about Nazi ideology and whose hands had remained unsullied by Nazi crimes. Again the late 1950s and early 1960s witnessed a politicisation of the German cinema, as reflected, for example, in Wolfgang Staudte's *Roses for the State Prosecutor* or Kurt Hoffmann's *Wir Wunderkinder (Aren't We Wonderful)*. Above all an attempt was made to break out of the sterile conventionalism of the early postwar years. By the 1970s, the next generation of film-makers had achieved its breakthrough and had re-established Germany's international reputation in the field of 'serious' cinema. Werner Fassbinder, Werner Herzog, Alexander Kluge, Margarethe von Trotta and Volker Schlöndorff rose to fame at home and abroad. Meanwhile American productions like the James Bond series or *E.T.* attracted the largest audiences, just as many West Germans, while dutifully praising West German television for its highbrow drama productions, are more anxious not to m. the latest weekly instalment of *Dallas* or *Dynasty*. As elsewhere in the world, one can only speculate about the long-term impact of the 'electronic revolution' in people's living rooms.

Notable shifts in content and style have also taken place in German literature. The early postwar period was dominated by writers who had lapsed into silence during the Third Reich, among them Werner Bergengruen and Rudolf Hagelstange. Next to them there appeared after 1945 a generation which felt compelled to write about their experience as soldiers and POWs. Wolfgang Borchert's *Outside the Door* may be cited as a typical and particularly moving example. It took another decade for the self-pitying undertones to disappear which pervaded the literature of the Zero Hour and for 'critical' treatments of the German past to be published. Günter Grass's *Tin Drum*, Heinrich Böll's novels and Siegfried Lenz's dissections of provincial Germany had a great impact. Other authors of the 1960s politicised their portrayals of peculiarly German themes even more openly. The 1970s then experienced a partial reversal of this tide of an explicitly committed literature. Some authors, such as Grass, reflected the disillusionment with the optimistic reformism of the preceding decade, while others retreated into a 'new sensibility' and subjectivism – a movement in which a number of women played leading roles.

Yet however strikingly West German *litterati* and intellectuals may have articulated and mirrored changing concerns of their environment, there emerged in the Federal Republic, just as elsewhere in the West, a type of popular literature which appealed to the less educated who were still interested in reading. This type of literature had a long tradition, and in comparison with other countries West Germany has remained a reading society. Certainly per head of population publishers achieve print-runs for non-academic books which English-language publishing houses find incredibly high. Bookshops tend to be well stocked and crowded, with the latest cheap paperback novel or science fiction volume stacked right next to the entrance. Sentimental literature which would not appear on any book-list for a German Studies course will also be serialised in one of the many *Illustrierten* whose weekly circulations run into millions. Finally, and apart from the quality dailies, there are the tabloids headed by the Springer Trust's *BILD*. This paper, whose journalistic methods have aroused serious criticism and even violent opposition, sold more than 5 million copies a day in the first quarter of 1985.

There is no absolutely reliable research to tell us conclusively what is the

261

impact on the population at large of this kind of mass circulation press and the values put across in its pages. Certainly, it would be naive to dismiss this influence as irrelevant. On the other hand, there is evidence that, though not creating new attitudes, tabloids and television reinforce particular ideological positions and prejudices latent within the population. The last aspect of contemporary Germany to be investigated in this chapter, therefore, concerns social movements and the mentalities of the 'man (and woman) in the street'.

Overall it must be admitted that it has become increasingly difficult to make the kind of firm statement concerning the country's social and sociopsychological structures which one is used to finding in histories of the Wilhelmine or Weimar period. This is not merely because fewer analyses are available but also because the Federal Republic, at least in outward appearance, is a more 'pluralistic' society than its predecessors. This pluralism does not mean that socioeconomic and political power has become more polycentric, but there is a greater variety of life-styles. Formerly insignificant fringe movements and phenomena have advanced more towards the centre of the stage; new forces have come to the fore, adding to a colourful and confusing picture. The sources of this development are not too difficult to pinpoint. Although there was some cracking up of old structures, the late 1940s and the 1950s remained a conventional and conformist period in terms of social mores and attitudes. But from the 1960s onwards a number of major issues became a matter of public debate which raised the question of the whole 'ethos' of the Western systems of society, their values and their practices. In the United States, the war in Vietnam and Civil Rights became the focal points of campaigns for a reorientation of policy-making. In the Federal Republic, though the broader questions of American power abroad and discrimination against ethnic minorities on the other side of the Atlantic also acted as a mobilising force, demands soon centred upon the idea that capitalism should be 'democratised' and society further liberalised. Discussion revolved around the need to reform the presumed authoritarian structures of the educational system, of industry, the judiciary, the churches and the family. Ultimately, the aim was to complete the 'emancipation from yesterday' (K. D. Bracher), that is, from the mentalities and practices of the pre-1945 period. The Allies and Adenauer had begun this emancipation process in some spheres of economic and political life but had arrested it in others. The SPD/FDP coalition came to power with a pledge to overhaul those institutions, codes and practices which seemed in need of modernisation. In fact, many of them had not been changed since the late nineteenth century. The basic intention behind this programme was not to turn everything upside-down but, rather, to create a more viable society whose institutional arrangements regulating the interactions of its members in various spheres of life were not creakingly out of joint with the highly complex structures that had meanwhile evolved within the economy. It is undeniable that this strategy has in many ways been a considerable success. By the end of the 1970s, West Germany was a more 'modern' society than before, and not only in respect of its industrial organisation and technological infrastructure. It was more 'pluralistic', albeit not in the sense that economic and political power has become diffuse. On the contrary, large-scale organisations and bureaucratised interest groups play a major role in the political economy of the Federal Republic. And yet, although conformist pressures exerted by these organisations have increased in some areas, other spheres of life were successfully 'liberated'. If they choose to, West Germans can live more freely today than at any previous time in German history. Using this historical yardstick may be rather modest, but it does belie the frequently heard argument that nothing has changed at all.

The question of the changing position of women and children in society is a case in point. Both in the family and at school, authoritarian conventions which continued to be powerful down to the 1960s have been eroded. Social relations are more relaxed and informal. Obviously, relative affluence has made it easier to experiment with new life-styles or to reject the strictness and self-righteousness with which previous generations of parents and teachers treated their children. The main parental pressure on children in the 1980s appears to consist of sometimes relentless exhortations to obtain the highest marks in school and to acquire further qualifications in the hope that they may have a more satisfying career than their fathers and mothers. In most other respects, teenagers have themselves become opinion-makers and creators of their own values, often helped by the media. This means that traditional authority patterns have to some extent even become reversed. Now it is many parents who vie for the love and support of their offspring. In 1955 some 16 per cent of the younger generation still took one of their parents as their model; the figure for 1984 was 3 per cent. In 1954 more than 50 per cent of German parents thought corporal punishment to be a good thing; in 1984 it is overwhelmingly frowned upon. Instead, some 35 per cent of all fathers and some 46 per cent of all mothers feel free to discuss their worries and family crises with their children. Another study, by the Hanover Youth Research Centre, found that in 1979 some 60 per cent of young people over 14 judged the family atmosphere to be 'partnerly, open-hearted and helpful', whereas some 28 per cent harboured ambiguous feelings and 12 per cent were on bad terms with their parents. Clearly, the dynamism of a modern industrial society has begun to destroy the traditional balance of power in the family as far as parents and their offspring are concerned.

While girls have also benefited from this trend, the experience of their mothers has been rather more ambiguous. As we have seen, women had long been integrated into the process of industrial production. This trend continued after 1945. At first there were the so-called *Trümmerfrauen*, the women who lived amid the rubble of Germany's bombed cities. With their husbands killed or interned as POWs, they had to make a living as well as raise their children. The contrast between their struggle against great odds and the ideology of an intact family-life purveyed by the Churches and conservative politicians could not have been starker. Nor did the welfare policies adopted by the Christian Democrats reverse the prewar development towards working women. As Robert Moeller has written: 'At least for working-class families, the "normal family" of family policy of the 1950s could not be re-established because it had never existed.' Between 1950 and 1969, the number of female employees grew from 4.2 million to 9.6 million. By 1978, well over a third of the total workforce (10.2 million out of 26.9 million) were women, of whom 3.5 million had children under the age of 18. Some features of female labour look familiar. Their pay is lower; they tend to be overrepresented in sectors of the economy which have traditionally been their domain. Nor has male predominance in higher and better-paid positions been challenged nearly as successfully as in the United States.

Still, if not in the world of labour, there have been marked changes in general attitude and behaviour, particularly among young women since the early 1970s. Thus the decline in the West German birth rate which began in the 1960s may be taken to signify that for many of them children are no longer a must. In 1960 women still bore an average of 2.4 children; by 1976 the figure had slumped to less than 1.5. Next to the GDR, the Federal Republic had the lowest reproductive rate in the whole of Europe. Considering that life expectancy increased dramatically, it is not surprising that the low birth rates began to alarm the social welfare statisticians. The so-called net reproduction rate was below unity, putting a strain on pension fund planning. More important for the immediate situation were the attitudes of women of childbearing age which lie behind the fertility figures. For as elsewhere, women in West Germany, too, began to engage in wide-ranging and at times emotional debates about their position and role in family, politics and society at large. They revived the old and unresolved topics of female emancipation and the 'feminine mystique'; they provided the permanent pressure to reform key paragraphs of the Criminal Code of 1871 and the Civil Code of 1900. In June 1976 the criminal code on abortion was liberalised. A year later, legislation came into force modifying the 'Equality of the Sexes Law' of 1957. Most of the feminist campaigns met with fierce opposition, with the Catholic Church launching an extensive counter-offensive against the widespread use of the contraceptive pill and the legalisation of abortion. But just as Church membership has been declining since the 1970s, it is clear that even younger couples who are still practising Catholics ignore the teachings of their Church on sexual morality. This is not to imply, however, that the Churches are no longer capable of wielding considerable influence in the 'corridors of power'. Especially the Catholic hierarchy, supported by a number of conservative lay organisations, has done so with considerable success in the educational field.

While the Vatican's response to libertarian trends has been completely negative, the attitude of 'the German man' has shown signs of being affected by the vigorous public argument about the 'other half' of society. Thus a representative study by two Dortmund University sociologists, Sigrid Meckel-Göckel and Ursula Müller, came to the conclusion: 'The old image of a patriarchal society is becoming more blurred. Men notice that women are changing and forced to confront new pressures.' More significantly, 'bit-by-bit' they were found to have begun to compromise. It is on the basis of these general observations that the two investigators developed a typology of male behaviour ranging from egalitarianism to outright male chauvinism. On the whole, however, the average German no longer sees his wife as a child-rearing homemaker and prefers her as an independent partner. Yet, he will do little to support her aspiration after independence; and once children are under way, 80 per cent of German men believe that women should abandon their career and devote themselves to 'their' children. Similarly, traditional attitudes prevail towards the sharing of household chores and towards contraception, both of which are overwhelmingly deemed to be a woman's responsibility.

On the other hand, a tangible shift appears to have occurred with respect to responsibility for children, in the sense that fathers tend to be more involved with their offsprings' weekend leisure activities and bedtime rituals than they were in previous generations. If the 'maternal fathers' (R. Just) have remained the exception, during the 1970s something like a rapprochement did set in between the sexes. The generation of the grandfathers is probably incapable of shedding its authoritarian ways; their sons have in their majority become, if nothing else, more civil as well as civilian; further differentiations will have to be made by reference to social background and educational achievement. A good deal of roughness has survived in many lower-class families, and child abuse statistics provide pointers as to how far this extends beyond certain strata.

If violence in the family, whether verbal or physical, tells us something about the general state of the society in which it takes place, attitudes towards ethnic and religious minorities offer further clues. One does not merely have to ponder the fate of the European Jews under Nazism to realise just how poor the Germans' record is on this score. From the 1960s, as we have seen, foreigners came to the Federal Republic in large numbers as so-called guest workers – in itself an intriguing term. Whether these workers arrived as individuals or with their families, they created major social problems, be they housing or the education of children whose first language was not German and who came from very different cultural backgrounds. In these circumstances the 'guest workers', by their mere existence, fanned resentments among the German majority. Racist prejudice was never far from the surface, and demands to repatriate the country's unwelcome newcomers reached a crescendo during times of economic recession. *Herrenmenschen* postures of the 1930s were still prevalent, especially among the older generation, and it took the Federal Republic some time to realise that they had imported human beings and their families for whom special provision had to be made. By and large, the authorities have been more flexible than many average citizens who expect foreigners either to be exactly like themselves or not to be in Germany.

Although it is difficult to quantify how widespread these over-reactions are, there persists an intolerance which is prone to show indifference towards criminal acts of violence against Turks or Spaniards by some of the ubiquitous youth gangs or which tempts right-wing radicals to beam their campaigns at the petty xenophobe. So far the courts have meted out harsh punishments against youth gang criminality directed at foreigners, while the agitation of the neo-Nazis does not appear to have inflated their ranks. More dangerous, perhaps, is the language used by some leading politicians in their Sunday speeches. The Bavarian Minister President Strauß has been in the forefront of this agitation, which, in his case, is not only openly xenophobic but also generally designed to polarise society.

If one follows Strauß's argument, the choice is not just between being 'swamped' by foreigners and maintaining a 'healthy' demographic balance; it is also between 'freedom and socialism', 'anarchy and order', 'Christianity and godlessness'. The themes and also the calculated method of mobilising fears which pervade the propaganda of the conservatives in West Germany are, of course, familiar ones. Nor have they made a secret of the objectives behind their strategy: their interpretations of past and present are designed to arrest and, if possible, reverse the reformist tendencies of the early 1970s. Reading the programmatic statements and listening to the speeches of leading CDU/CSU politicians, on the one hand, and those of some Social Democrats, on the other, it is often difficult to believe that they are, in fact, writing and talking about the past, present and future of the same society. It is not enough to explain the gulf across which the politicians stare and shout at each other in the Federal Republic in terms of electoral politics. The West Germans may have succeeded fairly well in managing their immediate economic and social problems, but they became more deeply divided during the 1970s over how to deal with their turbulent history in the first half of this century and how to look ahead into their future.

The practical results of this combative conservative propaganda have not been inconsiderable. By the 1970s, literally hundreds of thousands of applicants to the public services, teaching professions and other jobs in the state sector had their political reliability rigorously screened. There have been a number of verdicts which can only be explained in terms of the indiscriminate anti-Left feeling which has been encouraged in Bavaria and other CDU-dominated *Länder*. It is ironical that the original political impulse behind the *Radikalenerlass* came from the SPD, but it is also symptomatic. For the whole issue arose in connection with the debate on the political reliability of the SPD during the controversy over the Eastern Treaties in 1972. And was there a better way of refuting the conservative charge that the 'socialists' were conspiring with the Russians against German national interests than to demonstrate that the SPD-led *Länder* governments were eagerly hunting down left-wing teachers, civil servants, postal workers and engine drivers?

Thanks to the violence perpetrated by the extreme Left, the conservatives have also succeeded in vastly expanding the law enforcement apparatus of the State. The all-out effort to apprehend the urban terrorists has resulted in the creation of a police force which can call on the latest developments of the computer industry. Although Bonn and other cities no longer look like beleaguered fortresses, as they did in 1976/7, the anti-terrorist legislation which was hastily ratified, the sophisticated technology and the highly trained personnel are there to stay, to be used against future threats to 'law and order'.

There are inevitably many other aspects of contemporary West Germany which this chapter has not been able to deal with. If it has ended with a discussion of the law and order complex and the peculiar polarity which characterises the treatment of fundamental socioeconomic problems of the future in the Federal Republic, it is not merely because the dogmatism and fervour with which the two sides present their arguments contrasts strikingly with the pragmatic and measured ways in which immediate economic and social questions are being tackled; it is also because this complex refers to generational conflicts which are rooted in modern German history and raise, at the end of this book, once more the question of the extraordinarily violent course of Germany's development in this century. There would appear to be little doubt that this record of violence was connected with the experience of very rapid industrialisation. It unleashed a social and political crisis which overstretched the capacity of the existing institutions. Günter Grass, an astute commentator, once drew attention to what he called the country's 'inability to live through a crisis'. The social historian can be more specific than this: in the first half of this century it was in the first place the political and economic elites which suffered from this inability. Most of them resisted acceptance of the political consequences of industrialisation and succeeded in linking up with the lower middle classes against reformist forces in German society. More seriously, instead of adopting a conciliatory line towards the working class and its aspirations, this alliance, precarious as it was, displayed

267

a growing propensity to resolve by force the conflicts that inevitably arose. It is at this point that a connection may be made between the foreign policy methods of the dominant groups, on the one hand, and their politics of violence at home, on the other. After the turn of the century, if not before, talking of civil war or actually waging it and pursuing an aggressive foreign policy or actually resorting to military conflict were the two sides of the same coin, even if it was not until the 1930s that this unity became abundantly clear. The reverberations of the Nazi orgy of violence can be felt in Germany to this day. After all, many of those who were protagonists of such solutions to conflict are still alive and have failed to reflect upon the experience of the Third Reich.

However, they have also lost their former dominance both in the field of foreign policy formulation and in domestic politics. The balance of forces has shifted against the use of external violence, and the two Germanies are firmly tied into the international structures which have emerged in East and West since the Second World War. This conclusion applies in principle also to the internal situation of the Federal Republic, where the responses to the economic shocks of the past decade may provide a guide that the West Germans have learned better to live with major crises. As we have seen, they have been relentless in their drive for technological and economic modernisation. But this strategy, which all governments have pursued, has also revealed the old split between those, especially among the different elite groups, who press for an equally relentless adaptation of the social and political structures (in the widest sense) to shifting economic and ecological realities, on the one hand, and those who are as reluctant as their conservative predecessors during the Second Industrial Revolution to accept these consequences of technological change. It will be interesting to see how this dichotomy will develop, as the two Germanies pass through the Third Industrial Revolution.

Statistical tables

Introductory note
It is hoped that the tables in this appendix are set out clearly enough not to look too daunting to the non-economist. It is also well known that statistics are often problematical and inaccurate. For example, it was very difficult to obtain reliable data for Tables 35 and 44. There is obviously always a problem with the accurate recording of strikes and lock-outs; nor is there much agreement on the amounts spent by the Third Reich on the rearmament programme of the 1930s. Nevertheless, even if some of the data in various tables are open to correction, they point up general trends and ought to provide material for further discussion. Most figures have been compiled from standard sources listed below, to which specialists may also wish to refer for more detailed descriptions of the criteria of computation. Eight new tables have been added. For technical reasons, however, it was impossible to integrate them into the systematic pattern adopted for Tables 1–47 in the first edition. This is why the new material appears in Tables 48–55. Other tables have been updated.

Sources
Abelshauser, W., *et al.* (eds.), *Sozialgeschichtliches Arbeitsbuch, 1914–1945*, München 1978
Balfour, M., *The Kaiser and His Times*, New York 1972
Bergemann, J. (ed.), *Beiträge zur Soziologie der Gewerkschaften*, Frankfurt 1979
Bundesministerium für Gesamtdeutsche Fragen (ed.), *A bis Z*, Bonn 1969
Clapham, J. H., *The Economic Development of France and Germany 1815–1914*, Cambridge 1936
Claessens, D., *et al.* (eds.), *Sozialkunde der Bundesrepublik Deutschland*, Reinbek 1985
Connor, I., 'The Attitudes of the Bavarian Authorities towards the Refugee Problem', University of East Anglia, Ph.D. thesis, 1981
Cornelsen, D., *et al.* (eds.), *Handbuch der DDR-Wirtschaft*, Reinbek 1977
Fischer Weltalmanach '84, Frankfurt 1983
Fürstenau, J., *Entnazifizierung*, Neuwied 1969
Groh, D., *Negative Integration und revolutionärer Attentismus*, Frankfurt 1973
Guttsman, W. L., *The German Social Democratic Party, 1875–1933*, London 1980
Hoffmann, W. G., *et al.* (eds.), *Das Wachstum der deutschen Wirtschaft seit der Mitte des 19. Jahrhunderts*, Heidelberg 1965
Hohorst, G., *et al.* (eds.), *Sozialgeschichtliches Arbeitsbuch, 1870–1914*, München 1975
Holtfrerich, C.-L., *Die deutsche Inflation, 1914–1923*, Berlin 1980
Inter Nationes (ed.), *Prozeduren, Programme, Profile* (Sonderdienst SO 3/80), Bonn 1980
Jacobsen, H.-A., *et al.* (eds.), *Drei Jahrzehnte Aussenpolitik der DDR*, München 1979
Jungblut, M., *Die Reichen und die Superreichen in Deutschland*, Reinbek 1973

269

Statistical tables

Kaack, H., *Geschichte und Struktur des deutschen Parteiensystems*, Opladen 1971

Kocka, J., and Mütter, B. (eds.), *Wirtschaft und Gesellschaft in Zeitalter der Industrialisierung*, München 1984

Köllner, L., 'Wirtschaftsempirische und wirtschaftshistorische Bemerkungen zur langfristigen Entwicklung von Militärausgaben in Deutschland', in: E. Helmstädter (ed.), *Die Bedingungen des Wirtschaftswachstums in Vergangenheit und Zukunft*, Tübingen 1984

Kommission für wirtschaftlichen und sozialen Wandel (ed.), *Wirtschaftlicher und sozialer Wandel in der Bundesrepublik*, Bonn 1976

Kursbuch Deutschland 85/86, München 1985

Milatz, A., *Wähler und Wahlen in der Weimarer Republik*, Bonn 1965

Müller-Jentsch, W., *Soziologie der industriellen Beziehungen*, Frankfurt 1986

Pitz, K. H. (ed.), *Das Nein zur Vermögensbildung*, Reinbek 1974

Pritzkoleit, K., *Gott erhält die Mächtigen*, Düsseldorf 1963

Rausch, H., and Stammen, T. (eds.), *DDR – Das politische, wirtschaftliche und soziale System*, München 1978

Schäfers, B., *Sozialstruktur und Wandel der Bundesrepublik Deutschland*, Stuttgart 1976

Schönhoven, K., *Expansion und Konzentration*, Stuttgart 1980

Statistisches Bundesamt (ed.), *Datenreport 1985*, Bonn 1985

Tormin, W., *Geschichte der deutschen Parteien seit 1848*, Stuttgart 1967

Voß, W., *Die Bundesrepublik Deutschland. Daten und Analysen*, Stuttgart 1980

Winkler, D., *Frauenarbeit im 'Dritten Reich'*, Hamburg 1977

Witt, P.-Chr., *Die Finanzpolitik des Deutschen Reiches von 1903 bis 1913*, Lübeck 1970

270

Table 1. *Population growth and movements, 1870–1983*

Year	Pop.[a] (000s)	Average annual growth rate in decade following (%)	No. of emigrants in decade following (000s)
1871	40,997	1.01	626
1881	45,428	0.89	1,342
1891	49,762	1.30	530
1901	56,874	1.42	280
1911	65,359		
1922	61,900	0.60	
1933	66,027	0.71[b]	
1938	68,558		
1946	43,289	(18,350)[c]	
1951	47,456	(17,286)	
1959	51,747	(17,040)	
1965	58,619	(17,068)	
1970	60,651	(16,820)	
1975	61,832	(16,786)	
1980	61,566		
1983	61,423		

Notes: [a] 1871–1911: German Empire, incl. Alsace-Lorraine.
1922–1938: German Empire, frontiers of 1935, incl. Saar.
1946–1959: Fed. Rep., excl. West Berlin and Saar.
1960–   : Fed. Rep., incl. West Berlin and Saar.
[b] For period 1933–1938.
[c] Bracketed figures: GDR, incl. East Berlin.
Sources: Hoffmann, 173f.; Kommission, 83; Bundesministerium, 109; Rausch, 192; Statistisches Bundesamt, 35.

Table 2. *Percentages of population, 1871–1970, living in communities of*

Year	Under 2,000	2,000–5,000	5–20,000	20,000–100,000	Over 100,000
1871	63.9	12.4	11.2	7.7	4.8
1910	40.0	11.2	14.1	13.4	21.3
1925	35.6	10.8	13:1	13.7	26.8
1957[a]	20.7	12.2	18.2	16.4	32.5
1970[a]	18.7	11.7	18.9	18.8	32.4

Note: [a] Federal Republic.
Sources: Hohorst, 52; Kommission, 598.

Table 3. *Growth of some major cities, 1875–1973 (000s)*

	1875	1890	1910	1925	1939	1973[a]	1983	% increase 1875–1910	% increase 1910–1939
Berlin	967	1,588	2,071	4,024	4,339			114	109
Bremen	103	126	217	295	354	582	540	112	43
Breslau	239	335	512	557	629			114	23
Chemnitz	78	139	288	332	338	1,962		268	17
Cologne	135	282	516	700	772	1,022	941	282	50
Dortmund	58	90	214	322	542	639	590	271	153
Dresden	197	276	548	619	630	1,825		178	15
Duisburg	37	59	229	273	435	602		514	90
Düsseldorf	81	145	359	433	541	718	570	344	51
Essen	55	79	295	470	667	688	631	438	126
Frankfurt	103	180	414	467	553	658	610	302	34
Hamburg	265	324	931	1,079	1,712	1,742	1,610	252	84
Kiel	37	69	212	214	274	264		468	29
Leipzig	127	295	590	679	707	1,435		363	20
Munich	193	349	596	681	829	1,322	1,283	209	39
Nuremberg	91	142	333	392	423	513		266	27
Stuttgart	107	140	286	342	458	619	567	167	60

Note: [a] Figures for cities in East Germany = 1976.
Sources: Hohorst, 45; Abelshauser, 38; Rausch, 171; Statistisches Bundesamt, 39.

Table 4. *Numbers of refugees, displaced persons and evacuees, 1946–1949 (000s)*

Land	Refugees (on 1.7.49)	DPs[a] (on 1.4.1947)	Evacuees[b] (on 1.4.47)
Bavaria	1,914	390	624
Württemberg-Baden	698	101	193
Württ-Hohenzollern	75	} 30	} 365
South Baden	55		
Rhine Pd.-Palatin.	70		
Hesse	656	83	369
North Rhine Westph.	1,095	56	580
Lower Saxony	1,812	165	657
Schleswig-Holstein	956	49	465
Bremen	31	1.3	10
Hamburg	86	5.6	32
Total (excl. Berlin)	7,449	880.9	3,295

Notes: [a] Estimates for 1945/6 range from 6 million (M. Balfour) to 8.5–11 million (W. Jacobmeyer).
[b] Incl. evacuees from Soviet Zone and Berlin.
Source: Connor, passim.

Table 5. *Distribution of 10,000 residents according to religious denomination, in 1871 and 1910 (Reich territory) and in 1970 (Federal Republic)*

State	1.12.1871					1.12.1910			
	Evang.	Cathol.	Other Christ.	Jews	Other/ without	Evang.	Cathol.	Other Christ.	Jews
Prussia	6,497	3,349	22	132	0.3	6,182	3,631	47	104
Prov. East Prussia	8,609	1,278	34	79	0.1	8,434	1,409	84	3
Prov. West Prussia	4,819	4,880	98	203	0.3	4,632	5,182	99	82
City of Berlin	8,904	626	31	436	3	8,155	1,173	53	434
Prov. Brandenburg	9,760	170	14	56	0.1	8,984	734	50	150
Prov. Pomerania	9,761	118	30	91	0.0	9,536	328	70	52
Prov. Posnania	3,228	6,374	7	391	0.1	3,079	6,773	20	126
Prov. Silesia	4,749	5,115	10	126	0.3	4,208	5,669	25	86
Prov. Saxony	9,351	603	18	28	0.1	9,161	753	23	25
Prov. Schleswig-Hol.	9,894	60	10	36	0.1	9,556	330	61	21
Prov. Hanover	8,727	1,191	17	65	0.1	8,513	1,372	43	63
Prov. Westphalia	4,543	5,347	13	97	0.1	4,722	5,143	58	51
Prov. Hesse-Nassau	7,056	2,655	28	259	2	6,839	2,824	56	233
Prov. Rhineland	2,534	7,343	16	107	0.1	2,946	6,903	41	80
Hohenzollern	269	9,618	5	108	—	503	9,437	2	57
Bavaria	2,761	7,123	11	104	1	2,821	7,061	20	80
Saxony	9,755	209	19	13	3	9,405	491	53	37
Württemberg	6,867	3,044	21	67	0.2	6,856	3,036	53	49
Baden	3,359	6,449	16	176	0.2	3,856	5,932	62	121
Hesse	6,852	2,803	46	297	2	6,615	3,101	52	188
Mecklenburg-Schwerin.	9,921	24	2	53	0.4	9,618	320	20	22
Hamburg	9,044	229	93	407	227	9,163	503	42	199
Alsace-Lorraine	1,744	7,973	14	264	5	2,178	7,629	21	165
Total Reich	6,231	3,621	20	125	5	6,159	3,669	46	95
Fed. Rep. (1970)	4,900	4,460	110	10	520				

Sources: Hohorst, 54ff.; Schäfers, 78.

Table 6. Net agricultural production[a] at current prices, 1870–1959 (Mill. marks)

Year	Cereals & veg.	Meat	Milk, eggs, etc.	Total
1870	1,698	976	1,406	4,080
1871	1,775	1,176	1,507	4,458
1872	2,094	1,296	1,802	5,192
1873	2,173	1,414	1,911	5,498
1874	2,692	1,495	1,622	5,809
1875	2,073	1,417	1,579	5,069
1876	2,061	1,419	1,814	5,294
1877	2,270	1,355	1,933	5,558
1878	2,291	1,454	1,578	5,323
1879	1,994	1,455	1,484	4,933
1880	2,316	1,426	1,677	5,419
1881	2,426	1,428	1,574	5,428
1882	2,206	1,471	1,570	5,247
1883	2,258	1,557	1,732	5,547
1884	2,185	1,634	1,676	5,495
1885	2,085	1,653	1,558	5,296
1886	2,035	1,695	1,484	5,214
1887	2,061	1,670	1,714	5,445
1888	2,078	1,767	1,629	5,474
1889	2,048	1,911	1,744	5,703
1890	2,451	2,019	2,042	6,512
1891	2,304	1,880	1,894	6,078
1892	2,798	1,922	1,782	6,502
1893	2,447	1,950	1,959	6,356

Year	Cereals & veg.	Meat	Milk, eggs, etc.	Total
1894	2,206	2,073	2,009	6,288
1895	2,287	2,119	1,787	6,193
1896	2,224	2,282	1,809	6,315
1897	2,397	2,534	2,122	7,053
1898	2,738	2,753	2,251	7,742
1899	2,655	2,704	2,054	7,413
1900	2,842	2,647	2,115	7,604
1901	2,544	2,744	2,142	7,430
1902	2,832	2,640	2,452	7,924
1903	2,827	2,645	2,440	7,912
1904	3,129	2,803	2,297	8,229
1905	3,082	3,275	2,675	9,032
1906	2,845	3,495	2,970	9,310
1907	3,400	3,185	3,041	9,626
1908	3,693	3,539	2,875	10,107
1909	3,470	3,592	3,206	10,468
1910	3,168	3,986	3,545	10,699
1911	3,116	4,110	3,680	10,906
1912	3,931	4,606	3,847	12,384
1913	3,540	4,593	3,607	11,740
1924	2,891	3,839	4,153	11,951
1925	3,288	4,510	3,924	11,241
1926	2,428	4,889		

Year	Cereals & veg.	Meat	Milk, eggs, etc.	Total
1927	3,735	4,939	4,299	12,973
1928	4,583	5,421	4,519	14,523
1929	3,714	6,193	4,300	14,207
1930	2,973	5,504	3,842	12,319
1931	3,111	4,234	3,433	10,778
1932	3,317	3,235	3,149	9,701
1933	3,352	3,137	3,517	10,006
1934	3,449	3,830	3,665	10,944
1935	3,492	4,178	3,791	11,461
1936	3,608	4,238	4,184	12,030
1937	3,743	4,500	4,280	12,523
1938	4,252	4,638	4,350	13,240
1950	3,115	4,309	4,003	11,427
1951	3,632	5,411	4,715	13,758
1952	3,718	5,619	4,975	14,312
1953	4,028	6,327	5,054	15,409
1954	3,959	6,355	5,450	15,764
1955	3,732	7,128	5,705	16,565
1956	4,013	7,270	6,032	17,315
1957	4,349	7,579	6,854	18,782
1958	4,492	8,679	6,862	20,033
1959	4,828	8,610	7,198	20,636

Note: [a] After deduction of seeds, animal feedstuffs and processing losses.
Source: Hoffmann, 313.

Table 7. *Index of industrial production 1913–1974, respective; Reich territory (1928=100) and Federal Republic (1950=100)*

Year	Cap. goods	Consum. goods	Total	Year	Cap. goods	Consum. goods	Total
1913	99	97	98	1932	47	74	58
1914			81	1933	56	80	66
1915			66	1934	81	93	83
1916			63	1935	99	91	96
1917			61	1936	114	98	107
1918			56	1937	130	103	117
1919	32		37	1938	144	108	125
1920	56	51	54	1939	148	108	132
1921	65	69	65	1940	144	102	128
1922	70	74	70	1941	149	104	131
1923	43	57	46	1942	157	93	132
1924	65	81	69	1943	180	98	149
1925	80	85	81	1944	178	93	146
1926	77	80	78				
1927	97	103	98	1950			100
1928	100	100	100	1960			248
1929	102	97	100	1965			327
1930	84	91	87	1970			435
1931	62	82	70	1974			486

Sources: Abelshauser, 101; Dresdner Bank figures.

Table 8. *Production indices of key industries 1870–1959 (1913 = 100)*

Year	Coal	Lignite	Iron	Steel	Shipbldng	Cars	Chemicals
1870	13.9	8.7	7.2	6.0			
1875	19.7	11.9	10.5	8.8			
1880	24.7	13.9	14.1	10.9			
1885	30.7	17.7	14.1	13.4			
1890	36.9	21.9	24.1	18.0			
1895	41.7	28.4	28.3	22.4			
1900	57.5	46.4	43.6	33.4			
1905	63.8	60.2	56.9	47.0			
1910	80.4	77.5	76.6	75.8	63.8	51.1	80.5
1913	100.0	100.0	100.0	100.0	100.0	100.0	100.0
1915	77.2	100.8	61.1	69.8	56.6	—	—
1920	69.1	128.3	33.1	48.5	73.8	—	—
1923	32.8	136.2	25.6	36.0	71.9	—	—
1925	69.8	160.2	52.7	69.8	62.1	329.4	133.0
1930	75.1	167.4	50.2	65.7	54.2	403.0	172.2
1932	55.1	140.6	20.4	32.6	12.7	236.4	138.4
1935	75.2	168.5	66.5	93.2	61.5	815.5	201.9
1940	97.0	257.9	72.3	110.3	—	—	—
1945	18.7	27.9	10.9[a]	14.6[a]	—	—	—
1950	58.3	86.9	49.1	69.1	42.6	936.6	240.6
1955	68.8	103.6	85.4	121.4	153.9	2,656.0	439.8
1959	66.1	107.1	95.3	147.3	151.9	4,266.0	630.9

Note: [a] Figure for 1946.
Source: Hoffmann, 340ff., 353f., 358, 362.

Table 9. *Production of coal and steel in Britain and Germany, 1880–1976 (000s tons)*

Year	Britain Coal	Germany Coal	Lignite	Britain Steel	Germany Steel
1880	149,000	47,000	12,100	982[a]	1,548
1890	184,000	70,200	19,100	3,579	2,195
1900	228,000	109,300	40,500	4,901	6,260
1910	268,700	152,800	69,500	5,300[b]	10,900[b]
1913	292,000	191,500	87,500	6,903	18,654
1936					19,175[c]
1938	230,648				22,656[c]
1940					
1945		35,484[d]			300[e]
1946		53,946			2,551
1947		71,124			3,060
1948		87,033			5,561
1949		103,208			9,156
1950[f]		111,118	21,721		12,121
1954	227,637	129,041	25,148		17,434
1958	219,275	133,532	26,817		22,785
1962[g]	200,556	141,899	28,958		32,562
1964				26,200	36,700
1976		89,000	135,000		

Notes:
[a] Figure for 1878.
[b] Figure for 1908.
[c] Reich within frontiers of 1937
[d] Figure for Ruhr, Aachen and Lower Saxony.
[e] Western Zones/Fed. Rep.
[f] Excl. Saar.
[g] Incl. Saar.

Sources: Clapham, 281; Balfour, 439; Pritzkoleit, 142, 153, 294, 348; Voß 72.

Table 10. *Exports/imports in current prices (mill. marks) and by volume (1913 = 100),*
1880–1985

Year	Current prices		Volume	
	Exports	Imports	Exports	Imports
1880	2,923.0	2,813.7	22.4	25.5
1885	2,854.0	2,922.6	25.9	31.8
1890	3,335.1	4,162.4	29.8	44.0
1895	3,318.0	4,119.0	31.7	52.0
1900	4,611.2	5,768.6	44.7	63.2
1905	5,731.6	7,128.8	58.2	75.1
1910	7,474.7	8,926.9	77.4	88.3
1913	10,097.5	10,750.9	100.0	100.0
1923		6,150.1		
1925	9,284.0	12,429.2	66.4	82.3
1930	12,035.6	10,348.7	92.2	86.0
1932	5,741.1	4,652.8	55.6	62.5
1935	4,178.0	4,156.2	51.5	60.8
1940				
1945				
1950	8,363.1	11,373.9	34.3	47.4
1955	25,716.8	24,461.1	85.6	99.4
1959	41,062.4	35,485.7	120.6	153.7
1960	47,900.0	42,700.0		
1965	71,700.0	70,400.0		
1970	125,300.0	109,600.0		
1975	221,600.0	184,300.0		
1980	350,300.0	341,400.0		
1985	537,100.0	463,800.0		

Sources: Hoffmann, 520ff.; Statistisches Bundesamt, 240; *Die Zeit,* 21.2.1986.

Table 11. *Exports/imports in current prices, Fed. Rep. 1960–1980 (mill. marks) and GDR,*
1960–1974 (mill. Valuta-marks, excl. trade with Fed. Rep.)

Year	Exports	Imports	Year	Exports	Imports
1960	47,900.0	42,700.0	1960	9,270.8	9,216.6
1965	71,700.0	70,400.0	1965	12,892.9	11,800.4
1970	125,300.0	109,600.0	1970	19,240.2	20,357.2
1974	230,500.0	179,700.0	1974	30,443.2	33,569.5
1976	256,600.0	222,200.0			
1980	350,300.0	341,400.0			

Sources: Dresdner Bank figures; Bundesministerium, 71; Jacobsen, 901; *Die Zeit,*
4.12.1981.

Statistical tables

Table 12. *Real growth of the West German economy, 1951–1984 (%)*

Year	%	Year	%
1951	10.4	1970	5.8
1952	8.9	1971	3.0
1953	8.2	1972	3.4
1954	7.4	1973	5.1
1955	12.0	1974	0.4
1956	7.3	1975	− 2.7
1957	5.7	1976	5.8
1958	3.7	1977	2.7
1959	7.3	1978	3.3
1960	9.0	1979	4.5
1961	5.4	1980	1.8
1962	4.0	1981	− 0.2
1963	3.4	1982	− 1.0
1964	6.7	1983	1.3
1965	5.6	1984	2.6
1966	2.9		
1967	− 0.2		
1968	7.3		
1969	8.2		

Sources: Die Zeit, 29.8.1975; Voß, 69; Statistisches Bundesamt, 232.

Table 13. *Sources of Gross Domestic Product in East Germany, 1960–1975 (in mill. marks at 1967 prices)*

Sector	1960	1965	1970	1975[a]
Industry	51.3	64.2	86.5	114.6
Agriculture	11.9	12.2	13.5	15.6
Commerce and Transp.	13.9	16.5	21.6	28.5
Services	4.1	4.5	5.0	5.6
Health, Education, State	9.3	11.0	13.3	15.9
Total	90.5	108.4	139.9	180.2

Note: [a] Provisional figures.
Source: Cornelsen, 307.

Table 14. *Occupational distribution of the labour force (%)*

Year	Manual workers	White collar/ C.S.	Self-employed	Helping family members
1895	57	8	25	10
1950[a]	49	20	16	15
1979[a]	42	44	10	4

Note: [a] Fed. Rep.
Source: Die Zeit, 31.10.1980.

Table 15. *Structure of the labour force by sector, 1907–1984 (%)*

Year	Agriculture	Industry and handicraft	Tertiary sector	
			Total	Commerce/ Banking
1907	35.2	40.1	24.8	12.4
1925	30.5	42.1	27.4	16.4
1933	28.9	40.4	30.7	18.5
1939[a]	25.9	42.2	31.9	17.5
1950[b]	23.1 (26)	(45)	(29)	
1960	13.2 (19)[c]	(48)	(33)	
1962	12.5	46.0	41.2	17.5
1970	8.3			
1972	7.7	46.1	46.2	16.5
1975	(12)	(49)	(37)	
1984	5.4	41.6	53.0	

Notes: [a] Reich Territory of 31.12.1937.
[b] Fed. Rep.; figures for GDR in brackets.
[c] GDR figure for 1959.
Sources: Abelshauser, 55; Kommission, 164; *Die Zeit,* 23.7.1971; Statistisches Bundesamt, 81.

Table 16. *Structure of the labour force in occupational groups, 1875–1983 (000s)*

Sector	1875	1885	1895	1905	1913	1925	1935	1955[a]	1970	1983
Agriculture	9,230	9,700	9,788	9,926	10,701	9,778	9,030	4,257	2,262	1,371
Mining	286	345	432	665	863	743	525	637	551	502
Industry and handicraft	5,153	6,005	7,524	9,572	10,857	11,708	11,011	10,265	12,436	10,012
Transport	349	461	620	901	1,174	1,472	1,461	1,327 }		
Commerce/banking	1,116	1,457	1,970	2,806	3,474	3,864	4,056	3,777	7,688	7,389
Insurance, hotels,[b] domestic services	(1,490)	1,488	1,571	1,541	1,542	1,357	1,211	638 }		
Other services	589	659	894	1,159	1,493	1,969	2,645	2,386	2,978	4,005
Defence	430	462	606	651	864	142		303		
Total	18,643	20,577	23,405	27,221	30,968	31,003		23,590		

Notes: [a] Federal Rep.
[b] Incl. restaurants etc.
Sources: Hoffmann, 206; *Die Zeit*, 26.4.1985.

Table 17. *Distribution of labour force according to number employed per enterprise in different years in the Reich and the Federal Republic*

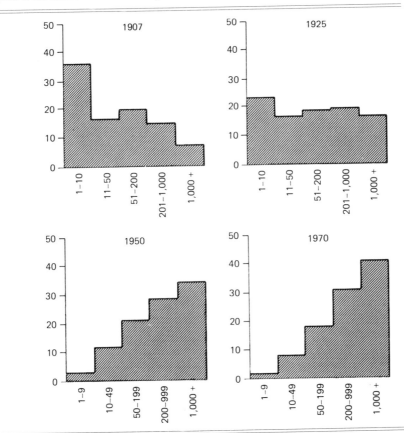

Sources: Guttsman, 26; Pitz, 73.

Statistical tables

Table 18. *Unemployment, 1900–1985 (annual averages)*

Year	No. (000s)	% of working pop.	Year	No. (000s)	% of working pop.
1900[a]	183	1.9	1934	2,718	13.5
1901	631	6.7	1935	2,151	10.3
1902	272	2.9	1936	1,593	7.4
1903	268	2.7	1937	912	4.1
1904	211	2.1	1938	429	1.9
1905	166	1.6	1939	119	0.5
1906	128	1.2	1940	52	0.2
1907	175	1.6			
1908	319	3.0	1946		
1909	307	2.9	1948		
1910	211	1.9	1950[b]	1,869	8.1
1911	215	1.9	1955	1,074	4.2
1912	239	2.0	1960	271	1.0
1913	348	3.0	1965	147	0.5
			1971	185	0.7
1921	346	1.8	1975	1,110	4.1
1922	215	1.1	1978	993	
1923	818	4.1	1980	865	3.8
1924	927	4.9	1981[c]	1,210	5.5
1925	682	3.4	1982[c]	1,810	7.5
1926	2,025	10.0	1983[c]	2,360	9.1
1927	1,312	6.2	1984[c]	2,370	
1928	1,391	6.3	1985[c]	2,440	
1929	1,899	8.5			
1930	3,076	14.0			
1931	4,520	21.9			
1932	5,603	29.9			
1933	4,804	25.9			

Notes: [a] Statistics for 1900–1913 for industry only, excl. handicrafts and only as far as recorded by trade unions. Actual figures probably much higher.
  [b] 1950–85 = Fed. Rep.
  [c] Av. for Jan.–May.
Sources: Witt, 384; Abelshauser, 119; Voß, 83; *Die Zeit*, 12.9.1980 and 20.6.1986.

Table 19. *Indices of producers' prices for agricultural produce, 1870–1959 (1913=100)*

Year	Cereals/veg.	Meat	Milk/eggs etc.	Total av.
1870	79.6	55.6	70.1	69.1
1875	80.7	65.4	76.2	74.3
1880	101.8	63.6	78.7	81.3
1885	72.7	63.2	69.3	68.4
1890	88.3	71.5	85.4	81.3
1895	74.2	65.7	68.5	69.3
1900	82.8	65.1	73.7	73.2
1905	92.2	78.0	84.7	84.4
1910	95.8	85.6	104.4	94.1
1913	100.0	100.0	100.0	100.0
1915				
1920				
1923				
1925	123.5	115.2	159.4	130.0
1930	114.5	114.3	119.6	115.8
1932	106.1	66.5	88.3	83.8
1935	114.7	80.0	105.5	96.5
1940				
1945				
1950[a]	188.9	193.4	192.7	191.4
1955[a]	240.0	210.8	234.2	222.2
1959[a]	288.7	225.3	255.1	247.9

Note: [a] Fed. Rep.
Source: Hoffmann, 561.

Table 20. *Return on capital in joint stock companies of the commercial and industrial sector, 1926–1959*

Year	Total capital	Profits	Profit rate (%)
1926	20,849	564	2.71
1927	22,130	1,422	6.43
1928	23,704	1,293	5.45
1929	24,561	1,351	5.50
1930	24,981	773	3.09
1931	25,294	135	0.53
1932	22,036	−2,208	−10.02
1933	21,991	− 497	− 2.26
1934	22,151	504	2.28
1935	23,222	1,704	7.34
1936	24,239	1,835	7.57
1937	25,616	3,182	12.42
1938	27,884	4,066	14.58
1950	32,753	2,931	8.95
1951	37,755	4,117	10.90
1952	42,277	4,939	11.68
1953	47,917	5,619	11.73
1954	50,557	6,725	13.30
1955	57,588	7,619	13.21
1956	64,388	8,172	12.69
1957	70,029	8,979	12.82
1958	51,215	8,971	11.93
1959	83,110	11,637	14.00

Source: Hoffmann, 503.

Table 21. *Fluctuations in share prices quoted on the stock market and in dividends, 1900–1943*

Year	Share prices (1926/8=100)	% dividend	Year	Share prices (1926/8=100)	% dividend
1900–	113	9.61	1933	48	3.27
1913			1934	56	3.53
1924	91		1935	66	4.26
1925	86		1936	81	5.17
1926	101	5.58	1937	83	5.70
1927	98	7.14	1938	78	6.40
1928	101	8.29	1939	82	6.55
1929	77	8.35	1940	106	6.60
1930	55	8.05	1941	106	6.38
1931	32	6.51	1942	98	5.35
1932	41	2.83	1943	97	5.25

Source: Abelshauser, 70.

Table 22. *Fluctuations in share prices quoted on the stock market 1951–1970, and in dividends, 1960–1979*

Year	Share prices (31.12.1965=100)	% dividend	Year	Share prices (31.12.1965=100)	% dividend
1951	16		1966	94	
1952	20		1967	98	
1953	18		1968	130	
1954	25		1969	144	
1955	39		1970	132	15.7
1956	37		1971		
1957	37		1972		
1958	48		1973		
1959	84		1974		13.8
1960	134	11.8	1975		
1961	138		1976		
1962	107		1977		
1963	107		1978		
1964	120		1979		9.1
1965	112	13.2	1980		

Sources: Die Zeit, 26.11.1971; Dresdner Bank figures.

Table 23. *Average annual wages and salaries, 1870–1982 (marks)*

Year	All industries and handicrafts	Mining		Administration	Reich Civil Service		
		Miners	All employees	Law, Education	Postal ass.	engine driver	Postal directors
1870	506	767	798	1,306			
1875	669	929	966	1,647			
1880	565	721	750	1,778			
1885	622	768	799	1,877			
1890	711	966	1,005	1,947			
1895	738	908	944	1,986			
1900	834	1,173	1,220	2,055			
1905	928	1,159	1,205	2,115			
1910	1,063	1,299	1,347	2,409			
1913	1,163	1,496	1,667	2,607	1913:	3,852	6,300
					1.12.1924:	3,818	5,892
					1. 4.1926:	3,912	6,024
					1. 7.1931:	3,756	5,940
					1. 1.1932:	3,372	5,340
1925	1,677	1,838	2,036	3,639			
1930	2,131	2,252	2,580	4,456			
1932	1,651	1,689	1,969	3,630			
1933	1,586	1,692	2,014	3,583			
1935	1,697	1,948	2,202	3,572	1. 4.1936:	3,372	5,340
1939	1,986	2,280	2,642		1. 7.1938:	3,492	5,496
1950[a]	3,046	3,627	3,908	4,328			
1955[a]	4,475	5,113	5,700	6,641			
1960[a]	6,148[b]						
1965[a]	9,336[b]						
1970[a]	13,841[b]						
1975[a]	22,063[b]						
1980[a]	29,923[b]						
1982[a]	32,624[b]						

Notes: [a] Fed. Rep.   [b] All workers and employees.
Sources: Hoffmann, 461, 469, 489f.; Abelshauser, 101; *Kursbuch Deutschland 85/86*, 201.

Table 24. *Indices of real wages of some workers and of real income of some civil servants living in cities, 1913–1923 (1913=100)*

Year	Railway workers		Printers	Miners	Civil Servants		
	Skilled	Unskilled			High-ranking	Middle rank	Low rank
1913	100.0	100.0	100.0	100.0	100.0	100.0	100.0
1914	97.2	97.2	97.2	93.3	97.2	97.2	97.2
1915	79.7	80.8	77.3	81.3	77.3	77.3	77.3
1916	69.2	73.8	60.6	74.4	58.9	58.9	58.9
1917	63.9	74.2	49.4	62.7	42.9	48.6	53.6
1918	83.9	99.8	54.1	63.7	46.8	55.0	69.6
1919	92.2	119.8	72.3	82.4	40.2	54.8	89.3
1920	66.7	89.1	60.8	77.6	31.7	44.0	71.3
1921	74.5	100.0	68.9	89.1	39.3	52.2	82.3
1922	64.2	87.6	60.9	69.9	35.6	46.4	72.9
1923	50.9	69.1	69.1	70.1	38.0	49.5	69.9

Source: Holtfrerich, 230ff.

289

Statistical tables

Table 25. *Indices of cost of living (prices)[a] and of workers' wages, 1913/14–1943 (1928=100)*

Year	Wages[b] Hourly	Weekly	Cost of living	Real wages[c]
1913/14	53	61	66	93
1924			86	
1925	77	75	93	81
1926	82	78	93	84
1927	90	88	97	89
1928	100	100	100	100
1929	106	103	101	102
1930	103	95	97	97
1931	95	84	89	94
1932	80	69	80	86
1933	77	71	78	91
1934	79	76	80	94
1935	80	77	81	95
1936	81	80	82	97
1937	83	83	82	101
1938	86	87	83	105
1939	89	90	83	108
1940	91	93	86	108
1941	95	99	88	113
1942	96	100	90	111
1943	97	101	91	109

Notes: [a] Calculated for working-class family of 5 (1934) with averages for food, drink, rent, heating, electricity, clothing.
[b] 'Effective wages' per hour and per week.
[c] Calculated on basis of cost-of-living index per week.
Source: Abelshauser, 98, 107.

Table 26. *Indices of nominal and real wages, 1950–1984, in Federal Republic (1976 = 100)*

Year	Nominal	Real
1950	14.5	31.4
1960	28.6	51.4
1965	44.0	69.0
1970	63.0	88.1
1975	92.3	96.3
1980	127.5	109.9
1981	133.3	108.6
1982	137.7	106.6
1983	141.0	106.0
1984	145.8	106.3

Source: Statistisches Bundesamt, 308.

Table 27. *Income distribution in the Federal Republic in 1970 (%)*

Net monthly income	Workers	Employees	Civil servants	Self-employed[a]
Over 1,800 DM	0.1	10.8	14.7	33.1
1,200–1,800 DM	3.6	27.9	31.2	24.1
800–1200 DM	39.1	39.6	40.5	24.8
600–800 DM	39.3	12.1	10.4	10.6
under 600 DM	17.8	9.6	2.9	7.3

Note: [a] Excl. farmers.
Source: Die Zeit, 2.7.71.

Statistical tables

Table 28. *Distribution of wealth by occupational group, 1950–1963*

	Wealth in milliard marks	% of total nat. wealth	No. of households	% of all households
Workers	27.1	17	6.6 mill.	33.7
White-collar employees	21.6	13	2.8 mill.	14.3
Civil servants	11.1	7	1.2 mill.	6.1
Pensioners	26.5	16	5.9 mill.	29.8
Total	86.3	53	16.5 mill.	83.9
Farmers	12.4	8	1.1 mill.	5.4
Self-empl.	63.9	39	2.1 mill.	10.7
Total	76.3	47	3.2 mill.	16.1

Source: Jungblut, 41.

Table 29. *Expenditure pattern of average disposable incomes in West Germany, 1957–1985 (%)*

	1957	1967	1977	1985
Food	36.6	29.3	23.0	17.4
Clothing	12.5	9.4	8.2	6.5
Housing	9.3	13.5	14.4	15.6
Furniture, cars Travel, leisure etc.	33.6	36.1	40.7	47.8
Savings	8.0	11.7	13.7	12.7

Sources: Voß, 135; *Die Zeit*, 23.5.1986.

Table 30. *Number of consumer durables per 100 households in East Germany, 1955–1985, and West Germany, 1975–1984*

	East Germany						West Germany	
	1955	1960	1965	1970	1975	1985	1975	1984
Cars	0.2	3	8	16	29		55	64
Motorbikes	11	13	17	19	19		7	
Mopeds			16	27	33			
Radios	77	90	87	92	97		99	
TV sets	1	17	49	69	84	93	89	82[a]
Fridges	0.4	6	26	56	90	99	93	82[b]
Washing machines	0.5	6	28	54	76	92	75	87

Notes: [a] colour TV
 [b] Plus fridge/freezer = 31; freezer = 40.
Sources: Rausch, 181; Cornelsen, 237; *Die Zeit*, 28.12.1984; *Die Zeit*, 20.6.1986.

Table 31. *Average hours of work per week in major branches of industry, 1895–1983*

Year	Total	Coal mining	Metals	Chemicals	Textiles
1895	64	51.5	63	60	65
1900	62	53	63	60	62.5
1905	60	46		60	61
1910	59	48.5			59
1914	57	50	60	58	
1919	48		48	48	47
1925	50.5	42			
1930	44	40	45.5		43
1935	44.5	41.5	47	44	41
1940	50	47.5			
1950	48	42	51	48.5	47
1955	49	38.5	51	49	46.5
1959	45.5		45	47	44
1961	46.2[a]				
1965	45.2[a]				
1969	44.9[a]				
1975	41.2[a]				
1979	42.4[a]				
1983	39.6[a]				

Note: [a] Average for male industrial workers, incl. overtime.
Sources: Hoffmann, 214; *Die Zeit*, 27.4.1984.

Table 32. *Mobilisation of civilian workforce, 1939–1944, Reich incl. Sudetenland and Austria (millions)*

Month/Year	Male	Female	Foreign	Total
May 1939	24.5	14.6	0.3	39.4
May 1940	20.4	14.4	1.2	36.0
May 1941	19.0	14.1	3.0	36.1
May 1942	16.9	14.4	4.2	35.5
May 1943	15.5	14.8	6.3	36.6
May 1944	14.2	14.8	7.1	36.1
Sept. 1944	13.5	14.9	7.5	35.9

Source: Abelshauser, 153.

Table 33. *Collectivisation of East German agriculture, 1952–1960*

Year	No. of collectives	% of farmed area
31.12.1952	1,906	3.3
31.12.1953	4.691	11.6
31.12.1954	5,120	14.3
31.12.1955	6,047	19.7
31.12.1956	6,281	23.2
31.12.1957	6,691	25.2
31.12.1958	9,637	37.0
31.12.1959	10,465	45.1
31.12.1960	19,261	84.2
31.12.1961	17,860	84.5
30. 9.1965	15,139	85.7
30. 9.1967	13,073	85.8

Source: Bundesministerium, 383.

Table 34. *Ordinary Reich revenue, 1901–1918 (mill. marks)*

Source	1901	1906	1909	1913	1914	1916	1918
Death duties	—	4.2	38.5	46.4	43.6	65.0	77.8
Capital gains	—	—	—	15.3	2.8	0.5	0.7
Property tax	—	—	—	—	—	—	89.1
Stamp duties	84.0	138.6	171.4	258.6	183.1	252.8	510.8
Tariffs	478.9	557.7	660.2	679.3	560.8	348.3	133.0
Taxes on consumption[a]	333.2	378.4	485.7	659.7	775.8	668.8	2,032.8
Matricular contrib.	15.2	24.2	48.5	51.9	51.9	51.9	51.9
Wehrbeitrag (1913)					637.4	19.5	·1.3
War contrib. 1916						45.6	791.8
War contrib. 1918							1,617.2
Post Office/railways	42.2	85.4	24.1	5.5	43.6[b]	365.1[b]	1,929.7[b]
Reich Bank	12.8	29.2	16.4	34.7	118.3	85.0	8.6
Special levies					(see above, pp. 48f)		
Other	94.4[c]	93.3[c]	196.6[c]	229.9[c]			
Loans	332.8	258.4	639.0	109.3			

Notes: [a] Incl. tobacco, beer, sugar, spirits.
[b] Incl. Reich Bank, *Darlehenskassen* levy, export levy, transport levy, Post Office levy.
[c] Incl. Reich Stationery Office, administrative fees, fund income.

Sources: Witt, 378f.; Holtfrerich, 108.

Statistical tables

Table 35. *Growth in military expenditure, 1900–1978*

Year	Expenditure (mill. marks)	% of Nettosozialprodukt[a]
1900	1,080	3.7
1906	1,359	3.8
1910	1,659	3.9
1913	2,312	4.7
1925	3,933	7.0
1930	4,688	6.8
1932	2,494	5.9
1933	2,772	6.3
1934	6,143	12.0
1935	8,017	14.1
1936	12,325	19.4
1937	13,360	18.7
1938	22,000	25.3
1939	37,340	38.1
1940	66,445	60.4
1941	86,500	72.1
1942	110,400	88.3
1943	132,800	98.4
1944	149,800	115.2
1951	13,916[b]	15.3
1955	13,217	13.8
1956	12,397	8.0
1961	22,862	8.9
1965	27,708	7.8
1969	25,300	5.4
1973	33,400	4.6
1977	48,200	5.2
1978	49,600	4.9

Note: [a] Net Social Product = GNP minus social benefits and indirect taxes, but incl. subsidies.
[b] Fed. Rep.
Source: Köllner, 207f.

Table 36. *Growth of Reich debt, 1933–1938 (1,000 mill. marks)*

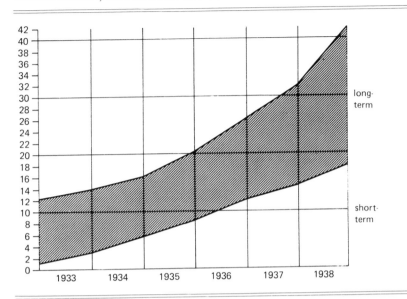

Source: Deist, 249.

Table 37. *Pupil/class, pupil/teacher and pupil/inhabitant ratios in state schools in Prussia, 1901–1911; Reich, 1921–1938; Federal Republic, 1950–1970*

Year	Volksschule[a]			Mittelschule[a]			Höhere Schule[a]		
	A[b]	B[c]	C[d]	A[b]	B[c]	C[d]	A[b]	B[c]	C[d]
1901	54	63	16	33	29.8	0.54		19.9	0.51
1906	53	60	16	32.1	28.2	0.57		20.4	0.60
1911	51	56	(16)[e]	30.4	29.5	(0.45)[e]		20.7	0.65
1921/2	43	45	14	26	27	0.5	30.0	18.7	1.3
1926/7	35	37	11		21	0.4		18.7	1.3
1931/2	39	40	12	25	20	0.4		15.5	1.2
1938	40	42	11				25.7	15.2	1.0
1950[f]	44			38			31		
1960[f]	37			33			28		
1970[f]	34			32			28		

Notes: [a] See above pp. 13f.   [d] Pupils per 100 inhabitants.
          [b] Pupils per class.   [e] Figure for 1910.
          [c] Pupils per teacher.   [f] Figures for Fed. Rep.
Sources: Hohorst, 157ff.; Abelshauser, 165ff.; Schäfers, 297.

Table 38. *Students in higher education, 1891–1939*

Year	Total	Universities	Technical univ.	Others[a]	Women %
1891	33,992	27,398	4,209	2,385	
1902	52,538	35,857	13,151	3,530	
1912	71,710	56,483	11,349	3,878	*c.* 3.6
1928[b]	110,808				11.6
1936[c]	71,850				13.7
1939[b]	56,477				11.1

Notes: [a] Academies of Mining, Forestry, Agriculture and Vet. Med.
         [b] Summer Semester.
         [c] Winter Semester.
Sources: Hohorst, 161; Abelshauser, 171, 169.

Table 39. *Father's profession of students at universities in Baden-Württemberg during the winter semester, 1952/3 and 1966/7 (%)*

Father's profession	1952/3	1966/7
Civil servants	39.2	30.8
with university degree[a]	(15.1)	(16.4)
without university degree[b]	(24.1)	(14.4)
Salaried employees	23.4	31.4
with university degree[c]	(5.3)	(8.2)
without university degree[d]	(18.1)	(23.2)
Professionals	11.7	13.8
with university degree[e]	(9.0)	(11.4)
without university degree	(2.7)	(2.4)
Farmers	3.7	2.2
Self-employed	17.9	12.8
with university degree[f]	(1.1)	(0.5)
without university degree[g]	(16.8)	(12.3)
Workers[h]	3.8	5.5
Unknown/others	0.3	3.5
	100.0	100.0
Total number of students	20,761	44,405

Notes:
[a] Incl. university and high school teachers, judges, medical and technical C.S.
[b] Officers, teachers, C.S. of all ranks.
[c] Teachers, doctors, engineers, lawyers, architects, accountants.
[d] Teachers, managers, works supervisors, white-collar workers.
[e] Solicitors, doctors, accountants, architects.
[f] Factory owners, traders, retailers.
[g] Factory owners, traders, retailers, publicans, self-employed craftsmen.
[h] Skilled and semi-skilled workers, employed craftsmen, land labourers.

Source: Mannheimer Morgen, 27.2.1969.

Table 40. *Conservative and Social Democratic voting strength and Reichstag representation,* *1881–1912*

Election	Conservatives		SPD	
	% of vote	% of seats	% of vote	% of seats
1881	16.3	12.6	6.1	3.0
1884	15.2	19.6	9.7	6.0
1887	15.2	20.1	10.1	2.8
1890	12.4	18.4	19.7	8.8
1893	13.5	18.1	23.3	11.1
1898	11.0	14.1	27.2	14.1
1903	10.0	13.6	31.7	20.4
1907	9.4	15.1	29.0	10.8
1912	9.2	10.8	34.8	27.7

Source: Guttsman, 80.

Table 41. *Reichstag election results, 1898–1912 (000s)*

	1898		1903		1907		1912	
Eligible	11,441		12,531		13,352		14,442	
Turnout	7,752		9,495		11,262		12,207	
% voting	67.7		75.8		84.3		84.5	
	Votes	Seats	Votes	Seats	Votes	Seats	Votes	Seats
SPD	2,107	56	3,011	81	3,259	43	4,250	110
Centre	1,455	102	1,875	100	2,180	105	1,997	91
Left. Lib.	863	49	872	26	1,234	49	1,497	42
Nat. Lib.	971	46	1,317	51	1,631	54	1,663	45
Free Cons.	344	23	333	21	472	24	367	14
Conservat.	859	56	949	54	1,060	60	1,126	43
RWSp.[a]	284	13	245	11	249	16	52	3
Minorities[b]	471	34	559	32	651	29	706	33
Sp. P.[c]	397	18	334	11	528	17	550	16

Notes: [a] Right-wing splinter groups, e.g. *Christlich-Soziale.*
[b] Poles, Danes, Guelphs, Alsatians.
[c] Other splinter parties.
Source: Tormin, 284.

Table 42. *Reichstag election results, 1920–1933 (000s)*

	6.6.1920[a]		4.5.1924		7.12.1924		20.5.1928		14.9.1930		31.7.1932		6.11.1932		5.3.1933	
Eligible	35,950		38,375		33,987		41,224		42,958		44,211		44,374		44,665	
Turnout	28,196		29,282		30,290		30,754		34,971		36,882		35,471		39,343	
% voting	78.4		76.3		77.7		74.6		81.4		83.4		79.9		88.1	
	Votes	Seats	Votes	Seats	Votes	Seats	Votes	Seats	Votes	Seats	Votes	Seats	Votes	Seats	Votes	Seats
KPD	590	4	3,693	62	2,709	45	3,265	54	4,592	77	5,283	89	5,980	100	4,848	81
USPD	5,047	83	235	—	99	—	—	—	—	—	—	—	—	—	—	—
SPD	6,104	103	6,009	100	7,881	131	9,153	153	8,578	143	7,960	133	7,248	121	7,181	120
Centre	3,910	64	3,914	65	4,092	69	3,712	61	4,128	68	4,589	75	4,230	70	4,425	74
BVP	1,173	21	947	16	1,134	19	946	17	1,059	19	1,193	22	1,095	20	1,074	18
DDP[b]	2,334	39	1,655	28	1,920	32	1,479	25	1,322	20	372	4	336	2	334	5
WP[c]	219	4	530	10	639	17	1,388	23	1,362	23	147	2	110	1	—	—
DVP	3,919	65	2,728	45	3,049	51	2,680	45	1,578	30	136	7	661	11	432	2
DNVP	4,249	71	5,697	95	6,206	103	4,382	73	2,458	41	2,177	37	2,959	52	3,137	52
NSDAP[d]	—	—	1,918	32	907	14	810	12	6,383	107	13,769	230	11,737	196	17,277	288
R.Sp.[e]	709	5	608	5	708	4	956	3	683	3	219	—	353	1	246	—
RWSp.[f]	—	—	666	10	545	8	1,025	23	2,373	46	552	9	510	10	384	7
Sp.P.[g]	161	—	682	4	401	—	958	2	455	—	185	—	252	—	5	—

Notes:
a Incl. by-elections in Schleswig-Holstein and East Prussia (20.2.1921) and Upper Silesia (19.11.1922).
b From 1930=*Staatspartei.*
c *Wirtschaftspartei.*
d In May 1924: *Deutsch-Völkische Freiheitspartei;* December 1924: *Nat. Soz. Freiheitsbewegung.*
e Regional splinters, e.g. *Bayerischer Bauernbund,* Guelphs, Polish Party.
f Right-wing splinter parties, e.g. *Landvolkpartei, Konservative Volkspartei.*
g Other splinter parties.

Sources: Tormin, 286; Milatz, 151.

Table 43. Bundestag election results,, 1949–1987 (000s)

| | 14.8.1949 31.2 mill. 24.5 mill. 78.5 | | | 6.3.1953 33.1 mill. 28.5 mill. 85.8 | | | 15.9.1957 35.4 mill. 31.1 mill. 87.8 | | | 17.9.1961 37.4 mill. 32.8 mill. 87.7 | | | 19.9.1965 38.5 mill. 33.4 mill. 86.8 | | | 28.9.1969 38.7 mill. 33.0 mill. 86.7 | | |
Eligible Turnout % voting	a	b	c	a	b	c	a	b	c	a	b	c	a	b	c	a	b	c
CDU/CSU	7,359	31.0	139	12,440	45.2	243	15,008	50.2	270	14,298	45.3	242	15,524	47.6	245	15,195	46.1	242
SPD	6,935	29.2	131	7,945	28.8	151	9,496	31.8	169	11,427	36.2	190	12,813	39.3	202	14,066	42.7	224
FDP	2,83	11.9	52	2,628	9.5	48	2,307	7.7	41	4,029	12.8	67	3,097	9.5	49	1,903	5.8	30
KPD/DKP	1,362	5.7	15	0,607	2.2	—	—	—	—	—	—	—	—	—	—	0,197	0.6	—
DP[d]	0.94	4.0	17	0,898	3.3	15	1,007	3.4	17	GDP 0,871	2.8	—	—	—	—	—	—	—
BHE[d]	—	—	—	1,614	5.9	27	1,374	4.6	—				—	—	—	—	—	—
Centre[d]	0.728	3.1	10	0,217	0.8	2	0,086	0.3	—	—	—	—	—	—	—	—	—	—
Bavaria Party[d]	0.986	4.2	17	0,466	1.7	—	0,168	0.5	—	—	—	—	—	—	—	—	—	—
WAV[d]	0.682	2.9	12	—	—	—	—	—	—	—	—	—	—	—	—	—	—	—
DRP/NPD	0.429	1.8	5	0,296	1.1	—	0,309	1.0	—	0,263	0.8	—	0,664	2.0	—	1,422	4.3	—
DFU[d]	—	—	—	—	—	—	—	—	—	0,61	1.9	—	0,434	1.3	—	—	—	—
Others	1,481	6.2	4	0,433	1.4	—	0,15	0.5	—	0,052	0.2	—	0,088	0.3	—	0,022	—	—

302

Table 43 (cont.)

	19.11.1972 41.4 mill. 37.8 mill. 91.2			3.10.1976 42.0 mill. 38.1 mill. 90.7			5.10.1980 43.2 mill. 38.3 mill. 90.7			6.3.1983 44.1 mill. 39.3 mill. 89.1			25.1.1987 45.3 mill. 38.2 mill. 84.4		
Eligible															
Turnout															
% voting	a	b	c	a	b	c	a	b	c	a	b	c	a	b	c
CDU/CSU	16,794	44.8	225	18,397	48.6	244	16,900	44.5	226	18,996	48.8	246	16,761	44.3	223
SPD	17,167	45.9	230	16,099	42.6	213	16,262	42.9	218	14,866	38.2	191	14,023	37.0	186
FDP	3,129	8.4	41	2,995	7.9	39	4,030	10.6	53	2,705	6.9	34	3,440	9.1	46
KPD/DKP	0,114	0.3	—	0,141	0.4	—	0,080	0.2	—	0,066	0.2	—	—	—	—
Greens	—	—	—	—	—	—	—	—	—	2,165	5.6	27	3,125	8.3	42
Centre	—	—	—	—	—	—	—	—	—	—	—	—	0,019	0.1	—
Bavaria Party	—	—	—	—	—	—	—	—	—	—	—	—	0,027	0.1	—
DRP/NPD	0,207	0.6	—	0,122	0.3	—	0,067	0.2	—	0,090	0.2	—	0,226	0.6	—
Others	0,027	0.1	—	0,070	0.2	—	0,599	1.6	—	0,044	0.1	—	0,240	0.6	—

Notes: [a] Total votes gained (000s).   [c] Number of seats, excl. deputies of West Berlin.
[b] Percentage of vote.   [d] Disappeared or included in 'Others'.
Sources: Tormin, 288; Kaack, 356; Inter Nationes, 25; *Fischer Weltalmanach '84*, 282; *Das Parlament*, 11.10.1980, 31.1.1987.

Table 44. *Strikes and lock-outs, 1900–1932 (based on trade union statistics [A] and Reich statistics [B]*

Year	No. of strikes and lock-outs		No. of employees (000s)		Working days lost (000s)	
	A	B	A	B	A	B
1900	852	1,468	115,7	141,1	1,234,0	3,712,0
1901	727	1,091	48,5	68,2	1,194,5	2,427,0
1902	861	1,106	55,7	70,7	964,3	1,951,0
1903	1,282	1,444	121,6	135,5	2,622,2	4,158,0
1904	1,625	1,990	135,9	145,5	2,120,1	5,285,0
1905	2,323	2,657	508,0	542,6	7,362,8	18,984,0
1906	3,480	3,626	316,0	376,3	6,317,7	11,567,0
1907	2,792	2,512	281,0	286,0	5,122,5	9,017,0
1908	2,052	1,524	126,9	119,8	2,045,6	3,666,0
1909	45	1,652	131,2	130,9	2,247,5	4,152,0
1910	3,194	3,228	369,0	390,7	9,037,6	17,848,0
1911	2,914	2,798	325,3	385,2	6,864,2	11,466,0
1912	2,825	2,834	479,6	493,7	4,776,8	10,724,0
1913	2,600	2,464	249,0	323,4	5,672,0	11,761,0
1915		141		15,2		46,0
1916		240		128,9		245,0
1917		562		668,0		1,862,0
1918		532		391,6		1,453,0
1919		3,719		2,132,5		33,083,0
1920		3,807		1,508,4		16,755,0
1921		4,485		1,617,2		25,874,0
1922		4,755		1,895,8		27,734,0
1923		2,046		1,626,8		12,344,0
1924		1,973		1,647,1		36,198,0
1925		1,708		771,0		2,936,0
1926		351		97,1		1,222,0
1927		844		494,5		6,144,0
1928		739		775,5		20,339,0
1929		429		189,7		4,251,0
1930		353		223,9		4,029,0
1931		463		172,1		1,890,0
1932		648		129,5		1,130,0

Sources: Hohorst, 132f.; Abelshauser, 114; Bergemann, 54.

Table 45. *Strikes and lock-outs in Federal Republic, 1950–1984*[a]

Year	No. of strikes and lock-outs	No. of employees	Working days lost
1950	1,344	79,270	380,121
1951	1,528	174,325	1,592,892
1952	2,529	84,097	442,877
1953	1,395	50,625	1,488,218
1954	538	115,899	1,586,523
1955	866	597,353	846,647
1956	268	25,340	263,884
1957	86	45,134	2,385,965
1958	1,484	202,483	782,123
1959	55	21,648	61,825
1960	28	17,065	37,723
1961	119	21,052	65,256
1962	195	79,177	450,948
1963	791	316,397	1,846,025
1964	34	5,629	16,711
1965	20	6,250	48,520
1966	205	196,013	27,086
1967	742	59,604	389,581
1968	36	25,167	25,249
1969	86	89,571	249,184
1970	129	184,269	93,203
1971	1,183	536,303	4,483,740
1972	54	22,908	66,045
1973	732	185,010	563,051
1974	890	250,352	1,051,290
1975	201	35,814	68,680
1976	1,481	169,312	533,696
1977	81	34,437	23,681
1978	1,239	487,050	4,281,284
1979	40	77,326	483,083
1980	132	45,159	128,386
1981	297	253,334	58,398
1982	40	39,981	15,106
1983	114	94,070	40,842
1984	1,121	537,265	5,614,360

Note: [a] 1950–7 excl. Saar and West Berlin; 1957–9 excl. West Berlin; 1960–78 incl. West Berlin.
Source: Müller-Jentsch, 172.

Table 46. *Trade union membership, 1890–1978 (000s) and SPD membership, 1905–1984 (000s)*

Year	Free T.U.s	Christian	Hirsch-Duncker	Total	SPD
1890	278	—	63[a]	357	
1895	259	5	67	327	
1900	680	77	92	849	
1905	1,345	192	116	1,653	384[b]
1910	2,017	316	122	2,455	720
1913	2,549	343	107	3,024	983
1914	2,076	283	78	2,437	1,086
1915	1,159	176	61	1,396	
1916	967	174	58	1,199	
1917	1,107	244	79	1,430	
1918	1,665	405	114	2,184	249
1919	5,479	858	190	6,527	
1920	7,890	1,077	226	9,193	1,180
1921	7,568	986	225	8,779	
1922	7,895	1,049	231	9,175	
1923	7,138	938	216	8,292	
1924	4,618	613	147	5,378	940
1925	4,156	588	158	4,902	
1926	3,977	532	163	4,672	806
1927	4,150	606	168	4,924	
1928	4,654	647	169	5,469	867
1929	4,906	673	169	5,740	
1930	4,822	659	198	5,679	1,021
1931	4,418	578	181	5,177	
1949					736
1950	5,450[c]				
1955	6,105				
1960	6,379				
1965	6,574				649
1970	6,713				710
1975	7,365				780
1978	7,752	249			
1980	7,883				
1981	7,958				
1982	7,849				
1983	7,746				
1984	7,660				

Notes: [a] Figure for 1891.
[b] Figure for 1906.
[c] From 1950 = DGB
Sources: Groh, 734; Schönhoven, 101; Guttsman, 153; Kaack, 496; Müller-Jentsch, 91.

Table 47. *Distribution of de-Nazified persons by categories in the three Western Zones of Occupation, 1949/50 (%)*

Zone	Cat. I and II	Cat. III	Cat. IV	Cat. V	Abandoned
US	2.5	11.2	51.1	1.9	33.3
British	*	1.3	10.9	58.4	29.4
French	0.1	2.5	44.7	0.5	52.2

Source: Fürstenau, 227.

Table 48. *Numbers of foreign workers in West Germany,*[a] *1973–1983 (000s)*

Citizenship	1973	1976	1978	1980	1982	1983[b]
Total[c]	2,595	1921	1869	2072	1784	1714
Greek	250	173	147	133	116	109
Italian	450	279	289	309	259	239
Yugoslav	535	387	369	357	313	306
Portuguese	85	62	59	59	51	46
Spanish	190	108	93	86	76	72
Turkish	605	521	515	591	554	540

Notes: [a] Excl. other family members.
[b] As of 30.6.1983.
[c] Total of foreign workers; total of all foreigners in 1983 = 4.67 million.
Source: Kursbuch Deutschland 85/86, 413.

Table 49. *Structure of exports and imports by major trading partners, 1900–1985 (mill. marks)*

Country	1900	1913	1925	1930	1938[a]	1950[b]	1960[c]	1971[c]	1985[c]
Exports									
France	278	790	462	1,149	217	614	4,202	16,975	64,000
Netherlands	396	694	996	1,206	448	1,164	4,210	14,522	46,300
Britain	912	1,438	937	1,219	351	361	2,147	5,449	46,000
Italy	127	395	423	484	301	486	2,847	11,451	41,800
Belgium/Lux.	253	551	264	601	227	677	2,890	11,581	37,000
Russia/USSR	325	880	251	431	32	0	778	1,608	10,500
USA	440	714	604	685	149	430	3,723	13,140	55,600
Imports									
France	306	583	558	519	144	691	3,998	15,919	49,300
Netherlands	215	333	743	561	198	1,246	3,638	15,769	58,300
Britain	841	876	944	639	283	489	1,956	4,413	37,200
Italy	196	318	496	365	246	507	2,631	12,692	37,200
Belgium/Lux.			416	325	194	405	2,441	11,638	29,100
Russia/USSR	717	1,425	230	436	47	1	673	1,277	13,600
USA	1,021	1,711	2,196	1,307	405	1,735	5,974	12,420	32,300

Notes: [a] Reich territory at 31.12.1937
[b] Fed. Rep. excl. Saarland
[c] Fed. Rep. incl. Saarland
Sources: Kocka and Mütter, 142f.; *Die Zeit*, 28.3.1986.

Table 50. *Growth of net incomes and price rises, 1972–1985 (%)*

Year	Net incomes	Price rises[a]	Purchasing power (gains/losses)
1972	9.5	5.3	4.0
1973	7.7	6.8	0.8
1974	9.4	6.9	2.3
1975	6.8	6.1	0.7
1976	4.4	4.4	0.0
1977	5.7	3.6	2.1
1978	6.5	2.5	3.9
1979	6.1	3.9	2.1
1980	5.2	5.3	− 0.1
1981	4.5	6.3	− 1.7
1982	2.4	5.4	− 2.4
1983	2.2	3.2	− 1.0
1984	1.6	2.4	− 0.8
1985	1.7	2.1	− 0.4

Note: [a] Based on consumption patterns of medium-income employee household.
Source: Die Zeit, 21.3.1986.

Table 51. *Mobilisation of female workforce by sector, 1939–1944 (000s)*

Sector	May 1939	May 1940	May 1941	May 1942	May 1943	May 1944	Sept. 1944
Agriculture	6,049	5,689	5,369	5,537	5,665	5,694	5,756
Industry/handicrafts	3,836	3,650	3,677	3,537	3,740	3,592	3,636
Banking/commerce/ insurance/transp.	2,227	2,183	2,167	2,225	2,320	2,219	2,193
Domestic services	1,560	1,511	1,473	1,410	1,362	1,301	1,287
Publ. admin./ services	954	1,157	1,284	1,471	1,719	1,746	1,748
Total	14,626	14,386	14,167	14,437	14,806	14,808	14,897

Source: Winkler, 201.

Table 52. *West Germany's social welfare budget, 1950–1983*

Year	Budget (milliard marks)	% of GNP
1950	16.8	17.1
1960	62.8	20.7
1970	174.7	25.7
1975	347.0	33.7
1980	476.7	32.1
1983	537.2	32.3

Sources: Müller-Jentsch, 255; *Die Zeit*, 13.1.1984.

Table 53. *Number of pupils in primary and secondary schools and in vocational training colleges, 1960–1985 (000s)*

Types of school	1960	1970	1975	1978	1980	1985[a]
Grundschulen	3,096.9	3,977.3	3,912.3	3,299.7	2,764.7	2,367.2
Hauptschulen	2,122.4	2,370.2	2,512.8	2,488.9	2,322.6	1,660.1
Realschulen	430.7	863.5	1,179.9	1,350.7	1,292.7	932.3
Gymnasien	853.4	1,379.5	1,863.5	2,013.4	2,019.0	1,590.5
Sonderschulen	142.8	322.0	393.8	387.8	363.6	291.3
Gesamtschulen	–	–	165.8	206.9	206.4	208.2
Abendschulen and Kollegs	8.8	25.1	37.8	35.6	37.3	37.9
Berufs- and Berufssonderschulen	1,661.9	1,599.8	1,607.5	1,732.2	1,817.5	1,499.1
Berufsaufbauschulen	–	40.4	27.8	16.1	26.6	26.8
Berufsfachschulen	139.2	205.0	269.6	316.2	307.7	340.3
Fachoberschulen	–	59.0	118.7	113.1	130.5	140.4
Fachschulen	141.8	167.5	211.1	173.2	173.4	184.5
Berufsgrundbildungsjahr	–	–	30.5	83.5	182.1	267.9
Total	8,598.0	11,009.3	12,327.3	12,146.8	11,644.1	9,546.5

Note: [a] Estimate.
Source: Claessens et al., 366.

Table 54. *Students in higher education in West Germany, 1960–1984*

Year	Total	Universities[a]	Gesamthochschulen	Art Coll.	Fachhochschulen[b]
1960	247,000	239,000	–	7,000	–
1970	422,000	412,000	–	10,000	–
1980	1,036,000	749,000	69,000	18,000	200,000
1984	1,314,000	915,000	86,000	21,000	292,000

Notes: [a] Incl. Technical Univ., Colleges of Education and Theological Seminaries.
　　　 [b] Excl. students at former Engineering Academies.
Source: Statistisches Bundesamt, 64.

Table 55. *West Germany's largest industrial enterprises, 1984–1985*

Rank 1985	Rank 1984	Name	Branch	Turnover 1985 Mill. marks	Turnover 1985 Change from 1984 (%)	Profits (−losses) 1985	Profits (−losses) 1984	No. of employees End of 1985	No. of employees Change from 1984 (%)
1.	2.	Siemens	Electrics	54,616	19.2	1,528	1,066	348,000	6.1
2.	3.	VW	Cars	52,502	15.0	596	228	259,047	8.7
3.	4.	Daimler-Benz	Cars	52,409	20.5	1,682	1,104	231,077	15.6
4.	1.	Veba	Energy	47,523	− 2.2	790	697	68,689	−10.6
5.	6.	BASF	Chemicals	46,610	9.4	998	895	130,173	12.4
6.	5.	Bayer	Chemicals	45,926	6.7	1,436	1,174	176,080	0.8
7.	7.	Hoechst	Chemicals	42,722	3.1	1,468	1,352	180,561	1.5
8.	8.	Thyssen	Steel/Manuf. Engin.	34,784	7.3	472	181	127,969	− 3.7
9.	9.	RWE	Energy	28,426	6.2	602	575	70,249	− 0.2
10.	10.	Ruhrkohle	Mining	22,515	0.4	129	138	133,157	− 2.0
11.	12.	Bosch	Electrics	21,223	15.5	402	446	140,374	6.4
12.	11.	Deutsche Shell	Oil	19,908	6.6	466	415	3,895	− 5.7
13.	13.	Krupp	Steel/Manuf. Engin.	18,479	1.3	124	108	67,402	1.6
14.	17.	Mannesmann	Manuf. Engin.	18,170	15.2	256	188	107,804	4.0
15.	16.	BMW	Cars	18,078	9.7	—	—	53,925	3.8
16.	19.	Ruhrgas	Energy	16,711	12.8	462	434	2,958	0.7
17.	18.	Esso	Oil	16,583	7.8	190	350	3,670	− 5.3
18.	14.	Deutsche BP	Oil	15,928	− 9.4	34	7	5,860	−16.8
19.	15.	GHH	Manuf. Engin.	14,978	−10.0	502	− 59	54,887	−25.7
20.	21.	Opel	Cars	14,795	14.9	−135	−695	57,273	− 4.0

Source: Die Zeit, 15.8.1986.

Chronological table

1871	18 January	Wilhelm I proclaimed German Emperor
	16 April	Reich Constitution received
1875	22–27 May	German Social Democratic Party founded
1878	18 October	Anti-socialist laws ratified
1879	12 July	Agricultural and industrial tariffs introduced
1888	15 June	Wilhelm II becomes German Emperor
1890	15 March	Reich Chancellor Otto von Bismarck dismissed
	1 October	Anti-socialist laws lapse
1893	17 January	Franco-Russian Alliance signed
	13 July	German Army Bill ratified
1898	10 April	First Navy Law passed by Reichstag
1900	14 June	Reichstag accepts Second Navy Law
	17 October	Bernhard von Bülow becomes Reich Chancellor
1902	15 December	Agricultural tariffs increased
1903	16 June	Reichstag elections with gains for the SPD
1904	8 April	Entente Cordiale between Britain and France
1907	25 January	Reichstag elections
	31 August	Anglo-Russian Entente
1908	15 May	Reich Association Law comes into force
1909	24 March	Collapse of Bülow bloc
	14 July	Theobald von Bethmann Hollweg nominated Reich Chancellor
1910	27 May	Reform of Prussian three-class voting system fails
1912	January	SPD emerges from Reichstag elections as strongest party
	8 December	Wilhelm II calls 'War Council'
1913	30 June	German Army Bill and Tax Compromise passed
	Oct.–Nov.	Zabern Affair
1914	28 June	Assassination of Archduke Francis Ferdinand and his wife at Sarajevo
	23 July	Austro-Hungarian ultimatum handed to Serbia
	31 July	Russian general mobilisation becomes known in Berlin
	1 August	Germany declares war on Russia
	3 August	Germany declares war on France
	4 August	British Ambassador asks for passport
	5 September	First Battle of the Marne
1916	27 January	Spartacus League founded in Berlin
	31 May	Battle of Jutland

Chronological table

	December	Auxiliary Service Law introduced
1917	7 April	Wilhelm II promises reform of suffrage system
	11 April	Independent Socialists founded
	19 July	Peace Resolution by Reichstag
1918	3 March	Treaty of Brest-Litovsk
	21 March	German offensive in the west
	18 July	Allied counter-offensive begins
	3 October	Prince Max von Baden becomes Reich Chancellor
	3 November	German Fleet mutinies
	9 November	Collapse of monarchy; Ebert-Groener Pact
	11 November	Armistice signed
	15 November	Stinnes–Legien Agreement
1919	5 January	Spartacist Uprising
	19 January	National Assembly elected
	April	Soviet Republic in Bavaria
	28 June	Treaty of Versailles signed
	31 July	Weimar Constitution adopted
1920	4 February	Works' Councils Bill ratified
	13 March	Kapp Putsch
1921	24 January	Paris Conference on reparations
1922	16 April	Rapallo Agreement between Germany and Russia
	24 June	Walther Rathenau assassinated
1923	11 January	France and Belgian troops occupy Ruhr
	8 November	Hitler–Ludendorff Putsch
1924	4 May	Reichstag elections
	29 August	Reichstag approves Dawes Plan
1925	25 April	Hindenburg elected President of Weimar Republic
	1 December	Locarno Pact signed
1926	8 September	Germany joins League of Nations
1928	28 June	Cabinet of Hermann Müller formed
1929	6 August	Young Plan agreed
	3 October	Gustav Stresemann dies
1930	30 March	Heinrich Brüning becomes Reich Chancellor
	14 September	Reichstag elections with major gains by Nazis
1931	1 July	Hoover Moratorium on reparations
	11 October	Anti-Republicans meet at Bad Harzburg
1932	10 April	Hindenburg re-elected President
	1 June	Franz von Papen becomes Reich Chancellor
	20 July	Coup d'état by Papen against Prussian government
	4 December	Kurt von Schleicher succeeds Papen
1933	30 January	Adolf Hitler nominated Reich Chancellor
	27 February	Reichstag Fire
	5 March	Reichstag elections
	23 March	Enabling Act ratified
	2 May	Trade unions proscribed
	14 July	All non-Nazi parties banned
	14 October	Germany leaves League of Nations
1934	30 June	Purge of Nazi SA (Night of the Long Knives)
	19 August	Hitler proclaims himself Führer and Reich Chancellor
	24 October	German Labour Front founded

1935	17 March	Universal military service reintroduced
	15 September	Anti-Semitic Nuremberg Laws promulgated
1936	7 March	Remilitarisation of the Rhineland
	19 October	Four Year Plan
1937	5 November	Hitler outlines his views on German foreign policy
1938	11 March	Annexation of Austria
	29 September	Conference of Munich
	1 October	Germany occupies Sudetenland
	7/8 November	Anti-Semitic pogroms
1939	15 March	Germany occupies Czechoslovakia
	22 August	Nazi–Soviet Pact concluded
	1 September	Germany invades Poland
	3 September	Britain and France declare war on Germany
1940	22 June	France signs armistice with Germany
	11–18 August	Battle of Britain
1941	9 February	Rommel crosses into North Africa
	22 June	Germany invades the Soviet Union
	11 August	Atlantic Charter signed
	7 December	Japan attacks Pearl Harbor
1942	20 January	Wannsee Conference on 'Final Solution' opens
	13 February	Albert Speer takes over as Armaments Minister
	27 July	German Army reaches northern Caucasus
	December	Battle of Stalingrad
1943	27 January	Civil conscription for women
	26 July	Fall of Mussolini
	6 November	Red Army retakes Kiev
1944	2 April	Red Army enters Roumania
	6 June	Allied invasion in Normandy (D-Day)
	20 July	Stauffenberg Plot
	1 August	Warsaw Uprising begins
1945	4–11 February	Big Three confer at Yalta
	30 April	Hitler commits suicide
	7/8 May	German Armed Forces surrender to Allies
	5 June	Allied Control Commission assumed control
	17 July	Potsdam Conference of Big Four opens
	20 November	Nuremberg Trials of Major War Criminals begin
1946	21/22 April	East German SPD and KPD merge to form SED
1947	1 January	Bi-zone formed between Britain and US
	5 June	George Marshall announces ERP
1948	18 June	Currency Reform in Western zones
	24 June	Berlin Blockade begins
1949	25–28 January	First SED Party Conference (SED becomes new-type Party)
	23 May	Basic Law comes into force; Federal Republic set up
	15 September	Konrad Adenauer elected Federal Chancellor
	21 September	Occupation Statute introduced
	7 October	East German Republic founded
1950	September	German rearmament debated in public
1951	18 April	Treaty to set up European Coal and Steel Community signed
	May	Coal and Steel Co-Determination Law passed
1952	10 March	Russia proposes reunification of Germany

1953	19 March	European Defence Community approved by *Bundestag*
	17 June	Uprising in East Germany
	6 September	Adenauer wins Federal elections
1954	25 March	Soviet declaration on East German sovereignty
	3 October	West Germany invited to join NATO
	23 October	Western Allies end occupation (Germany Treaty)
1955	11–14 May	Warsaw Pact concluded with East Germany as a member
	23 September	*Bundestag* votes to resume diplomatic relations with Russia
1956	18 January	East German Army (NVA) formed
	18 August	Communist Party outlawed in West Germany
1957	25 March	Treaty of Rome signed, setting up EEC
	15 September	Adenauer gains further victory at polls
1959	5 July	Saar reincorporated into West German economy
	November	Godesberg Programme of SPD approved
1960	14 April	Collectivisation of East German agriculture completed
1961	17 August	Berlin Wall built
	17 September	Elections to the *Bundestag*
1962	Oct./Nov.	'Spiegel' Affair and subsequent government crisis in FRG
1963	24/25 June	SED approves NÖSPL economic programme
	15 October	Ludwig Erhard succeeds Adenauer as Federal Chancellor
1964	10 January	First Berlin Passes agreement between East and West Germany
1965	19 September	Federal elections
1966	11 February	Correspondence between SED and SPD begins
	30 November	Erhard resigns
	1 December	Kurt-Georg Kiesinger heads Grand Coalition Cabinet
1967	11 May	East German Minister President Willi Stoph starts correspondence with Kiesinger
1968	14 April	Student protest movements in West German universities
	30 May	*Bundestag* passes Emergency Laws (*Notstandsverfassung*)
1969	5 March	Gustav Heinemann (SPD) elected Federal President
	28 September	SPD/FDP coalition government formed after Federal elections
	21 October	Willy Brandt elected Federal Chancellor
1970	12 August	Russia and West Germany formally agree to refrain from violence in international relations
	7 December	West German–Polish Treaty signed
1971	3 May	Erich Honecker succeeds Walter Ulbricht as First Secretary of SED Central Committee
	16 September	Brandt–Breshnev talks open in Crimea
1972	27 April	Brandt survives 'constructive vote of no-confidence'
	17 May	*Bundestag* ratifies Eastern Treaties
	June	Leaders of Baader-Meinhof Gang arrested
	19 November	Federal elections; continuation of SPD/FDP coalition
1973	11 May	*Bundestag* ratifies Basic Treaty between East and West Germany
	11 December	Treaty between West Germany and Czechoslovakia; Munich Agreement of 1938 declared void
1974	16 May	Helmut Schmidt succeeds Brandt as Federal Chancellor
	3 October	Stoph becomes chairman of DDR State Council

1975	25 July	*Bundestag* approves of results of Helsinki Conference
1976	18 March	Co-determination Law ratified
	3 October	SPD/FDP coalition emerges from elections with reduced majority
	14 November	Violent clashes between police and opponents of Brokdorf nuclear power station
	15 December	Helmut Schmidt re-elected Federal Chancellor
1977	28 June	Employers file suit against Co-determination with Federal Constitutional Court
	Sept./Oct.	Height of terrorist activity (H.-M. Schleyer kidnapped; Mogadishu hostage crisis; suicides of members of Baader-Meinhof Gang)
1978	16 February	Anti-terrorist laws passed by *Bundestag*
	July	Rise of 'Green' parties in *Land* elections
1979	1 March	Constitutional Court declares Co-determination Act to be constitutional
	24 May	F.-J. Strauß announces intention to compete for Chancellorship in 1980 elections
	1 July	Karl Carstens succeeds Walther Scheel to Federal Presidency
1980	end June	Schmidt/Genscher visit to Moscow
	15 October	SPD/FDP coalition maintains majority against CDU/CSU led by Strauß
	November	Pope visits Germany for the first time in 198 years
1981	11 June	Richard von Weizsäcker elected Governing Mayor of West Berlin after CDU poll victory
	20 August	FDP chief Hans-Dietrich Genscher proclaims need for change of policy and coalition
	end November	Leonid Brezhnev visits Bonn
1982	9 May	Ronald Reagan addresses *Bundestag*
	17 September	Four FDP ministers leave Schmidt Cabinet
	1 October	Helmut Kohl elected Chancellor after successful constructive vote of no-confidence in *Bundestag*
1983	6 March	Kohl's CDU/CSU/FDP coalition obtains clear majority in national elections
	25 April	Storm over 'Hitler Diaries' breaks
	22 November	NATO's 'double track' policy on East–West relations upheld in *Bundestag* vote
1984	end January	Helmut Kohl visits Israel
	Spring	Lengthy and major industrial dispute over 35-hour week in printing and metal industries
	23 May	Richard von Weizsäcker elected Federal President
1985	early May	Reagan attends Bonn economic summit and visits Bitburg cemetery and Bergen-Belsen
	16 July	Death of Heinrich Böll
	October	'Red-Green' coalition formed in Hesse
1986	April/May	Chernobyl fall-out affects Germany
	Summer	Major public debate on growing stream of refugees seeking political asylum in West Germany

Select bibliography

This bibliography attempts to provide some further reading in English. It is arranged broadly to accord with the themes covered in the sub-sections of each chapter rather than in single alphabetical order.

Introduction

Carr, W., *A History of Germany, 1815–1945*, London 1969
Craig, G. A., *Germany, 1866–1945*, Oxford 1978
Holborn, H., *A History of Modern Germany*, 2 vols., London 1969
Mann, G., *The History of Germany Since 1789*, London 1968
Ramm, A., *Germany, 1789–1919*, London 1967
Ryder, R. J., *Twentieth-Century Germany*, London 1973

1. Wilhelmine Germany, 1900–1914

Industry and agriculture

Bade, K. (ed.), *Population, Labour and Migration in 19th- and 20th-Century Germany*, New York 1987
Barkin, K. D., *The Controversy over German Industrialization, 1890–1902*, Chicago 1970
Borchardt, K., 'Germany 1870–1914' in: C. M. Cipolla (ed.), *The Fontana Economic History of Europe*, vol 4 (I), London 1973
Bruck, W. F., *Social and Economic History of Germany, 1888–1938*, Oxford 1938
Bry, G., *Wages in Germany, 1871–1945*, Princeton 1960
Cecil, L., *Albert Ballin*, Princeton 1969
Clapham, J. H., *The Economic Development of France and Germany 1815–1914*, Cambridge 1936
Desai, A. V., *Real Wages in Germany, 1871–1913*, Oxford 1968
Evans, R. J. (ed.), *The German Peasantry*, London 1985
Farr, I., ' "*Haberfeldtreiben*" and Rural Society in the Bavarian *Oberland* in the later 19th Century', MS, 1977
Gerschenkron, A., *Bread and Democracy in Germany*, New York 1965
Henderson, W. O., *The Rise of German Industrial Power, 1834–1914*, London 1975
Lee, W. R. (ed.), *Industrialisation and Industrial Growth in Germany*, London 1986
Stern, F., *Gold and Iron*, London 1977
Stolper, G., *The German Economy from 1870 to the Present*, London 1967

318

Tilly, R., 'German Banks and German Industry', *Journal of Economic History*, 1976, 180–8.

Veblen, T., *Imperial Germany and the Industrial Revolution*, London 1915

Wehler, H.-U., *The German Empire*, Leamington Spa 1985

Wunderlich, F., *Farm Labor in Germany, 1810–1945*, Princeton 1961

State and society in Imperial Germany

Albisetti, J. C., *Secondary School Reform in Imperial Germany*, Princeton 1983

(Angel-)Volkov, S., *The Rise of Popular Antimodernism in Germany*, Princeton 1978

Blackbourn, D., 'The *Mittelstand* in German Society and Politics, 1871–1914', *Social History*, 1977, 409–33

  Class, Religion and Local Politics in Wilhelmine Germany, New Haven 1980

Cecil, L., *The German Diplomatic Service*, Princeton 1976

Crew, D., *Town in the Ruhr*, New York 1979

Dahrendorf, R., *Democracy and Society in Germany*, London 1968

Demeter, K., *The German Officer Corps*, London 1965

Eley, G., and Blackbourn, D., *The Peculiarities of German History*, Oxford 1985

Evans, R. J. (ed.), *Society and Politics in Wilhelmine Germany*, London 1978

Gellately, R., *The Politics of Economic Despair*, London 1974

Guttsman, W. L., *The German Social Democratic Party, 1875–1933*, London 1981

Herwig, H., *The German Naval Officer Corps*, Oxford 1973

Hughes, D. J., 'Occupational Origins of Prussia's Generals, 1871–1914', *Central European History*, 1980, 3–33

Iggers, G. G. (ed.), *The Social History of Politics*, Leamington Spa 1986

Jarausch, K. H., 'Liberal Education as Illiberal Socialization: The Case of Students in Imperial Germany', *Journal of Modern History*, 1978, 609–30

  Students, Society and Politics in Imperial Germany, Princeton 1982

Kaelble, H., 'Social Mobility in Germany, 1900–1960', *Journal of Modern History*, 1978, 439–61

McClellan, D., *State, Society and Universities in Germany, 1700–1914*, Cambridge 1980

Ringer, F. K., *The Decline of the German Mandarins*, Cambridge (Mass.) 1969

Ritter, G. A., *Social Welfare in Germany and Britain*, Leamington Spa 1986

Röhl, J. C. G., 'Higher Civil Servants in Germany, 1890–1900', *Journal of Contemporary History*, 1967, 101–21

Sagarra, E., *A Social History of Germany, 1648–1914*, London 1977

Snell, J. L., *The Democratic Movement in Germany, 1789–1914*, Chapel Hill 1976

Spencer, E. G., 'Employer Response to Unionism', *Journal of Modern History*, 1976, 397–412

Spree, R., *Health and Social Class in Imperial Germany*, New York 1987

Witt, P.-C. (ed.), *Wealth and Taxation in Central Europe*, Leamington Spa 1987

Parliamentary and extra-parliamentary politics

Chickering, R., *Imperial Germany and a World Without War*, Princeton 1975

  We Men Who Feel Most German, London 1984

Eley, G., *Reshaping the German Right*, New Haven 1980

  From Unification to Nazism, London 1985

Epstein, K., *Matthias Erzberger and the Dilemma of German Democracy*, Princeton 1959

Evans, E. L., *The German Center Party*, Carbondale 1981

Select bibliography

Levy, R. S., *The Downfall of the Anti-Semitic Political Parties in Imperial Germany*, New Haven 1975

Mosse, G. L., *The Nationalization of the Masses*, New York 1975

Nichols, J. A., *Germany After Bismarck*, Cambridge (Mass.) 1958

Peck, A., *Radicals and Reactionaries*, New York 1979

Pulzer, P. J., *The Rise of Political Antisemitism in Germany and Austria*, New York 1964

Röhl, J. C. G., *Germany Without Bismarck*, London 1967

Sheehan, J., *German Liberalism in the 19th Century*, Chicago 1978

Sperber, J., *Popular Catholicism in 19th-Century Germany*, Princeton 1984

Suval, S., *Electoral Politics in Wilhelmine Germany*, Chapel Hill 1985

Tirrell, S. R., *German Agrarian Politics After Bismarck's Fall*, New York 1971

Zeender, J. K., *The German Center Party, 1890–1906*, Philadelphia 1976

(Social Democracy)

Evans, R. J. (ed.), *The German Working Class*, London 1982

Fletcher, R., *Revisionism and Empire*, London 1984

Gay, P., *The Dilemma of Democratic Socialism*, New York 1962

Guttsman, W. L., *The German Social Democratic Party, 1875–1933*, London 1981

Hall, A., *Scandal, Sensation and Social Democracy*, Cambridge 1977

Lidtke, V., *The Alternative Culture*, Oxford 1985

The Outlawed Party, Princeton 1965

Moses, J. A., *German Trade Unionism from Bismarck to Hitler*, 2 vols., London 1981

Roth, G., *The Social Democrats of Imperial Germany*, Totowa 1961

Schorske, C. E., *Germany Social Democracy, 1905–1917*, New York 1972

(Women and the family)

Evans, R. J., *The Feminist Movement in Germany, 1894–1933*, London 1976

'German Social Democracy and Women's Suffrage, 1891–1918', *Journal of Contemporary History*, 1980, 533–57

Evans, R. J., and Lee, W. R. (eds.), *The German Family*, London 1980

Hackett, A. K., *The Politics of Feminism in Wilhelmine Germany, 1890–1918*, New York 1979

Quaetert, J. H., *Reluctant Feminists in German Social Democrracy*, Princeton 1979

(Youth)

Becker, H., *German Youth. Bond or Free*, London 1946

Laqueur, W., *Young Germany*, New York 1962

Stachura, P. D., *The German Youth Movement, 1900–1945*, London 1981

(Cultural life)

Allen, A. T., *Satire and Society in Wilhelmine Germany*, Louisville 1985

Gray, R., *The German Tradition in Literature*, Cambridge 1965

Pascal, R., *From Naturalism to Expressionism*, New York 1973

Select bibliography

Weltpolitik *and the spectre of encirclement*

Anderson, P. R., *The Background to Anti-English Feeling in Germany, 1890–1902*, Washington 1939
Balfour, M., *The Kaiser and His Times*, London 1964
Berghahn, V. R., *Germany and the Approach of War in 1914*, London 1973
Crothers, G. D., *The German Elections of 1907*, New York 1967
Dehio, L., *Germany and World Politics in the 20th Century*, New York 1959
Eley, G., 'Sammlungspolitik, Social Imperialism and the Navy Law of 1898', *Militärgeschichtliche Mitteilungen*, 1974, 29–63
Fink, C., et al. (eds.), *German Nationalism and the European Response, 1890–1945*, London 1985
Fischer, F., *War of Illusions*, London 1975
Geiss, I., *German Foreign Policy, 1871–1914*, London 1976
Gordon, M., 'Domestic Conflict and the Origins of the First World War', *Journal of Modern History*, 1974, 191–226
Heckart, B., *From Bassermann to Bebel*, New Haven 1974
Hull, I. V., *The Kaiser and his Entourage*, Cambridge 1982
Jarausch, K., *The Enigmatic Chancellor*, New Haven 1973
Kehr, E., *Battleship Building and Party Politics in Germany*, Chicago 1973
  Economic Interest, Militarism and Foreign Policy, Berkeley 1977
Kennedy, P. M., *The Rise of the Anglo-German Antagonism*, London 1980
Lambi, I., *The Navy and German Power Politics, 1862–1914*, London 1984
McClellan, D., *The German Historians and England*, Cambridge 1971
Mommsen, W. J., 'Domestic Factors in German Foreign Policy before 1914', *Central European History*, 1973, 3–43
Röhl, J., and Sombart, N. (eds.), *Kaiser Wilhelm II*, Cambridge 1982
Smith, W. D., *The German Colonial Empire*, Chapel Hill 1978

2. War and civil war, 1914–1923

The beginning of the First World War

Clarke, I. F., *Voices Prophesying War*, London 1970
Farrar Jr, L. L., *The Short-War Illusion*, Santa Barbara 1973
Fischer, F., *War of Illusions*, London 1975
Kennedy, P. M., (ed.), *The War Plans of the Great Powers, 1880–1914*, London 1979
Kitchen, M., *A Military History of Germany*, London 1975
Ritter, G., *The Sword and the Sceptre*, London 1973
Stone, N., *The Eastern Front*, London 1975

The strains of total war

Armeson, R. B., *Total War and Compulsory Labor*, The Hague 1964
Berghahn, V. R., and Kitchen, M. (eds.), *Germany in the Age of Total War*, London 1981
Englander, D., 'The Armed Forces and the Working Class', *Historical Journal*, 1978, 593–622
Feldman, G. D., *Army, Industry and Labor in Germany, 1914–1918*, Princeton 1966
Fussell, P., *The Great War and Modern Memory*, Oxford 1975

Select bibliography

Kocka, J., 'The First World War and the Mittelstand', *Journal of Contemporary History*, 1973, 101–23
Leed, E. J., *No Man's Land*, Cambridge 1979
Mendelssohn-Bartholdy, A., *The War and German Society*, New York 1971

Reaction, reform and revolutionary ferment

Carsten, F. L., *War Against War*, London 1982
Epstein, K., *Matthias Erzberger and the Dilemma of German Democracy*, Princeton 1959
Fedyshin, O. S., *Germany's Drive to the East and the Ukrainian Revolution, 1917–1918*, New Brunswick 1971
Fischer, F., *Germany's War Aims in the First World War*, London 1969
Gatzke, H., *Germany's Drive to the West*, Baltimore 1950
Goodspeed, D. J., *Ludendorff*, London 1966
Horn, D. (ed.), *War, Mutiny and Revolution in the German Navy. The World War I Diary of Seaman Richard Stumpf*, New Brunswick 1967
Jarausch, K., *The Enigmatic Chancellor*, New Haven 1973
Kitchen, M., *The Silent Dictatorship*, London 1976
Kocka, J., *Facing Total War*, Leamington Spa 1984
Meyer, H. C., *Mitteleuropa in German Thought and Action*, The Hague 1955
Wheeler-Bennett, J., *Brest Litovsk. The Forgotten Peace*, London 1938

The Revolutions of 1918/19

Berlau, A. J., *German Social Democracy, 1914–1921*, New York 1949
Burdick, C. B., and Lutz, R. H., *The Political Institutions of the German Revolution*, Stanford 1968
Carsten, F. L., *Reichswehr and Politics*, Oxford 1966
  Revolution in Central Europe, London 1972
Comfort, R. A., *The Politics of Labor in Hamburg, 1918–1924*, Princeton 1962
Horn, D., *The German Naval Mutinies of World War I*, New Brunswick 1969
Mishark, J. W., *The Road to Revolution*, Detroit 1967
Mitchell, A., *Revolution in Bavaria*, Princeton 1965
Morgan, D. W., *The Socialist Left and the German Revolution*, Ithaca 1975
Rosenberg, A., *A History of the German Republic*, London 1936
Rürup, R., 'Problems of the German Revolution', *Journal of Contemporary History*, 1968, 109–26
Ryder, A. J., *The German Revolution of 1918*, Cambridge 1967
Waldman, E., *The Spartacist Uprising*, Marquette 1958

Economic dislocation and counter-revolution

Bresciano-Turroni, C., *The Economics of Inflation*, London 1937
Feldman, G. D., 'Economic and Social Problems of German De-Mobilization, 1918–1919', *Journal of Modern History*, 1975, 1–47
  Iron and Steel in the German Inflation, Princeton 1977
Felix, D., *Walter Rathenau and the Weimar Republic: The Politics of Reparations*, Baltimore 1971
Fergusson, A., *When Money Dies*, London 1975
Graham, F., *Exchange, Prices and Production in Hyperinflation Germany*, Princeton 1930

Holtfrerich, C. L., *The German Inflation, 1914–1923*, Berlin 1985
Jones, L. E., 'Inflation, Revaluation and the Crisis of Middle-Class Politics', *Central European History*, 1979, 143–68
Keynes, J. M., *The Economic Consequences of the Peace Treaty*, London 1919
Laursen, K., and Pedersen, J., *The German Inflation, 1918–1923*, Amsterdam 1964
Maier, C. S., *Recasting Bourgeois Europe*, Princeton 1975
Mantoux, E., *The Carthaginian Peace*, London 1946
Marks, S., 'The Myths of Reparations', *Central European History*, 1978, 231–55
Moeller, R. G., *German Peasants and Conservative Agrarian Politics, 1914–1924*, Chapel Hill 1985
Nicholls, A. J., *Weimar and the Rise of Hitler*, London 1968
Ringer, F. K. (ed.), *The German Inflation of 1923*, New York 1969
Schmidt, R. J., *Versailles and the Ruhr*, London 1968
Wheeler-Bennett, J., *The Wreck of Reparations*, London 1933

(Counter-revolution)

Angress, S., *The Stillborn Revolution: The Communist Bid for Power in Germany, 1921–1923*, Princeton 1963
Cornebise, A. E., *The Weimar Republic in Crisis: Cuno's Germany and the Ruhr Occupation*, Washington 1977
Gordon, H. J., *The Reichswehr and the German Republic*, Princeton 1957
Hitler and the Beer Hall Putsch, Princeton 1972
Rupieper, H.-J., *The Cuno Government and Reparations*, The Hague 1979
Waite, R. G. L., *Vanguard of Nazism*, Cambridge (Mass.) 1952

3. *The Weimar Republic, 1924–1933*

Intellectual and cultural activity

Bullivant, K. (ed.), *Culture and Society in the Weimar Republic*, Manchester 1978
Deak, I., *Weimar Germany's Leftwing Intellectuals*, Stanford 1968
Gay, P., *Weimar Culture*, New York 1968
Guttsman, W. L., *The German Social Democratic Party, 1875–1933*, London 1981
Herf, J., *Reactionary Modernism*, Cambridge 1984
Klemperer, K. von, *Germany's New Conservatism*, Princeton 1957
Laqueur, W., *Weimar: A Cultural History*, New York 1975
Manvell, R., and Fraenkel, H., *The German Cinema*, London 1971
Mosse, G. L., *The Crisis of German Ideology*, New York 1964
Patterson, M., *The Revolution in German Theatre, 1900–1933*, London 1981
Stern, F., *The Politics of Cultural Despair*, New York 1961
Taylor, R., *Literature and Society in Germany, 1918–1945*, Brighton 1980

Party politics

Dorpalen, A., *Hindenburg and the Weimar Republic*, Princeton 1964
Eschenburg, T., *et al.*, *Road to Dictatorship*, London 1970
Eyck, E., *A History of the Weimar Republic*, 2 vols., London 1962
Fischer, R., *Stalin and German Communism*, Cambridge (Mass.) 1948
Fowkes, B., *Communism in Germany Under the Weimar Republic*, London 1984

Select bibliography

Gratwohl, R. P., *Stresemann and the DNVP*, Lawrence 1980
Hertzman, L., *DNVP*, Lincoln (Nebr.) 1963
Hunt, R. N., *German Social Democracy, 1918–1933*, New Haven 1964
Nicholls, A. J., and Matthias, E. (eds.), *German Democracy and the Triumph of Hitler*, London 1971
Wheeler-Bennett, J., *The Wooden Titan*, London 1936

Weimar foreign policy

Bretton, H. L., *Stresemann and the Revision of Versailles*, Stanford 1953
Cornebise, A. E., 'Gustav Stresemann and the Ruhr Occupation', *European Studies Review*, 1972, 43–67
Dawson, P., *Germany's Industrial Revival*, London 1938
Dyck, H. L., *Weimar Germany and Soviet Russia*, London 1966
Freund, G., *The Unholy Alliance, 1918–1926*, London 1957
Gatzke, H., *Stresemann and the Rearmament of Germany*, Baltimore 1954
Haigh, R. H., *et al.*, *German-Soviet Relations in the Weimar Era*, Aldershot 1986
Homer, F. X. J., and Wilcox, L. D. (eds.), *Germany and Europe in the Era of Two World Wars*, Charlottesville 1986
Jacobson, J., *Locarno Diplomacy*, Princeton 1971
Laqueur, W., *Russia and Germany*, London 1965
Lee, M., and Michalka, W., *German Foreign Policy*, Leamington Spa 1987
Post Jr, G., *The Civil–Military Fabric of Weimar Foreign Policy*, Princeton 1973
Stehlin, S. A., *Weimar and the Vatican, 1918–1933*, Princeton 1983
Turner, H. A., *Stresemann and the Politics of the Weimar Republic*, Princeton 1963

Economic tensions and the rise of the Nazis

Abraham, D., *The Collapse of the Weimar Republic*, Princeton 1981
Bessel, R., and Feuchtwanger, E. J. (eds.), *Social Change and Political Development in Weimar Germany*, London 1981
Brady, R., *The Rationalization Movement in German Industry*, Berkeley 1933
Coyner, S. J., 'Class Consciousness and Consumption: the New Middle Class during the Weimar Republic', *Journal of Social History*, 1977, 310–37
Evans, R. J., and Geary, D. (eds.), *The German Unemployed, 1918–1936*, London 1986
Farquharson, J. E., *The Plough and the Swastika*, London 1976
Feldman, G. D., 'Big Business and the Kapp Putsch', *Central European History*, 1971, 99–130
Fromm, E., *The Working Class in Weimar Germany*, Leamington Spa 1984
Gessner, D., 'Agrarian Protectionism in the Weimar Republic', *Journal of Contemporary History*, 1977, 759–78
Holt, J., *German Agricultural Policy, 1918–1934*, Chapel Hill 1936
Patch. W. L., *Christian Trade Unions in the Weimar Republic*, New Haven 1985
Pool, J., and Pool, S., *Who Financed Hitler?* London 1979
Sohn-Rethel, A., *Economy and Class Structure of German Fascism*, London 1978
Stachura, P. D. (ed.), *Unemployment and the Great Depression in Weimar Germany*, London 1986
Thyssen, F., *I Paid Hitler*, London 1941
Turner, H. A., 'Emil Kirdorf and the Nazi Party', *Central European History*, 1968, 324–44

'Big Business and the Rise of Hitler', *American Historical Review*, 1969, 56–70

'The *Ruhrlade*', *Central European History*, 1970, 195–228

German Big Business and the Rise of Hitler, Oxford 1985

Weisbrod, B., 'Economic Power and Political Stability Reconsidered', *Social History*, 1979, 241–63

Winkler, H. A., 'From Social Protectionism to National Socialism', *Journal of Modern History*, 1976, 1–18

(Rise of Nazism)

Fest, J., *Hitler*, London 1974

Kater, M. H., *The Nazi Party*, Cambridge (Mass.) 1983

Merkl, P. H., *The Making of a Storm-Trooper*, Princeton 1980

Noakes, J., *The Nazi Party in Lower Saxony*, Oxford 1971

Nyomarkay, J., *Charisma and Factionalism in the Nazi Party*, Minneapolis 1967

Orlow, D., *The History of the Nazi Party*, 2 vols., Newton Abbot 1973

Pridham, G., *Hitler's Rise to Power*, London 1973

(Social basis of Nazism)

Angress, W., 'The Political Role of the Peasantry in the Weimar Republic', *Review of Politics*, 1959, 530–50

Bessel, R., *Political Violence and the Rise of Nazism*, New Haven 1984

Chanady, A. 'The Disintegration of the German National People's Party, 1924–1930', *Journal of Modern History*, 1967, 67–90

Childers, T., 'The Social Bases of the National Socialist Vote', *Journal of Contemporary History*, 1976, 17–42

The Nazi Voter, Chapel Hill 1984

(ed.), *The Formation of the Nazi Constituency, 1918–1933*, London 1986

Fischer, C., *Stormtroopers*, London 1983

Hamilton, R. F., *Who Voted for Hitler?* Princeton 1981

Jones, L. E., 'The Dying Middle', *Central European History*, 1972, 23–54

Kele, M. H., *Nazis and Workers*, Chapel Hill 1972

Lebovics, H., *Social Conservatism and the Middle Classes in Germany*, Princeton 1969

McKibbin, R., 'The Myth of the Unemployed', *Australian Journal of Politics and History*, 1969, 25–40

Mühlberger, D., 'The Sociology of the NSDAP', *Journal of Contemporary History*, 1980, 493–511

O'Lessker, K., 'Who Voted for Hitler?' *American Journal of Sociology*, 1968/69, 63–9

Shively, W. P., 'Party Identification, Party Choice and Voting Stability', *American Political Science Review*, 1972, 1203–25

Speier, H., *German White-Collar Workers and the Rise of Hitler*, New Haven 1986

From Brüning to Hitler

Bennett, F. W., *Germany and the Diplomacy of the Financial Crisis*, Cambridge (Mass.) 1962

Breitman, R., 'German Social Democracy and General Schleicher', *Central European History*, 1976, 352–78

Broszat, M., *Hitler and the Collapse of Weimar Germany*, Leamington Spa 1987

Select bibliography

Clark, R. T., *The Fall of the German Republic*, New York 1964

Diehl, J. M., *Paramilitary Politics in Weimar Germany*, Bloomington 1977

Dobrowski, M. N., and Wallimann, I. (eds.), *Towards the Holocaust. The Social and Economic Collapse of the Weimar Republic*, Westport (Conn.) 1983

Eksteins, M., *The Limits of Reason*, London 1975

Gates, R. A., 'German Socialism and the Crisis of 1929–1933', *Central European History*, 1974, 332–59

Halperin, S. W., *Germany Tried Democracy*, London 1946

Hayes, P., 'A Question Mark with Epaulettes? Kurt von Schleicher and Weimar Politics', *Journal of Modern History*, 1980, 35–65

James, H., *The Reichsbank and Public Finance in Germany, 1924–1933*, Frankfurt 1985
The German Slump, Oxford 1986

Petzina, D., 'Germany and the Great Depression', *Journal of Contemporary History*, 1969, 59–74

Stachura, P. D., 'The Political Strategy of the Nazi Party', *German Political Studies*, 1980, 261–88

Winkler, H. A., 'German Society, Hitler and the Illusion of Restoration, 1930–1933', *Journal of Contemporary History*, 1976, 1–16

4. The Third Reich, 1933–1945

The face of the Nazi dictatorship

Allen, W. S., *The Nazi Seizure of Power*, Chicago 1965

Bessel, R., 'The rise of the NSDAP and the Myth of Nazi Propaganda', *Wiener Library Bulletin*, 1980, 20–9

Beyerchen, A. D., *Scientists Under Hitler*, New Haven 1977

Bleuel, H. P., *Sex and Society in Nazi Germany*, Philadelphia 1973

Fest, J., *The Face of the Third Reich*, London 1970

Giles, G. J., *Students and National Socialism in Germany*, Princeton 1986

Grunberger, R., *A Social History of the Third Reich*, London 1974

Koch, H. J., *The Hitler Youth*, London 1975

Mosse, G. L., *Nazi Culture*, New York 1966

Noakes, J. (ed.), *Government, Party and the People in Nazi Germany*, Exeter 1980

Pois, R. A., *National Socialism and the Religion of Nature*, London 1986

Ritchie, J. M., *German Literature under National Socialism*, London 1983

Schoenbaum, D., *Hitler's Social Revolution*, London 1967

Stachura, P. D., *The German Youth Movement, 1900–1945*, London 1981
    (ed.), *The Nazi Machtergreifung*, London 1983

Steinberg, M. S., *Sabres and Brownshirts*, Chicago 1977

Weber, R. G. S., *The German Student Corps in the Third Reich*, London 1986

Welch, D., *Nazi Propaganda*, London 1983

(Explanations of Nazism)

Aygoberry, P., *The Nazi Question*, London 1979

Hiden, J., and Farquharson, J., *Explaining Hitler's Germany*, London 1983

Hildebrand, K., *The Third Reich*, London 1984

Kershaw, I., *The Nazi Dictatorship*, London 1985

(Women)

Bridenthal, R., *et al.* (eds.), *When Biology Became Destiny*, New York 1984
Evans, R. J., 'German Women and the Triumph of Hitler', *Journal of Modern History*, 1976 (microfilm)
Mason, T., 'Women in Nazi Germany', *History Workshop*, 1976, I:74–113 and II:5–32
Rupp, L., *Mobilizing Women for War*, Princeton 1978
Stephenson, J., *Women in Nazi Society*, London 1975
  The Nazi Organisation of Women, London 1981

(Churches)

Conway, J. S., *The Nazi Persecution of the Churches*, London 1968
Helmreich, E. C., *The German Churches under Hitler*, Detroit 1979
Lewy, G., *The German Catholic Church and Nazi Germany*, London 1964
Rhodes, A., *The Vatican in the Age of the Dictators*, London 1973
Walker, L. D., *Hitler Youth and Catholic Youth, 1933–1936*, New York 1979
Wright, J. R. C., *Above Parties*, Oxford 1974
Zahn, G., *German Catholics and Hitler's Wars*, London 1962

Economic conditions and mobilisation for war

Borkin, J., *The Crime and Punishment of I. G. Farben*, London 1979
Deist, W., *The Wehrmacht and German Rearmament*, London 1981
Farquharson, J. E., *The Plough and the Swastika*, London 1976
Klein, B. H., *Germany's Economic Preparations for War*, Cambridge (Mass.) 1959
Mason, T. W., 'Some Origins of the Second World War', *Past and Present*, 1964, 67–87
  'Labour in the Third Reich', *Past and Present*, 1966, 112–41
  'The Primacy of Politics', in S. J. Woolf (ed.), *The Nature of Fascism*, New York 1969, 165–95
Müller, K.-J., 'The Army in the Third Reich', *Journal of Strategic Studies*, 1979, 123–52
O'Neill, R., *The German Army and the Nazi Party*, London 1966
Overy, R., *The Nazi Economic Recovery, 1932–1938*, London 1982
Schweitzer, A., *Big Business in the Third Reich*, New York 1972
Sweezy, M., 'German Corporate Profits, 1926–1938', *Quarterly Journal of Economics*, 1940, 384–98
Turner, H. A. (ed.), *Nazism and the Third Reich*, New York 1972
Wheeler-Bennett, J., *The Nemesis of Power*, London 1953
Witt, T. E. de, 'The Economics and Politics of Welfare in the Third Reich', *Central European History*, 1978, 256–78

Nazi foreign policy and Hitler

Carr, W., *Arms, Autarky and Aggression*, London 1972
Compton, J. V., *The Swastika and the Eagle*, Boston 1967
Friedländer, S., *Prelude to Downfall*, New York 1967
Hildebrand, K., *The Foreign Policy of the Third Reich*, London 1973
Hitler, A., *Mein Kampf*, London 1969
Jäckel, E., *Hitler's Weltanschauung*, Middletown 1972
Leach, B., *German Strategy Against Russia*, Oxford 1973

Select bibliography

Rich, N., *Hitler's War Aims*, 2 vols., New York 1973
Schmokel, W. W., *Dream of Empire*, New Haven 1964
Stoakes, G., *Hitler and the Quest for World Dominion*, Leamington Spa 1987
Trevor-Roper, H. R. (ed.), *Hitler's Table Talks*, London 1953
Weinberg, G. L., *The Foreign Policy of Hitler's Germany*, Chicago 1970

(Biographies)

Binion, R., *Hitler among the Germans*, New York 1976
Bullock, A., *Hitler*, New York 1964
Carrr, W., *Hitler*, London 1978
Fest, J., *Hitler*, London 1974
Stone, N., *Hitler*, London 1980
Waite, R. G. L., *The Psychopathic God*, New York 1977

(Structure of the regime)

Bracher, K. D., *The German Dictatorship*, New York 1970
Broszat, M., *Hitler's State*, London 1981
Fraenkel, E., *The Dual State*, New York 1969
Hirschfeld, G., and Kettenacker, L. (eds.), *The 'Führer State'*, Stuttgart 1980
Koehl, R., *The Black Corps*, Middletown (Conn.) 1983
Neumann, F., *Behemoth*, New York 1966
Peterson, E. N., *The Limits of Hitler's Power*, Princeton 1969
Stachura, P. D., *The Shaping of the Nazi State*, London 1978

Occupation, exploitation and extermination

Bartov, O., *The Eastern Front, 1941–1945*, London 1986
Dallin, A., *German Rule in Russia, 1941–1945*, London 1957
Gross, J. T., *Polish Society under German Occupation*, Princeton 1979
Höhne, H., *The Order of the Death's Head*, London 1969
Homze, E. L., *Foreign Labour in Nazi Germany*, Princeton 1967
Kogon, E., *The Theory and Practice of Hell*, London 1950
Krausnick, H., *et al.*, *Anatomy of the SS State*, London 1968
Milward, A., *The New Order and the French Economy*, Oxford 1970
  The Fascist Economy of Norway, Oxford 1972
Reitlinger, G., *The SS*, New York 1957
  The House Built on Sand, New York 1960
Warmbrunn, W., *The Dutch under German Occupation*, Stanford 1963

(Nazism and the Jews)

Arendt, H., *Eichmann in Jerusalem*, New York 1963
Baum, R. C., *The Holocaust and the German Elite*, London 1982
Dawidowicz, L. S., *The War Against the Jews, 1939–1945*, Harmondsworth 1976
Fleming, G., *Hitler and the Final Solution*, Stanford 1984
Gordon, S., *Hitler, Germans and the 'Jewish Question'*, Princeton 1984
Hilberg, R., *The Destruction of the European Jews*, London 1961
Laqueur, W., *The Terrible Secret*, London 1980

Massing, P., *Rehearsal for Destruction*, New York 1967
Mosse, G. L., *Germans and Jews*, London 1971
Reitlinger, G., *The Final Solution*, London 1953
Schleunes, K., *The Twisted Road to Auschwitz*, Champaign–Urbana 1970
Sereny, G., *Into That Darkness*, London 1974
Steiner, J. M., *Power Politics and Social Change*, The Hague 1976
Stokes, K. D., 'The German People and the Destruction of the European Jews', *Central European History*, 1973, 167–91
Trunk, I., *Judenrat*, New York 1977

The final years

Baird, J. W., *The Mythical World of Nazi War Propaganda*, Minneapolis 1974
Balfour, M., *Propaganda in War*, London 1979
Bramsted, E. K., *Goebbels and National Socialist Propaganda*, London 1965
Hale, O. J., *Captive Press in the Third Reich*, Princeton 1964
Milward, A. S., *The German Economy at War*, London 1965
Speer, A., *Inside the Third Reich*, London 1970
Zeman, Z. A. B., *Nazi Propaganda*, London 1973

(The German resistance)

Deutsch, H. C., *The Conspiracy against Hitler in the Twilight War*, London 1968
Graml, H., et al., *The German Resistance to Hitler*, London 1970
Prittie, T., *Germans Against Hitler*, London 1964
Ritter, G., *The German Resistance*, London 1958

5. Occupation and division, 1945–1960

The Western Zones of Occupation

Balabkins, N., *Germany under Direct Controls*, New Brunswick 1964
Balfour, M., *Four-Power Control in Germany and Austria*, London 1956
Braunthal, G., 'The Anglo-Saxon Model of Democracy in the West German Political Consciousness after World War II', *Archiv für Sozialgeschichte*, 1978, 245–77
Clay, L. D., *Decision in Germany*, London 1950
Edinger, L. J., *Kurt Schumacher*, Stanford 1965
Farquharson, J., *The Western Allies and the Politics of Food*, Leamington Spa 1985
FitzGibbon, C., *Denazification*, London 1969
Gimbel, J., *The American Occupation of Germany*, Stanford 1968
The Origins of the Marshall Plan, Stanford 1976
Kennedy, E., *After the Holocaust*, London 1981
Marshall, B., 'German Attitudes to British Military Government, 1945–1947', *Journal of Contemporary History*, 1980, 655–81
Merritt, A. J., and Merritt, R. L., *Public Opinion in Occupied Germany*, Champaign-Urbana 1970
Peterson, E. N., *The American Occupation of Germany*, Detroit 1977
Pronay, V., and Wilson, K. (eds.), *The Political Re-education of Germany and Her Allies after World War II*, London 1985

Select bibliography

Schlauch, W., 'American Policy Towards Germany in 1945', *Journal of Contemporary History*, 1970, 113–28
Schmitt, H. A. (ed.), *U.S. Occupation in Europe after World War II (Papers and Reminiscences)*, Lawrence 1973
Spotts, F., *Churches and Politics in Germany*, Middletown 1973
Tent, J. F., *Mission on the Rhine*, Chicago 1983
Zayas, A. de, *Nemesis at Potsdam*, New York 1975
Zeitschrift für die gesamte Staatswissenschaft, Special Issue in English on German Economic Reconstruction, 3/1979
Zink, H., *The United States in Germany*, Westpoint 1957

The Soviet Zone of Occupation and East Germany

Baring, A., *Uprising in East Germany*, Ithaca 1972
Childs, D., *East Germany*, London 1969
Krisch, H., *German Politics under Soviet Occupation*, New York 1974
Leonhard, W., *Child of the Revolution*, London 1956
Nettl, J. P., *The Eastern Zone and Soviet Policy in Germany, 1945–1950*, Oxford 1951
Sanford, G. W., *From Hitler to Ulbricht*, Princeton 1983
Stern, C., *Ulbricht*, London 1965

The shaping of the Federal Republic, 1949–1960

Adenauer, K., *Memoirs*, London 1966
Almond, G., 'The Political Attitudes of German Business', *World Politics*, 1955/6, 157–86
Arndt, H.-J., *West Germany: Politics of Non-planning*, New York 1973
Balfour, M., *West Germany*, London 1968
Berghahn, V. R., *The Americanisation of West German Industry, 1945–1973*, Leamington Spa 1986
Braunthal, G., *The Federation of German Industry in Politics*, Ithaca 1965
Bunn, R. F., 'The Federation of German Employers' Associations', *Western Political Quarterly*, 1960, 652–69
Childs, D., *From Schumacher to Brandt*, Oxford 1966
Cullingford, E. C. M., *Trade Unions in West Germany*, London 1973
Edinger, L. J., 'Post-Totalitarian Leadership. Elites in the German Federal Republic', *American Political Science Review*, 1960, 58–82
  'Continuity and Change in the Background of German Decision-Makers', *Western Political Quarterly*, 1961, 17–36
Erhard, L., *Prosperity Through Competition*, London 1958
Golay, J. F., *Founding the Federal Republic of Germany*, Chicago 1958
Graf, W. D., *The German Left Since 1945*, Cambridge 1976
Grosser, A., *The Federal Republic of Germany*, New York 1964
Hartmann, H., *Authority and Organization in German Management*, Princeton 1959
Heidenheimer, A., *Adenauer and the CDU*, The Hague 1960
Loewenberg, G., *Parliament in the German Political System*, Ithaca 1967
Merkl, P. H., *The Origins of the West German Republic*, Oxford 1963
Pridham, G., *Christian Democracy in Western Germany*, London 1977
Prittie, T., *Adenauer*, London 1972
Spiro, H. J., *The Politics of German Codetermination*, Cambridge (Mass.) 1958

Stahl, W. (ed.), *The Politics of Postwar Germany*, New York 1963
Tauber, K. P., *Beyond Eagle and Swastika*, 2 vols., Middletown (Conn.) 1967
Thayer, C. W., *The Unquiet Germans*, New York 1957
Tilford, R. B., and Preece, R. J., *Federal Germany*, London 1969
Wallich, H. C., *Mainsprings of the German Revival*, New Haven 1955
Wighton, C., *Adenauer. Democratic Dictator*, London 1963

Foreign policy and rearmament

Bölling, K., *Republic in Suspense*, New York 1964
Hanrieder, W. F., *West German Foreign Policy, 1949–1963*, Stanford 1967
  The Stable Crisis, New York 1970
Kelleher, C. M., *Germany and the Politics of Nuclear Weapons*, New York 1975
Knorr, K. (ed.), *Nato and U.S. Security*, New York 1959
Paterson, W. E., *The SPD and European Integration*, Lexington 1974
Smith, J. E., *The Defense of Berlin*, Baltimore, 1963
Speier, H., *German Rearmament and Atomic Warfare*, Evanston 1957
Windsor, P., *City on Leave*, London 1963
  German Reunification, London 1969

6. The two Germanies since the 1960s

Economics and politics in East Germany

Bahro, R., *The Alternative in Eastern Europe*, London 1978
Baylis, T., *The Technical Intelligentsia and the East German Elite*, Berkeley 1974
Childs, D., *The GDR. Moscow's German Ally*, London 1983
  (ed.), *Honecker's Germany*, London 1985
Edwards, G. E., *GDR. Society and Social Institutions*, London 1985
Forster, T. M., *The East German Army*, London 1980
Hangen, W., *The Muted Revolution*, New York 1966
Honecker, E., *From My Life*, London 1981
Krisch, H., *The German Democratic Republic*, Boulder 1981
Legters, L. H. (ed.), *The GDR*, Boulder 1978
Leptin, G., *Economic Reform in East German Industry*, Oxford 1978
Ludz, P. C., *The Changing Party Elite in East Germany*, Cambridge (Mass.) 1973
McCardle, A. W., *East Germany*, London 1984
McCauley, M., *Marxism-Leninism in the German Democratic Republic*, London 1979
  The German Democratic Republic since 1945, New York 1983
Moore-Rinvolucri, M. J., *Education in East Germany*, London 1973
Sontheimer, K., and Bleek, W., *The Government and Politics of East Germany*, London 1975
Steele, J., *Socialism with a German Face*, London 1977
Woods, R., *Opposition in the GDR under Honecker, 1971–1975*, London 1986

West Germany and the international system

Berghahn, V. R., *The Americanisation of West German Industry*, New York 1986
Calleo, D., *The German Problem Reconsidered*, Cambridge 1979

Select bibliography

Cooney, J. A., et al. (eds.), *The Federal Republic of Germany and the United States*, Boulder 1984

Crawley, A., *The Rise of Western Germany*, London 1973

Griffith, W., F., *The Ostpolitik of the Federal Republic of Germany*, Cambridge (Mass.) 1978

Grosser, A., *Germany in Our Time*, London 1971

Hanrieder, W. F. (ed.), *West German Foreign Policy*, Boulder 1980

Hartrich, *The Fourth and Richest Reich*, London 1980

Keithly, D. M., *Breakthrough in the Ostpolitik*, Godstone 1986

Krippendorff, E., and Rittberger, V., *The Foreign Policy of West Germany*, Beverly Hills 1980

Morgan, R., *The United States and West Germany, 1945–1973*, London 1974

  West Germany's Foreign Policy Agenda, Beverly Hills 1978

Smith, E. O., *The West German Economy*, New York 1983

Tilford, R. (ed.), *The Ostpolitik and Political Change in Germany*, Farnborough 1975

Vogl, F., *German Business After the Economic Miracle*, London 1973

West German politics since the 1960s

Baker, K. L., et al. (eds.), *Germany Transformed*, Cambridge (Mass.) 1981

Becker, J., *Hitler's Children*, London 1977

Beyme, K. von, and Kaase, M. (eds.), *Elections and Parties*, London 1978

Beyme, K. von, and Schmidt, M. G. (eds.), *Policy and Politics in the Federal Republic of Germany*, Aldershot 1985

Burkett, T., *Parties and Elections in West Germany*, London 1975

Chalmers, D., *The Social Democratic Party of Germany*, New Haven 1974

Child's D., and Johnson, J., *West Germany*, London 1981

Conradt, D. P., *The German Polity*, New York 1978

Dahrendorf, R., *Democracy and Society in Germany*, London 1968

Döring, H., and Smith, G. (eds.), *Party Government and Political Culture in West Germany*, London 1982

Dyson, K., *Party, State and Bureaucracy in Western Germany*, Beverly Hills 1977

Edinger, L. J., *Politics in Western Germany*, Boston 1977

Goldman, G., *The German Political System*, New York 1974

Graf, W. D., *The German Left Since 1945*, London 1974

Johnson, N., *Government in the Federal Republic of Germany*, Oxford 1973

Kolinsky, E., *Parties, Opposition and Society in West Germany*, London 1984

Loewenberg, G., *Parliament in the German Political System*, Ithaca 1966

Nagle, J. D., *The National Democratic Party*, Berkeley 1970

Neven-Dumont, J., *After Hitler*, London 1969

Papadakis, E., *The Green Movement in West Germany*, London 1984

Paterson, W. E., and Smith, G. (eds.), *The West German Model*, London 1981

Pridham, G., *Christian Democracy in Western Germany*, London 1977

Schweigler, G., *National Consciousness in Divided Germany*, Beverly Hills 1975

Smith, G., *Democracy in Western Germany*, London 1979

Sontheimer, K., *Government and Politics in West Germany*, London 1972

Tilford, R., and Preece, R. J. (eds.), *Federal Germany*, London 1969

Wallach, H. G. P., and Romoser, G. K., *West German Politics in the Mid-Eighties*, New York 1985

Culture and society in East and West Germany

Bullivant, K., *Realism Today*, Leamington Spa 1987
Burdick, C., *et al.* (eds.), *Contemporary Germany*, Boulder 1984
Demetz, P., *Postwar German Literature*, New York 1972
Gachnang, J., *New German Painting*, Milan 1982
Hearnden, A., *Education in Two Germanies*, Oxford 1974
Hinton-Thomas, R., and Bullivant, K., *Literature in Upheaval*, New York 1975
Huebner, T., *The Literature of East Germany*, New York 1970
Huettich, H. G., *Theater in a Planned Society*, Chapel Hill 1978
Krejci, J., *Social Structure in Divided Germany*, London 1976
Parkes, K. S., *Writers and Politics in West Germany*, London 1986
Sanford, J., *The Mass Media of the German-speaking Countries*, London 1976
    The New German Cinema, Totowa (N.J.) 1980
Wild, T. (ed.), *Urban and Rural Change in West Germany*, London 1983

Index

Index

Brecht, B., 85, 235f.
Brest-Litovsk, Treaty of, 55, 57
Brüning, H., 93ff., 102, 115ff., 125, 127
Bücher, H., 103
Bülow, B. von, 32, 35
Bund der Industriellen (BdI), 88, 103
Bund Deutscher Frauenvereine (BDF), 27, 140
Bund Deutscher Madel (BDM), 134
Bundesrat: in Second Empire, 20, 32, 60; in West Germany, 199
Bundesverband der Deutschen Industrie (BDI), 204, 206
Bundesvereinigung deutscher Arbeitgeberverbände (BdA), 206
Bundeswehr, 209ff.
Bundy, M., 227
Burckhardt, C., 156
Burgfrieden, 42, 45, 51, 53

Calleo, D., 250
Carnaris, W., 163
Carte Blanche, 210
cartels, 103f., 153, 184, 204, 241
Centre Party (*Zentrumspartei*), 11, 24f., 32, 35, 58, 66, 74, 89f., 91f., 94, 102, 106, 110, 113, 121f., 188, 199
Chamberlain, N., 158
Christlich-Demokratische Union (CDU): in West Germany, 188ff., 199, 215, 224, 247ff., 266f.; in East Germany, 193ff., 221f.
Christlich-Soziale Union (CSU), 189, 199, 215, 247ff.
Churches: under Nazism, 133f.; in West Germany, 187, 198, 247, 262; in East Germany, 235
Churchill, W., 158, 173, 179, 218
Ciano, Count G., 158
Civil Service, 7, 13, 49, 62, 70, 98, 116, 127, 132, 135f., 140, 144ff., 202, 244
Class, H., 79
class, *see* stratification
Clay, L. D., 209
Co-determination (*Mitbestimmung*), 205f., 243
Cold War, 183f., 187, 192, 195, 212, 215, 249
COMECON (East European Common Market), 238
Commissar Order, 164f.
Conservatives, 20, 24, 32, 35f., 53, 90, TT.40–42
Conservative Revolution, 84
Constitution: of Second Empire, 10, 18ff., 51f., 54; reform of, in First

World War, 54, 58ff.; of Weimar Republic, 66f., 88, 92ff., 119, 122, 125, 127, 140; of West Germany (Basic Law), 197ff.
Craig, G. A., vii
Crown Prince, 36, 51, 101
Cuno, W., 89
Currency reform, of 1948, 182, 197

Darré, R. W., 142f., 153
Dawes Plan, 90f., 100f., 104
Delbrück, C. von, 41
demographic change, 3ff., 19, 31, 68, 109, 177f., 232, 253f., TT.1–3
de-Nazification, 179, 182, 185ff., 191, 200, 202, 211, 220, T.47
denomination, 66, 11, 23, T.5; Catholics, 11ff., 24f., 110, 114, 133; Protestants, 11, 110ff.; Jews, 11, 13; *see also* anti-Semitism
Dertinger, G., 222
Deutsch-Nationale Volkspartei (DNVP), 71, 74f., 86, 90ff., 104, 108ff., 123f., 189
Deutsch-Völkische Freiheitspartei (DVFP), 90
Deutsche Arbeitsfront (DAF), 141
Deutsche Demokratische Partei (DDP), 66, 74, 91, 94
Deutsche Partei (DP), 199
Deutsche Reichspartei (DRP), 200
Deutsche Volkspartei (DVP), 74, 87ff., 102, 113, 189
Deutsche Wirtschafts-Kommission (DWK), 196
Deutscher Frauenbund, 27f.
Displaced Persons (DPs), 179, 181
Disraeli, B., 7
Dönhoff, M., Countess, 203
Doenitz, K., 176
Dual Alliance, 36
Dürrenmatt, F., 260
Düsseldorf Guidelines, of CDU, 198
Duesterberg, Th., 119
Duisberg, C., 103

Ebert, F., 55ff., 59, 61ff.; as President of Weimar Republic, 75, 80, 88ff., 92, 198
Ebert-Groener Pact, 65
'Economic Miracle', 201f., 204, 246
education, 13f., 80, 86, 92, 136, TT.37–39, TT.53–54; in West Germany, 200, 265f., TT.37–39, TT.53–54; in East Germany, 220f., 233f.
Ehrhardt, H., 75f., 78
Einsatzgruppen (EG), 162, 167
Eisner, K., 62, 64, 76

Index

Riezler, K., 51
Röhm, E., 77, 144
Röhm Purge (1934), 144, 154
Rommel, E., 161, 174
Roth, G., 26
Rubenstein, R., 169
Ruhr Occupation, 77f., 99
Rundstedt, G. von, 165

Sarajevo, 37
Sauckel, F., 165f.
Schacht, H., 146, 151
Scheel, W., 249
Scheer, R., 60f.
Scheidemann, Ph., 61f., 88
Schiller, K., 247
Schirdewan, K., 223
Schleicher, K. von, 93, 95, 102, 116f., 121ff.
Schlieffen Plan, 43
Schlöndorff, V., 261
Schlüter, L., 214f.
Schmokel, W. W., 159
Schumacher, K., 138, 189f., 224
Schumann, R., 208
Schutzstaffel (SS), 133, 144, 162ff., 187, 213
Schweigler, G., 251
Schwerin, G. von, 210
Seeckt, H. von, 75ff., 96, 98, 101
Seghers, A., 235
Sitte, W., 236
Social Darwinism, 31, 130, 145, 150, 152
Social Democratic Party (SPD): in Second Empire, 12, 15ff., 19f., 22f., 25ff., 30ff., 38ff., 53, 55f., 58; in Weimar Republic, 61ff., 66, 73f., 79, 85, 88ff., 93, 95, 97, 102, 104, 106, 109, 111, 113f., 117, 121; in Third Reich, 129f., 137, 140; in West Germany, 189ff., 204, 212, 215, 247ff.; in East Germany, 194f.
Social Democratic Party programmes: of Erfurt, 17, 67; of Heidelberg, 105; of Godesberg, 247
social mobility, 5f., 12ff., 143ff., 200f., 220f., 233f., 242ff.
social security, 9, 66, 107, 115, 118, 141, 172, 231f., 244f.
Sozialistische Arbeiterpartei (SAP), 130
Sozialistische Einheitspartei (SED), 195f., 197, 217ff., 226ff.
Sozialistische Reichspartei (SRP), 214
Sozialistischer Deutscher Studentenbund (SDS), 248
Spartacus League, 55, 66f.

Spartacus Uprising, 66f.
Speer, A., 159, 170, 174
Spiller, J. O., 108
Springer, A., 261
Stab in the Back (Legend of), 59
Stahlhelm, 119
Stalin, J., 161, 179, 193, 195f., 209, 216, 223
Staritz, D., 231
Staudte, W., 260
Stauffenberg, C. von, 175
Stinnes, H., 65, 68, 79
Stinnes-Legien Agreement, 65, 68
Stolberg-Wernigerode, U., Count, 7
Stoph, W., 229
Strasser, G., 122
stratification, viii, 6, 10ff., 17ff., 45, 51, 143, 172, 233ff., 242ff.
Strauß, F.-J., 251, 266
Streicher, J., 132
Stresemann, G., 88f., 91, 95, 97ff., 102ff., 109, 116, 153
Stülpnagel, J. von, 96, 101f.
Stülpnagel, K. H. von, 165
Stumpff, H.-J., 176
Sturmabteilung (SA), 77, 80, 110, 120, 129f., 144
Supreme Headquarters Allied Expeditionary Forces (SHAEF), 180

T 4 Action, 168f.; *see also* extermination
taxation, 7f., 34f., 48, 70, 108, 118, 147f., 197, 278
Thälmann, E., 92, 119
Thomas, G., 173
Thomas, R., 233
Tirpitz, A. von, 96
Todt, F., 174
total war, 44ff., 51, 102, 174ff.
trade unions, 12, 49, 65, 105, 118, 146, 243, T.46; in West Germany, 204ff., 243f.; in East Germany, 196, 217; Catholic, 12, 106, 204; Hirsch-Duncker, 12, 106, 204; Social Democratic, 12, 16, 105ff., 117
Triple Alliance, 36f.
Trotha, A. von, 61
Trotta, M. von, 261

Ulbricht, W., 212, 223ff., 230
unemployment, 9, 49, 68, 107, 113, 115, 118, 138f., 182, 202, 245, T.18
universities, 14, 136, 233, T.39, T.54
university fraternities, 27, 201
university students, 14, T.39, T.54
Uprising of 1953, 219f., 223

340